Differentiated Literacy Instruction for English Language Learners

Alice L. Quiocho
California State University, San Marcos

Sharon H. Ulanoff
California State University, Los Angeles

TOURO COLLEGE LIBRARY
Kings Hwy

WITHDRAWN

D1275621

Allyn & Bacon
is an imponint of

PEARSON

Boston   New York   San Francisco
Mexico City   Montreal   Toronto   London   Madrid   Munich   Paris
Hong Kong   Singapore   Tokyo   Cape Town   Sydney

KH

Vice President and Executive Publisher: Jeffery W. Johnston
Senior Editor: Linda Ashe Bishop
Senior Managing Editor: Pamela D. Bennett
Senior Project Manager: Mary M. Irvin
Editorial Assistant: Demetrius Hall
Senior Art Director: Diane C. Lorenzo
Cover Designer: Bryan Huber
Cover Image: Susan Courtney
Operations Specialist: Matthew Ottenweller
Director of Marketing: Quinn Perkson
Marketing Manager: Krista Clark
Marketing Coordinator: Brian Mounts

Photo Credits: Sharon H. Ulanoff: pp. 20, 47, 67, 118, 149, 160, 194, 234; Alice L. Quiocho: p. 105; Susan Courtney: p. 252

For related titles and support materials, visit our online catalog at www.pearsonhighered.com

Copyright © 2009 Pearson Education, Inc.
All rights reserved. No part of the material protected by this copyright notice may be reproduced or utilized in any form or by any means, electronic or mechanical, including photocopying, recording, or by any information storage and retrieval system, without written permission from the copyright owner.

To obtain permission(s) to use material from this work, please submit a written request to Allyn and Bacon, Permissions Department, 501 Boylston Street, Suite 900, Boston, MA 02116 or fax your request to 617-671-2290.

Library of Congress Cataloging-in-Publication Data
Quiocho, Alice L.
    Differentiated literacy instruction for English language learners/Alice L. Quiocho, Sharon H. Ulanoff.
        p. cm.
    Includes bibliographical references and index.
    ISBN-13: 978-0-13-118000-0
    ISBN-10: 0-13-118000-2
    1. English language—Study and teaching—Foreign speakers. I. Ulanoff, Sharon H. II. Title.
    PE1128.A2Q56 2009
    428.2'4—dc22   2008000239

Printed in the United States of America
10 9 8 7 6 5 4 3 2 1   [HAM]   12 11 10 09 08

**Allyn & Bacon
is an imprint of**

10/5/09

DEDICATIONS

I dedicate this book to my four sons, Kevin, Ken, Keith, and Kris, who have always believed in me. I include my parents, Sam and Alice Lujan, who inspired me to be the best I can be, and my brother Herm Lujan for his constant love, encouragement, and unwavering support.

Alice L. Quiocho

For my best friend, Mary Lou, for all her support and encouragement throughout this long process. Even when we drove her crazy, she always brought chocolate.

Sharon H. Ulanoff

Preface

Too many times English language learners (ELLs) are perceived as a monolithic entity—what is "done" for one ELL will surely work for all ELLs. We look for programs to "fix" all ELLs only to be disappointed in the results and then blame the students and their families. We write this book because there are no monoliths among our children in schools today. ELLs are not all alike. Grouping and separating them does not work. Differentiating instruction by providing one modification doesn't work either. Each child is unique with specific strengths and needs. We must know them and learn from them to best teach them. As so, we write this book.

Alice L. Quiocho

Whenever I introduce myself to my pre- and in-service teachers, I always tell them that the reason I get to stand before them mostly has to do with the years I spent as a bilingual teacher. During those years, I got to work with amazing ELLs who taught me things everyday about their strengths and their needs. They taught me how I needed to differentiate instruction for each of them in a dynamic way that shifted from day to day, and even minute to minute. Although I now work with amazing teachers, like Alice, I find that some of them have been indoctrinated into thinking that the best way to work with their students is to be "difference-blind" and to look for the one-size-fits-all "answer" to their students' needs. We hope to dispel that myth by adding our work to the dialogue.

Sharon H. Ulanoff

We talked about writing this book for a long time. Both of us have been educators for more than 30 years, working first in K–12 bilingual classrooms and for the last 15 or so years as teacher educators in southern California. Central to our work is the preparation of teachers who go out into the field to work with ELLs. This book is written to provoke deeper thought in the educational community about meeting the instructional needs of ELLs in literacy teaching and learning. In education, there is presently a focus on differentiating instruction for all students. However, methods and models of differentiation used with English-only students, developed from work with at-risk English-only students, are being superimposed on instruction for ELLs. In the search for quick answers and simple methods that will solve the challenge of improving student achievement, we need to closely analyze how differentiated instruction would best benefit ELLs. For example, teachers often neglect cultural ways of communicating and knowing, differences ELLs use to make sense of academic content. In addition, many teachers are unfamiliar with the process of second language acquisition as well as the structure of the students' primary languages (such as whether the language is alphabetic or not). As a result, during instructional planning, many teachers, inadvertently or not, refer to ELLs as "less capable," a term that reinforces a deficit model and contributes to lower expectations for students.

This book is intended for classroom teachers, building administrators who understand their academic role as instructional leaders, teacher educators, and curriculum planners. It is also intended for preservice teachers in methodology courses, including language and literacy, ESL, and/or second language literacy. The book fits these audiences because we concretely address the concept of differentiated instruction—what it means and what it looks like for ELLs. We further present a model for looking at, planning for, and delivering differentiated instruction to meet the needs of ELLs, with specific attention to culture, language, assessment, planning, scaffolding student learning, and the delivery of instruction. We introduce readers to teachers and students from schools with large numbers of ELLs in order to situate our *model for a new pedagogy* in the context of real examples from the field.

Organization of the Text

This text addresses issues specifically related to the use of differentiated instruction to support literacy development for ELLs. We offer practical suggestions for implementing such instruction and provide examples of effective practice. Each chapter begins with a discussion based on current theory and practice and continues by offering both suggestions for planning and implementation as well as classroom cases that showcase teachers and students working together.

In Chapter 1 (What Differentiation Should Be for English Language Learners), we begin the book with an in-depth look at the concept of differentiation in general and as it applies to classroom practice for ELLs, specifically as that practice relates to literacy acquisition and learning. We expand this definition to explore what differentiated literacy instruction for ELLs should look like in the classroom. We introduce the *Model for a New Pedagogy* (Quiocho & Ulanoff, 2005) as well as some of the students and teachers that become the focus of subsequent chapters.

Chapter 2 (The Role of Culture in Planning) describes the role of culture in planning and implementing effective differentiated instruction. Children's cultural experiences affect how they "see" the world and what the texts that are available in school and at home "reveal" to them. In this chapter we emphasize that teachers must start with the students rather than standards and textbooks that may be part of mandated curricula. With the students as the center of instruction, teachers can analyze how to approach the teaching/learning process as well as how the other students in the class will benefit from being in a diverse classroom.

Chapter 3 (The Role of Language in Planning and Delivering Differentiated Instruction to English Language Learners) explores the role of language in planning, implementing, and analyzing differentiated literacy instruction for ELLs. Research has shown (Cummins, 1994, 2005; Willig, 1985) that language, including native language proficiency, plays an important role in second language literacy development. Students who learn to read and write in a second language before acquiring academic language in their primary language (Cummins, 1994) often struggle when exposed to literacy instruction in the second language (Short & Fitzsimmons, 2007). This chapter emphasizes the importance of examining students' language proficiency, including the surface features of the language spoken by the children in the classroom and school, language skills that transfer from the first to the second language, as well as the language skills that do not transfer in order to design lessons that meet their linguistic and content needs. We discuss how to scaffold ELLs' learning experiences so that they will develop enough academic language to learn content.

Chapter 4 (Effectively Assessing ELLs) focuses on the role of assessment in planning and implementing instruction as well as how differentiated instruction can allow for multiple ways of knowing and demonstrating what is known. The chapter also presents a planning scheme that teachers can use to look at different assessments to find out what students know and how they can demonstrate that knowledge. We describe how teachers can look at patterns that emerge from multiple assessments to identify students' strengths and areas of need to support them when learning the scaffolding process. We further discuss how the information obtained through the assessment process can then be used to identify the skills students will need to learn academic content and how students can demonstrate their success in literacy.

Chapter 5 (Teaching and Learning the Necessary Skills for Literacy Success) explores skills that are necessary for students to show their academic success through carefully constructed lessons. It presents a scheme for analyzing objectives based on standards and the assessment data gleaned from the students. This chapter then provides practical examples of cognitive objectives as well as language objectives at different grade levels so teachers can determine the cognitive and linguistic skills or scaffolds that ELLs need before they can meet lesson objectives.

Chapter 6 (Strategies That Count) focuses on effective strategies for ELLs. It explores the need to examine strategies closely to determine why each one has been selected and to use data analysis to explore how the strategy will use the strengths of students as a starting point to address their academic needs. It further describes the role of the questioning process that can help teachers develop quality lesson plans that differentiate instruction to meet the needs of all students.

Given the move toward standards-based instruction throughout the United States, Chapter 7 (Making Content Accessible Through Standards-Based Instruction) explores the ways in which teachers align instruction with both content and language standards to develop effective lessons to meet their students' needs. With examples from the field, we demonstrate how the teachers in one school reformed the district-mandated curriculum, aligning it with state standards and setting up student-centered classrooms. This chapter further contains examples of model lessons and content alignment guides.

Chapter 8 (You Mean I Have to Scaffold the Scaffolds? Learning from Myra and Roberto) suggests ways to scaffold instruction so that students have access to content knowledge. It begins by defining scaffolding and scaffolds (Wood, Bruner, & Ross, 1976) and emphasizes three necessary components of scaffolding: (1) that scaffolds are temporary and supportive structures that help students accomplish a task they would not have been able to accomplish without the scaffold or support; (2) that a scaffold must place a learner in the zone of proximal development (Vygotsky, 1978) and, (3) that a scaffold must be dismantled and taken away with responsibility for completing the learning task taken over by students. This chapter further emphasizes that ELLs should be taught grade level content that is based on their language needs and not watered down; rather it should be scaffolded according to language and content proficiency levels. The scaffolding process and the numbers and types of scaffolds ELLs require—to learn grade level content—influence how teachers support and differentiate instruction.

Chapter 9 (Differentiating Instruction for Exceptional ELLs), authored by Lorri Santamaría, describes effective differentiated instruction for exceptional ELLs (eELLs), focusing on those who have been placed in special day classes or have qualified for special education resource services. It looks at how to meet the students' educational and linguistic needs through instructional practices that scaffold content and language, allowing for support so that ELLs with special needs can also have access to the content and demonstrate what they know.

Chapter 10 (Putting It All Together) ties it all together. This chapter revisits the model for a new pedagogy (Quiocho & Ulanoff, 2005) and uses the principles of multicultural education and scaffolding to test the design of lessons. It further explores the expansion of the traditional assessment model, suggesting a close examination of content objectives and attention to language development before, during, and after lessons to ensure that ELLs have access to the curriculum. It further makes the case that the principles of scaffolding lead to differentiation and that, in turn, has a direct effect on the formation of groups, the rotation of groups, the flexibility of groups, and the necessary opportunities for learning support required by different students.

Features of the Text

This text includes a variety of theoretical and practical features, including:

- **Chapter Objectives:** Each chapter is introduced with a description of the objectives for that chapter to serve as an anticipation guide.
- **Building Background Knowledge:** This feature provides a theoretical framework to contextualize the content of the chapter.
- **Linking Theory to Practice:** This feature links the theoretical framework of the chapter to classroom practice. It includes such things as
  - lesson plans;
  - descriptions of skills and strategies;
  - checklists and charts; and
  - teacher dialogues.
- **Examples from the Field:** In this feature, we further demonstrate the links between theory and practice with
  - cases of individual students;
  - vignettes of classroom practice;
  - student work samples;

- descriptions of planning for individual students; and
- descriptions of lessons in action.
- **Practical Applications and Individual Inquiries:** This feature includes questions and activities that ask readers to apply the content from each chapter.

Acknowledgments

This book is the result of many years of teaching and learning in K–University classrooms. We would like to thank the many teachers and students with whom we have worked over the years for all that we have learned and also for the questions that they have asked that have pushed us to write this book. Their insights and questions have inspired us to move forward.

We further thank the teachers of the classrooms into which we bring our readers: Kelli, Tessie, Dionna, Violetta, Raeanna, and Kris. By allowing us into your rooms, your meetings, and your discussions, you permitted us to show, not tell, things about effective instruction that words alone could not demonstrate. In addition, we thank Susan and Richard for allowing us not only to move freely through their classrooms during instruction, but also to photograph them and their students for this book.

We must also thank the students who serve as the main actors in this text: Roberto, Myra, Dire, Teddy, Ramón, Chau, Luz, Aida, Ricardo, Esteban, Elena, and the rest. You served as the inspiration and impetus for this book. As you showed us how ELLs can and will succeed in supportive classroom contexts, you also show our readers the effects of differentiated literacy instruction for ELLs.

And finally, we want to thank Lorri Santamaría, who contributed her expertise to the chapter on eELLs. We would also like to express our thanks to the reviewers whose constructive criticism and insightful comments helped us to make sense of our task and construct a cohesive text: Denise Fleming, California State University-Hayward; Deanna Gilmore, Washington State University; Margot Kinberg, National University; Maria H. Koonce, Florida Atlantic University; Ana H. Macias, University of Texas-El Paso; Linda Montes, California State University–Chico; Debra Price, Sam Houston State University; Lettie Ramirez, California State University-East Bay; Janet C. Richards, University of South Florida; and Paula M. Selvester, California State University-Chico. Their expertise contributed greatly to the final product.

References

Cummins, J. (1994). Primary language instruction and the education of language minority students. In C. F. Leyba (Ed.), *Schooling and language minority students: A theoretical framework.* Los Angeles: EDAC.

Cummins, J. (2005). Teaching the language of academic success: A framework for school-based language policies. In C. F. Leyba (Ed.), *Schooling and language minority students: A theoretico-practico framework* (3rd ed., pp. 3–32). Los Angeles: LBD Publishers.

Quiocho, A., & Ulanoff, S. (2005). What differentiation should be for English language learners: A new pedagogy. In B. Bartlett, F. Bryer, and D. Roebuck (Eds.), *Stimulating the "action" as participants in participatory research, Volume III* (pp. 62–72). Brisbane, Australia: Griffith University.

Short, D. J., & Fitzsimmons, S. (2007). *Double the work: Challenges and solutions to acquiring language and academic literacy for adolescent English language learners—A report to Carnegie Corporation of New York.* Washington, DC: Alliance for Excellent Education.

Vygotsky, L. S. (1978). *Mind in society: The development of higher psychological processes* (M. Cole, V. John-Steiner, S. Scribner, & E. Souberman, Eds. and Trans.). Cambridge, MA: Harvard University Press.

Willig, A. C. (1985). A meta-analysis of selected studies on the effectiveness of bilingual education. *Review of Educational Research, 55*(3), 269–317.

Wood, D., Bruner, J., & Ross, G. (1976). The role of tutoring in problem solving. *Journal of Child Psychology and Psychiatry, 17,* 89–100.

Brief Contents

Chapter 1 *What Differentiation Should Be for English Language Learners* 1

Chapter 2 *The Role of Culture in Planning* 25

Chapter 3 *The Role of Language in Planning and Delivering Differentiated Literacy Instruction to English Language Learners* 52

Chapter 4 *Effectively Assessing ELLs* 82

Chapter 5 *Teaching and Learning the Necessary Skills for Literacy Success* 109

Chapter 6 *Strategies That Count* 123

Chapter 7 *Making Content Accessible Through Standards-Based Instruction* 153

Chapter 8 *You Mean I Have to Scaffold the Scaffolds? Learning from Myra and Roberto* 187

Chapter 9 *Differentiating Instruction for Exceptional ELLs (eELLs) (by Lorri Santamaría)* 221

Chapter 10 *Putting It All Together* 242

References 267

Index 279

Contents

Chapter **1** ***What Differentiation Should Be for English Language Learners* 1**

Building Background Knowledge About Differentiated Instruction for ELLs 2

Defining Differentiation 2

Why Differentiation for English Language Learners Is Different 2

Differentiated Instruction, Language, and Culture 3

What Is Differentiation? A Traditional Model of Differentiated Instruction 5

The Instructional Needs of ELLs 7

Linking Theory to Practice 8

Components Necessary to Differentiate Instruction for ELLs 8

Culturally Responsive Teaching 9

A Focus on Critical Thinking 10

Scaffolded Instruction 11

Planning 11

Considerations for Differentiating Instruction for ELLs 14

Planning and Delivering Differentiated Literacy Instruction for ELLs 17

Examples from the Field 19

Planning for Ramón, Chau, Luz, and Aida 19

Meet the Students: Ramón, Chau, Luz, and Aida 20

Planning for a New Pedagogy: Instructional Reform at Edge Lake School 22

Practical Applications and Individual Inquiries: Cases to Think About and Investigate 24

Chapter **2** ***The Role of Culture in Planning* 25**

Building Background Knowledge About the Role of Culture in Planning 26

Why Should We Talk About Culture? 26

What Is Culture? 26

Why Is Culture Important for Teaching and Learning? 27

Culturally Responsive Teaching 28

Culturally Responsive Differentiated Instruction for ELLs 29

Linking Theory to Practice 34

Using Stories as Cultural Responsiveness: The Power of Storytelling 34

Using Multicultural Children's Literature as Cultural Responsiveness 38

Bias in Children's Literature 40

Guidelines for Developing Culturally Responsive Differentiated Lessons for ELLs 43

Planning for Effective Instruction 44

Examples from the Field 46

A Bird's-Eye View of Culturally Responsive Teaching 46

Practical Applications and Individual Inquiries: Cases to Think About and Investigate 51

Chapter **3** *The Role of Language in Planning and Delivering Differentiated Literacy Instruction to English Language Learners* 52

Building Background Knowledge About the Role of Language in Literacy Development 53

What Is Language and Why Is It Important? 53

Issues in First and Second Language Acquisition and Development 54

L1 Acquisition and Development 54

L2 Acquisition and Development: A Look at Language Issues for ELLs Who Learn to Read in English 56

Factors That Impact Learning to Read in a Second Language 57

Language Structure and Use: Examining the Surface and Content Features of L1 and L2 57

Exploring Prior Literacy Experiences 60

Scaffolding Access to Language and Text 60

Demonstrating Knowledge 61

Teaching ELLs to Read in English 61

Writing Instruction for ELLs 62

Linking Theory to Practice 63

Facilitating Language and Literacy Development 63

Nonexamples: Strategies That Can Inhibit Language and Literacy Development 66

Examples from the Field 66

Meet Ricardo and Esteban 66

Esteban's Story 67

Ricardo's Story 75

What We Learned from Ricardo's and Esteban's Journals 79

What Esteban's and Ricardo's Stories Tell Us About Differentiating Writing Instruction 80

Practical Applications and Individual Inquiries: Cases to Think About and Investigate 80

Chapter **4** *Effectively Assessing ELLs* 82

Building Background Knowledge About Effectively Assessing ELLs 83

What Is the Purpose of Classroom Assessment? 83

What Kinds of Assessments Are Used in Classrooms? 84

Norm-Referenced and Criterion-Referenced Assessments 84
Formative and Summative Assessment 85
Diagnostic Assessments 86
Diagnostic Language Assessments 86
The CELDT 88
The SOLOM 91
Issues of Bias and Validity in Assessing ELLs 93
Authentic Assessment 94
The Use of Portfolios 95
Ensuring Quality in Assessing ELLs 96

Linking Theory to Practice 96
Retelling 97
Barrier Games 99
Assessing Reading Comprehension 99
Checklists 99
Think Alouds 100
Reading Pictures 101
Conferences 102
Assessing Student Writing 103

Examples from the Field 105
Summing It Up 107

Practical Applications and Individual Inquiries: Cases to Think About and Investigate 108

Chapter **5** *Teaching and Learning the Necessary Skills for Literacy Success 109*

Building Background Knowledge About Teaching and Learning the Necessary Skills for Literacy Success 110
What Are Skills? 110
What Are Strategies? 111
The Relationship Between Skills and Strategies 111

Linking Theory to Practice: Differentiating Skills Instruction for ELLs 114
Find Out What Students Know 114
Preteach Critical Vocabulary 114
Build on Background Knowledge 114
Provide Explicit Instruction in Collaborative Settings 115
Plan for Language, Then Model and Demonstrate 115
Practice, Practice, Practice 115
Check for Understanding 116

Examples from the Field 118
Discussing Skills and Strategies with Teachers 118
Watching Kelli Teach 119
What We Learned from the Teachers 122

Practical Applications and Individual Inquiries: Cases to Think About and Investigate 122

Chapter **6** *Strategies That Count* *123*

Building Background Knowledge About Strategies 124

The Context for Using Strategies with ELLs 124

What Do We Mean by Strategies? 125

Choosing Appropriate Strategies for ELLs 125

Metacognition 127

Linking Theory to Practice 130

Strategies That Count and How They Work 130

A Word About Word Work 148

Examples from the Field 149

Kelli Teaches Word Work 150

Practical Applications and Individual Inquiries: Cases to Think About and Investigate 151

Chapter **7** *Making Content Accessible Through Standards-Based Instruction* *153*

Building Background Knowledge About Making Content Accessible Through Standards-Based Instruction 154

Linking Theory to Practice 155

One School's Guiding Principles 156

The Change Process at Edge Lake 156

Examples from the Field 160

Aligning Skills and Topics with Standards and Materials 161

Understanding the Role of Assessment 172

Lessons Learned 185

Practical Applications and Individual Inquiries: Cases to Think About and Investigate 186

Chapter **8** *You Mean I Have to Scaffold the Scaffolds? Learning from Myra and Roberto* *187*

Building Background Knowledge About Scaffolding the Scaffolds 188

Scaffolding Student Learning 188

Linking Theory to Practice 189

Meet Myra and Roberto 190

Examples from the Field 194

Myra's Story 194

Scaffolds to Support Myra's Writing *196*

Content Area Reading Support for Myra   198

Summary of the Scaffolds Myra Received   201

Roberto's Story   202

Poetry   203

Scaffolds the Teacher Used to Teach Poetry   204

Extending the Writing/Reading Experience   204

Beginning Content Area Writing   206

Scaffolds the Teacher Used   211

Extending the Reading/Writing Process   211

More Content Area Writing   212

Summary of Scaffolds Roberto Received   214

Strategies to Scaffold the Scaffold   215

Prediction   215

Visualization   217

Cause and Effect   218

Practical Applications and Individual Inquiries: Cases to Think About and Investigate   219

Chapter 9   *Differentiating Instruction for Exceptional ELLs (eELLs) (by Lorri Santamaría)*   221

Building Background Knowledge About Differentiated Instruction for eELLs   222

Welcome to Bienvenidos: A Case Study as Context to Discuss Differentiation for eELLs   222

Differentiation with eELLs: Some Concepts and Definitions   223

Managing Differentiated Instruction for eELLs   224

Linking Theory to Practice   226

In What Ways Does Assessment Inform Instruction? Debunking Assumptions and Using Assessment to Address Student Needs   226

Exceptional Education Programs as Resources to the Mainstream: The Value of Co-Teaching   228

Scaffolded Instruction for Exceptional Students   230

Lessons Learned   232

Examples from the Field   233

Practical Applications and Individual Inquiries: Cases to Think About and Investigate   241

Chapter 10   *Putting It All Together*   242

What Have We Learned About Differentiated Literacy Instruction for ELLs?   243

Teaching from a Multicultural Perspective   244

Promoting Multilingualism   245

Understanding Culture   245

Using Assessment Appropriately   245

Linking Theory to Practice 246

 The Students, the Teachers, and the Classroom   246

 Culturally and Linguistically Appropriate Diagnostic and Ongoing Assessment   247

 Language and Content Standards and Objectives   248

 Skills, Strategies, and Scaffolds   248

 Differentiated Instruction Revisited   248

 Summative Assessment Linked to the Content and Language Standards   251

Examples from the Field   251

 Cindi's Writing Development   259

 Daniel's Writing Development   261

 Ignacio's Writing Development   263

 Important Factors to Consider as We Reflect on Writing Development   263

Practical Applications and Individual Inquiries: Cases to Think About and Investigate 265

References 267

Index 279

About the Authors

Alice L. Quiocho is a professor of language and literacy in the College of Education at California State University, San Marcos. She received her doctorate from the University of Washington in reading/language arts and bilingual education.

Dr. Quiocho has more than 30 years of experience in California's public schools as a classroom teacher, elementary and middle school principal, district administrator, and County Office administrator. Dr. Quiocho's areas of specialty and experience are language and literacy, multicultural literature, bilingual education, and school change. She trains reading specialists and beginning teachers in second language acquisition, oral language development, and reading and writing strategies. Dr. Quiocho continues her work in public schools working at school sites with teachers and principals.

Sharon H. Ulanoff is a professor of bilingual/multicultural and literacy education at California State University, Los Angeles, where she coordinates the Graduate Reading Programs and teaches in the areas of language acquisition, cultural diversity, and literacy education. She received her doctorate from the University of Southern California in language, literacy, and learning.

Dr. Ulanoff also has 30 years of experience in California's public schools as a bilingual teacher aide, bilingual teacher, and now bilingual teacher educator. Her research interests include literacy and biliteracy acquisition, cultural identity development, narrative inquiry, and practitioner research. Dr. Ulanoff is a frequent presenter at state, national, and international conferences.

Chapter One

What Differentiation Should Be for English Language Learners

My reading book was called Getting Ready to Read. *I was in a group with four other kids. Mrs. Lynn called us the green group.* Getting Ready to Read *was not an easy book. Most of the time I did not know what the picture was called. I could identify the object in Spanish but not in English. I did not understand why a "gato" began with a /c/. I thought, "Mrs. Lynn is wrong, she doesn't know that a "gato" begins with /g/."*

Sometimes I would be able to figure out some initial sounds. The word flower *begins with /f/ for "flor." I really did not know how I could explain my reasoning to Mrs. Lynn. I decided to keep quiet, follow directions, and circle whatever she asked me to. Besides all that mattered was that I was a step away from reading. A step away from being like the blue group.*

Elena, former ELL, currently a teacher

Changing demographics in classrooms throughout the United States make it necessary for teachers to understand how to make content accessible for linguistically and culturally diverse students, especially those who come to school speaking a language other than English—English language learners (ELLs). This book will examine the concept of differentiated instruction—what it means, and what it looks like in terms of who the students are, and what they specifically need. We propose an overall model for a new pedagogy that includes the dynamic elements of culture, language, and assessment in order to address student needs (Quiocho & Ulanoff, 2005). This model looks at the skills students already possess and can be built upon as well as competencies that can be developed based on the content students already know. The pedagogy also includes scaffolding instruction and practice to ensure that content being taught is mastered by students; that knowledge can be put in students' own words and thus, becomes theirs.

This chapter presents an in-depth look at differentiation in general and as it applies to classroom practice for ELLs, specifically as that practice relates to literacy acquisition and learning. We will:

- Look at differentiation and why differentiation is different for ELLs.
- Describe the instructional needs of ELLs.
- Review the necessary components of differentiating instruction for ELLs and model for a new pedagogy.
- Plan for differentiated instruction for ELLs.

Building Background Knowledge About Differentiated Instruction for ELLs

Defining Differentiation

Tomlinson (2000) defines differentiated instruction as the efforts teachers make to address differences among students in the classroom. She further describes four elements that should be differentiated to best meet the needs of those students: instructional content, instructional processes, student products, and the learning environment. Differentiated instruction, then, is instruction that is targeted to meet the needs of the individual students in the classroom, scaffolding instruction so that it is accessible for all.

Differentiated instruction is typified by flexible groupings and varied tasks within and among groups. Teachers are called upon to link assessment to instruction and modify instruction as needed. Furthermore, there is a focus on different products for different students, so that students can find ways to effectively demonstrate what they know.

Inherent in differentiated instruction is a system of scaffolding that helps students succeed at the different tasks they are asked to complete (Tomlinson, 1999). Tomlinson describes some of these scaffolds. For example, she suggests modifying instruction to give either more or less structure, depending on individual needs; using tape recorders to help with reading and writing beyond the student's grasp; using icons to help interpret print; reteaching or extended learning; modeling; giving clear criteria for success; using reading buddies (with appropriate directions); using text survey strategies; and teaching through multiple modes. She further recommends the use of manipulatives (when needed), leveled reading materials, and study guide organizers.

Why Differentiation for English Language Learners Is Different

Although there are similarities between differentiating instruction for mainstream English speakers and English language learners, instruction for ELLs has to be different from the differentiation model that has been used with gifted students and mixed-ability students in mainstream classrooms. Traditional models of differentiated instruction, as outlined above, were developed in response to the needs of English-only students, often those with special needs who are mainstreamed into the regular classroom. Tomlinson (1999, 2004) notes that whenever teachers do something to meet the needs of individual students, differentiation is occurring. Technically that is accurate, and the models, guiding graphics, classroom scenarios, and examples of contracts provided by Tomlinson are helpful. However, ELLs have additional needs that must be met and usually are not considered in the equation.

Naturally, one important difference for ELLs is related to issues of language proficiency and how students will be able to access the instruction regardless of differentiation. A further difference is related to the cultural context of the instruction, including the background knowledge that students bring to the lesson. And finally, the need for scaffolding of both content and language is critical to meeting the needs of ELLs.

Differentiated Instruction, Language, and Culture

It is important to explicitly teach academic language to ELLs. Every lesson must contain a language objective that builds on preassessment of students' language abilities in terms of the content to be taught in each lesson as well as fluency of listening, understanding, and practical/academic use of the second language. Language teaching must move beyond the preteaching of vocabulary. English as a second language methodology recommends that teachers first focus on vocabulary before teaching ELLs. Findings from classroom observations conducted by the authors indicate that although students engage in word work, they often do not carry that knowledge beyond the word work to make explicit application within the context of the text. It makes more sense to teach students how to find meaning for unfamiliar vocabulary within the context of the content area text, rather than have them use worksheets or activities with words in isolation. Additionally, if cognates—words that mean the same in a student's first language and the second language being learned—exist, they should be used and recorded on a word wall to support connections between both languages and the text (see Chapters 6 and 7 for specific strategies to build and activate prior knowledge as well as how to develop vocabulary within the text itself).

In terms of scaffolding for ELLs, sometimes it is necessary to make provisions for students to have extended work periods or to work within one or more groups to complete a task. It is important to either activate or build background knowledge for students before they engage in learning content. Although mention of flexible grouping structures is made in traditional models that all students will experience over time, there are few or no provisions for multiple grouping experiences. These experiences include the use of two or three different grouping structures that support the completion of an assigned task to scaffold ELLs. Because other students will complete the same task in a different group configuration, it is important to provide opportunities for ELLs to share their learning with others, rather than use traditional models where group membership usually remains the same for one assigned task. Instead of a focus on identifying learning modalities such as visual, auditory, or holistic modes, proficiency in English and the ability to understand the instruction with the necessary linguistic and cognitive supports are the keys to providing effective differentiation for ELLs.

When working with ELLs it is also critical to examine cultural ways of making meaning, which may vary from student to student. Students who come from different cultures make meaning in different ways. Additionally, materials with which students can make connections that touch their hearts and lives are indispensable components of culturally relevant curriculum (Banks, 1999). For example, children from some cultural groups must be provided time to observe others learning as well as the teacher modeling the task that must be completed. For Native American children, it is not sufficient for the teacher to model a task once and review it repeatedly if students do not understand. Instead time must be allowed for students to observe, think, and be ready to take risks as they become more comfortable about trying a classroom task.

Classroom observations (Quiocho, Dantas, & Mackintosh, 2001) indicate that observation and opportunities to talk with peers about what a task looks like and sounds like is supportive of the cultural ways of knowing of Native American children. Other students such as Pacific Islanders must be provided time to talk about learning, or as Au (1998) refers to this cultural communication process, talking story, before they engage in learning any unfamiliar content. Talk story provides children time to share their personal connections to content. As children talk to their peers, they begin to see the relevance of the material to be learned. Thus, students activate prior knowledge in ways that are culturally relevant to them, if not to others. That is, the talk occurs with a minimum amount of turn taking. As children think of ideas, they share them, a process that may be considered as interruptive and rude in other cultures. In addition, Native American and Pacific Islanders seem to make more immediate connections with stories of real people than with unfamiliar notes, charts, or videos.

In addition to language proficiency, prior educational experience, and academic achievement, teachers must closely analyze and pay attention to ELLs' instructional needs. Therefore, while some students might receive opportunities to design their own projects and work at their own pace, others may be given a variety of worksheets to complete in order to become familiar with vocabulary in context that is related to grade level content. Although high expectations are consistent throughout instruction regardless of language proficiency level, students must demonstrate what they know in a manner that is culturally and linguistically congruent with their abilities. Too often when ELLs are present in the mainstream classroom, they are not involved in activities that promote academic oral language development or real writing because there is no specific attention paid to their unique needs. ELLs can achieve academic success when teachers differentiate instruction specifically targeting their needs.

It is important to consider scaffolding within each student's zone of proximal development (Vygotsky, 1978) as a way to ensure access to the curriculum and academic success. According to Vygotsky, the zone of proximal development is the distance between what students can do on their own and what they are capable of in the presence of a more capable other, such as a teacher, peer, or other more "expert" person. Within the zone of proximal development, students can learn content otherwise not accessible to them with the guidance and feedback from someone who has already demonstrated competence in the particular area. Teaching within each student's zone of proximal development does not assume limits or lower expectations for any student. Rather, the zone of proximal development assumes that the "expert" will teach students the skills, create experiences, and develop the academic language necessary for success and improved achievement. It assumes that the necessary academic support or scaffolds (Wood, Bruner, & Ross, 1976) will be offered by the expert who sees his or her role as one who actively supports students in their zone of proximal development and moves them out of the zone to independent learning.

Given this cultural and linguistic stance, the traditional model of differentiation lacks some very important components. In this book, we address each of those components using the overall structure or *new learning* proposed by Shulman (2002) as well as the critical dimensions of multicultural education suggested by Banks and McGee Banks (2003). To this we add second language acquisition concerns (Droop & Verhoeven, 2003; Crawford, 2003; Krashen, 2003; Cummins, 2003) as well as the problem-solving roles and literacy responsibilities students assume in their homes (Orellana, Reynolds, Dorner, & Meza, 2003).

In our observational and advisory work in schools and classrooms we have often found that teachers focus on teaching a strategy to students with little attention to the academic, linguistic, and cultural needs of the students. This is especially true in today's classrooms, where teachers are encouraged, if not directed, to use scripted programs targeted at English-only students. These programs, taught exclusively in English, pay little attention to the needs of ELLs and are often based on the premise that in order to become proficient in English and successful in literacy activities, students need to be fully "immersed" in all-English instruction, ignoring the notion that input needs to be comprehensible for students to make sense of the input and learn language and content (Krashen, 1994, 2005).

Teachers often select an instructional strategy for the sake of the strategy itself after they "learn" of the strategy from the teacher's guide or during a professional development inservice where the strategy was modeled as being effective in classrooms without ELLs. When asked why the strategy was selected, what students would learn from the strategy being taught, and how the language level of the students would be supported in the learning process, teachers either had difficulty answering the question or provided superficial answers that did not get to the heart of the question. Teachers need to use robust strategies with ELLs, ones that support language, culture, and academic content learning. They also need to use strategies that target student strengths to address areas of need. Complex strategies that provide the cognitive academic language proficiency or CALP (Cummins, 1994, 2005) as well as academic proficiency are central to effective differentiated instruction for ELLs.

In this text, we take a critical look at the components of differentiation and discuss how and/or whether the components meet the needs of ELLs in the regular classroom as well as ELLs who have been identified as qualifying for special education resources. The remainder of this chapter describes the various components that are critical to developing a model of differentiated instruction for ELLs. These components include a definition of a traditional model of differentiated instruction, the components of differentiated instruction for ELLs including the use of culturally responsive teaching, a focus on critical thinking, the notion of scaffolded instruction, and how to plan for differentiated instruction for ELLs.

What Is Differentiation? A Traditional Model of Differentiated Instruction

The notion of differentiation is based on the assumption that teachers modify instruction for student success. Some of the guiding principles include the following (Tomlinson, 1999, pp. 9–14):

- The teacher focuses on the essentials.
- The teacher attends to student differences.

- Assessment and instruction are inseparable.
- The teacher modifies content, process, and products.
- All students participate in respectful work.
- The teacher and students collaborate in learning.
- The teacher balances group and individual norms.
- The teacher and students work together flexibly.

When teachers plan for differentiation in the classroom, they make decisions related to the fundamental concepts, principles, and skills that must be taught in each content area. Teachers must pay special attention to the dynamic needs of all students, including struggling learners and advanced learners for each subject. Upon deciding which are the critical content area concepts, principles, and skills to include in the lesson, the teacher must then clearly introduce the content to create linkages among teachers, students, content, teaching, and assessment to ensure success for all students (Tomlinson, 1999).

Within the traditional model of differentiation, student differences are presented as paying attention to ways in which we are all alike, such as sharing the same basic needs for nourishment, shelter, safety, belonging, achievement, contribution, and fulfillment. Note is made of experiences, culture, gender, genetic codes, and neurological wiring, with limited reference to how they affect instructional experiences for ELLs.

Skills inventories, class discussions, and homework assignments are included as means for formative assessment, and benchmark points in learning are explored through formal evaluation, including teacher-made tests and more standardized assessments. These assessments allow teachers to examine where students are at any given time and use the information to accelerate learning for some students and reteach content to others.

Differentiated instruction places emphasis on the content or what students will learn, the process or activities through which they will learn content, and the product or how students will demonstrate that they have learned specific content. Within content, process, and product a variety of activities are appropriate for students who are not quite ready to learn specific content. Many of these activities are based on student interest to promote success. Furthermore, teachers are encouraged to examine the learning profile of each student to look for differences in gender, culture, intelligence preference, and learning style (Gardner, 1999) to modify instruction to best meet their needs. Teachers are not encouraged to pay a great deal of attention to oral and written language development or academic language development, factors that are critical to academic achievement for ELLs. In the next section we will discuss these factors and others that are crucial to differentiated instruction for ELLs.

Differentiated instruction pays careful attention to the readiness levels of students. It is based on the expectation that all students will grow and therefore need to be supported, that there will be opportunities for students to explore essential understandings and develop skills while being involved in interesting and engaging tasks. Learning is a collaborative effort between teachers and students, and weaknesses and strengths are critical in planning groups and individual norms in assessment, instruction, feedback, and grading. Work is flexible, and time is allotted accordingly for students to complete the tasks assigned.

On the surface, the principles of differentiated instruction appear to meet the needs of all students. These principles recognize students' unique learning styles and a variety of factors as listed above. Within the framework of the mainstream classroom, teachers have traditionally tried to meet the needs of ELLs by focusing on ways in which they are like other students. This can be seen in specific programs schools and districts use for instruction as well as in the types of training that teachers receive in order to work with the students in their classrooms. It can even be seen in methods textbooks that are used in preservice teacher education programs where issues of linguistic diversity are often included as after-thoughts or "alerts." Then when ELLs do not achieve at the same levels as their English-only counterparts, they are often viewed from a deficit perspective and blamed for their own lack of success. It is important to examine how programs fail students, not why students don't achieve. Through the use of differentiated instruction directly targeted at the needs of ELLs, teachers can improve their language proficiency and academic achievement.

The Instructional Needs of ELLs

Although the instructional needs of all students can be considered unique, we argue here that the needs of ELLs are very different and must be based on their language acquisition, content mastery, and background experiences. All instruction for ELLs must be based on a variety of assessment results as well as careful, yet complex planning.

Several standardized instruments provide feedback about the language proficiency level of ELLs in several areas of literacy. For example, the California English Language Development Test or CELDT (California Department of Education, 2003a) provides information about students' language proficiency levels (1 through 5) in listening and speaking in kindergarten and first grade and in two additional areas in the other grades, specifically, reading and writing. This information can be used as a general guideline; however, when one considers the raw scores and scale scores within each level of proficiency, it becomes clear that a student at the beginning (or scoring lower) in level one, a student at the middle of level one, and a student ready to move into a level two, cannot receive the same instruction because they are not at the same level of proficiency in the second language. In addition, teachers receive an overall CELDT score that is a conglomeration of the listening/speaking, reading, and writing scores of students in second grade on up. That is, an overall score of 2 does not tell the teacher how the student scored in listening/speaking, reading, and writing. Neither the strengths of students nor their areas of need in language development are identified.

Standardized assessments cannot provide the teacher with a clear picture of what students can do. Instead, many times the results urge us to focus on weaknesses of students rather than strengths. Therefore, we should look at standardized test results as one source of information about students. As we think about appropriate literacy instruction for ELLs, we must use and analyze authentic assessments such as retellings, checklists of expected performance, writing samples, running records, think alouds, and other measures that help teachers understand how students are using the second language to make meaning and get things done in the classroom and as members of that classroom community.

BOX 1.1

In this text when we discuss mastery we mean that students have learned content and language in depth, to the extent that they are able to talk about the content in their own words (not the author's) and can generate new perspectives and transfer what they have learned to other content areas.

BOX 1.2

The CELDT is used throughout California to assess the language proficiency of ELLs. Tests are administered and scored individually by classroom teachers who rate students' English language proficiency on a scale of 1 (limited) to 5 (proficient). Students take the test annually in the fall until they are redesignated as Fluent English Proficient (FEP).

Planning must be focused, based on feedback from multiple assessments. Chapter 4 provides tools teachers can use to gather and analyze data based on assessments to inform their instruction. All lesson plans must consider the following instructional components:

- Cognitive objectives that are focused on access to grade level content.
- Language objectives that target the academic language of the content to be learned.
- Consideration of grouping configurations that provide opportunities for ELLs to receive scaffolded instruction and opportunities to observe, learn, discuss, summarize, and share learning and thinking with other groups. Thus, attention to a model of differentiation that is appropriate for ELLs, not one that is meant to address the needs of mainstream students.
- Attention to the critical academic skills, thinking, and problem solving necessary to learn grade level content.
- Attention to which students have the necessary skills and which students do not. The point is to teach students what they don't know rather than teach all students at the same level of language acquisition the same thing and in the same way.
- Consideration of and attention to the critical concepts that students need to learn in order to acquire learning skills that transfer to other areas of schooling and provide them with information they will master. In other words, the emphasis is to teach for depth and mastery of understanding.
- Attention to necessary scaffolds that support student learning of academic content as well as academic language and an understanding of when and how to release the scaffold or help students assume more personal responsibility for their own learning. Students who need step-by-step guidance as they write should receive it; students who do not need such focused assistance should not receive it.
- Use of ongoing assessment that provides students with feedback about what they are doing that is "right" as well as feedback about areas that need improvement.
- Consideration of future grouping configurations that provide opportunities for all students to master grade level content.

In this book, we focus specifically on each of the critical points delineated above. We provide specific planning techniques, strategies for analyzing data, and instructional strategies that serve as scaffolds to support cognitive academic language learning.

Linking Theory to Practice

Components Necessary to Differentiate Instruction for ELLs

Differentiating instruction for ELLs should give respectful attention to the following components:

- Teaching that is culturally responsive.
- A focus on critical thinking that is to include students' learning about the biases of a content area and engaging in prejudice reduction activities as well as multiple

opportunities to adopt a variety of perspectives with the freedom to offer solutions that may not coincide with mainstream perspectives.

- Opportunities to construct knowledge and be able to support learning with content and research, including results of their own research and inquiries.

- An equitable pedagogy where teaching is modified in ways that facilitate academic achievement of diverse racial, cultural, gender, and social-class groups.

- Scaffolding student learning at a variety of levels, with as many scaffolds as students require, and in a variety of ways as needed by students, based on academic language needs and content area assessment.

- Attention to the primary language structure of students and the components that transfer to a second language as well as those that do not transfer.

- A complex process of planning that takes the components listed above into consideration with the intent to implement them into instruction.

Culturally Responsive Teaching

Examining issues of both language and culture is critical to understanding what students bring to classroom tasks. Too often schools ignore students' language and culture, creating a disconnect between how students make sense of a task and demonstrate what they know and what is expected in terms of school outcomes (Au, 1998; Moll, 2001). Those who make decisions in the school setting need to redefine the goals of instruction not only to include all students, but also to engender a culture that promotes school success (Cummins, 1989; Irvine, Armento, Causey, Jones, Frasher, & Weinburgh, 2001). Whereas teachers can construct school failure as a result of misinformation, negative attitudes, and low expectations, they can also become "sociocultural mediators" and facilitate student success by making explicit connections for students and scaffolding curriculum so that all students have access to learning (Díaz & Flores, 2001).

Culturally responsive teaching (Gay, 2000; Jordan, Irvine, & Armento, 2001) begins with students themselves. Student strengths, cultural capital or understandings of their world as well as other world experiences, their communities, interests, and languages are central to the curriculum. Students and their communities are important in all learning. Teachers see their roles as giving back to the communities in which they teach and encourage their students to do the same. The belief that all students can succeed permeates the classroom environment, and students are encouraged as well as taught how to support each other in the learning process where they make connections among identities they have developed in their communities, the nation, and the world. Students understand that knowledge is something that is constructed, reconstructed, recycled, and shared, and that knowledge comes from students' experiences as well as how they make sense of content (Ladson-Billings, 1994). In culturally responsive teaching, knowledge is viewed passionately and critically where all biases are unmasked for what they are and are open for discussion. Skills that students need to be critical thinkers, discussers, readers, and writers are taught and instructional scaffolds meet and bridge between where students are "intellectually and functionally and where they need to be to participate fully in meaningful construction of knowledge" (Ladson-Billings, 1994, p. 96).

Culturally responsive pedagogy is important in that it offers educators an understanding of why students from diverse backgrounds may not achieve in mainstream educational situations (Nieto, 2001). However, many students from ethnically and linguistically diverse backgrounds succeed despite the cultural differences between home and school (Nieto, 2001). Furthermore, there is little evidence to suggest that any sort of "cultural mismatch" negatively impacts the linguistic and academic success of ELLs (Cummins, 1989). Rather, other sociocultural factors, including the belief by many parents of ELLs that they should not talk or read to their children in their native language in order to promote success in school, often serve to influence academic success. Teaching that is truly responsive to the cultural and linguistic needs of students is one aspect of differentiation that is important for ELLs.

A Focus on Critical Thinking

Tasks with open-ended questions that address controversial issues that are aligned with student interest are a part of differentiated instruction. Tasks should promote critical thinking to include learning about the biases of a content area being studied. Tasks should encourage students to question text and the viewpoints of authors who many times represent the accepted biases of the content being studied. Students (and teachers) should analyze text from the perspectives of both the microculture to which a student belongs as well as the macroculture in order to promote active engagement and critical thinking. Teachers should also include prejudice-reduction activities in differentiated instruction. Teachers should encourage students to look at their own biases as well as biases presented in material being used.

Students must be provided with multiple opportunities to adopt a variety of perspectives and feel free to offer solutions that may not coincide with mainstream views. Service learning projects, for example, provide students opportunities to integrate content and real-life experiences in their local communities and to communicate with leaders and elders in their communities as well. Differentiated instruction focused on quality instruction for ELLs means that students will have opportunities to construct knowledge and be able to elaborate on and support their learning with data derived from research, including results of their own research and inquiries. Thus teaching is modified in ways that facilitate academic achievement for diverse racial, cultural, gender, and social-class groups. When students are encouraged to analyze data and situations, to think critically, and to understand how to support and elaborate their answers, content standards as well as reading and language arts standards will be met. Rather than starting with the standards, we advocate starting with the students themselves. When we start with student experiences we look for ways in which the standards match the skills students need to survive in their own personal lives. We advocate thinking about learning as how the specific skills we want students to learn in order to master content as well as meet standards help students make sense of and navigate the situations in their own personal lives.

Sternberg (1982) notes that schools teach students to think about and solve problems that have been created for them with little or no attention to the problems they actually have in their everyday lives. For example, if they are concerned about being treated fairly, how do they approach the adult or peer without making that person defensive? How do they say how they feel and open a dialogue that will help them talk about bias, social justice, and equity in ways that make the conversation productive?

Gardner (1999) identifies multiple intelligences closely related to cultural ways of knowing. If a person likes music and learns better either when music is playing or having content arranged in a musical score, that medium of learning should be used as a scaffold to learning unfamiliar content. If students learn content through the use of storytelling, that is, if they have linguistic strengths, teachers need to use storytelling as a way to teach content (Dyson & Genishi, 1994). Capitalizing on the strengths of students and the cultures from which they come will help create classrooms that not only are equitable but also provide quality access for all students to grade level content.

Scaffolded Instruction

Scaffolded instruction is critical for ELLs. Since it is the teacher's responsibility to make sure that all students have access to the curriculum, if the students cannot understand the teacher or the text, there is no access to that content (see Chapter 6 for a broader explanation of the process of scaffolding with attention to the language as well as skill needs of ELLs). Wood, Bruner, and Ross (1976) define scaffolding as "a process that enables a child or novice to solve a problem, carry out a task, or achieve a goal, which would be beyond his unassisted efforts" (p. 90).

Scaffolding has been referred to as temporary supports provided for students. Usually the temporary support refers to one supportive strategy such as modeling; however, scaffolding for ELLs is much more complicated. Scaffolding instruction for ELLs at a variety of language development and skill levels means that students are provided as many scaffolds as required to ensure that they learn academic language, acquire the skills needed to be successful in the assigned tasks, and understand how to use their cultures and perspectives to make meaning. In scaffolding, teachers must pay attention to the language structure of the primary languages students speak and to the components that transfer as well as those that do not transfer from the primary language to the second language. Teachers also must know when and how to remove scaffolds gradually to foster independent learning.

Scaffolding is one tool that teachers can use to ensure that students are able to operate in their zone of proximal development (Vygotsky, 1978). When an ELL cannot perform a task by herself or himself due to a lack of language proficiency, background knowledge, or cultural context, the teacher or another "expert" can provide scaffolds that support the student through the task and allow her or him to access the content. As time goes on and the ELL learns more language, develops more background knowledge, begins to understand the context, and becomes more proficient at the task, the expert can begin to remove scaffolds, giving the ELL more and more control until she or he can perform the task solo.

Planning

A complex process of planning that takes the components listed above into consideration with the intent to implement them into instruction is the foundation of differentiated instruction. All differentiated instruction requires complex planning. Differentiated instruction, intended to provide ELLs with pedagogy that is equitable, requires that the following factors be taken into consideration:

- Assessments that examine who students are—their cultures, home languages, and responsibilities.
- Assessments that explore the students' background knowledge.
- Assessments that provide data on student interests, literacy skills, writing skills, oral language development as well as literacy skills assumed in the home.
- Formal assessments (standardized tests) as well as any other informal assessments used in the classroom.
- Analysis of the cognitive/content (grade level) objectives students will learn and the standards—English Language Arts (ELA) and the English Language Development (ELD), grade level content—the cognitive/content objectives address.
- Identification of the language objectives (registers, functions, structures) that students will be expected to use to access grade level content and learn the cognitive objectives and standards.
- Identification of the skills required for students to access grade level content and learn the cognitive objectives and standards. The language demands of the task must be analyzed to identify the language structures, registers, and skills students will need to know and use. The literacy demands of the task must also be analyzed to ensure that the required skills are taught to students in the differentiation process to support active engagement and learning.
- Analysis and identification of ways to integrate the cultural perspectives of students in the critical thinking tasks.

Teachers must use all of the information listed above to determine the levels of scaffolds, the numbers of scaffolds necessary, and the groups of students who will receive the support. Once all of the factors have been determined, flexible groups are formed to support differentiated instruction. At times, mini lessons will be appropriate; at other times, groups may comprise two students or more who will integrate into other groups once they have acquired the requisite skills. Students should be able to group and regroup as they progress through different stages of task completion based on conferences with the teacher who is aware of where students are in the process of constructing knowledge and mastering content concepts.

All lessons for ELLs should have content as well as language objectives so that ELLs can learn the vocabulary and other language skills necessary to understand the curriculum. Teachers should constantly check for understanding with feedback for students who need it. Students should be able to move out of the zone of proximal development based on feedback and support from peers and the teacher. All student work should be calibrated using separate rubrics developed by grade level teachers to establish benchmark samples of excellent as well as substandard work based on the cognitive, content, and language objectives. These teachers should understand the complex issues related to both language development and subject matter proficiency. Figure 1.1 provides an overview of the process of differentiating instruction for ELLs.

FIGURE 1.1 Toward a New Pedagogy for Planning and Delivering Differentiated Instruction to ELLs

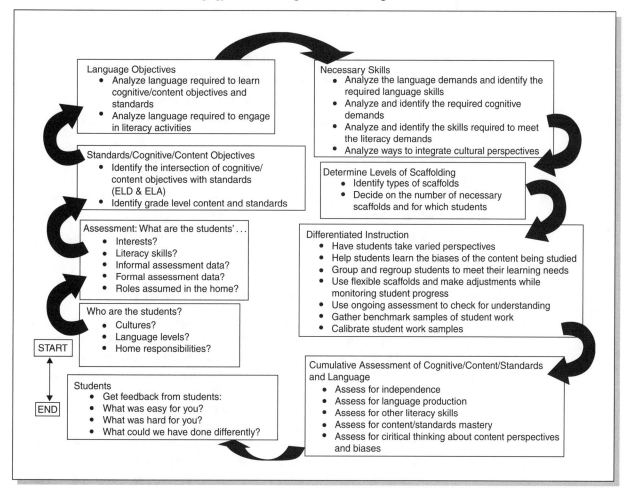

Differentiated instruction for ELLs begins with complex planning. The complex planning process culminates with assessments for independence of learning; appropriate academic language structure and production; appropriate literacy skills required to learn the cognitive, content, and language of the tasks; and the standards as well as assessment that help determine the level of critical thinking in which students have engaged. These informal assessments can take a variety of creative forms such as presentations for which students have been trained and allotted appropriate time to practice. They can ask students to create display boards, write research papers, develop newscasts, or engage in other creative ways to present content. However, the assessments must be guided by rubrics that assess for a specific factor, such as language structure and production, and take into consideration the student's English proficiency level. Assessments of ELLs should also take into account different ways of knowing and demonstrating what is known.

Figure 1.1 presents a visual description of the factors that teachers must take into consideration when planning for effective differentiated instruction for ELLs. The factors are

- the students themselves, their culture, homes, communities, strengths, and needs;
- the standards that students are expected to learn and master;
- access to and understanding as well as mastery of grade level content;
- the background knowledge students possess about academic content and personal life experiences;
- the assessment data that guides instruction before it begins, during instruction, and after instruction;
- the need to check for understanding frequently and to provide immediate feedback and scaffolds as appropriate for each student and flexible groups of students; and
- a focus on teaching that culminates in mastery of content because students are able to talk about content and write about it in their own words.

Considerations for Differentiating Instruction for ELLs

Students are always the center of planning and instruction. Teachers must get to know students on a personal basis: their interests, likes, dislikes, best ways to learn as well as things that get in the way of learning. It is especially helpful to get to know students' parents and the homes and communities in which they live—not to make any negative judgments about their lives and the circumstances in which they live, but to make connections between what students are learning in school and the positive factors in their personal lives.

Reviewing content specific standards to determine which standards are the most important to teach ELLs is the next critical step. Determine which standards are related to the assessment data that has been collected about students. Start with students' strengths and focus on standards that directly address the grade level concepts that students must learn. A review of which standards to teach first is integral to the process of making connections with the critical grade level concepts students must learn as well as the critical skills required to learn concepts. A planning chart is helpful to keep track of what assessments have been conducted, what skills need to be developed, and what instruction needs to occur for each student. Table 1.1 gives an example of a planning chart that focuses on four ELLs and their specific needs. We will talk about them later in the chapter.

To be effective, all instruction must begin with what students already know. If students do not possess the background knowledge, then it must be built through interactive, concrete, and/or kinesthetic activities in which students can experience the background required and then be able to activate the knowledge during the lesson or unit. Background knowledge can be determined in a variety of ways. This concept will be discussed in detail in Chapter 6, which focuses on strategies for differentiating instruction for ELLs.

Planning for instruction means strategically planning to check student understanding and then developing lessons that help students attach new meaning to what they already know and understand. What students already know and understand can be determined by preplanned checkpoints and during instruction as the teacher observes that some students disengaged from in the lesson or group work. When teachers notice that students

TABLE 1.1 A Planning Chart for Differentiated Instruction for Four ELLs

Student Name	What I Know About Each Student	Grade Level	Skills Required	Necessary Scaffolds
Ramón	Spanish is L1.*	Third grade	Understanding the similarities and differences between English and Spanish. Using cognates is helpful. Understanding the meaning units in English is helpful.	Use cognates to make connections between L1 and L2.
	Involved in soccer in the community.		Understanding how soccer strategies are related to learning strategies.	Use soccer stories and strategies.
	Parents want him to succeed.		Communicating with parents.	Reinforce parental desire for success.
	Syntax is difficult in writing; L1 vowel sounds substituted for L2 vowel sounds.		Understanding what transfers and what doesn't.	Conference. Use analogies between L1 and L2. Post reminders and expect student to use them.
	Getting the "gist" of a reading and comprehension of main idea is difficult.		Processing smaller chunks of text first facilitates understanding the meaning of larger pieces of text.	Use think alouds.
	Needs support on how to elaborate on ideas in writing.		Drawing on personal interests and background knowledge.	Begin writing in poetry about grade level content. Conference often with teacher and peers. Use post writing graphic organizers and rubrics.
Chau	Vietnamese is L1. Parents expect her to do well in school. Is a relentless worker. Asks questions often when she doesn't understand. Willing to take risks with language.	Fourth grade	Understanding that structures (syntax, semantics) do not transfer from Vietnamese to English.	Work on morphological units and demonstrate how words are made in English to address her curiosity and desire to learn the second language.
	She is angry sometimes because she is frustrated with making sense of L2 (English).		Understanding the meaning units in English is helpful. Acquiring an "ear" for the language is critical. Voluntary free reading is necessary.	Share stories of how others struggle to learn a second language and have succeeded. Use stories of ethnic authors.
	Syntax is difficult in writing. Needs additional help to elaborate and support main ideas in writing.		Noting how authors "use" English in their writing. Keeping a journal of phrases that are either misunderstood or sound "good."	Begin with poetry. Conference and ask her to read her writing. Focus on positives of writing, having her work on one area of difficulty at a time. Allow time for her to read and talk about one piece of work. Observe when she becomes frustrated and let her put the piece away to revisit later. Encourage parents to read in the L1 at home.

* L1 refers to the student's primary language or the language he or she speaks the most often.

(continued)

TABLE I.I (continued)

Student Name	What I Know About Each Student	Grade Level	Skills Required	Necessary Scaffolds
Luz	Tagalog is L1. Parents try to speak only English at home. Attended school in the Philippines and studied Tagalog, Spanish, and English.	Fourth grade	Understanding that knowing three languages is an asset and that all languages have form, function, and use that may differ, but are essential.	Use cognates when necessary. Work on morphemes, both bound and unbound as they appear in grade level text, and assist in decoding unfamiliar words.
	Has adapted well to the English curriculum. Is inquisitive about language. Needs support in elaboration of ideas writing.		Noting how authors "use" English in their writing. Keeping a journal of phrases that are either misunderstood or sound "good."	Provide positive feedback. Use graphic organizers or other organizational charts to illustrate the structure of grade level text and what authors do to help readers "see" the message they are trying to convey.
Aída	Spanish is L1. Parents only speak Spanish and do not write or read Spanish. They want Aida to do well but are unable to help her at home.	Third grade	Understanding that knowing two languages is an asset and that all languages have form, function, and use that may differ, but are essential.	Use primary language support when appropriate and cognates to make connections between oral language and written language. Encourage parents to tell stories in the L1 at home.
	Is shy and afraid to speak out—fears making errors.		Understanding that it is okay to wait and think about what you are going to say before you say it. Practicing taking risks with language.	Provide time for her to process information in her primary language. Talk no more than 10 minutes and allow her to process in Spanish for at least 2 or 3 minutes. Review information again in English prompting Aida to fill in vocabulary that is important to concept understanding—a kind of oral "cloze" procedure. Post word walls and let her use a personal word wall of cognates and other vocabulary essential to content understanding and to writing.
	Comprehension of main ideas is difficult.		Understanding that the meaning of larger pieces of text is facilitated by processing smaller chunks of text first.	Use a think aloud, illustrating how you think about making sense as you read. Model and let Aida try this process with coaching, not telling.
	Elaboration of main ideas in writing needs support.		Noting how authors "use" English in their writing. Keeping a journal of phrases that are either misunderstood or sound "good."	Begin with poetry writing, encouraging her to use both languages as she writes her poems about content. Conference, asking her what she wants to say and then helping her fill in the blanks with appropriate vocabulary. Have her work with a supportive partner who has been taught how to wait and support but not tell her the answers or do the work for her. Encourage parents to tell stories in the L1 at home.

are disengaged, they should explore whether gaps in understanding are related to content, language, or both in order to continue planning effective lessons. This ongoing assessment during instruction is necessary if we are to teach ELLs for mastery of grade level content, a goal that is attainable with appropriate instructional practices.

Students who are struggling with understanding content, either because of language or background knowledge, must be provided with instructional interventions at the time the gap in understanding occurs. Grouping must be flexible. Students need to be regrouped as often as needed and a variety of instructional interventions must be planned in advance to serve students' needs. As long as flexible grouping is a consistent practice in the classroom and students are mastering content, it poses no problem to classroom dynamics and relationships. Grade level content mastery and language acquisition are the goals of all instruction that occurs when the students themselves are the principal consideration in planning.

Planning should always begin and end with students' voices, which should be involved in providing constructive feedback on the ease or difficulty of the task and ways in which the task could be better mediated. We must become partners with students to create a respectful learning community where all voices count, all perspectives are honored, critical discussions can occur, and ELLs can fully participate.

Planning and Delivering Differentiated Literacy Instruction for ELLs

To effectively afford ELLs the necessary learning opportunities for them to be successful second language readers and writers, teachers must look at the instructional experiences they provide for students. We argue that effective instruction needs to begin and end with the students themselves and also needs to be situated within sociocultural, linguistic contexts that have high expectations and are aligned with national, state, and district standards. Figure 1.1 depicts our *model for a new pedagogy* as a basis for planning and delivering differentiated literacy instruction to ELLs.

This model includes the dynamic elements of culture, language, and assessments that address knowledge and skills that students already possess and competencies that can be developed to extend what they know. This model incorporates the concept of scaffolding instruction and practice to ensure that the content being taught is mastered by students and that it can be put in students' own words and thus becomes their own. Figure 1.2 demonstrates the role of assessment in planning and differentiating instruction.

To plan effective instructional experiences for students, teachers begin by examining who the students are and the strengths they bring to the classroom context. It is important to examine students' cultures, language proficiency levels, and the outside responsibilities they may have when designing lessons to best meet their needs. For example, students who come to school with limited English proficiency, but who are proficient readers in their native language, will have an easier time making sense of English print (see Chapter 3 for an in-depth discussion of the role of language in literacy development). Students who come to school from diverse cultural backgrounds may also be used to different types of school experiences and may approach school tasks in different ways than the teacher is used to (see Chapter 2 for a comprehensive discussion on the role of culture). It is critical that these factors are taken into consideration when planning instruction.

FIGURE 1.2 The Role of Assessment in Planning and Differentiating Instruction to Meet Student Needs

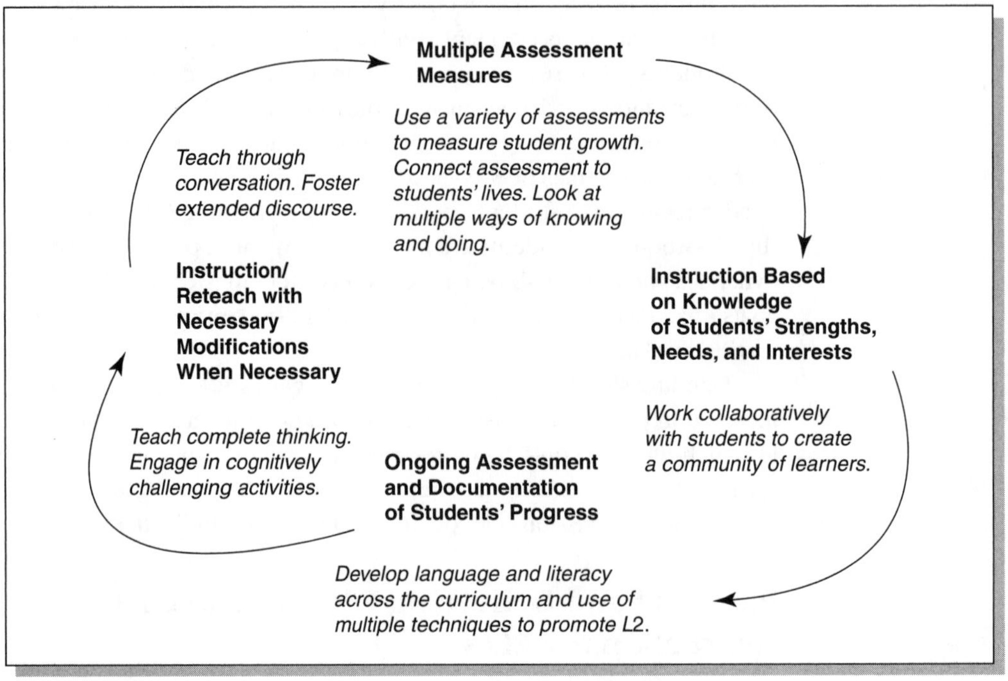

Source: From *Developing academic language in English for heritage language learners*, by A. Quiocho and L. Santamaria, November 2003. Paper presented at the annual meeting of the California Reading Association, San Diego, CA.

Assessment also plays a central role in planning differentiated literacy instruction that meets the needs of all students in the classroom (Figure 1.2). Teachers not only need to evaluate students' literacy skills, but also need to take students' interests into consideration as well as the different types of literacy activities they may have previously engaged in at home or another school. Furthermore, it is important to consider the student's literacy level in her or his native language as this can greatly impact success in L2 literacy. Both informal and formal assessments should be examined as well as the student's use of literacy in and around the home. For example, some ELLs serve as "language brokers" (Orellana et al., 2003) and engage in complex tasks that require the use of literacy skills *outside* of school, but then are challenged by English literacy during classroom tasks.

Education today is increasingly being linked to national, state, and district standards, which are generally posed as ways in which to ensure accountability for students and teachers (Darling-Hammond, 2000). Furthermore, programs are often criticized for their lack of evaluation, increasing assumptions that there is limited accountability. In the past decade, most, if not all, states developed curricular standards for all content areas, generally starting with language arts. For example, California has English Language Arts Standards (California Department of Education, 1997), English Language Development Standards (California Department of Education, 1999; see WestEd, 2001, for a concept map of the alignment between these two sets of standards), and an English Language Arts Framework (California Department of Education, 1999/2007) to guide instruction. Teachers in California design lessons that address these standards, which are also measured by an annual exam. Schools and districts operate on the assumption that teachers who use the standards are able to ensure that all students receive a similar content base.

Language objectives are equally important for all students, but especially ELLs. Apart from ensuring access to the content, teaching to language objectives ensures that the student can comprehend the new concepts because she or he understands the vocabulary. Chamot and O'Malley (1992) recommend that each content lesson include specific language objectives that include vocabulary development and linguistic background knowledge that contains related words and concepts. That way ELLs not only gain content knowledge but also increase their language proficiency.

Next, teachers need to plan for teaching the necessary skills to ensure successful learning of the content at hand. This includes analyzing what skills are needed before instruction begins, including background knowledge, language, and literacy levels. Once the teacher has decided what skills are needed, she or he has to plan the level of scaffolding that will be needed by each student in the class. For example, students with high native language literacy skills may need less language scaffolding and more content scaffolding, whereas students with little or no native language literacy skills may need scaffolding that initially focuses exclusively on language development (see Chapter 8 for a comprehensive discussion on scaffolding).

Within this new pedagogy, then, teachers differentiate instruction for ELLs based on the students' background knowledge, skills, and interests, scaffolding the content according to students' linguistic and content needs. Teachers hold high expectations for students and align curriculum to national, state, and district standards at the same time supporting ELLs so that they have access to the same curriculum as native English-speaking students. Teaching strategies, which are described in detail in Chapter 6, include grouping and regrouping students to meet their learning needs, using ongoing evaluation to check for understanding, and allowing for multiple ways of knowing and demonstrating that knowledge. It is also important to gather work samples from students. These work samples can then be calibrated and used as benchmarks that can be used to show what the students have learned.

And finally, it is important to include cumulative assessment to evaluate when students meet lesson objectives and acquire the knowledge described in both content and language standards. Cumulative assessments allow ELLs to demonstrate growth over time and are more valuable than on-demand one-time assessments. They take into account how ELLs take control of their own learning and move from needing more scaffolding to less scaffolding to no scaffolding; in other words, how they move through the zone of proximal development (Vygotsky, 1978) from novice to expert. In the model for a new pedagogy for planning and delivering effective instruction for ELLs (Figure 1.1), the cumulative assessment then leads to the next step, where teachers begin again to look at the students in their classrooms.

Examples from the Field

Planning for Ramón, Chau, Luz, and Aida

Welcome to Room 15 at Edge Lake School, the fourth-grade classroom where Ramón, Chau, Luz, and Aida spend their days. Throughout the book we will be visiting Edge Lake School and learning about these and other students, as well as the teachers who work

Discussing and responding to stories.

with them and the stance they take toward their practice. Edge Lake School is a K–5 (grades kindergarten to 5) school in southern California, not far from the Mexican border. Seventy-four percent of the students in Room 15 are ELLs like Ramón, Chau, Luz, and Aida. Most instruction is provided in English as a result of California legislation, Proposition 227, which calls for instruction to be "overwhelmingly in English" (García & Curry-Rodriguez, 2000), but the teachers do offer primary language support as needed.

Meet the Students: Ramón, Chau, Luz, and Aida

Ramón is a native speaker of Spanish. He has mastered word work, that is, the sounds and symbols of the English language. He knows the difference between decodable and nondecodable words. He understands that there are words in Spanish that mean the same as words in English. He is aware of cognates as he comes across them either in oral presentations or in reading. "Conquistadors," he says, beginning his sentence on explorers in a confident voice and suddenly stops mid sentence. "Oh, that's a cognate. In Spanish it's conquistadores."

Ramón has learned that when he reads, he needs to chunk text; if he tries to "digest" too much text at once, he won't understand everything. However, when he reads difficult text such as those in social studies and science, he struggles with the vocabulary that doesn't transfer from English to Spanish. He gets "lost" sometimes in comprehending complex concepts. Ramón works very hard at writing but feels insecure when it comes to actually placing his own words and thoughts on paper. He wants to be *right*. Fluency in writing is a challenge for him, and in his classroom and school all reading instruction is followed by writing.

Chau grew up speaking Vietnamese as her first language. She has great resiliency when it comes to learning English. She has learned to crack the code and can decode text quite well. She leaves off plurals and has trouble with irregular tenses such as "built." When it comes to comprehension, Chau becomes easily frustrated because of the syntactical structure of English. "In Vietnamese we have no adjectives or adverbs. I never see a period before I come here." She is very inquisitive about learning new words. "Teacher, teacher, I learn a new word last night. It is biome. Good word, no? That mean where things can grow, right?" She uses the dictionary and thesaurus in her classroom more than most of the other students. Her parents expect her to do well in school, and Chau knows she has to perform well and is not going to disappoint them.

She willingly shares her ideas one on one with her teacher, but is silent in a large group. "I listen," she confides in her teacher. "I think I learn lot that way." Writing, the focus of Chau's school, presents an obstacle to her learning. Her curiosity with new words helps her; however, many times the words she decides to use in her writing do not "fit" the context of the writing. Elaboration or providing explanatory support for her writing is necessary. When she describes what she is writing about orally, she includes details. She eliminates those details when she has to put pencil to paper. Perhaps letting Chau record herself before she begins writing and have her listen to her own narrative during the writing process might prove to be helpful.

Luz came to the United States knowing three languages. She attended school in the Philippines and is a newcomer to Edge Lake. Her grandparents live with the family and speak Tagalog at home. Her father speaks Spanish and Tagalog fluently. He uses English in the workplace and seems to be doing well, but he always notes in conferences that he is still learning English; that it is very hard to speak all day all of the time.

Luz likes school and works very hard. She tells her teacher how some words in Tagalog and Spanish sound the same and many times mean the same. She also notices the connections in English. Since the focus at her school is on writing, Luz needs ongoing and continued support through frequent conferences so she can understand the structure of the genre of writing she is being asked to produce. She also needs to adopt the habit of going back and rereading her own writing to check for sufficient elaborative details that will make her writing clear, complete, and inform her audience.

The language spoken in **Aida's** home is Spanish. Her father is learning some English at the construction site where he is working but since most of the other workers are Spanish speaking, they communicate in their language of comfort. Aida's mother speaks very little English. She cleans houses as an assistant for another woman who speaks English. When speaking with Aida's parents, it is very clear that they want Aida to learn all that the other students learn. They want her to study science and social studies and to do well in math, reading, and writing. "Pero, no podemos ayudarla" [but we are unable to help her], her parents say. They don't understand the work in English and neither of them completed school.

Because Aida does not receive assistance at home in the language of instruction at school, English, she is not a confident learner. She is quiet, shy, and rarely speaks out.

Sometimes her classmates speak out for her, and her teacher is working on teaching them how to wait so Aida can find the word on her own. She can decode words in English very well. Sometimes she memorizes the text. When asked why she memorizes, she replies, "The words stay in my brain." It is comprehension with which she struggles. If Aida has memorized the text, she will repeat it word for word. She is unable to put the text in her own words and can't answer inferential questions. She uses her background knowledge and responds in ways that are unrelated to the question. Consequently, when she writes in different genres it soon becomes evident that Aida does not fully comprehend the text and either cannot respond to or search through text for evidence and details to support her responses.

Planning for a New Pedagogy: Instructional Reform at Edge Lake School

The teachers at Edge Lake School structured their instruction to meet the needs of students like Ramón, Chau, Luz, and Aida. They worked together at weekly grade level meetings to plan instruction and, as a result of monthly professional development sessions, focused on research to inform their decisions about practice. They read the research on literacy and second language acquisition and decided that if they developed and taught a robust curriculum that integrated the critical components of interactive assessment to inform instruction, meeting state standards and raising test scores for the students would be a by-product of what happened in their classroom communities, not the goal.

As they guided their students through the literacy process (Kucer, 2001), the teachers at Edge Lake School focused on writing as one means of improving reading comprehension, and they implemented a cycle of observational checks, reflections, and decision making (Crumpler, Bertelsen, Bond, & Tierney, 2003). At those weekly meetings their reflections and conversations centered around student work, assessments results, student portfolios, development of rubrics using district guidelines, English language development standards, and comparison across grade levels by calibrating student writing.

Table 1.1 on pages 15–16 demonstrates how the teachers at Edge Lake School organized their planning for differentiated literacy instruction for ELLs. By creating planning charts such as this one, they were able to look at the students' needs *at a glance* as a tool to facilitate their work. The starting point for their planning was what they knew about each of the students, including background knowledge and assessment data. Figure 1.3 demonstrates one way to individualize planning to differentiate instruction for Ramón.

For example, the fourth-grade language arts standards for the state of California, as aligned with the English language development standards (California Department of Education, 1997, 1999), note that ELLs should demonstrate comprehension of simple vocabulary with an appropriate action, produce simple vocabulary to communicate basic needs in social and academic settings, recognize sound/symbol relationships in one's own writing, and develop fluency and systematic vocabulary development (WestEd, 2001).

Although Ramón needed the support demonstrated in Figure 1.3, Chau needed concentrated work on subject–verb agreement through the process of guided writing. Her writing needed to be scaffolded consistently over time. The teacher would model and she and Chau would read the sentences together. Then Chau would write her own sentences.

FIGURE 1.3 Individualized Planning for Ramón

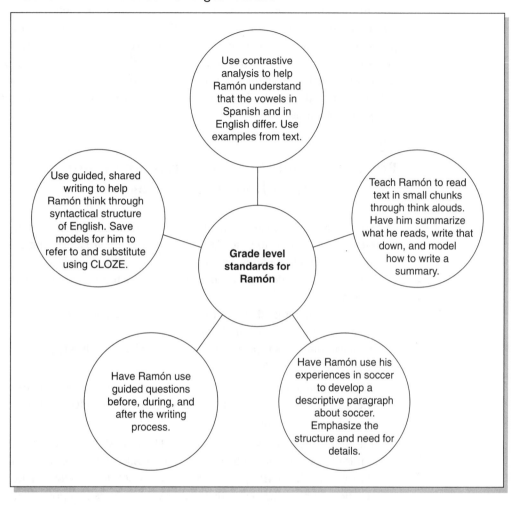

She and her teacher read the sentences together and wherever Chau made a syntactical "error," the teacher would look for a similar sentence in Chau's library books, have her read the sentences, and delete the kind of words Chau struggled with, such as plurals and pronouns. Chau then filled in the blanks and sought feedback from her teacher and writing partner. Finally Chau wrote either her responses or the understanding of text in a poem that could be shared with others and posted in the classroom.

On the other hand, Luz was doing well transitioning from her native language to English. She brought with her at least an intermediate skill level in English. She was ready for word study—to play with morphemes and build words using prefixes and suffixes. She received instruction in the structure of various genres of reading and writing and engaged in lessons where she was encouraged to "show" her writing using descriptive words, finally learning to combine sentences.

Aida needed much more support. She could decode but struggled with getting the main ideas and supporting information from text. Her teachers used her primary language to clarify meaning of concepts and directions. They understood that they needed to limit the amount of auditory input Aida received in a lesson. So, her group was allowed lots of time to process information and to discuss the content in their primary language if necessary. Refer to Table 1.1 for the format of the planning grid as well as the instructional plans for each student. The point to be made is that knowing students through observation and assessment is essential to all instructional planning. Focusing on student strengths is the best starting point for instruction. That is what happened for the students at Edge Lake, and Ramón, Chau, Luz, and Aida were successful because of the teachers' thoughtful planning.

Practical Applications and Individual Inquiries: Cases to Think About and Investigate

1. Spend time in a classroom with ELLs. Ascertain the students' English language proficiency levels by asking the classroom teacher. Create a drawing of the classroom and note which students are in which groups. Take anecdotal notes about what the students are doing in each group. Next, match what you actually see with the following:
   - Is the work at grade level, that is, is it about grade level content?
   - What standards does the work meet?
   - What kinds of support or scaffolds have been built into or are being explicitly provided for students?

2. Visit a school and ask to speak with the person in charge of assessment. Inquire about the way in which ELLs are assessed and how the results are used to help teachers differentiate instruction.

3. Interview a teacher who works with ELLs and ask how the writing process is different for ELLs than for English-only students. Ascertain whether guided writing, shared writing, or other writing supports such as CLOZE or poetry are being used. Ask the teacher whether the scaffolds have served students in a positive manner, contributing to their improved success.

4. Observe a classroom with ELLs where reading instruction is taking place. What are the group configurations? Do the groups ever change within the school day? When and if they do change, what kind of instruction occurs? Describe what you see.

Chapter Two

The Role of Culture in Planning

"Chinese, Japanese, look like these!" said the freckle-faced boy to the slanty-eyed immigrant. With mischievous glee, poster child of the Aryan nation pulled his eyes upwards, slightly at an angle. And for the first time I felt ashamed of where I came from. For the first time, I felt ashamed to see my parents pick me up at school. For the first time, I was afraid of every time they visited my teacher—afraid they'd mangle some simple question about my progress. For the first time, I felt ashamed and that is a sad, sad thing. Yet, I think such insecurities operated on such a subconscious level that my parents were never aware. What I do know is that from that time forward, I became a much quieter boy—what stupidity.

David, classroom teacher

The classroom context is being transformed daily as state and local demographics change. Although the United States has always been a diverse nation, statistics show that today's classrooms are more diverse than ever, and will continue in this manner well into the 21st century. Given the dynamic shifts in demographics, teachers today can expect to teach in classrooms vastly different from those that they experienced as children. Teacher candidates are challenged to explore both underlying assumptions about why certain things happen in schools and the ways in which they will approach both teaching and learning. Therefore, it is important to explore not only how teachers think, but also what they need to know about culture and language that will help them be effective teachers in ethnically and linguistically diverse settings. Despite the changing demographics in schools, the teaching force remains largely white and female. All teachers and prospective teachers need to examine the lenses through which they view the world in order to explore their own views of teaching and learning, teacher and learner, and what counts as demonstration of knowledge.

It is important to explore differentiated literacy instruction situated in a cultural context in order to describe not only the role of culture in planning but the ways in which teachers can create environments that support culturally relevant pedagogy (Gay, 2000). In this chapter we:

- Examine the concept of culture and its role in teaching and learning.
- Explore the use of stories and multicultural children's literature within the framework of culturally responsive teaching.
- Describe culturally relevant differentiated instruction for ELLs.

Building Background Knowledge About the Role of Culture in Planning

Why Should We Talk About Culture?

Children's cultural experiences affect how they "see" the world and what is revealed to them in texts. Considering the culture of the children in the classrooms is more than selecting books that represent the cultures of the children in the class. It is teaching the children in the class how to move within their own microcultures as well as in the macroculture in which they find themselves, where speaking English is the accepted mode of teaching and speaking. Considering the culture of the children means that we understand how to approach children from different cultures without stereotyping each culture and approach teaching with recipes that include dishing up only one way to relate to Latino students, one way to communicate with Asian students, etc. This chapter will focus on identifying who ELLs are and how we can best meet their needs in terms of curriculum and practice and the creation of a safe environment. To do so we explore the role of culture in planning effective instruction for ELLs and focus on three areas: what is culturally responsive teaching? What does it look like? And how does culturally relevant teaching intersect differentiated instruction for ELLs?

What Is Culture?

Culture is a dynamic, creative, and continuous process that consists of shared community beliefs and ways of doing things. Nieto (1999) states that "culture consists of the values, traditions, social and political relationships, and worldview created, shared, and transformed by a group of people bound together by a common history, geographic location, language, social class and religion" (p. 139). Culture is a dynamic concept that encompasses all that is created by people, including behaviors, values, attitudes, customs, viewpoints, and history, among other things (Valle, 1997). We are all the product of the culture that we experienced and, at the same time, we help facilitate the evolution of that culture. Delgado-Gaitán and Trueba (1991) argue that defining American culture is complex given its composition of varied cultural and social groups but suggest that "cultural transmission from one generation to another, and the role school plays in acculturation of minorities especially with regard to the values of American democracy and respect for cultural differences" (p. 17) is central to the dialogue surrounding the definition of culture.

All cultures have values that are specific to that particular culture and that also vary according to subgroups within the culture. Children learn culture from their families first (Ooka Pang, 2001) and later on from their peers. Their instantiation of culture influences how they view and react to the world. Children bring their own worldviews, based on culture, to the classroom and interact according to those views. These worldviews serve to influence how they perceive their teachers, their peers, and the school setting itself (Spindler & Spindler, 1994).

Why Is Culture Important for Teaching and Learning?

Researchers in multicultural education agree that to be effective, teachers need to consider the diverse cultural backgrounds that students bring to school as well as the specific culture that is inherent in the school setting (Banks, 2007; Ooka Pang, 2001). Schooling has long been considered the primary means of replicating cultural behaviors since it is at school that children learn not only content but also how to participate. Schools are generally organized, therefore, to maintain hierarchical structures already in place in the greater society (Carnoy, 1974). These structures include some students while excluding others.

To be effective educators, teachers need explicit knowledge about cultural diversity and the diverse backgrounds of their students (Gay, 2002). This knowledge includes information about specific cultural groups, multicultural instructional strategies, and multicultural content. Since teachers are often subjected to mandated programs with curricula that is written for white, monocultural students, they need to be able to analyze curriculum and make changes to meet the needs of their students. Teachers not only have to be aware of interaction strategies that may differ from group to group and be different from what they are used to, but also must understand that students may demonstrate different ways of knowing and show what they know in diverse ways.

Gay (2002) describes three kinds of curricula that are often present in today's classrooms: formal instructional plans, symbolic curriculum, and societal curriculum. Each plays a different role in education and all three work together to prepare students to take on adult roles in society.

Formal instructional plans are comprised of curriculum that is shared at the national, state, district, and/or school level. It includes such things as curricular standards issued by national, state, or local bodies; commercial programs that may be adopted for state or district use; and other curricular documents that influence the nature of instruction for students. For example, national initiatives, such as No Child Left Behind, have direct impact on what is instructed and how that instruction is delivered. The National Reading Panel Report (NRP, 2000) has also served to greatly influence how literacy instruction is constructed nationwide, despite its lack of attention to students from linguistically and culturally diverse backgrounds.

Students are also exposed to the symbolic curriculum (Gay, 2002; Ooka Pang, 2001), which includes "images, symbols, icons, mottoes, awards, celebrations, and other artifacts that are used to teach students knowledge, skills, morals and values" (Gay, 2002, p. 108). The symbols that are used in the classroom and the larger community serve to model what values are acceptable and what values are not. Gay (2002) also describes the societal curriculum as the body of knowledge about different groups that we see portrayed in the media.

Students spend much of their time in classrooms and are often bombarded with a variety of messages about what is important and what is not important. These messages generally promote traditional monocultural values and ideas and often look at diversity from a deficit perspective. Teachers need to make a commitment to teaching multiculturally, looking at the different levels of ethnic content (Banks, 2001, 2003) that is integrated into the curriculum. Rather than merely focus on heroes and holidays, teachers need to integrate a social action approach, one that advocates student decision making and action on critical social issues.

Culturally Responsive Teaching

One way to enhance teaching to incorporate curriculum and practice that meets the needs of students from diverse cultural backgrounds is to employ culturally responsive teaching (Gay, 2000). Culturally responsive teaching uses "the cultural characteristics, experiences, and perspectives of ethnically diverse students as conduits for teaching them more effectively. It is based on the assumption that when academic knowledge and skills are situated within the lived experiences and frames of reference of students, they are more personally meaningful, have higher interest appeal, and are learned more easily and thoroughly" (Gay, 2002, p. 106). Ooka Pang (2001) describes it as culturally relevant teaching, which "is an approach to instruction that responds to the sociocultural context and seeks to integrate cultural content of the learner in shaping an effective learning environment" (p. 192).

Teachers who teach in culturally responsive ways are looking to maximize learning for culturally diverse students (Irvine & Armento, 2001). Ooka Pang (2001) maintains that to be culturally responsive, teachers need to first make connections with their students and question how they perceive both the instruction and the classroom context. She suggests that sometimes there is a disconnect between the different contexts (e.g., sociocultural, linguistic, political) of the classroom experience and the learner's expectations of those contexts.

Heath (1983) argues that "the different ways children learned to use language were dependent on the ways in which each community structured their families, defined the roles that community members could assume, and played out their concepts of childhood that guided children's socialization. . . . In communities throughout the world, these and other features of the cultural milieu affect the ways in which children learn to use language" (p. 11). Teachers, therefore, need to take these different types of knowledge about language into consideration when they are planning for instruction with students from ethnically and linguistically diverse backgrounds. They need to understand that there are a variety of different contexts, but that none of these is inherently better or worse than any other—just different.

In addition to considering the various cultural and linguistic backgrounds that students bring to school, teachers need to think about both the content and the delivery of instruction. This includes understanding varied behaviors and ways of communicating as well as values children bring with them to school (Ooka Pang, 2001). Ooka Pang (2001) argues that teachers need to listen to students in addition to observing them in order to understand varied interactional structures, student and parent expectations, frustrations, and the values that support the manner in which the students relate to school.

Gay (2002) lists four elements that are critical to using culturally responsive teaching: developing a cultural diversity knowledge base, designing culturally relevant curricula, demonstrating cultural caring, and building a learning community and cross-cultural communications. Within this framework, culturally responsive teaching not only teaches to the strengths of children, but uses those strengths as a mechanism for teaching as well (Gay, 2000), at the same time validating the legitimacy of backgrounds different from the dominant culture. Culturally responsive teachers, then, learn to use "cultural referents to impart knowledge, skills and attitudes" (Ladson-Billings, 1992, p. 382 as cited in Gay, 2000) within the mainstream classroom.

Culturally responsive teachers, therefore, need a substantial knowledge base related to (1) the cultural characteristics and contributions of different groups (Gay, 2002) and (2) specific strategies to work with students from diverse backgrounds. This includes both multicultural content and multicultural instructional strategies, as well as strategies to work with students from diverse linguistic backgrounds. These teachers must be able to design culturally relevant curricula and critique existing curricula for biases and stereotypes. Furthermore, culturally responsive teachers need to be able to assess children's literature used in the classroom for these same cultural biases, exploring not only who is depicted in books but also the roles individuals play. In addition to their roles in classrooms, culturally responsive teachers can take an active role at the state and/or district level in textbook and curricula adoptions so that students may be exposed to more accurate representations of cultural and linguistic diversity.

Culturally responsive teachers need to make connections between classrooms and the community, inviting the families into the classroom for more than just back-to-school night and individual conferences. Too often, parents from diverse backgrounds, especially those who do not speak English well or at all, are excluded from the school community. Even when it is not intentional, certain things, such as having no one in the office that can communicate with the parents, or scheduling all meetings during the day when parents are working, can serve to eliminate parents from participating more fully in school. Culturally responsive teachers invite parents to be part of the classroom community in a variety of ways, at times by sharing their own expertise or funds of knowledge (Moll, Amanti, Neff, & González, 1992), at other times as classroom helpers, and during still other times as learners themselves. Care must be taken so that parent education is not approached from a deficit perspective, assuming that parents of students from diverse backgrounds do not know things needed to help their children, but rather from an additive perspective, acknowledging what parents can add to the educational experiences of their children.

There is a growing body of literature related to cultural diversity and culturally relevant pedagogy. Figure 2.1 includes a list of books that address issues related to constructing classroom practice to support students from diverse backgrounds.

Culturally Responsive Differentiated Instruction for ELLs

In addition to being culturally responsive, teachers must plan instruction that is also differentiated to meet the linguistic needs of students who come to school speaking a language other than English. The following values and beliefs regarding differentiated instruction for ELLs are central to this text and to all teaching and learning for ELLs. If instruction is

FIGURE 2.1 Selected Books About Cultural Diversity and Culturally Relevant Pedagogy

Applebee, A. N., Langer, J. A., & Foote, D. W. (1993). *Multicultural perspectives.* New York: McDougal, Littell.

Au, K. H. P. (1993). *Literacy instruction in multicultural settings.* Fort Worth: Harcourt Brace Jovanovich.

Banks, J. A. (Ed.). (1995). *Handbook of research on multicultural education.* London: Macmillan.

Banks, J. A. (2000). *Cultural diversity, education and teaching: Foundations, curriculum and teaching* (4th ed.). Boston: Allyn & Bacon.

Banks, J. A. (2002). *Teaching strategies for ethnic studies* (7th ed.). Boston: Allyn & Bacon.

Banks, J. A. (2007). *An introduction to multicultural education* (4th ed.). Boston: Allyn & Bacon.

Banks, J. A. (2007). *Educating citizens in a multicultural society* (2nd ed.). New York: Teachers College Press.

Banks, J. A., & McGee Banks, C. A. (Eds.). (2006). *Multicultural education: Issues and perspectives* (6th ed.). New York: John Wiley.

Bigelow, B. (Ed.). (1995). *Rethinking our classrooms: Teaching for equity and justice.* Milwaukee, WI: Rethinking Schools.

Campbell, D. E., & Delgado-Campbell, D. (2000). *Choosing democracy: A practical guide to multicultural education.* Upper Saddle River, N.J.: Merrill.

Cummins, J. (Ed.). (1994). *Cultural diversity in schools: From rhetoric to practice.* Albany: State University of New York Press.

Darling-Hammond, L., French, J., & Garcia-Lopez, S. P. (2002). *Learning to teach for social justice.* New York: Teachers College Press.

Davidman, L., & Davidman, P. T. (2001). *Teaching with a multicultural perspective: A practical guide.* New York: Longman.

Delpit, L. (1995). *Other people's children. Cultural conflict in the classroom.* New York: New Press.

Díaz, C. (2001). *Multicultural education for the 21st century.* New York: Longman.

Dietrich, D., & Ralph, K. S. (1995). Crossing borders: Multicultural literature in the classroom. *The Journal of Educational Issue of Language Minority Students, 15.* Retrieved May 19, 2003, from http://www.ncela.gwu.edu/miscpubs/jeilms/vol15/crossing.htm

Dyson, A. H., & Genishi, C. (Eds.). (1994). *The need for story. Cultural diversity in classroom and community.* Urbana, IL: National Council of Teachers of English.

Fraser, J. W. (Ed.). (1993). *Freedom's plow: Teaching in the multicultural classroom.* New York: Routledge.

García, E. E. (1999). *Student cultural diversity: Understanding and meeting the challenge.* Boston: Houghton Mifflin.

Gay, G. (2000). *Culturally responsive teaching: Theory, research, and practice.* New York: Teachers College Press.

Gollnick, D. M., & Chinn, P. C. (2005). *Multicultural education in a pluralistic society* (7th ed.). Boston: Prentice Hall.

Grant, C. A. (Ed.). (1993). *Research and multicultural education: From the margins to the mainstream.* London: Falmer Press.

Grant, C. A. (Ed.). (1995). *Educating for diversity. An anthology of multicultural voices.* Boston: Allyn & Bacon.

Grant, C. A., & Gomez, M. L. (Eds.). (1996). *Making schooling multicultural. Campus and classroom.* Indianapolis, IN: Merrill.

Grant, C. A., & Sleeter, C. E. (1999). *Turning on learning five approaches for multicultural teaching plans for race, class, gender, and disability.* New York: Wiley.

Hernández Sheets, R. (Ed.). (1999). *Racial and ethnic identity in school practices: Aspects of human development.* Mahwah, NJ: Erlbaum.

Hollins, E. R. (Ed.). (1996). *Transforming curriculum for a culturally diverse society.* Mahwah, NJ: Erlbaum.

Nieto, S. (1999). *The light in their eyes: Creating multicultural learning communities.* New York: Teachers College Press.

Nieto, S. (2002). *Language, culture, and teaching critical perspectives for a new century.* Mahwah, NJ: Erlbaum.

Nieto, S., & Bode, P. (2007). *Affirming diversity: The sociopolitical context of multicultural education* (5th ed.). New York: Allyn & Bacon.

Ooka Pang, V. (2001). *Multicultural education: A caring-centered reflective approach.* Boston: McGraw Hill.

Richard-Amato, P. A., & Snow, M. A. (Eds.). (1992). *The multicultural classroom. Readings for content-area teachers.* London: Longman.

Saville-Troike, M. (1978). *A guide to culture in the classroom.* Rosslyn, VA: National Clearinghouse for Bilingual Education.

Schlesinger, A. M. (1998). *The disuniting of America: Reflections on a multicultural society.* New York: Norton.

FIGURE 2.1 (continued)

Sleeter, C. E., & Grant, C. A. (2006). *Making choices for multicultural education: Five approaches to race, class, and gender* (5th ed.). New York: Wiley.

Sleeter, C. E., & McLaren, P. (Eds.). (1995). *Multicultural education, critical pedagogy, and the politics of difference.* Albany: State University of New York Press.

Spindler, G. D., & Spindler, L. S. (1990). *The American cultural dialogue and its transmission.* London: Falmer Press.

Spring, J. H. (2006). *Deculturalization and the struggle for equality. A brief history of the education of dominated cultures in the United States* (5th ed.). Boston: McGraw-Hill.

Tiedt, P. L., & Tiedt, I. M. (2005). *Multicultural teaching: A handbook of activities, information, and resources* (7th ed.). Boston: Allyn & Bacon.

Trueba, E. T., Guthrie, G. P., & Au, K. H. P. (1981). *Culture and the bilingual classroom. Studies in classroom ethnography.* Rowley, MA: Newbury House Publishers.

Villegas, A. M., & Lucas, T. (2002). *Educating culturally responsive teachers: A coherent approach.* Albany: State University of New York Press.

meant to make a difference for ELLs, all practice must spring from the desired habits of mind noted here.

Teachers must have high expectations for all students, no matter their linguistic, ethnic, or social background. At first glance, this statement appears to make sense and not arguable, but there are often inconsistencies in how instruction is designed to help students meet these expectations. Lessons should be designed to allow ELLs to succeed at school tasks.

A good way to begin is to learn about students' lives and the communities from which they come. Teachers must get to know parents and let parents get to know them so that a spirit of partnership develops between teachers and parents in spite of language differences. If possible, teachers should visit the communities where their students live to find out more about them. They should also attend community celebrations and set up situations where their families interact with their students and their families. They should let the parents know and see that they really do care about their children by being present in their communities (Ladson-Billings, 1995).

Understanding assessment is critical to designing effective instruction for ELLs. There must be a strong focus on quality assessment that is analyzed to uncover students' strengths and the background knowledge they bring to the classroom in order to differentiate instruction appropriately. Chapter 4 provides examples and guidelines on how to analyze data and use it to best benefit children. When most ELLs enter classrooms in the United States, they are given diagnostic assessments of their language proficiency. The results of these assessments must be examined in conjunction with observational data from classroom activities in order to best meet student needs. It is important to remember that all assessments for ELLs measure their content knowledge in addition to their language knowledge (Mercado & Romero, 1993), and it is generally difficult to evaluate whether they make mistakes because they don't know the content or the language. Teachers who provide culturally responsive differentiated instruction for students take this into account when using assessments to make decisions for practice.

Materials that reflect the lives and experiences of the children in the class must be used along with any state-adopted materials (Au, 1993). Comparisons must be drawn between what students know and the materials that reflect their cultures. Comparisons must be made among the standards students must learn, their daily lives, and the content they are learning in class. Teachers need to make special efforts to make instruction relevant and meaningful for students.

Furthermore, teachers must design activities that allow all students to participate, regardless of linguistic ability. They must also provide time for students to observe one another work and time to talk about the task so that students can take risks with learning and make sense of the tasks. Teachers should observe how students use their time to try to make sense of the language of the task and the task itself and provide supports or scaffolds that help facilitate this understanding.

Teachers must also plan activities that guarantee success for students. If instructional planning stems from assessment that focuses on student strengths, the activities that follow will provide for student participation and success. Rather than lowering standards, teachers provide instructional support for the critical concepts students must learn. For example, if students' papers will be scored using a rubric, the rubric should be introduced and taught ahead of time. It should also be posted clearly for students to see, and students should be reminded to check the rubric as they write. Teachers can teach mini-lessons and demonstrate how to write to a rubric, providing the students with specific tools to think about as they write. Table 2.1 can be used and adapted to support student writing for success. If the writing task itself is kept simple, with steps for writing posted where students can see them and opportunities for reviewing the steps, it will be easier for students to succeed. Finally, as students read and write, short individual conferences should occur (Graves, 1982).

Table 2.1 provides general guidelines for what teachers can do to support student success. Reading is reasoning; writing is thinking. Therefore, it is logical to support ELLs to be metacognitive and to think about their own reading as they read, their writing as they write, and words as they decode them or search for meanings.

Specific supports must be provided to students before they begin a task, and conferences that contain positive feedback must be provided as students proceed through their work. Students must see that they are on the "right track" and that the teacher values what they are doing. Suggestions for improvement must be a part of feedback. The number of suggestions is critical. Give students no more than one suggestion at a time so that students are not overwhelmed and find it difficult to begin. Once they have addressed that suggestion, provide positive feedback and add another suggestion. The idea is to instill in students that learning is always under "construction," that we continue to read, reread, write, rewrite, and think about our work before, during, and after the task is addressed. An environment of risk taking (Krashen, 1987) must be an integral part of instruction and the tone of the classroom.

Table 2.1 also addresses thinking/learning skills that must be explicitly taught to students. For example, if we want students to summarize, we must teach them to summarize. Begin with activities in which they engage on a daily basis. Have them list what happens first, second third, etc. Next have them put the steps together in shorter statements. Show them how that process leads to summary. As appropriate, lead students to practice and learn how to summarize their thoughts, the readings they do, and other activities in which they engage in the classroom. It is important to teach how to ask questions in the same manner that predicting, hypothesizing, and critical oral language functions (Gibbons, 1993) as well as reading and writing skills are taught. This will be further discussed in Chapter 5.

It is also important that teachers nurture positive self-esteem by focusing on what students do well and use their strengths to address areas of need. This does not mean

TABLE 2.1 Strategies for Supporting ELLs' Writing/Reading

Student Thinking About Writing/Reading	Strategies to Teach ELLs to Use
What can I do when I need to be clear about what I am doing and how I am going to get there?	• Have the student restate the task, goal, problem, or question. Support the academic language of ELLs as they do this. • Support the student to encourage him/her to restate what he or she wants to accomplish (goals). Ask: What do you want to tell your classmates and me about your reading/writing? • Support students to restate or summarize their goals—where it is, what is there, etc. This is important to encourage students to state their goals for their work in their own words and not the words of the teacher.

What can I do when I need to think about "seeing" the entire picture of what I am trying to do?	• Support ELLs in small groups or one on one to search for and list as many ideas as possible. Use cognate word walls and/or content word walls when appropriate.
	• Support ELLs to search for as many possibilities as they can think of or can find.
	• Ask questions such as:
	  • How else might I think about it? Ask "what if. . . ?"
	  • What are the causes? How do I know? What else do I know?
	  • What are the effects? How do I know? What else do I know? Has this happened in my life? When? What did it look like?
	  • Who might not agree with me or question what I have to say? How do I make sure they understand my viewpoint or perspective?
	  • What other questions do I have about what I am doing?
	  • What will I do with my information? How will I show it to my audience? What does it mean to me as a learner? So what?

What can I do when I need to assess or rate my work/thinking?	• Teach ELLs to think critically (evaluate) their questions, plans, facts they found, goals, and what they know.
	• Ask questions such as:
	  • Does my work tell my audience what I really know?
	  • Did I follow my plan?
	  • Did I answer my questions?
	  • Are my facts accurate?
	  • Did I meet my goals?
	  • Did I ask for all of the help I needed?

What can I do when I need to think or rethink the details of my project?	• Support ELLs to find more information from other sources. • Teach ELLs to add more explanations (elaboration). • Do I want to start all over again or should I just change a few things in my plan?

that ELLs should be doing the drawing in a group while everyone else is engaged in tasks that require higher level thinking skills. Rather it means that ELLs should be commended for the things they already have in their heads and the tasks they perform in their homes and communities (Moll, 2001; Orellana, Reynolds, Dorner, & Meza, 2003), and then those thoughts and tasks should be tied into what is being learned at that time. ELLs should be encouraged to bring their strengths, such as how they help their families by translating the English-speaking world and documents/directions written in English, to school assignments that ask them to write or orally describe what they have learned.

Teaching must also be differentiated in ways that are culturally responsive for ELLs. That means that planning, instruction, monitoring of student progress, and grouping structures must reflect on what we know about culturally responsive curriculum.

Linking Theory to Practice

Using Stories as Cultural Responsiveness: The Power of Storytelling

One way to approach cultural responsiveness is to teach lessons that incorporate what we know about the cultures of students through stories. Students listen to and hear stories from the time they are young children and understand these cultural narrative structures because they are part of their everyday life. For example, Cline and Necochea (2003) describe that although they were never read to as children, they heard stories from aunts, uncles, visitors to their homes, and family friends. Since books were not readily available in their homes, the stories that were told and the songs shared among family and friends on lazy Sunday afternoons and at parties provided their first induction into literacy and their understanding of how stories were culturally organized.

Our observations in classrooms where the majority of the population of students were Native Americans revealed that storytellers from the Native tribe told stories that did not always have resolutions. Instead, the stories provided a prelude to the creation of a new story. Stories that were shared included myths passed down through oral tradition and demonstrated the close connection the Native tribe had with nature. Other stories included lessons elders had to share with students. The stories ended with thought-provoking statements for students to consider and discuss. What did not occur in the classrooms was an effort to use the Native structure of stories and the thought-provoking statements to encourage students to talk, a method of learning that worked well with that group of children.

Many—including Augusta Baker, a renowned African American librarian from the New York Public Library system, and her colleague, Ellin Greene—argue that through storytelling, children understand the rhythms, structures, cadences, and conventions of the various forms of language (Baker & Green, 1997). Storytelling, due to its universal nature, is a key to cultural understanding both within and among groups (Baker & Green, 1997). With storytelling children create their own mental images from the words that they hear and thus come to understand narrative, sometimes before they even pick up a book.

Therefore, storytelling can be one way to bring the child's culture into the classroom in a variety of ways. Although stories of culture are often not part of the classroom context (George, Rafael, & Florio-Ruane, 2003) and, in fact, are often excluded from the classroom dialogue except during "show and tell" time (Wertsch, 1990), storytelling is one way to bring students' backgrounds and literacy knowledge to school.

The storyteller and the purpose of storytelling may vary at different grade levels. Stories provide opportunities for teachers to demonstrate to children the similarities among cultures. Through this process, students should be able to identify recurring archetypes and themes that are evident across cultures, such as creation stories (Roe, Alfred, & Smith, 1998). (See Roe et al., 1998, for a reference list of creation stories told in different cultures; Givens, 1998, for African American stories and songs for girls; and West, 1989, for a collection of Mexican American folklore.)

Children more readily create mental images from stories and process the language of stories if they hear and use stories with which they have been familiar since birth.

Furthermore, the power of storytelling can help children develop their own oral histories (Edinger & Fins, 1998) as they help children think about the past, compare the past to their present lives, and learn from the people they meet in stories told and songs shared. Children's own personal experiences or their true stories (Duthie, 1996; Barton, 2000) shared with others in classrooms, once children are encouraged to use their cultural frames of reference, serve as another authentic source for culturally relevant curriculum. Students can thus use personal storytelling (Miller & Mehler, 1994) to talk about events they recall from their daily lives, embedded in the contexts of home, family, and culture.

Stories can be used as an entry point to teaching (Egan, 1986, 1988). The stories, both personal and imaginary, that children tell are often ignored in the school curriculum. Yet, it is easy to see that storytelling and stories can be an effective way to hook students into content lessons (Egan, 1986, 1988) when linked to content and students' interests or experiences. Stories can be used to foster thinking, reflection, and problem solving in the classroom (Carreiro, 1998). Cultural stories validate the students' communities (Moll, 2001) and demonstrate for them the connections among their background knowledge, experiences, and school.

If we are to really utilize culturally responsive curriculum to help students make connections among who they are, where they come from, and the values of their families and communities, we need to investigate the cultural structure of stories told in students' families and communities. We need to use the cultural story structures to expose all students to the ways stories from different cultures vary in organization. Cultural story structures should be used in storytelling and immediately transferred to writing using the same structure. As students become fluent in oral language and writing, comparisons and contrasts should be made between the cultural story structures and Western story grammars to expose all students to the breadth and depth of literacy as transmitted through stories. The following is an overview of a lesson on using storytelling in a culturally relevant format (Lesson 2.1). The lesson does not follow a specific lesson plan format; however, it describes what a teacher would do before, during, and after a lesson that uses cultural storytelling as a vehicle for learning. It also includes the following teaching tools: think-pair-share (Kagan, 1994; see Figure 2.2) and storyboards (Figure 2.3).

LESSON 2.1 | A Culturally Responsive Lesson Using Storytelling

Step 1. Tell students that they are going to tell their own personal stories about themselves, their communities, and people in their lives. Emphasize that it is our personal experiences that influence who we are and how we see the world. Support this by either having a storyteller in the room that represents the culture of students or reading a short story that is culturally aligned in organization and language. Point out how the storyteller draws on his or her own experiences in life for the story and those experiences represent who they are and their cultures.

Step 2. Validate experiences students have had by presenting them with pictures taken in their communities, for example, at powwows, soccer games, fiestas, and community landmarks such as churches, schools, stores, restaurants, or playgrounds. Commercial prints might work, but it is not recommended that they be used because they do not have the power of authentic pictures taken in the community. Connections with their families and communities provide opportunities for students to make immediate and direct connections. Provide time for students to look at the pictures, reflect on what they see, and talk about the people, places, and things that the pictures conjure up in their heads. Students may also relate an incident that just happened at school and talk about their personal responses to and perceptions of what happened.

Step 3. Use the think-pair-share strategy (see Figure 2.2) where students are provided time to reflect on pictures or other prompts. They can write their thoughts down or draw pictures to represent their thoughts with labels to "capture" the language that best represents their thinking. Next, each student pairs with another student and they talk about what they have on their "thinking sheets." Finally, students share the results of their talk with the entire class. The teacher should jot down students' thoughts and language to create a memory of the thinking that occurred and will give rise to as well as support the writing process.

Step 4. Build a story by modeling your own cultural story with students. Demonstrate how to begin by creating a storyboard (see Figure 2.3). On a storyboard, the events of a story are sketched and placed on the board sequentially. Key words and labels, including labels that utilize words in the student's primary language, are used to identify each event. Provide some guiding questions for students to use as they create the events for their storyboards. These guiding questions might include:

    a. What happened?
    b. When did it happen?
    c. Where did it happen?
    d. Who was there?
    e. What were the colors? Sounds?
    f. How did you feel about it?
    g. How do you feel about it now?

FIGURE 2.2 Think-Pair-Share

Think-Pair-Share is a cooperative discussion strategy. Students work in **pairs** to **think** through a strategy and **share** it with their partners. This is a good strategy to use for reviewing material or for finding out what students know.

Steps: Before the activity begins, the teacher divides the students into pairs. Then:

1. **Think.** The teacher asks students to think about a question or problem and then gives the students a few minutes to THINK about the answer or solution. The teacher may also ask the students to prepare a written response.

2. **Pair.** Students then PAIR up to talk about their answer with each other. They compare their mental or written notes and identify the answers they think are best, most convincing, or most unique.

3. **Share.** After students talk in pairs for a few minutes, the teacher asks the pairs to SHARE their answers (and how they reached those answers—their thinking) with the rest of the class. This can be done by having students share around the room orally, posting their responses for others to see or in any other way that allows for all students to hear each pair's answer. The teacher may also have someone record the responses for further use.

Sources: From *Cooperative learning* (2nd ed.), by S. Kagan, 1994, San Juan Capistrano, CA: Kagan Cooperative Learning; Lyman, F. T. (1981). The responsive classroom discussion: The inclusion of all students. In A. Anderson (Ed.), *Mainstreaming Digest* (pp. 109–113). College Park, MD: University of Maryland Press.

FIGURE 2.3 A Storyboard

h. How would you want to begin your story?

i. Think about what happened first, second, next, etc.

j. Does your story have an end? Remember that it doesn't have to have an ending.

Step 5. Create a talking circle that provides students opportunities to share their personal stories. In a talking circle, students have time to look at storyboards and to talk about and share their boards with a partner who can ask them questions about the story they will be sharing with the rest of the class.

a. Be sure to give students a purpose for listening to the stories of others. Have them look for commonalities between their own stories and the stories other students are telling to demonstrate that there are common experiences across people and cultures.

b. When it is time for students to tell their stories, they can hold a talking stick that symbolizes the voice and thoughts of the storyteller.

Step 6. Debrief with students about how their stories differed but shared some similar features. Point out the language used to begin stories. For example, some stories begin with "once upon a time . . ." while others begin differently. Make note of several ways stories are started and remind students that the various ways in which stories start represent the diversity in world literature.

Step 7. Follow Up Suggestions

    a. Practice storytelling until your students are comfortable with the process. Have them keep their sketches, storyboards, notes, keywords, beginnings, plots, and endings.

    b. Provide students with multiple opportunities to tell their favorite stories. Let them make changes if they want to. Told stories should naturally lead to writing, which is a natural sequence after the lesson and practice on storytelling.

    c. Have students write their stories, but before they write, have them tell the story and record it. As they listen to themselves on the recording they can use their thoughts and language to begin the writing process.

    d. Support your students by modeling and telling your own stories. Memorize a few short stories from different cultures and share them with students.

Step 8. Other Suggestions

    a. Evaluate the climate of your classroom to ensure that there are not so many times when you demand silence in classroom routines that your students lose their voices.

    b. Provide many opportunities for your students to value themselves and develop their imaginations from where they sit. Storytelling means that students have to be in contexts in which they feel validated for their thoughts and ideas. Only then will their voices emerge to reveal the rich stories that reflect their lives.

Using Multicultural Children's Literature as Cultural Responsiveness

In addition to the use of stories in a storytelling format, it is also important for students to both listen to and read children's literature so that they may develop a reading habit and interest in reading from an early age (Goodman, 1986; Krashen, 1987; Smith, 1986). While it makes sense that it is easier for students to develop reading proficiency in their native language, rather than one in which they are not proficient (Cummins, 1994; Thonis, 1994), it is most often the case that ELLs learn to read in English, their second language (Ulanoff & Vega-Castaneda, 2003). This would lead us to believe that it is beneficial for students to have access to a wide variety of books, both in English and their native language (Ulanoff & Pucci, 2005) to promote reading proficiency.

It is well documented (Athanases, 1998; Au, 1993; Ladson-Billings, 1995; McGinley et al., 1997; Sims Bishop, 2003) that the use of multicultural children's literature can have a positive impact on reading and attitudes toward reading for students from diverse backgrounds. So what is multicultural children's literature? First, there are many definitions of multicultural literature. Multicultural literature includes stories and books about people who come from a variety of different backgrounds related to culture, socioeconomic status, and religion (Salas, Lucido, & Canales, 2002). Children's literature is simply books that are read to and by children (Temple, Martinez, Yokota, & Naylor (2002). For the purpose of this chapter we expand and combine both definitions to consider multicultural children's literature to be those books that are read to and by children that depict people with diverse cultural, linguistic, socioeconomic, and religious backgrounds.

While Figure 2.4 is by no means an exhaustive list, it does include a variety of articles and books about multicultural children's literature, a short list of multicultural children's

FIGURE 2.4 Multicultural Children's Literature: Selected Resources

Books and Articles About Multicultural Children's Literature

Aoki, E. M. (1980). "Are you Chinese? Are you Japanese? Or are you a mixed-up kid?" Using Asian American children's literature. *Reading Teacher, 34*(4), 382–385.

Beilke, P. (1986). Selecting materials for and about Hispanic and East Asian children and young people. Hamden, CT: Library Professional Publications.

Dowd, F. S. (1992). Evaluating children's books portraying Native American and Asian cultures. *Childhood Education, 68*(4), 219–224.

Harada, V. H. (1995). Issues of ethnicity, authenticity, and quality in Asian-American picture books, 1983–93. *Journal of Youth Services in Libraries, 8*(2), 135–149.

Harris, V. J. (1991). Multicultural curriculum: African American children's literature. *Young Children, 46*(2), 37–44.

Jenkins, E. C., & Austin, M. C. (1987). *Literature for children about Asian and Asian Americans*. New York: Greenwood Press.

Pang, V. O., Colvin, C., Tran, M., & Barba, R. H. (1992). Beyond chopsticks and dragons: Selecting Asian-American literature for children. *The Reading Teacher, 46*(3), 216–224.

Multicultural Children's Books

Ancona, G. (1993). *Pablo remembers: The fiesta of the day of the dead*. New York: Lothrop, Lee & Shepard Books.

Beatty, P. (1981). *Lupita manana*. New York: Beech Tree Books.

Bunting, E. (1991). *Fly away home*. New York: Clarion Books.

Buss, F. (1991). *Journey of the sparrows*. New York: Dell Publishing.

Crew, L. (1989). *Children of the river*. New York: Dell Publishing.

Dooley, N. (1991). *Everybody cooks rice*. Minneapolis: Carolrhoda Books.

Fritz, J. (1982). *Homesick: My own story*. New York: Dell Publishing.

Gray, N. (1988). *A country far away*. New York: Orchard Books.

Lankford, M. (1992). *Hopscotch around the world*. New York: Morrow & Company, Inc.

Lord, B. (1984). *In the year of the boar and Jackie Robinson*. New York: Trumpet Club.

Morris, A. (1989). *Bread, bread, bread*. New York: Lothrop, Lee & Shepard Books.

Pinkley, A. (1993). *Seven candles for Kwanzaa*. New York: Dial Books.

Soto, G. (1991). *Taking sides*. San Diego: Harcourt Brace & Co.

Taylor, M. (1990). *Mississippi bridge*. New York: Bantam Skylark Book.

Taylor, M. (1976). *Roll of thunder, hear my cry*. New York: Bantam Books.

Waters, K., & M. Slovenz-Low (1990). *Lion dancer: Ernie Wan's Chinese new year*. New York: Scholastic.

Websites and Other Links About Multicultural Children's Literature

50 Multicultural Books Every Child Should Know: http://www.soemadison.wisc.edu/ccbc/50mult.htm#repro

The Anti-Defamation League: http://www.adl.org

Barahona Center for the Study of Books in Spanish for Children and Adolescents at California State University, San Marcos: http://www.csusm.edu/csb/

Bibliography of Multicultural Education: http://www.discourse-in-society.org/Bibliography%20Multicultural %20Education.htm

Celebrating Diversity Through Children's Literature: http://www.multiculturalchildrenslit.com/

Circle of Stories, A PBS website that has lessons on using storytelling in the classroom: http://www.pbs.org/ circleofstories/

¡Colorín Colorado!—Information and advice for Spanish-speaking parents (and educators, too): http://www. colorincolorado.org/homepage.php

Cooperative Children's Book Center: http://www.education.wisc.edu/ccbc/

Multicultural Children's Literature in the Elementary Classroom—An ERIC Digest: http://www.ericfacility.net/ ericdigests/ed423552.html

Multicultural Children's Literature (Teachers College, Columbia University): http://lweb.tc.columbia.edu/rr/cl/ topics2.html

Multiculturalism and Children's Literature: http://www.nea.org/readacross/multi/

Multicultural Literature for Children—The Internet Public Library: http://www.ipl.org/div/pf/entry/48493

Rethinking our schools: http://rethinkingschools.org

Small presses owned and operated by people of color—Publishers of Children's Books: http://www.education. wisc.edu/ccbc/pclist.htm

Sources: Lu, M. (1987). Multicultural children's literature in the elementary classroom. *ERIC Digest.* Bloomington, IN: ERIC Clearinghouse on Reading English and Communication; Dietrich, D., & Ralph, K. S. (1995). Crossing borders: Multicultural literature in the classroom. *Journal of Educational Issue of Language Minority Students, 15.* Retrieved Dec. 22, 2007, from http://www.nccla.gwu.pubs/jeilms.vol15/crossing.htm

books, and some websites about multicultural children's literature. These resources will help get you started.

Bias in Children's Literature

Although it is critical that the literature used in classrooms reflects the students' cultural backgrounds (Au, 1993; Shioshita, 1997), it is equally important that teachers select literature that is free from bias and stereotypes. One way to do this is for teachers to not only examine selections before bringing them into the classroom, but to also fully read them so that they may get the full impact of the text before using it with the children (Wilkerson & Kido, 1997). In this way teachers will be better prepared to teach the literature in meaningful ways that consider both the authors' perspective and connections to their students' lives (Mathis, 2001).

One concern that teachers must have about using children's literature is that of accuracy and authenticity, including the reflection of students' cultural and background knowledge related to their lives (Hefflin, 2002). Since children's literature affords students the opportunities to share the experiences of the characters as they glimpse the cultural context of the story (Salas, Lucido, & Canales, 2002), it is critical that this literature accurately depict the various cultural experiences it describes.

Several things need to be taken into consideration when developing guidelines for choosing and working with children's literature. We will present two versions of such guidelines to facilitate choosing appropriate multicultural children's literature in the classroom. Figure 2.5 lists five working guidelines put together by Hefflin (2002) to guide the selection of children's literature. These working guidelines are based on the works of various multicultural educators, including Banks (2003) and Sims Bishop (1997). Figure 2.6 is a series of guidelines from the Council on Interracial Books for Children (n.d.) and offers an extensive list of what to look for when selecting children's literature.

Both sets of guidelines allude to insider perspectives, and although it is not always necessary that multicultural children's literature be written by someone from inside the culture depicted, it is important to consider the ramifications of such literature that is written by outsiders. The Cooperative Children's Book Center in the School of Education at the University of Wisconsin–Madison began compiling statistics on children's books written by and about people of color in 1985 (see Table 2.2). It is interesting to note that

FIGURE 2.5 Five Working Guidelines for Selecting Multicultural Children's Literature

1. Select literature from authors and illustrators who have established reputations for publishing culturally sensitive material, and look at material that highlights the works of new and up-and-coming authors and illustrators.

2. Analyze how the characters are portrayed in the story.

3. Analyze the author's use of language.

4. Examine the illustrations for appeal, ethnic sensitivity, and authenticity.

5. Evaluate factual information for accuracy.

Source: From "Learning to develop culturally relevant pedagogy: A lesson about cornrowed lives," by B. R. Hefflin, 2002, *The Urban Review, 34*(3), p. 237.

FIGURE 2.6 10 Quick Ways to Analyze Children's Books for Racism and Sexism

Both in school and out children are exposed to racist and sexist attitudes. These attitudes—expressed over and over in books and other media—gradually distort their perceptions until stereotypes and myths about minorities and women are accepted as reality. It is difficult for a librarian or teacher to convince children to question society's attitudes. But if a child can be shown how to detect racism and sexism in a book, the child can proceed to transfer the perception to wider areas. The following ten guidelines are offered as a starting point in evaluating children's books from this perspective.

1. **Check the Illustrations**
   a. **Look for Stereotypes.** A stereotype is an over-simplified generalization about a particular group, race or sex, which usually carries derogatory implications. Some infamous (overt) stereotypes of blacks are the happy-go-lucky, watermelon-eating Sambo and the fat, eye-rolling "mammy"; of Chicanos, the sombrero-wearing peon or fiesta-loving, macho bandito; of Asian Americans, the inscrutable, slant-eyed "Oriental"; of Native Americans, the naked savage or "primitive brave" and his "squaw"; of Puerto Ricans, the switch-blade-toting teenage gang member; of women, the completely domesticated mother, the demure, doll-loving little girl or the wicked stepmother. While you may not always find stereotypes in the blatant forms described, look for variations, which in any way demean or ridicule characters because of their race or sex.
   b. **Look for Tokenism.** If there are racial minority characters in the illustrations, do they look just like whites except for being tinted or colored in? Do all minority faces look stereotypically alike, or are they depicted as genuine individuals with distinctive features?
   c. **Who's Doing What?** Do the illustrations depict minorities in subservient and passive roles or in leadership and action roles? Are males the active "doers" and females the inactive observers?

2. **Check the Story Line**

   Liberation movements have led publishers to weed out many insulting passages, particularly from stories with Black themes and from books depicting female characters; however, racist and sexist attitudes still find expression in less obvious ways. The following checklist suggests some of the subtle (covert) form of bias to watch for.
   a. **Standards for Success.** Does it take "white" behavior standards for a minority person to "get ahead"? Is "making it" in the dominant white society projected as the only ideal? To gain acceptance and approval, do persons of color have to exhibit extraordinary qualities—excel in sports, get As, etc.? In friendships between white and non-white children, is it the child of color who does most of the understanding and forgiving?
   b. **Resolution of Problems.** How are problems presented, conceived and resolved in the story? Are minority people considered to be "the problem"? Are the oppressions faced by minorities and women represented as related to social injustice? Are the reasons for poverty and oppression explained, or are they accepted as inevitable? Does the story line encourage passive acceptance or active resistance? Is a particular problem that is faced by a racial minority person or female resolved through the benevolent intervention of a white person or male?
   c. **Role of Women.** Are the achievements of girls and women based on their own initiative and intelligence, or are they due to their good looks or to their relationship with boys? Are sex roles incidental or critical to characterization and plot? Could the same story be told if the sex roles were reversed?

3. **Look at the Lifestyles**

   Are minority persons and their setting depicted in such a way that they contrast unfavorably with the unstated norm of white middle-class suburbia? If the minority group in question is depicted as "different", are negative value judgments implied? Are minorities depicted exclusively in ghettos, barrios, or migrant camps? If the illustrations and text attempt to depict another culture, do they go beyond over-simplifications and offer genuine insight into another lifestyle? Look for inaccuracy and inappropriateness in the depiction of other cultures. Watch for instances of the "quaint-natives-in-costume" syndrome (most noticeable in areas like clothing and custom, but extending to behavior and personality traits as well).

4. **Weigh the Relationships Between People**
   a. Do the whites in the story possess the power, take the leadership, and make the important decisions? Do racial minorities and females of all races function in essentially supporting roles?
   b. How are family relationships depicted? In Black families, is the mother always dominant? In Hispanic families, are there always lots of children? If the family is separated, are societal conditions—unemployment, poverty, for example—cited among the reasons for the separation?

(continued)

FIGURE 2.6 (continued)

5. **Note the Heroes**

   a. For many years, books showed only "safe" minority heroes—those who avoided serious conflict with the white establishment of their time. Minority groups today are insisting on the right to define their own heroes (of both sexes) based on their own concepts and struggles for justice.

   b. When minority heroes do appear, are they admired for the same qualities that have made white heroes famous or because what they have done has benefited white people? Ask this question: "Whose interest is a particular hero really serving?"

6. **Consider the Effect on a Child's Self-Image**

   a. Are norms established which limit any child's aspirations and self-concept? What effect can it have on images of the color white as the ultimate in beauty, cleanliness, virtue, etc., and the color black as evil, dirty, menacing, etc.? Does the book counteract or reinforce this positive association with the color white and negative association with black?

   b. What happens to a girl's self-image when she reads that boys perform all of the brave and important deeds? What about a girl's self-esteem if she is not "fair" of skin and slim of body?

   c. In a particular story, is there one or more persons with whom a minority child can readily identify to a positive and constructive end?

7. **Consider the Author's or Illustrator's Background**

   Analyze the biographical material on the jacket flap or the back of the book. If a story deals with a minority theme, what qualifies the author or illustrator to deal with the subject? If the author and illustrator are not members of the minority being written about, is there anything in their background that would specifically recommend them as the creators of this book?

8. **Check Out the Author's Perspective**

   No author can be wholly objective. All authors write out of a cultural, as well as a personal context. Children's books in the past have traditionally come from authors who were white and who were members of the middle class, with one result being that a single ethnocentric perspective has dominated children's literature in the United States. With any book in question, read carefully to determine whether the direction of the author's perspective substantially weakens or strengthens the value of his/her written work. Is the perspective patriarchal or feminist? Is it solely eurocentric, or do minority cultural perspectives also appear?

9. **Watch for Loaded Words**

   a. A word is loaded when it has insulting overtones. Examples of loaded adjectives (usually racist) are "savage," "primitive," "lazy," "superstitious," "treacherous," "wily," "crafty," "inscrutable," "docile," and "backward".

   b. Look for sexist language and adjectives that exclude or ridicule women. Look for use of the male pronoun to refer to both males and females. While the generic use of the word "man" was accepted in the past, its use today is outmoded. The following examples show how sexist language can be avoided: ancestors instead of forefathers; chairperson instead of chairman; community instead of brotherhood; firefighters instead of firemen; manufactured instead of manmade; the human family instead of the family of man.

10. **Look at the Copyright Date**

    a. Books on minority themes—usually hastily conceived—suddenly began appearing in the mid-1960s. There followed a growing number of "minority experience" books to meet the new market demand, but most of these were still written by the white authors, edited by white editors and published by white publishers. They therefore reflected a white point of view. Not until the early 1970s has the children's book world begun to even remotely reflect the realities of a multiracial society. The new direction resulted from the emergence of minority authors writing about their own experiences. Unfortunately, this trend has been reversing, as publishers have cut back on such books. Non-sexist books, with rare exceptions, were not published before 1973.

    b. The copyright dates, therefore, can be a clue as to how likely the book is to be overtly racist or sexist, although a recent copyright date, of course, is no guarantee of a book's relevance or sensitivity. The copyright date only means the year the book was published. It usually takes about two years from the time a manuscript is submitted to the publisher to the time it is actually printed and put on the market. This time lag meant very little in the past, but in a time of rapid change and changing consciousness, when children's book publishing is attempting to be "relevant," it is becoming increasingly significant.

Source: From *10 quick ways to analyze children's books for racism and sexism,* by Council on Interracial Books for Children, No Date. Available: http://birchlane.davis.ca.us/library/10quick.htm

TABLE 2.2 Children's Books By and About People of Color Published in the United States, 1994–2002

Year	Total Number of Books Published	African/African Americans		Asian/Pacific Asian/Pacific Americans	American Indians	Latinos
		By	About	By and About	By and About	By and About
2002	5,000	69	166	91	64	94
2001	5,000–5,500	99	201	96	60	76
2000	5,000–5,500	96	147	54	39	42
1999	5,000	81	150	61	41	64
1998	5,000	92	183	50	54	66
1997	4,500–5,000	88	216	66	64	88
1996	4,500	92	172	49	50	103
1995	4,500	100	167	91	83	70
1994	4,500	82	166	65	70	90
Total	43,000–58,000	799	1,568	623	525	693

Source: From *Children's books by and about people of color published in the United States*, by Cooperative Children's Book Center, 2003, Madison: University of Wisconsin. Courtesy of Cooperative Children's Book Center.

of the approximately 5,000 children's books published each year from 1994 to 2002, approximately 10% were written by and about people of color. When you look at the numbers written by people of color, the percentages are much smaller.

Given these numbers, and other issues surrounding the authenticity of multicultural children's literature, teachers must pay attention to the books they are using in the classroom as part of culturally relevant pedagogy; otherwise they may fall into the trap of perpetuating stereotypes and bias during lessons set up to do just the opposite.

Guidelines for Developing Culturally Responsive Differentiated Lessons for ELLs

In this section we provide guidelines for how to begin developing culturally responsive lessons for ELLs. Keep in mind that lessons for ELLs should be written to specific standards and include both content and language objectives (see Chapter 3 for a comprehensive discussion on the role of language in differentiating instruction for ELLs).

James Banks (1999), an expert in multicultural education, lists five guidelines for developing a multicultural conceptual curriculum that address issues of differentiation. This model presents a spiraling curriculum, where teachers start with the big picture and then spiral their curriculum down to smaller parts, all thematically related to the whole. The guidelines are as follows:

1. Identify key concepts to be taught. Theses concepts should be powerful and useful for organizing instruction in a variety of content areas. Teachers should also take the

developmental levels of their students into consideration (Banks, 1999). When working with ELLs, teachers must also take the student's language proficiency level into account when designing lessons to teach the key concepts.

2. Identify key or universal generalizations related to each of the key concepts (Banks, 1999). Teachers of ELLs also need to take into consideration their students' background knowledge as well as language levels. They should be sure to preteach any vocabulary related to theses generalizations to ensure access to the curriculum. Furthermore, teachers must plan to scaffold any content that is completely unfamiliar to the student and plan ways to make the content comprehensible to students who are limited in English proficiency (see Chapter 3 for a comprehensive discussion on the role of language in differentiating instruction for ELLs).

3. Identify an intermediate-level generalization for each of the key concepts (Banks, 1999). These intermediate-level generalizations serve as scaffolds, and therefore keys, to understanding the "big picture" at the end of the lesson or unit.

4. Identify a lower-level generalization related to the key generalization for each of the subject areas in which the key concept will be taught (Banks, 1999). Banks's model proposes that concepts should be interdisciplinary or thematic so that content is integrated and lessons span one or more content areas. Using a thematic approach has been shown to be effective with ELLs (Chamot & O'Malley, 1993) in that such an approach gives students a frame on which to hang their growing body of knowledge. ELLs, especially those with limited English proficiency, can build on what they know and what they are learning within the context of a shared theme.

5. Formulate teaching strategies and activities to teach the concepts and generalizations (Banks, 1999). This formulation is especially critical for ELLs since teachers must pay special attention to any language and the content objectives that are contained in the lesson or unit. These strategies and activities should pay close attention to the linguistic needs of the students as well as the background knowledge (linguistic, cultural, content) that the students bring to the lesson. They should also provide students with a variety of ways to access the curriculum, including varied grouping strategies, teacher and student demonstrations and modeling, and vocabulary building activities. Chapter 8 will focus on strategies and activities for effectively differentiating instruction for ELLs.

Planning for Effective Instruction

Instruction that is culturally responsive for ELLs requires careful, reflective planning. It is based on the assumptions made in the previous section and provides opportunities for students to examine issues, concepts, and ideas from multiple (cultural) perspectives and reflect on biases in text. Children's cultural experiences with text and their families also affect how they "see" the world as revealed to them in typical school tasks. Cheng (1987) cites examples of preschool children who were puzzled by questions asked by teachers who expected traditional answers. For example, a Cambodian child who was asked which bedroom she slept in responded with a puzzled look and queried, "What do you mean?" When the teacher repeated the question, the child responded, "Everywhere," clearly indicating that when educators have perceived ideas about what children should know there will be a mismatch as indicated in the example above and the story of the Chinese-speaking preschooler who pointed to two pencils when asked with what would she eat. Many times real-life experiences clash with school experiences for ELL students. In culturally responsive teaching, teachers learn from their students as traditional assumptions are held at bay.

It is important to consider grouping strategies, taking into account not only the group composition, but also the ways in which students understand their roles within the group. This is critical in heterogeneous language groups. While there are benefits to grouping ELLs and English-only students together, we frequently observed such groups where the English-only students have not been taught to work with ELLs and tend to take over and do the work for them. This can produce a sort of "learned helplessness" over time. All students need to be taught to work with others to mediate group structures. For example:

1. teach English-only students to be patient and wait while ELLs take the time to think through the prompts and find words in order to share their ideas;

2. teach ELL students to be politely assertive and tell English-only students they need extra time; and

3. teach both groups to understand that working together in a group is a supportive activity and not one driven by the clock.

Group numbers are also a consideration. Sometimes ELLs who have not acquired the confidence to speak in larger groups of students participate more actively if they are in pairs. Students also have to be trained to work in pairs in structures such as think-pair-share (see Figure 2.2 on page 36). In this structure (Kagan, 1994) students are asked a question or given a prompt. Time is given for them to think about the question or the prompt when they understand what they are being asked. Each student then briefly jots down his/her thoughts (approximately 2 to 4 minutes depending on the language proficiency of ELLs). Next, students pair by exchanging answers with their partners. Finally, each pair shares their ideas with the rest of the class. Student answers should be recorded for future review. The skills required for paired learning work should be reviewed and retaught to support a dyad structure. For example, both partners need time to think on their own. Both partners need to take turns to share their ideas. Both partners need to get ready to share ideas they have discussed with the rest of the class. All answers need to be validated through the recording process that produces a class memory of students' ideas.

Students need to be trained to work in other grouping structures such as triads. The same kinds of skills need to be taught—turn taking, time to think, time to share, and an understanding of the roles individuals in groups undertake. These roles can be assigned to students by the teacher or chosen by the students themselves and include such roles as leader, recorder, timekeeper, praise manager (in charge of giving out praise), or office manager (in charge of supplies) and may vary from task to task and group to group. Knowing the social rules of the group, as well as the class, will help students to succeed in group participation.

Teachers also need to pay attention to how the students participate in home and school (Heath, 1983), looking for ways to understand the households from which their students come (Moll, 2001). Too often teachers react to cultural diversity from a deficit perspective and complain about what is missing from their students' lives. Moll (2001) describes the need to look for what he calls the "funds of knowledge" (p. 17) that exist in families and households and how those funds can serve as resources for both students and teachers. As teachers come to view their students and their families as resources, they can create learning opportunities in their classrooms that draw on this cultural context and bring the home into the school.

One benefit of looking beyond the classroom is that teachers are given opportunities to observe their students in a different context and often are able to see them participate in ways that they do not demonstrate in schools. Often ELLs are called on to translate complex texts or conversations for parents and others. These translations often exhibit not only a linguistic sophistication beyond what the child may demonstrate during school tasks, but also an authoritative role where the child is providing varying degrees of support for the adult and being recognized as being both important and proficient (Orellana et al., 2003). Teachers need to look for ways to provide students with opportunities to engage in learning apart from traditional school interactions (Gutiérrez, Baquédaño-López, & Tejeda, 1999). This will help them organize instruction that is not only culturally, but linguistically, relevant.

Examples from the Field

A Bird's-Eye View of Culturally Responsive Teaching

The classroom at Blue Eagle Elementary School, a school near Edge Lake, was abuzz with soft voices. Children read books, wrote in journals, and worked on tasks in groups of one to four. The kindergarteners had been assigned their work, and the teacher sat on the floor with a small group of first graders. The assignment entailed kindergarteners finding words they were able to recognize in the room and other classroom materials. Students in this class had access to a variety of resources. They could *read the room*: the word walls, independent reading books that had been set aside for each of them based on individual assessments, posted news, and holiday words. Students could also read their own personal word lists, their journals, and the lists and journals of other students in the room. The day began with a Native American chant. Children beat the drums and chanted in their primary language.

In this classroom it was permissible to walk around the room and observe what was going on in other groups. Manipulatives, word cards, poems, audiotapes of Native American music, and stories told by Native American storytellers were available for the kindergarteners to use. They had to learn the alphabet. This was an area being tested at the school. They needed to know the sounds of the English language and be phonemically aware because that area of language development had been deemed by the state and district as critical to students learning how to read. It was assumed that kindergarteners who lived on the Indian reservation were disadvantaged or behind the norm, and would not be ready to read until first or second grade.

Dire was about to openly challenge this belief. Dire resides with his family on an Indian reservation. He is the youngest of five children. During the time of this study, Dire

A classroom library—the wonderful world of books.

was enrolled in a combination kindergarten/first-grade class. The class was composed of children from the same Indian tribe and children who came from homes where Spanish was the language most often spoken. Dire exhibited the characteristics of indigenous people, that is, he was quiet most of the time. He spent a lot of his time watching others in the classroom, stopping to observe when something really interested him and about which he was anxious to learn.

When Dire learned to write his name, he perceived writing as drawing. "Help me draw my name," he would say. He loved to draw and as the year progressed he began to differentiate between drawing and writing. At first, he needed to learn to control his fine motor skills so he could write legibly. He copied a lot from the bulletin boards in his classroom, and this helped him develop his fine motor skills. His classroom was filled with print and cultural objects such as drums, the headdresses of his Indian tribe, and recorded music to which the children could listen. Once a month Indian storytellers would come to the school and share stories from the tribe with the children. Dire would sit cross legged, mouth open, eyes fixed on the storyteller, completely enthralled with the stories, the drums, and the dances. When he was ready to read, he slowly approached the reading circle and waited for the teacher to invite him into the circle.

An inquisitive young man, he walked up to the teacher and asked her to help him "draw" those things. The "things" he referred to were the letters he saw posted on the walls and around other areas in the classroom. Dire knew that the letters on the wall communicated ideas when put together, and if he could just learn how to manipulate them, he could "draw" his name. We spent one day a week during an entire school year observing Dire's classroom. His teacher worked one on one with him in response to his request. In time, Dire referred to "drawing" his name as writing it.

One day Dire stopped what he was doing and left his seat. He slowly made his way toward the first-grade reading group, with a few detours. First he walked over to the window ledge and looked at the ant farm. He talked to himself, asking questions as he watched the ants busy themselves trying to exist in an environment where they had been placed on display for the world to see. Next Dire walked over to the tubs in which the independent reading books had been placed. As he glanced through the books, his gaze repeatedly shifted from what he was doing to the first-grade reading group. After about 5 minutes of looking at the independent reading books, Dire finally made his way to the first-grade reading group.

He circled the group observing what the other children were doing. They were reading and following along in the text as needed. The children were reading at their individual reading rates. The teacher monitored their reading, providing assistance as the children needed it. Dire closed in on the group. He moved closer to his teacher who reached out to him. He sat in her lap. She had the book the first graders were reading open on the floor in front of her. Dire watched the others read and the teacher offer assistance. Help was provided as students looked at her in a silent prompt for help. She waited and observed their use of picture clues and decoding skills. Then she offered a prompt.

Dire began to imitate the first graders. He looked at the book the teacher had open on the floor, put his finger on a word, looked at his teacher and waited for her to respond to him. She helped him decode the word, sometimes told him the word. He began to "read," haltingly at first and with numerous appeals for help. He was ready to get started.

The teacher in this classroom understood Dire's needs and responded to them appropriately. She understood that the Native American children she taught might appear to be cautious about learning. She discovered that they learned through observations. They were motivated about school when experiencing learning. She learned that to stay motivated about school and learning, they had to make connections between school and their personal lives. She found out that the children in this classroom had to talk about things that affected their lives as well as their work.

Teddy's story is another example. Teddy was the youngest child in his family. His mother passed away at the age of 35 and Teddy was sent to live with an aunt. He was very close to his mother and her death sent him into a state of seclusion. He would rock back and forth in his kindergarten/first-grade classroom. Music would calm him and he knew that he could go to the listening station at any time. When he became agitated, he would cry and be unable to focus on completing his assigned tasks. For days, Teddy sat and listened to Native American music and other music he could choose on his own. He was encouraged to sit in his teacher's lap whenever he felt he needed her comfort. He could read and write the room. Materials were available to him to do his work, but whenever grief became too much for this kindergartener, Teddy would and could seek other activities that calmed him. Although the tears would flow, they dissipated when he found a comforting activity in which to engage.

When he became anxious, Teddy would take a clipboard and walk around the room copying words and sentences from the walls of his print rich classroom. He worked well with his classmates in a small group where the other children would talk and sing. This environment calmed Teddy and he was able to get his work done. Teddy could write his name and was a beginning reader. He struggled with mastering high frequency words. He was not reading at the end of his kindergarten year.

One day Teddy decided to join a group of children at a table. He picked up his pencil and phonics worksheet. The children were repeating the beginning sounds of each picture and giving each other feedback as to the accuracy of the beginning sounds. They were aware that Teddy had joined them and each child in the group of four made sure he had everything needed to become a member. The children continued their work for a few minutes until one of them began to talk about the issue that weighed heavily on their hearts and minds.

"I think that when people leave this earth, they go to other places where they are happy. I think the earth keeps them warm," he began.

"Yeah," replied another student, "that's what my grandma says. We can be sad, but it's okay if they go, because they have to."

"I know," retorted another child, "we'll see them some day."

Teddy did not engage in the talk, but he was listening. His eyes darted from his work to the other children. One would expect Teddy to burst into tears at any moment because of the exchange. But he didn't. The conversation could have been interpreted as forbidden or cruel. But it was not. It seemed the other children knew that Teddy needed a different kind of comforting, and they began to talk about what they had heard about death in their community. The word *death* was not mentioned. No one specifically referred to Teddy's mom. They didn't have to. It was as if they all knew what to say and when to say it. Comfort emerged from the cultural talk.

This exchange and Dire's nontraditional way of approaching text on his own terms may never have happened in a classroom where the teacher did not understand what culturally relevant classroom experiences looked and sounded like. Dire's teacher went beyond traditional practice to organize culturally relevant pedagogy that explored different ways of knowing and learning so that her students were able to demonstrate competence and achieve beyond expectations. Both teachers planned instruction based on what they knew about the students (see Table 2.3).

In this chapter we discussed the role of culture in planning for differentiated instruction for ELLs and explored how to look beyond the classroom at what students bring to the classroom that can help teachers design effective lessons that provide opportunities for all students to learn. It is critical that teachers consider culture when they are planning for instruction. We all bring our own personal lenses to our roles as teachers and it is important to understand the cultural contexts within which teaching exists. Children spend a good deal of their time in classrooms and it is up to teachers to make those classrooms places where learning takes place. Given the constraints placed on teachers as well as the changing face of their students, culture plays a larger and larger role in their everyday lives. We must also remember that language and culture are intricately related, which is evident from the sections in this chapter that discuss storytelling and multicultural children's literature. Chapter 3 will focus on the role of language in differentiating instruction for ELLs and will provide a link between the issues of culture and language and their relation to planning effective instruction.

TABLE 2.3 A Planning Chart for Differentiated Instruction for Dire and Teddy

Student Name	What I Know About Each Student	Grade Level	Skills Required	Necessary Scaffolds
Dire	Native California Indian tribe member. English is his primary language.	Kindergarten	Understanding that parents expect their children to be independent, find their way to school and back home without escorts.	Encourage and support his tribal culture through Native songs, poems, stories, use of drums, attention to powwow rituals.
	Sees writing as drawing.		Understanding that drawing is a part of writing. Let him observe the role of drawing in books and talk about how the drawing helps the reader understand the story.	Show him how writing is different from drawing. Encourage him to mix writing and drawing.
	Is a keen observer and curious about many things in the classroom such as the ant farm, books, music.		Understanding that areas of interest such as the ant farm can be found in books and on the Internet. Understanding that music is a form of communication.	Use oral language as a way to scaffold him into reading. Have him dictate stories.
	Parents believe his educational growth is the school's responsibility.		Communicate regularly and consistently with parents in the home to establish cordial relationships.	Involve Dire in home visits.
	Is also an auditory learner who likes to listen to stories.		Understanding that storytelling helps us understand how stories are constructed and that Native stories have a different structure than Western stories.	Use story maps to visually show how stories in different cultures are structured. Add pictures and drawings.
	Will engage in activities when he feels confident and ready.		Understanding that interest and observation are cultural ways of knowing for the children of this tribe. Encourage Dire's curiosity.	Help him understand that it is okay to observe. Ask questions about his observations to increase interest.
Teddy	Is withdrawn and shy. Needs nurturing and time to heal after his mother's death.	Kindergarten	Understanding that tragedies make us sad and that is a natural response.	Provide a safe place to be alone in the classroom or with others.
	Responds to firm requests with anger and perceived stubbornness.		Understanding that drawing about how one feels is a way to put our feelings into visual symbols so we can feel better.	Help Teddy to express how he is feeling and that he needs some space for a short time.
	Calms down when listening to music.		Understanding that music is communication that tells stories just like books do.	Help Teddy create poems and songs that can be communicated with drums and chants.
	Likes to copy words from the room environment.		Understanding that lists of words can be turned into poems, songs, and stories.	Use language experience creating his own stories through dictation. This becomes his reading.

Practical Applications and Individual Inquiries: Cases to Think About and Investigate

1. Search the Internet to locate a checklist for biases in children's literature. Get three children's books and use the checklist as the criteria for evaluating children's books for biases. Do a brief write up about what you found, citing evidence from the children's books.

2. Search the Internet for a list of criteria that can be used to investigate the use of cultural stereotypes in literacy materials. Select an anthology that is used in schools, such as a social studies book, and use the criteria to evaluate the materials. Write your personal definition of stereotypes, using the criteria list and what you located in the literacy materials.

3. Read the book *The New Circles of Learning: Cooperation in the Classroom and School* (Johnson, Johnson, & Holubec, 1994). Find the roles the authors define as necessary for cooperative learning to be successful. Teach the roles to a group of students and evaluate how well they do. Have students evaluate themselves.

The Role of Language in Planning and Delivering Differentiated Literacy Instruction to English Language Learners

When I was in elementary school I use[d] to translate for my landlady. She could not speak a word in Spanish and the people living in her houses did not speak English. Therefore, I translated. Not only was I practicing, I was also being paid for translating. Translating [into English] somehow helped me get better in my fluency when I read, therefore, I was able to pronounce words better and better every day. . . .

Ámparo, teacher candidate

Given the changing demographics in today's schools, teachers are increasingly being called on to teach students from a variety of ethnic and linguistic backgrounds who come to school with varying experiences in language and literacy, regardless of their native language. Teachers often find themselves teaching students to read and write in a language they do not yet understand or in a language variety that is different from the Standard English used in schools nationwide. Furthermore, children come to school differentially prepared to use language for learning purposes (Schleppegrell, 2004).

Fillmore and Snow (2002) argue that teachers need training in the use of specific strategies to deal effectively with linguistic diversity in the classroom.

Teachers need to examine the surface features of the language spoken by the children in the classroom and school to explore the language skills that transfer to a second language as well as the language skills that do not transfer. They can then use this knowledge to create effective lessons that target both language and content. To differentiate literacy instruction for ELLs, teachers need to pay close attention to students' academic language needs when planning instruction.

In this chapter, we examine the importance of exploring each student's language to best meet his or her academic needs through differentiated instruction. We will:

- Define language and its importance in differentiating literacy instruction for ELLs.

- Explore issues in first and second language acquisition that are critical to designing effective literacy lessons for ELLs.

- Examine literacy instruction and opportunities to learn for ELLs who learn to read in English.

- Give examples of language objectives and descriptions of how teachers mediate language during instruction.

- Give examples of scripts from classrooms where teachers have thought about, learned about, and become metacognitive about students' language during the teaching/ learning process.

- Describe the second language writing development of two ELLs, one who received initial literacy instruction in Spanish and one who received initial literacy instruction in English.

Building Background Knowledge About the Role of Language in Literacy Development

What Is Language and Why Is It Important?

It is easy to take language for granted, because most humans are capable of producing language and begin to acquire language shortly after birth. In fact, given the apparent ease with which most children acquire their first language, it seems puzzling why many struggle when it comes to acquiring a second language. Although many argue that it is difficult to put together a fixed definition of language, experts agree on some basic characteristics for defining language.

As early as 1921 experts described language as a way for humans to communicate using arbitrary symbols (Hall, 1964; Sapir, 1921; Trager, 1949). Chomsky (1968) also noted that language involves the construction of sentences from a fixed set of elements. Halliday (1973) described language as varied behavior options taking place in a social context and linked to culture. Most experts also argue that language is not necessarily instinctual, but is passed down from parent to child from birth. Parents use specialized talk sometimes called *mothereze* to "teach" their young children language.

Children come to school with varying language proficiency, and it is the teacher's role to facilitate students' growing language proficiency in ways that help them to succeed in school.

Peregoy and Boyle (2005) define language proficiency as "the ability to use a language effectively and appropriately throughout the social, personal, school, and work situations required for daily living in a given society" (p. 34). Peregoy and Boyle also describe the teacher's role as one that helps students become proficient in listening, speaking, reading, and writing.

Language proficiency, therefore, is not solely based on grammar and form; rather it is a complex process that requires students to understand word and sentence meanings as well as the social conventions and rules that govern linguistic interactions in school and other settings. Peregoy and Boyle (2005) use the term *communicative competence* to describe the way proficient language users manipulate correct grammatical forms, the understanding of language functions, as well as the social conventions needed to communicate effectively. Students who are proficient language users coordinate all language subsystems: phonology, the sound system of language; morphology, the rules of word formation; syntax, the rules of word order; semantics or meaning; and pragmatics, the sociolinguistic rules that influence communication (Peregoy & Boyle, 2005).

In addition to being able to use language to communicate, students need to be able to use language to learn once they get to school. This language that students use to learn is often called *academic language*. Although children begin acquiring communicative language at birth, they learn academic language at school from teachers and textbooks, as well as from peers in formal and informal learning situations (Fillmore & Snow, 2002).

Issues in First and Second Language Acquisition and Development

But what about students who come to school speaking a language other than English, or who come to school speaking a nonstandard variety of English? Historically, these students are viewed from a deficit perspective, at times even as having a language disorder! Research in first and second language acquisition (Krashen, 1994, 2005) tells us that languages are equal and students who come to school speaking a language other than English bring skills in their native language to school. The teacher's job is to teach students English through English language development activities, show students how to make connections between their native language and English, and help students gain access to the curriculum through scaffolded instruction that allows ELLs to comprehend oral and written language. What students learn in their native language transfers to their second language (Cummins, 1994; Thonis, 1994) once they become proficient in that language.

L1 Acquisition and Development

Most children are successful in acquiring their native language. In fact, children begin to acquire language early on as they start to babble and coo, sometimes by 2 months of age. Generally by the time a child reaches 1 year of age, he or she has uttered his or her first word or words, and the process continues until the child is able to communicate with language. A variety of theories related to first language acquisition and development attempt to explain just how children acquire language. These include the behaviorist theory (Skinner, 1957), the innatist theory (Chomsky, 1957), and the interactionist theory (Halliday, 1975).

The behaviorist theory relies on the concepts of imitation and reinforcement to describe how children acquire or learn language and does not account for the fact that children often speak sentences that they have never heard before as well as sentences that are approximations of correct speech, which they have not heard before (Peregoy & Boyle, 2005). The innatist theory argues that language development is innate and each child has a "biological language acquisition device" (Chomsky, 1968; Peregoy & Boyle, 1997, p. 33) that "prewires" them to acquire language. This theory, therefore, discounts the role of social context in language acquisition and development.

The interactionist theory acknowledges the role of social context in addition to some form of innate capacity for language learning. According to this theory, caregivers of young children play an important role in language acquisition as they scaffold language through modeling during communication (Halliday, 1975). However, Chomsky (2001) reminds us that even young children talk in ways that are "innovated and rule-governed" (p. 52). The rules that govern language, although not directly taught to young children, are modeled in ways that facilitate acquisition. Children then experiment with language in ways that help them use language in socially acceptable ways, which may vary according to specific social and cultural rules. Heath (1983) examined the communication patterns of children in two communities and found differences in language usage that were specific to each community. Children in both communities grew up speaking English, but parents and other adults and older peers modeled specific rules for communication. The children in both communities "came to have different ways of communicating, because their communities had different social legacies and ways of behaving in face-to-face interactions" (p. ii). In other words, children in each community learned to use language in socially acceptable ways for that community.

Cummins's (1981, 1991, 1994) work helps us to explore first language acquisition and development in relationship to success in school. If we look at his description of basic interpersonal communication skills (BICS)—the language that children (and adults) use in daily face-to-face communications—and cognitive *academic language* proficiency (CALP)—the language necessary to be successful in school, we can see that these concepts describe two aspects of language proficiency (Cummins, 1989). Both aspects are naturally connected and interrelated. As children come to understand and use language, they develop their BICS and learn to communicate in the socially acceptable ways described above. Their BICS, then, help them to develop the academic language or CALP that is necessary to be successful in school. If we look at these two aspects as a sort of fuzzy continuum, we can see that children continually develop their BICS, but as they become more proficient language users and enter school or engage in tasks that require them to use language to learn, they begin to develop their CALP. By the time children are in the second grade, they are expected to be able to use language to learn, in other words, use CALP to make sense of school tasks.

Although some argue against there being two types of language proficiency (MacSwan, Rolstad, & Glass, 2002; Wiley, 1996), Cummins (n.d.) continues to make the case that there is a difference between the language children use to communicate with one another and the language that teachers use in the classroom. He states,

> In monolingual contexts, the distinction reflects the difference between the language proficiency acquired through interpersonal interaction by virtually all 6-year old children and the proficiency developed through schooling and literacy, which continues to expand throughout our lifetimes. For most children, the basic structure of their native language is in place by age 6

or so but their language continues to expand with respect to the range of vocabulary and grammatical constructions they can understand and use and the linguistic contexts within which they function successfully. (Cummins, n.d., p. 5)

Looking at BICS as a means of facilitating a child's development of CALP makes sense when differentiating literacy instruction for ELLs. In other words, when children develop BICS in their L1, that BICS will help them to gain CALP in their L1 once they enter school or encounter academic language for learning purposes. As Cummins (1981, 1994) argues, it can take *up to* 7 years for CALP to develop, but if we think of a young child, this also makes sense. Most 7-year-olds are in the second grade, and it is at the end of first and the beginning of second grade that children engage in tasks that ask them to use language to learn. By that time, they are not only learning language and literacy in school, but also using that language and literacy to learn in and out of school. It makes sense, then, that when ELLs come to school speaking a language other than English, they can use that language to help them learn English. The more fully developed their CALP in the L1 is, the faster the path to the successful use of academic language in English. Therefore, when students can fully use academic language or CALP in their L1, that CALP will support the development of both communicative and academic language in the L2.

L2 Acquisition and Development: A Look at Language Issues for ELLs Who Learn to Read in English

This notion of a continuum of language learning also is important when we look at students who come to school speaking a language other than English. Imagine coming to school and learning to read in a language that you don't understand. Think about listening to a teacher you know is saying something important but for you it sounds like nonsense. This is what happens for many ELLs who come to school with limited English language proficiency, but who are being taught to read in English. Although these students make remarkable progress in learning English, they often struggle with learning to read at first. Furthermore, teachers who lack training in how to effectively teach ELLs to read in English may be unaware of the ways in which they limit access to the curriculum. Marina, currently a principal in California, describes her experience as a young ELL in a mainstream English second-grade class.

Marina's Literacy Story

I remembered hoping that just maybe this class and above all this teacher might be different than my first grade teacher. I remember feeling so very sad that I had another teacher that could not pronounce my name "María" instead of "Marina." "Oh well" I thought, it's ok in other areas she will be different. I need time to know her more and she needs time to know me.

As I looked around me I felt happy inside to see some familiar faces, but at the same time I felt my heart beating very fast and the palms of my hands sweating because those familiar faces, Anna and Tilly, were two faces I wish so much I would have never seen—they were the ones I spoke Spanish to and got in trouble with; I was tired of the spankings I received by our principal and I wanted to be a good girl and not a bad girl and these two girls were going to get me in trouble. There was still a hope that this teacher would be different.

That week the teacher called names on who would be in the high group, middle group and low group in reading. My name and the names of about seven other Hispanic children were never called on; my heart sank, "yes, I am stupid. How can I read if I don't even speak English?" The seven of us were guided by the teacher's index finger, a sign to come with her to a corner. We were given crayons and paper to color. That went on for a long time. The teacher always met with the high group, middle group and low group. One day as she was still with the reading group, I stood up to select a book from a shelf. The teacher stood up, yelled across the room, "go back to your group," pointing to the corner (where the other Hispanic children were coloring) "and put that book back."

I froze and never again did I ever get up to even open or look at a book in that class for the remainder of the year.

Although a large, established body of literature addresses the concept of how to teach students to read (Kamil, Mosenthal, Pearson, & Barr, 2000; McArdle & Chhabra, 2004; NICHD, 2000; Snow, Burns, & Griffin, 1998; Unrau & Ruddell, 2004), the research on teaching ELLs to read in English is now emerging as a separate field (August & Shanahan, 2006; Genesee, Lindholm-Leary, Saunders, & Christian, 2006). Proponents of bilingual education have long supported the use of the primary language for initial literacy instruction (Cummins, 1994, 2003, Thomas & Collier, 1997), making the commonsense assertion that it is easier to learn to read in a language that is already understood and arguing that literacy skills transfer from the L1 to the L2 (Thonis, 1994). Critics (Baker, 1992; Rossell, 1992, 2004–2005), argue that students often languish in bilingual programs and need to be instructed in English upon entering school. Issues related to initial literacy experiences are further compounded by national, state, and district mandates that increasingly dictate how students are to be taught.

Factors That Impact Learning to Read in a Second Language

When teaching students to read in their second language, teachers must be aware of several things in order to provide quality instruction and ensure that students have access to the curriculum. These include examining the surface features of language that signal differences in the languages students already speak and the second language in which they are being taught; exploring prior literacy experiences; providing appropriate scaffolds so that students have access to the texts used in class; and allowing students to use multiple means to demonstrate what they know.

Language Structure and Use: Examining the Surface and Content Features of L1 and L2

The structure of the English language needs to be an essential part of reading instruction, especially for those students who come to school speaking a language other than English. Effective direct, systematic reading instruction recognizes and uses the inherent organizational patterns in spoken and written English. Effective teaching of English as a second language is also organized according to language form, function, and use. Teachers must consider how children learn the alphabetic principle and what to do to ensure that students understand the principle. For example, children who have seen and been exposed to a language that is logographic and tonal will need ongoing support to understand how an alphabetic language works. They may not *hear* the sounds we are trying to teach them because the sounds may not exist in their native tongue.

Therefore, lessons for ELLs must not only teach content, but also focus on language learning specific to the individual student. For example, when teaching ELLs, especially those whose native language is Spanish, teachers must think about the structure of both languages. Although Spanish is an alphabetic system like English, the two languages have several key differences. The main difference is that Spanish is phonetically more consistent. Graphemes and phonemes in Spanish have one-to-one correspondence.

Another phonological difference between Spanish and English is that Spanish has more graphemes (letters) that represent a single phoneme (sound) than English does. Spanish has only five vocalic phonemes: /a/, /e/, /i/, /o/, and /u/. Spanish contains fewer sounds and only five different consonant sounds in word endings: d, l, n, r, and s. The following consonant blends never appear at the beginning of a Spanish word: sl, st, sp.

As with dialects in English, there are phonological variations among Spanish-speaking cultures. For example, just as some New Englanders substitute /er/ for the /a/ at the ends of words like tuba, some Spanish speakers from the Caribbean may pronounce the /r/ at the end of a word as /l/, such as amol for amor, mal for mar, and comel for comer (Pérez & Torres-Guzmán, 2002).

Spanish and English share many prefixes (re, des, dis, im, in, co, extra, inter, trans, anti) and some suffixes (plural s and es, ado, able), and the concept of compound words (abrelatas, rascacielo, chupaflor, etc.), and syntax.

There is also a difference in the position of the noun and adjective. In Spanish the noun precedes the adjective, as in "El papel amarillo" (The paper yellow), whereas in English the adjective usually precedes the noun. However, the situation is not so simple, since we can also say "Paint the paper yellow." Another difference involves the use of "have." In Spanish one would literally say, "I have 11 years" (tengo 11 años) and "I have thirst" (tengo sed), whereas in English, one would say, "I am 11 years old" and "I'm thirsty."

Spanish employs double negatives, literally to say "He doesn't have nothing" (El no tiene nada). Other differences also exist. In Spanish, we can literally "open the faucet" (abrir la llave) rather than turn it on, and "put attention" (poner atención) rather than pay attention. As children gain experience in English, they may go through a phase in which they use these literal translated language forms.

Much of this will depend on how much academic language and literacy students have in their native language (Short & Fitzsimmons, 2007). A child in the early grades who has never had instruction in Spanish, for example, would benefit little from such comparisons since there would be no background knowledge base with which to compare. Transitional readers, however, should be given explicit instruction about items that do not transfer from the first language, such as apostrophes in contractions and possessives, use of "s" in simple present (the boy runs), and capital letters for days and months.

True competence in a language, however, involves much more than understanding its structure. Knowing how and when to use informal slang or how to begin and end a conversation with normal social conventions can be just as important to communication as word order (syntax), grammatical rules of sounds (phonology), word forms (morphology), and semantics (word meaning). To communicate orally or in writing, people must coordinate all their knowledge of these systems in a way that fits the social context. Language carries meaning through a shared understanding of rules regarding sounds (including pitch, intonation, etc.), word order, and word forms. However, as anyone who has taken a language course that focused on grammar can tell you, an understanding of language rules does not empower one to carry on a conversation in that language.

The meanings and forms of words are reflections of the cultures that use them; culture and language are closely interwoven. Linguists tell us that by comparing even the amount of words devoted to a certain item or concept, one can tell a great deal about the culture surrounding a language. Consider, for example, the number of words in Spanish devoted to corn in its various forms (and that many are borrowed from the indigenous Nahuatl language): xilotes (the corn on the stalk newly formed), elotes (from elotl, the ear of corn), mazorca (the full ear), miahuatl (grains from which corn syrup is taken), granos (the grains), nixtamal (grains cooked in water with lime), esquites (soft grains in their own water), masa (the nixtamal ground and mashed), to name a few, and not to mention the dozens of elaborate recipes involving corn: pinole (corn flour with sugar—a candy), atole (corn flour with water or milk, sugar, and cinnamon), many types of tortillas (blanditas, tlayudas, totopos, tostadas, sopes, etc.).

In English, rice is rice, whereas many Southeast Asian languages use different words depending on whether it is in the field, cut or threshed, or prepared to eat. In English we eat breakfast, lunch, or dinner, whereas in Cambodia, their words literally mean to eat rice. Other words also reflect daily culture—in English we can carry something, but in Cambodia there are at least 15 words to express the action depending on whether it is on the head, shoulder, a pole, in the hand, on the hip, etc. (Bliatout, Downing, Lewis, & Yang, 1988). In the United States consider how many ways we can express the concept of a transportation vehicle: car, automobile, SUV, compact, full size, convertible, coupe, van, truck, not to mention the names of specific makes and models. Teachers need to consider the possibility of creating an unintended mental image in the minds of students when using words with shades of meaning that are unfamiliar to someone from a different culture.

The semantics can be even more complicated for an ELL when we consider the many meanings of the same word. For example, in English we can carry on, carry out (a plan), carry a disease, carry over, carry (in addition), carry off, carry our own weight, and get carried away, all different concepts using the same word. Students need to hear this type of idiomatic speech within comprehensible contexts, and teachers need to be prepared to clarify when the context itself has failed to communicate the meaning.

Becoming literate in any language is a complicated and multifaceted task. Children who begin formal reading instruction in kindergarten have already enjoyed thousands of hours mastering the sounds, syntax, grammatical rules, and social nuances of their language. They have already developed an expansive oral vocabulary. As previously mentioned, the more proficient children are in their native language—in other words, if they have developed CALP in that language—the faster the road to fluent English proficiency. Children who begin the process of becoming literate in a language they know since birth have a tremendous advantage because most of the skills of reading and writing are transferable to a second language (Cummins, 1994; Thonis, 1994). Children who begin reading in a language they do not yet speak or understand learn to focus on the mechanics of decoding without gathering meaning from the text. This overemphasis on graphophonic cues (and underutilizing of syntactic and semantic cues) often results in comprehension that lags behind native speakers throughout their years in school.

Exploring Prior Literacy Experiences

All children (barring physical or environmental barriers) learn to speak their first language without any formal instruction, but the same cannot be said about reading and writing. Because of the universality of spoken language, Chomsky (1957) theorized that language acquisition can only be explained by an inherent "language acquisition device" (LAD). By first generalizing those rules they come to understand about grammar and syntax (such as adding "ed" to every word to make it past tense—"I telled him a story"), children gradually refine their knowledge by testing and listening. Parents and others help children to acquire language through using "caretaker speech," paraphrasing their statements, expanding on their expressions, and ensuring comprehension through whatever means. Rather than telling young children, "Today we are going to learn the present perfect tense," we expose them to meaningful language forms in a natural context. Teachers can build on these initial experiences in language and literacy development to help ELLs make sense of school activities.

Research shows that we learn our second (or third) language much in the same way as we learned our first. Dulay and Burt (1974) examined the grammatical errors made by native Spanish- and Chinese-speaking children. Their analysis showed that the types of errors, rather than being due to the influence of their first language, were mostly the same types of errors made by young English speakers acquiring their first language. Contrastive linguistics, comparing structural differences between the first language and the second, is less likely to predict the difficulties a child will have with English as a second language than is a knowledge of how young native speakers "creatively construct" the rules and structure of English early on (Dulay, Burt, & Krashen, 1982). However, because ELLs generally acquire their first and second languages in different contexts and use them in different ways, they often demonstrate differences in proficiency between their L1 and L2 (Valdés, 2005).

Krashen (1994, 2005) draws a distinction between learning and acquiring a language. Learning focuses on direct and formal teaching of the grammar and structure of a language in an academic environment. Acquisition occurs in a natural context, in much the same way as we learn our first language. According the Krashen's Natural Order hypothesis, we acquire (rather than learn) morphemes in a predictable sequence. We acquire certain morphemes early in the acquisition process, whereas we may not master others until later. Formal learning does little to affect the order.

Scaffolding Access to Language and Text

Students learn a great deal about language through meaningful context. Therefore, teachers must provide meaningful and comprehensible content to facilitate language and literacy development. The key is to afford students access to texts in ways that help them to learn language. Regardless of students' language proficiency level, if they cannot make meaning of a text in use, little language or literacy acquisition is taking place.

Krashen's (1994, 2005) work also helps us to understand this phenomenon. In his Input hypothesis, he introduces us to the concept of comprehensible input or $i + 1$, which he describes as "structures that are just beyond our current level of competence" (1994, p. 61). This useful concept tells us that ELLs (and other students) can read and understand text with words and structures that they don't yet know, but that are only just outside what they currently know. Krashen also tells us that if there is enough comprehensible input in a specific text, i + 1 is automatically provided and it is not necessary to teach every grammatical structure. Krashen further argues that within this framework, teachers do not need to directly teach grammatical structures. Instead, ELLs acquire new grammatical structures by reading texts with i + 1. Although the Input hypothesis has implications beyond reading instruction, we can also see its application here.

Demonstrating Knowledge

Because it may be challenging for ELLs to demonstrate what they know as a result of their emerging language proficiency, it is important that they be given multiple opportunities to show what they know. ELLs in the early stages of L2 acquisition are able to understand and appropriate complex English language concepts through the use of scaffolded instruction by skilled teachers who provide opportunities for them to use language in meaningful ways (Ulanoff, Gopalakrishnan, Brantley, & Courtney, with Rogers, 2007). Thus students of diverse linguistic, economic, and cultural backgrounds succeed when they have opportunities to engage in "a continuum of teaching strategies that involves them in motivating, meaningful reading [and learning] experiences" (Au, 2002, p. 409).

Teaching ELLs to Read in English

Children come to school with a great deal of knowledge about literacy, and often their prior experiences with language and print can have a significant impact on their emerging reading success (Liebling, 1998). For ELLs, oral language development and proficiency is also a predictor of subsequent reading proficiency (Peregoy & Boyle, 2005, Proctor, Carlo, August, & Snow, 2005), although some recent studies argue against the use of oral language proficiency as a construct for measuring linguistic competence (see MacSwan et al., 2002, for a comprehensive discussion of this issue). Initial literacy instruction today often focuses on concepts about print (Clay, 1993), phonemic awareness, and phonics, rather than the underlying meaning of the text (Chall, 1983). As evidenced by the recent incarnation of the reading wars nationwide (Allington, 2002; Allington & Woodside-Jiron, 1999; Coles, 2000; Foorman, Fletcher, Francis, & Schatschneider, 2000; Garan, 2002), some arguments support the importance of developing automatic decoding skills to promote reading success (Adams, 1990; Konold, Juel, & McKinnon, 1999; NIHCD, 2000), whereas others support reading instruction situated in a more holistic understanding of the words in context (Goodman, 1986; Smith, 1986). These issues related to effective initial literacy instruction become even more compelling when examined within the context of their application to ELLs.

Much has been written about how ELLs can best learn to speak, read, and write English (August & Shanahan, 2006; Bialystock, 2002; Collier & Thomas, 2004; Cummins, 1994; Genesee, Lindholm-Leary, Saunders, & Christian, 2006; Krashen, 1994; Willig, 1985). Although not without contradictory argument (Rossell, 2004–2005; Rossell & Baker, 1996), most proponents of bilingual education accept that the use of L1 instruction as students are becoming literate greatly facilitates L2 acquisition (Cummins, 2005; Krashen, 2005; Ramírez, 1992; Thonis, 1994; Ulanoff, 1995), as it makes sense that it is easier to learn to read and write in a language that is already understood. Studies in California (Krashen & Biber, 1988; Ramírez, 1992) demonstrated successful academic achievement for ELLs who had the benefit of L1 instruction. Other studies reported similar success for students outside of California (Collier & Thomas, 2004; Willig, 1985).

Regardless of specific research on effective ways to teach reading to ELLs, initial literacy instruction for many, if not most, ELLs takes place in English. Although there are parallels between first and second language literacy development, there are also specific issues that ELLs encounter when they learn to read in their second language. Bernhardt (2003) argues that students who learn to read in their second language have a "cultural memory" that enables them to have a different understanding of the meaning of words. This different understanding renders the L2 reading process inherently different from the L1 reading process due to the knowledge base already stored in memory in the L1. These differences in understanding have a direct effect on literacy acquisition in terms of what ELLs bring to the task of learning to read in their second language (Bernhardt, 2003). This difference and its effect on L2 literacy development are inextricably related to the language of initial literacy instruction and the age at which ELLs learn to read in their L2.

Cummins (1994) argues that students who learn to read and write in a second language before they have acquired proficiency in their L1 are likely to struggle with elements that do not transfer from the L1 to the L2. To effectively teach L2 learners to read proficiently in English, teachers must know a great deal about language and literacy (Adger, Snow, & Christian, 2002), understand that learning to read in the L2 relies on the structure of that language, and understand how to teach students with whom they do not share a common language (Droop & Verhoeven, 2003). Rather than focus on teaching grammar, teachers need to examine the regularities and irregularities between, among, and within second languages, second language learning, and the learners. These factors can have a great impact on students' emerging reading development.

Writing Instruction for ELLs

Most children come to school with a great deal of knowledge about written language (Bissex, 1980; Calkins, 1994; Carrasquillo, Kucer, & Abrams, 2004; Clay, 1975; Edelsky, 1986; Samway, 2006; Wells, 1986; and others). Krashen (1991) argues that children acquire writing subconsciously, much the same way as they acquire a second language, through comprehensible input. He stresses that reading in L1 as well as in L2 assists in the development of writing. This language then becomes the base on which the second language learners draw when they write. Their experiences with reading facilitate their writing by demonstration; the text that is read demonstrates proficient writing to the novice (Ray, 1999; Smith, 1983, 1994).

ELLs are therefore exposed to varied forms of print, initially in their first and eventually their second language. These print forms serve as comprehensible models of writing, demonstrating both the form and function of written language. As the students begin to engage in written communication, they are able to use their knowledge of print to facilitate the construction of meaning.

Dialogue journals—written conversations between teacher and student (Peyton & Reed, 1990)—offer the student, as well as the teacher, a means of generating authentic written communication instead of practice exercises. Through the dialogue journal, the teacher and student develop a relationship that is mediated by the continuous writing,

writing that is situated in the social context of the dialogue itself. The student, therefore, becomes an active participant in a continuing writing event, one that not only has elements of both written and oral language in that it is conversation that is written down, but also by its very nature facilitates writing development and growth.

Dialogue journals can be an effective way to help students with L2 acquisition as they allow ELLs at the beginning levels of English language proficiency to express themselves in writing before they have complete control over English (Staton, 1983, Ulanoff, 1995). Dialogue journals serve as an arena for both reading and writing as the student reads the teacher's response and then responds to the teacher in a comprehensible manner (Peyton, 1990).

That children become literate within a context of reading and writing authentic language (Freeman & Freeman, 1992; Nassaji & Cumming, 2000) is especially significant for ELLs who may rely on this real language context even more so. Dialogue journals afford students who are learning a second language an opportunity to express themselves by communicating a message. This interactive communication then becomes the basis for the shared meaning making that exists between journal writer and reader/respondent. ELLs are able to write in a second language before they exhibit complete control over all the systems of that language (Hudelson, 1986). Dialogue journals give students an avenue for experimenting with written language within the framework of a socially mediated, interactive activity.

Linking Theory to Practice

Facilitating Language and Literacy Development

Teachers can facilitate ELLs' L2 and literacy development in a variety of ways by effectively linking students' experiences and language proficiency in the L1 with instruction in English. The following are examples that demonstrate ways to make such connections.

Word Walls. One important resource that teachers can easily use is the word wall. Word walls can be organized in a number of ways that facilitate understanding the structure of the language. Using different colors for different types of words (blue for contractions, red for adjectives, etc.) is a simple way to remind students of the formal names.

Personalized Word Banks. Students can also have their own personal lists of words. Have students select a few words from each story or text that they read to become a part of their personalized word bank. Model the many ways that words can be selected and organized—homonyms, synonyms, contractions, compound words, silent letters, by how they sound, or even by how they feel on the tongue when you pronounce them, or visual images they provoke. These word banks can and should be shared with other students on a regular basis so that all can learn from the collections.

Color-coded Poetry. Use "color-coded poetry" and other ways to generate word lists that students can use in their writing. Hang five sheets of butcher paper or other large paper, preferably each of a different color.

On day one, brainstorm lists of words that have to do with a unit of study, book, science topic, etc. On one piece of colored paper, list words that are "person or thing" words, on another piece of colored paper list "describing" words that tell, on another write "action" words that end in "ing," on the fourth write words that end in "ly," and on the last list "time and place" words. There is no need to tell students that these are lists of nouns, verbs, etc.; that can happen later during special mini-lessons. For now, write these brief headings on each colored paper and save them.

On day two, show examples of how students can create "word paintings" by choosing a word off each piece of colored paper (choose a blue word to start, then an orange, etc.). For the second line of the poem, choose different words and write them in a different order (choose an orange word first, followed by a blue word, etc.). The students will add appropriate prepositions and connecting words as necessary, but have them stick as much as possible to words that are or could be on the list. After a unit on the ocean, we observed one ELL use a colored word list to write this poem:

> Ocean blue sailing silently at midnight
> Barely blowing wet storms by morning
> Floating quietly, boats safe in the harbor
> Makes me feel alive again

In this type of writing, it is helpful to have a way to end the poem, such as "It makes me feel . . ." or I wonder how. . . ." The parts of speech become clear as the students write and share their creations. After writing this way a few times, the students are ready for mini-lessons that put formal names on each type (color) of word, now that they have experience with using them.

Substituting Words. Using a Big Book, cover certain types of words with sticky notes and let students insert words that might make sense. This can be done with or without using the formal names for the substituted words. The idea is to help ELLs focus on the syntax of the language. More proficient students can use *Mad Libs*, a series of one-page stories with words left out that students fill in with random words. Syntactically the random words fit since they are the same parts of speech, but the meaning is sure to be comical. Initially, rather than saying, "Give me a noun" the leader will ask for a person, place, or thing word, or rather than asking for an adjective, the leader will ask for a describing word. Later on the teacher can say, "You know, there is a name for these types of words. They are called nouns." These can be read with the whole class or laminated and left at a center for students to work with in pairs or small groups.

Jazz Chants. *Jazz Chants for Children* by Carolyn Graham provides excellent practice that internalizes the forms of words and structure of sentences. Many are organized with special focus on language forms that are chanted or sung. Using these as "performance pieces" greatly enhances their value and makes for a more authentic experience, especially for older children.

Music. The *Schoolhouse Rock* series of cassettes and videos, especially the language video Grammar Rock (with such classics as "Conjunction Junction, what's your function?"), serves dual purposes for ELLs. For students with enough English proficiency to access the meaning of the grammar, the videos allow them to develop their understanding of syntactic and semantic clues as the videos provide ample visual scaffolding. For those with less English proficiency, the songs and chants are an excellent tool for acquiring language through the Natural Approach (Krashen & Terrell, 1988).

Dialogue Journals. Dialogue journals are like diaries where students write to the teacher or another student on a daily basis. Peyton and Reed (1990) liken dialogue journals to conversations between a teacher and student and describe the journals as having the characteristics of both written and oral language. Guidelines for using dialogue journals describe their use as a risk-free activity where students can feel free to experiment with language. Through dialogue journals, the teacher and students develop a relationship mediated by the continuous writing. Because the student writes first everyday and the teacher responds, the student begins to view writing as a means of communication with authentic reasons for writing. Figure 3.1 shows an example of a dialogue journal.

FIGURE 3.1 A Simulated Dialogue Journal

	March 20

	Dear Ms G.
	    Yesterday I went to the park with my mom and got in the tree. Tomorrow I am going to the zoo.
	                    Esteban

	March 21

	Dear Esteban,
	    Who else went to the zoo with you and your mom? Do you go there a lot?
	                    Ms. G.

Part-to-whole Reading. First, break written text into small parts to analyze before giving ELLs an opportunity to experience the text as a whole. Then give children a chance to hear natural comprehensible language as a whole, especially in stories read aloud. They will not only pick up the subsystems of the language, but enjoy the experience more as well.

It is important that teachers take into consideration language structure and students' experiences with L1 and L2 when planning effective literacy lessons for ELLs. Table 1.1 in Chapter 1 provides a framework for developing effective, differentiated literacy lessons for ELLs. It demonstrates how to organize instruction based on student needs, skills to be taught, and scaffolds that need to be provided in order for ELLs to access the curriculum.

Nonexamples: Strategies That Can Inhibit Language and Literacy Development

Some teaching practices will not help facilitate L2 acquisition. The following is a list of activities to be avoided.

Grammar Worksheets. Worksheets tend to focus on one structure at a time in an environment that inhibits meaningful interaction between people (which is what communication is all about). Furthermore, Krashen's (1994, 2005) Input and Monitor hypotheses tell us that teaching specific grammatical structures does not facilitate L2 acquisition.

Verb Conjugation and Substitution Drills. The old audiolingual method is still alive and well in foreign language instruction, and still does no better at preparing students to communicate through a language. This method was developed during World War II to quickly teach U.S. Army personnel foreign languages (Celce-Murcia, 1991) and consists of dialogue memorization and practice, repetitive pattern drills, and conversation. Such a focus on form and repetitive practice does not demonstrate language use in authentic, interactive settings.

Overemphasis on Rules Instead of Meaning and Communication. An overemphasis on language rules causes the "language monitor" to run overtime. Aside from the increase in tension caused by this approach, according to Krashen's (1994, 2005) five hypotheses, formal study of a language (learning as opposed to acquisition) leads to a sort of mental grammar monitor that inhibits language expression. Although this monitor is more effective for writing, it is better left for "polishing up" a language rather than its initial acquisition.

Examples from the Field

Meet Ricardo and Esteban

In this section, we will explore the writing development of two ELLs over 3 years (see Table 3.1 for the planning chart for these students). At the time this exploration took place, the school had a transitional bilingual education program in which the children were separated according to language dominance for initial reading instruction and later "transitioned"

Writing workshop.

or changed over to English language arts instruction when they reached a certain proficiency level in the L1 reading and in English. These two students are unique in that they participated in a pilot program where they remained with the same teacher from the second through fifth grades, so we were able to look closely at their writing during that time.

Ricardo and Esteban are both ELLs with Spanish as their primary language. We looked at their work from third to fifth grade. Though both students were able to read and write in English by the fifth grade, their routes to literacy were quite different. One student, Ricardo, was placed in an English-only program upon arriving at Edge Lake; the other, Esteban, received initial literacy instruction in Spanish before "transitioning" to all English instruction in the beginning of the third grade.

Dialogue journals for Ricardo and Esteban were collected from the beginning of third grade until the second half of fifth grade. Ricardo and Esteban wrote in their dialogue journals on a daily basis for 20 minutes immediately following recess. Their teacher responded to their journals twice every week. In all, 771 journal entries were examined, 383 for Esteban, 388 for Ricardo. Ricardo and Esteban were also interviewed and observed.

Esteban's Story

Esteban entered Edge Lake School in kindergarten. He received initial literacy instruction in Spanish and transitioned to English reading in the third grade. He is a very verbal child who talks constantly. He engages in literate activities all the time, reading and writing and using literacy to accomplish communicative goals. Dialogue journals are part of his repertoire of literate behaviors, and he writes in his journal on a daily basis. As such, he is aware of the purpose for journal writing. Listen as he talks to his teacher about dialogue journals.

TABLE 3.1 A Planning Chart for Differentiated Instruction for Ricardo and Esteban

Student Name	What I Know About Each Student	Grade Level Concept	Skills Required	Necessary Scaffolds
Ricardo	Spanish is L1. Was instructed in English in K, changed schools and began instruction in Spanish in first grade, moved again and was placed in English instruction in second grade.	Fifth grade	Needs to build CALP in his L2.	Develop vocabulary through use of visuals.
	Very good with math, especially problems that call for understanding spatial relationships.		Understanding how to use what he knows about spatial relationships in math to make meaning of text.	Use math word problems.
	Parents want him to succeed.		Communicating with parents.	Reinforce parental desire for success.
	Relies heavily on L2 and has trouble with both reading and writing.		Understanding what transfers and what doesn't.	Conference. Use analogies between L1 and L2. Post reminders and expect student to use them.
	Getting the "gist" of a reading and comprehension of main idea is difficult.		Understanding that the meaning of larger pieces of text is facilitated by processing smaller chunks of text first.	Use think alouds.
	Needs support on how to elaborate on ideas in writing.		Drawing on personal interests and background knowledge.	Begin writing in poetry about grade level content. Conference often with teacher and peers. Use post writing graphic organizers and rubrics.
Esteban	Spanish is L1. Was enrolled in L1 reading K–2 and then in a transitional reading class for third grade. Very verbal in both English and Spanish, but more comfortable in Spanish.	Fifth grade	Listening and speaking English in meaningful conversations with peers in order to receive comprehensible input.	Use cooperative group work.
	Relies heavily on Spanish syntax and spelling as the basis for his writing in English.		Understanding the structures that do and do not transfer from Spanish to English.	Use contrastive analysis between Spanish and English. Allow free voluntary reading and listening to stories. Use journal writing.

Interview: Part One

(Adapted from Burke, 1987, 2005; Kucer, 1989)

Teacher: What is a dialogue journal?

Esteban: Where we write like what we did and like what we did and what we want to talk to our teachers about.

Teacher: What else can you tell me about dialogue journals?

Esteban: That sometimes they're kind of private, sometimes like other teachers can't read it, just your own teacher could read it.

Teacher: Explain a little bit more to me.

Esteban: Like sometimes they're personal, sometimes other persons could read it, or um, some friends.

Teacher: What do you mean when they're personal?

Esteban: Like sometimes you write something to a teacher that you wouldn't like somebody else to see or read.

It is easy to see that Esteban is aware of the personal nature of his dialogue journal and that he also views it as a means of communicating with the teacher. Within the framework of his classroom setting, the privacy of the journal is important. Students are not required to share their journals with anyone but the teacher, and all other people who view the journals must ask for and receive permission.

Esteban's journal entries are interesting to read in that he often elaborates on topics that interest him. In his journal writing, he repeatedly asks for feedback from the teacher (see Figure 3.2) a phenomenon that parallels his oral behavior in class. Esteban wrote this entry in response to the teacher's questioning why the class misbehaved after a student teacher had been absent one day.

Examination of the entry shows a focus on the communicative aspects of the writing, with limited, if any focus on graphophonics or syntax. This sample has 16 inventions with some based on Spanish ("rily" for really, "ger-nal" for journal) and others based on English ("isint" for isn't, "whrit" for write), and the unconventional segmentation in the word "besiseing" for busy seeing. Esteban uses his journal as a form of written communication, and he believes that there is a responsive audience for his writing.

During interviews, Esteban discusses writing as a process but appears to view his dialogue journal as something that is somewhat exempt from this process of writing.

Interview: Part Two

Ms. G: Do you think that you write better in your dialogue journal or in other writing?

Esteban: In my other writing. Cause in my journal sometimes that I know I'm gonna write something long, I write it really fast cause I know I'm just gonna have one day to do that. If you're doing a story you could have time for like a week.

Even though he perceives his journal writing as one-time writing (perhaps like drafts) he says that he brainstorms before he writes: *"Um, I brainstorm then I write the, down,*

FIGURE 3.2 Esteban's Entry: Requesting Teacher Response, End of Third Grade

> 3/29: beacase Miss H isint hir thats why wher
> ackting so crase thats why ha rily Miss g you
> havent whrit in my ger-nal in page 13 plese
> whrite to me Miss G I dident whrite to you
> becas I was so besiseing the film how you put
> it
>
> [Because Miss H. isn't here that's why we're
> acting so crazy that's why, ha, really Miss G.,
> you haven't written in my journal on page 13.
> Please write to me Miss G. I didn't write to you
> because I was so busy seeing the film and how
> you put it.]

what I'm going to talk to my teacher about." He also does some editing, *"Um, I um, try to put periods but sometimes I forget because sometimes I know I'm going to write a lot and I write really fast."* During one observation he did revise/edit, but those changes seemed to be for graphophonic reasons, in other words, to correct spelling (see Figure 3.3). He also had a new "white-out" pen that day, so he may have made the mistakes so that he would be able to use the pen.

The spaces indicate his corrections and are in the actual text (words covered by white-out). As can be seen from this entry, Esteban is aware of his audience and writes the "letter" or entry directly to the teacher. This entry has relatively few inventions (3 out of 33 words, and all three apparently based on English). The only punctuation, an apostrophe in the word "din't," is conventionally placed although the word is unconventionally spelled. This entry asks the teacher a question, once again supporting the notion of journal writing as a form of interactive, written communication.

Esteban feels that the problems he has in his journal writing are based on semantics, that he might have problems thinking of something to write. Furthermore, although he seems unconcerned with the surface features of his writing, he does discuss the fact that "sloppy" writing might affect the communicative abilities of that writing.

FIGURE 3.3 Esteban's Entry: Mid Fifth Grade

February 19
Dear Ms G
When are we going to see the lion the   witch
and the wardrobe the play was fun to bad
Lumina din't see   it beocase it was so   fun

[Ms. G,
    When are we going to see "The Lion, the
witch and the wardrobe?" The play was fun. Too
bad Lumina didn't see it because it was so fun.]

Interview: Part Three

Ms. G: What is the process of writing like? What do you do as a writer?

Esteban: Um, think really hard because sometimes you don't know how to write.

Ms. G: When you are writing in your journal, what kinds of troubles or problems do you have?

Esteban: Sometimes I get stuck with words or I get, I have problems about, or sometimes I don't know what to write.

Ms. G: What do you do about the problems?

Esteban: I try to brainstorm really hard until I remember something that happened yesterday or that I'm gonna do during the weekend.

Ms. G: Do you ever go back when you are having trouble and reread some of the things that you wrote?

Esteban: Yeah.

Ms. G: Why would you reread?

Esteban: Um because sometimes you can't read it so sloppy and sometimes you don't know what word it is because it's not correct and sometimes you don't know what word so you try to reread so it could be better.

Esteban does not feel that this is too big a problem for him, as he has no difficulty in making his entries legible and therefore readable. He feels capable of judging whether an entry is legible and makes the connection between that which both he and the teacher can understand. He feels that a good entry is one that is interesting to the reader, perhaps mysterious, but at the same time realizes that he generally bases his entries on things that have happened to him.

Esteban feels that journal writing has helped him to learn and views this writing as a process that helps a person to write or read better. He views journal writing as an arena for writing practice. He is consistent in acknowledging the writing process in his answers.

Interview: Part Four

Ms. G: If you knew someone was having a hard time writing something in their journal, how would you help him or her?

Esteban: By telling them to brainstorm as hard as they can, till like they remember what happened yesterday or the past weekend or what you're gonna do in the weekend.

Ms. G: How would a teacher help that person?

Esteban: By like asking them questions.

This is an interesting observation on Esteban's part in that teachers often instigate brainstorming by asking questions of the class in order to activate background knowledge. Esteban makes the connection between the brainstorming and questioning activities that he attributes to himself and to the teacher.

Esteban is aware of both the process and product involved in dialogue journal writing. He views it as an interactive process whose purpose is that of improving reading and writing. He also seems to fully understand the context in which journal writing lies, that of ongoing communication between himself and the teacher. He understands the importance of using background knowledge to facilitate writing as evidenced by the fact that he often uses prior or future experiences as a basis for his writing. He also views himself as a good writer.

Let's look at the difference in Esteban's writing between third and fifth grade to see how it changes. Esteban wrote the entry in Figure 3.4 at the beginning of third grade.

Esteban wrote this entry immediately following his transition to English reading after 3 years of reading instruction in Spanish. There are several inventions based on Spanish ("jis" for he's, "jand" for hand, "alrayd" for already, etc.), a limited reliance on the English language, and no use of Spanish words in the entry. Esteban rarely uses Spanish words in his entries and only does so to describe things for which he does not yet know English words.

In his journal writing at the beginning of the third grade, Esteban only averages about 50% conventionally spelled words, and he bases the majority of his inventions on what he knows about Spanish. By the middle of fifth grade, almost 90% of his words in journal entries are conventionally spelled; of the remaining 10% of words that are not spelled conventionally, less than one-fifth of them are based on Spanish word knowledge. By fifth grade, he also writes longer entries, averaging 75 words per entry compared with an average of 32 words per entry in the beginning of the third grade. Figure 3.5 shows one of Esteban's entries in mid fifth grade. He wrote it on a day the teacher was absent and after

FIGURE 3.4 Esteban's Entry: Beginning Third Grade

10/18: Dear Ms. G my unclel lives in san francisco
and ay cold jim and ji was alitolbit jurt from jis leyg
and in jis jand but jis alrayd and dat brig folt daun
but gut tinget der is anoder wan in da botem aybin
in day brig about wan gir agou and it is ay hiys
pleys but ay liych da brig da wan det fal daun beter
dat da gol den brig bicos

[Dear Ms. G, My uncle lives in San Francisco and I
called him and he was a little bit hurt from his leg and
in his hand but he's all right and that bridge fell down
but good thing it there is another one in the bottom. I
been in that bridge about one year ago and it is a nice
place but I like the bridge that one that fall down better
than the golden bridge because.]

a particularly difficult student returned from suspension. The student teacher was in charge of the class and the vice principal came to the class to help avoid a confrontation.

Notice the difference in readability of this entry. Although almost completely devoid of punctuation, the few nonconventionally spelled words are based almost entirely on English ("whent" for went, "wornt" for weren't). This entry also shows that Esteban is experimenting with punctuation. Although he ignores the need for simple periods at the end of sentences and at the end of the entry, he correctly uses a colon in "11:11 AM." and attempts a period at the end of that abbreviation and that of "mr." His writing is clearly approaching conventional syntax and spelling.

By the middle of fifth grade, Esteban is a competent writer who exhibits control over writing in the English language. Considering the difference between this writing and that of 3 years ago, it is easy to see that he has grown as a writer. Esteban elaborates on his topics, explaining, describing, predicting, etc. Rarely does Esteban write just one or two sentences; rather he discusses his topic with details and sometimes gives opinions to accompany his topic. Esteban is a writer; he participates in literacy events and sees himself as a writer.

FIGURE 3.5 Esteban's Entry: Mid Fifth Grade

3/6 Dear Mis G today mister Dancer came to the class to tell us to treat steven like if nothing had hapend beocase miss brown told us not to get close to steven and mr. dancer found out that whe wornt treating steven normally so He came emidiatly and told miss brown to wait out side and He told us that He was going to behave or else he whould have to visit progect hope again but meanwile that He ackted right whe should treat him like one of us then He whent out side to talk with miss brown to tell her that mean wile he ackted nice and not bothering nobody people could get close and help him on his problems and if he bothered you just walk away but meanwile treat him nice so far he hasent got no blue slips our botherd nobody I hope he stais that way for ever meanwille the substitute hasent come yet it 11:11 AM. in the morning and the substitute hasent come I ges she aint going to come

[Dear Ms. G., Today Mr. Dancer came to the class to tell us to treat Steven as if nothing had happened because Miss Brown told us not to get close to Steven. Mr. Dancer found out that we weren't treating Steven normally so he came immediately and told Miss Brown to wait outside. He told us that he (Steven) was going to behave or else he would have to visit Project Hope again. But meanwhile when he acted right we should treat him like one of us. Then he went outside to talk with Miss Brown to tell her that meanwhile he (Steven) acted nice and not bothering anybody, people could get close and help him on his problems. And if he bothered you just walk away. But meanwhile treat him nice. So far he hasn't gotten any blue slips or bothered nobody. I hope he stays that way forever, Meanwhile the substitute hasn't come yet. It is 11:11 a. m. in the morning and the substitute hasn't come. I guess she isn't going to come.]

Ricardo's Story

Ricardo came to Edge Lake School in the first grade. In kindergarten, he received initial literacy instruction in Spanish (his native language and the language spoken at home) but due to a clerical error at his present school he was placed in an English reading program in first grade. Since that time he has been placed in an English-only literacy program, although he received primary language support in other subjects from his classroom teacher. He is a likable child who has many friends. He also is excellent at tasks incorporating spatial relationships (e.g., he was the first to finish a tangram puzzle, often quite challenging for children). Ricardo is a verbal child who reads and writes frequently. Dialogue journals are part of his daily repertoire of writing, and he, too, is aware of the purpose for journal writing.

Teacher: What is a dialogue journal?

Ricardo: I would say a dialogue journal is something that you write to somebody sometimes; you write to somebody and you could use it like if it was a diary.

Teacher: What else can you tell me about dialogue journals?

Ricardo: That you can use them for diaries a lot and use it for lots of things like, like you can use the pages for pen pals, send the book back and forth.

Teacher: What is journal writing like?

Ricardo: It's like writing to a pen pal.

Ricardo seems to understand the communicative nature of his journal and views it as a diary that is passed back and forth between himself and the teacher. Ricardo also keeps a journal at home.

Teacher: What kinds of things do you write in your journal?

Ricardo: Like secrets and secrets and sometimes I write questions like about to like, like when I lost my soccer ball I wrote questions about if anybody had seen it in my journal and I got it home to another and I said that I lost it in my other journal.

Ricardo views the purpose of journal writing as documentation of what is happening to him in and out of the class.

Teacher: What is the purpose of journal writing?

Ricardo: So we know what is happening, what happened in the past.

Ricardo does not elaborate on his topics. His entries at the beginning of third grade are short, averaging approximately 15 words per entry. Ricardo expresses an idea and then either moves on to another topic or is finished. He also asks questions of the teacher, indicating that he does have some awareness of audience and the interactive nature of the journals (see Figure 3.6).

Ricardo's entries show some developing control over both graphophonics and syntax, but it is not until the middle of fifth grade that he begins to demonstrate control over capital letters and spelling. He bases his few nonconventionally spelled words on English

FIGURE 3.6 Ricardo's Questioning/Interactive Entries: Fourth and Fifth Grade

6/10: Dear Ms. G why can't we bering gloves to school evey boby is bring baseball gloves and tennis balls.

[Dear Ms. G, Why can't we bring gloves to school? Everybody is bringing baseball gloves and tennis balls.]

9/12: Ms. G Do you like fujicolor or Kodak I like kodak we buy Kodak and we use the cramer the picture comeing out those are very cool and they cost losts of money

[Ms. G, Do you like Fujicolor or Kodak? I like Kodak. We buy Kodak and we use the camera. The pictures that come out are very cool and cost lots of money.]

("bering" for bring, "comeing" for coming, etc.). Notice that in addition to questioning the teacher about both school and personal things, Ricardo does use her name in the beginning of each entry. That and responses to her questions are the only indications that he gives of his awareness of audience beyond the general notion of the journal's function as that of communicating back and forth.

Ricardo also makes connections to process writing by discussing revision, but does not always demonstrate this in his writing (see Figure 3.7).

Teacher: Do you ever make changes in what you have written in your journal?

Ricardo: Sometimes.

Teacher: What kinds of things get changed?

Ricardo: Like something that doesn't make sense in the thing I'm writing.

FIGURE 3.7 Ricardo's Entry: Mid Fifth Grade

Ms. G Oscar has a ball like an egg and every time
we cote it it start to crark and he almost lost it
by　　senden it to the gate of the freway.

[Ms. G., Oscar has a ball like an egg and every time
we caught it, it starts to crack and he almost lost it by
sending it to the gate of the freeway.]

This entry, as are all of his entries (except for those written when he purposely attempts writing in Spanish), is entirely in English and his inventions, 4 out of a total of 32 words ("cote" for caught, "crark" for crack, "senden" for sending, and "freway" for freeway), are based on English.

Ricardo indicates that problems he has with journal writing are related to both spelling and meaning.

> **Teacher:** When you are writing in your journal what kinds of troubles or problems do you have?
>
> **Ricardo:** Spelling. Remembering something to write.
>
> **Teacher:** What do you do about them?
>
> **Ricardo:** Spelling, I check over everything I write and or things I remember to write in the journal I just try to remember something in my mind about something I could write about.
>
> **Teacher:** What is the process of writing like? What do you do as a writer?
>
> **Ricardo:** I look for something good that happened in the day to write in it, something that might be interesting, like a secret. I just do drafts and maps and all.
>
> **Teacher:** In your journal?
>
> **Ricardo:** No, in my mind so then I write them in my journal like a little story.

It is possible that here Ricardo initially became confused between what he does when writing a story and writing in his journal and then related the two types of writing, one as having external and the other as having internal ("in my mind") planning. Ricardo generally stops to think several times during his journal writing, looking into space, and appearing to be thinking.

Ricardo often mentions the surface features of writing. He feels that the most difficult part of journal writing is spelling, and that journal writing has helped his spelling improve. He indicates that good entries are ones that are interesting or "weird."

Ricardo views himself as a good writer but would like to be able to write longer stories. Ricardo has no trouble finishing his assignments in class, but his responses are generally short and without elaboration, as are his journal entries.

Now let's compare a journal entry from the third grade with one from the fifth grade. Figure 3.8 is Ricardo's first third-grade entry.

Ricardo wrote this entry upon returning from summer vacation after the second grade and before teamed reading began in the fall. Asking whether he will read in English or Spanish is interesting in that it shows his confusion at first being instructed in Spanish and then in English, and he is wondering if the language of instruction will switch again. What is apparent is that Ricardo uses inventions (3 out of 12 words) based on English ("cown" for going, "ieglsh" for English, and "spnsh" for Spanish). Ricardo consistently bases his writing on English. Although Spanish is spoken in the home and in his classroom, all of his instruction takes place in English.

Ricardo's reliance on English as a basis for his writing is consistent throughout the 3 years. At the beginning of third grade, he uses approximately 80% conventionally spelled words with English as the basis for the nonconventionally spelled words. By the middle of the fifth grade, his writing is almost 90% conventional. He rarely uses inventions based on Spanish but does so on occasion. It is important to note, though, that his conventional writing consists of entries that still have an average of 15 words, an average that has remained the same over the 3 years. Figure 3.9 shows one of Ricardo's entries written toward the end of fifth grade.

Note how much more readable this entry is than the first one made almost 3 years prior. This entry only has two nonconventionally spelled words, one clearly a letter reversal ("wiht" for with) and one a simple substitution ("anly" for only). The only indication of

FIGURE 3.8 Ricardo's Entry: Beginning Third Grade

9/26 Ms. G I'm I cown to read in ieglsh or in spnsh.

[Ms. G, Am I going to read in English or in Spanish?]

FIGURE 3.9 Ricardo's Entry: Mid Fifth Grade

3/17 Ms. G it is fun playing basketball wiht Steven and he was the anly one that made Baskets

[Ms. G., It is fun playing basketball with Steven and he was the only one that made baskets.]

awareness of audience is his use of a greeting, and possibly the topic as he discusses a classmate.

Ricardo has grown as a writer, but still writes with little elaboration. Although on first appearance it would seem that Ricardo controls both the content and surface features of his writing, closer examination reveals that his writing is short, containing few elaborations and details. He often is successful communicating his messages, but what he says is short and to the point. Ricardo rarely demonstrates audience awareness beyond the initial greeting in his entries. Nevertheless, Ricardo perceives himself as a writer, and he engages in reading and writing activities on a daily basis.

What We Learned from Ricardo's and Esteban's Journals

Looking at Esteban's and Ricardo's writing growth from third to fifth grades, we can see how differently they grew as writers. Esteban was able to grow as a writer in his native language, Spanish, engaging in literacy events in that language before making the transition to reading and writing in English, whereas Ricardo experienced early literacy in his L2, one that was less developed at the time of his beginning experiences with literacy.

One of the main differences between their writing is the length of their journal entries. From the outset there was a difference in the mean length of entry between the two students, with Ricardo's entries averaging 15 words from third to fifth grade and Esteban's entries growing from an average of 32 to 75 words by the end of fifth grade. It is no surprise, then, that Esteban's entries are consistently more elaborate than Ricardo's entries.

Both students demonstrated steady patterns of growth toward controlling the mechanical features of their writing, however, Esteban's growth seems more dramatic. Although Esteban had less conventional spelling initially, by the end of the study there is little difference between the two boys—close to 90% conventional spelling for both of them.

Another important distinction, then, between the two students' writing is this initial reliance on the Spanish language as a basis for inventing spelling in English. Based on his extensive experience with Spanish literacy, Esteban uses his L1 to facilitate development in his second language. That Esteban bases his writing on Spanish is consistent with Edelsky's (1986) findings that bilingualism adds to rather than detracts from a child's repertoire of available language by allowing him or her a wider range of language choices. Interstingly, Edge Lake School no longer has a bilingual program.

What Esteban's and Ricardo's Stories Tell Us About Differentiating Writing Instruction

We used our knowledge about first and second language acquisition as we analyzed Esteban's and Ricardo's dialogue journals and looked at what they were doing with syntax and language in academic settings to develop and provide appropriate scaffolds to support their writing development in L1 and L2. The dialogue journals allowed us to look at growth in student writing ability and also to examine their linguistic needs from a different perspective over time. What we learned about their writing (and also their reading) was fed directly into the differentiation process and informed the planning process by helping us to use different phases of reflection and analysis (Shulman, 2003). As teachers, once we were able to get into the students' work, we reflected on their writing in relation to what we knew about L1 and L2 reading and writing, then critiqued the work to make judgments to design scaffolded/differentiated instruction that would uniquely support each of them in their academic development.

Practical Applications and Individual Inquiries: Cases to Think About and Investigate

1. Begin using dialogue journals with a small group of students in your classroom (see Figure 3.10 for suggestions about how to get started using dialogue journals). Collect the journals for a minimum of 4 weeks. Knowing that syntax is a nontransferable skill, use what you know about the structure of English sentences and compare that structure with the native language of the students.

FIGURE 3.10 How to Get Started Using Dialogue Journals

✓ Discuss the need to communicate.
✓ Discuss the importance of privacy.
✓ Brainstrom possible topics.
✓ Stress that entries can vary in length.
✓ Students should write first each day.
✓ Don't worry about content at first.

Source: From *Dialogue journal writing with nonnative English speakers: An instructional packet for teachers and workshop leaders,* by J. K. Peyton and J. Staton, 1992, Alexandria, VA: TESOL.

2. Set up a writing conference to give feedback to one of your ELL writers. Record your conference for analysis and reflection. Use the following prompts to question the student about his or her writing.

   - "Read your writing aloud to me." (As the student reads, listen for inflections and match the oral reading with the student's writing. Provide positive feedback and prompt the student if the writing and reading do not match.)

   - Ask the student, "Have you told me all that you want to tell me? What else can you tell me about this? Are there any colors you can remember about your writing? Are there any special ways that you feel about this writing?" (Continue to provide positive feedback as you ask probing questions and prompt the student to think about language he or she might use to describe his or her feelings.)

   - Make a list with the student of things, events, and ideas that need to be revised in the piece of writing. Have the student work on one thing at a time.

   - Provide opportunities for the student to share his or her writing with a writing/reading partner.

   - Provide opportunities for students to read mentor texts (Ray, 1999) that serve as models for writing.

Chapter Four _____

Effectively Assessing ELLs

I learned so much about assessment when I had to go back and look at how reading, oral language and writing data cannot be separated. Once I sat down with the data and did an in-depth analysis, focusing on student strengths, I began to see how I could develop interventions over time.

Monique, fourth-grade teacher

This chapter addresses how to effectively assess ELLs. Research shows us that assessing ELLs is a complex process because of the relationship between language learning and content learning (Mercado & Romero, 1993). When you assess ELLs using conventional exams that are dependent on students' proficiency in English, it is increasingly difficult to evaluate whether they make errors because they don't know the content or the language (Mercado & Romero, 1993). Furthermore, language is such a complex issue, in and of itself, that it is necessary to look at all the functions of language when assessing ELLs (Gibbons, 1993; Halliday, 1989; Peregoy & Boyle, 2005).

Students who come to school speaking a language other than English undergo a variety of assessments from the time they enter school. In this chapter, we argue that authentic assessments, those in which students are called upon to demonstrate what they know as they engage in classroom tasks, are better measures of success for ELLs. We listen to classroom teachers as they evaluate their students to see what they know. In this chapter we will:

- Describe the types of assessments used in classroom settings, including language proficiency exams, such as the California English Language Development Test (CELDT) and the Student Oral Language Observation Matrix (SOLOM).
- Discuss challenges inherent in assessing ELLs.
- Discuss the use of authentic assessment with ELLs through the integration of assessment and instruction.
- Review authentic assessments in oral language, reading, and writing.

- Explore the interdependency of oral language, reading, and writing.
- Discuss/describe quality student assessment for ELLs.
- Demonstrate how assessments inform teachers' decisions about curriculum and instruction at one school.

Building Background Knowledge About Effectively Assessing ELLs

What Is the Purpose of Classroom Assessment?

Classroom assessment is used for a variety of purposes, from something as simple as a quick informal test or checklist used as a task analysis for a specific lesson to formal standardized assessments that measure student achievement. In general, the purpose of classroom assessment is to find out what students know in order to plan instruction. Teachers and researchers alike agree that teaching and learning are intricately linked and dependent on each other (Kellough & Kellough, 1999). Teachers use assessment to identify their students' strengths and weaknesses so that they can help them learn. Teachers also use assessment to evaluate the work they do: Do the strategies and curriculum they are using meet the needs of the students? Are they effective teachers? Finally, teachers and administrators use assessment to gather data to help them with decision making and also to work with parents (Kellough & Kellough, 1999). Given the multiple purposes of assessment, the American Association of Higher Education (AAHE) developed a series of guidelines for implementing effective assessment (see Figure 4.1).

FIGURE 4.1 Nine Principles of Good Practice for Assessing Student Learning

1. The assessment of student learning begins with educational values.
2. Assessment is most effective when it reflects an understanding of learning as multidimensional, integrated, and revealed in performance over time.
3. Assessment works best when the programs it seeks to improve have clear, explicitly stated purposes.
4. Assessment requires attention to outcomes but also equally to experiences that lead to those outcomes.
5. Assessment works best when it is ongoing not episodic.
6. Assessment fosters wider improvement when representatives from across the educational community are involved.
7. Assessment makes a difference when it begins with issues of use and illuminates questions that people really care about.
8. Assessment is most likely to lead to improvement when it is part of a larger set of conditions that promote change.
9. Through assessment, educators meet responsibilities to students and to the public.

Source: From "9 principles of good practice for assessing student learning," by A. W. Astin, T. W. Banta, K. P. Cross, E. El-Khawas, P. T. Ewell, P. Hutchings, T. J. Marchese, K. M. McMClenney, M. Mentkowski, M. A. Miller, E. T. Moran, and B. D. Wright, 1996, *AAHE Assessment Forum, July 25.* Retrieved September 7, 2005, from http://www2.oakland.edu/secure/oira/AAHE_Principles.pdf

What do these guidelines mean in terms of classroom assessment for ELLs? First, teachers need to examine student needs to create effective assessments and to design instruction to meet their needs. It is also critical to use multiple modes of assessment to ensure that students are given many opportunities to demonstrate what they know. But wait, this may not be the way you remember assessment. Many of us can still remember sitting down with our number 2 pencils, filling in bubbles on the standardized test given toward the end of the year. We remember end-of-unit tests and spelling tests where we had only one chance to pass or fail.

Many feel that the current national and state trend toward accountability has moved us away from assessment's original goals, to find out what students know in order to plan for instruction, and toward a system that is geared toward sorting students according to their test scores. High-stakes testing most often ends up labeling students into one category or another.

Standardized testing has become a "scientifically sound" way of reinforcing our societal beliefs that some people are deserving and worthy, and others, because of their own inabilities or unwillingness, are not. In the hierarchy created by current assessment practices, as in the parallel hierarchy created by our societal practices, ELLs are most often found at the bottom, with the most to lose (Houk, 2005).

And although classroom teachers administer the batteries of exams required by state and federal regulations, they also use assessment on a daily basis to inform their practice and assist their students. Testing begins early in the school year as teachers try to find out what students know in order to plan effective instruction. Teachers use diagnostic assessments, formative and summative assessments, norm- and criterion-referenced tests, and alternative assessments that are more authentic. As they use each of these assessments, they must make them relevant for ELLs.

What Kinds of Assessments Are Used in Classrooms?

Teachers use a variety of assessments throughout the school year, from diagnostic assessments to formative assessments to summative assessments. Norm-referenced and criterion-referenced tests are two major types of assessments used to measure student achievement. Teachers also use diagnostic language assessments to measure language proficiency. The National Research Council (2001) lists a variety of ways teachers can assess student learning in the classroom based on the work of McTighe and Ferrara (1998). Table 4.1 describes a framework of assessment approaches and methods.

Norm-Referenced and Criterion-Referenced Assessments

Norm-referenced tests (NRTs) generally measure student achievement as compared to a larger group, which is usually a national sample or norming group that is representative of a wide cross-section of students (Bond, 1996; CRESST [National Center for Research on Evaluation of Standards and Student Testing], n.d.). Although some NRTs use open-ended and/or short-answer questions, most NRTs use multiple-choice questions (FairTest, 2005b). For the most part, NRTs are commercially published tests. Some examples of commercial NRTs are the Comprehensive Test of Basic Skills (CTBS) and the Iowa Test of Basic Skills (ITBS).

TABLE 4.1 Assessing Student Learning in the Classroom

Selected-Response Format	Constructed-Response Format			Process-Focused Assessment
	Brief-Constructed Response	Performance-Based Assessment		
		Product	Performance	
Multiple-choice	Fill in the blank	Research paper	Oral presentation	Debate
True-false	Word(s)	Story/play	Dance/movement	Musical recital
Matching	Phrase(s)	Poem	Science lab demonstration	Keyboarding
Enhanced multiple choice	Short answer	Portfolio	Athletic skill performance	Teach-a-lesson
	Sentence(s)	Art exhibit	Dramatic reading	Oral questioning
	Paragraphs	Science project	Enactment	Observation ("kid watching")
	Label a diagram	Model		Interview
	"Show your work"	Video/audiotape		Conference
	Visual representation	Spreadsheet		Process description
	Essay	Lab report		"Think aloud"
				Learning log

Source: From *Classroom assessment and the National Science Education Standards*, by J. M. Atkin, P. Black, and J. Coffey (Eds.), National Research Council, Committee on Classroom Assessment, and the National Science Education Standards, 2001. Center for Education, Division of Behavioral and Social Sciences Education. Washington, DC: National Academy Press. Retrieved February 19, 2006, from http://books.nap.edu/html/classroom_assessment/ch14_t1.html. Reprinted with permission from the National Academies Press, Copyright 2001, National Academy of Sciences.

NRTs rank-order students in comparison to the norming group and discriminate between high and low achievers (FairTest, 2005b). The tests measure general skills, which are tested by one or more items on the test. Scores are reported as percentile ranks ranging from the 1st to the 99th percentile and most often conform to the normal curve (FairTest, 2005b). Most high-stakes testing and standardized tests used in schools are NRTs.

Criterion-referenced tests (CRTs) measure whether individual students have learned specific skills or concepts and find out what students already know. With CRTs skills are stated as instructional objectives, and all students can learn the skill and thereby receive a passing grade on the test (Huitt, 1996). Although CRTs are usually thought of as "teacher-made tests" they can also be standardized like the California Standards Tests (CSTs), which measure progress toward California's state-adopted academic content standards. The CSTs include multiple-choice tests and writing assignments.

Formative and Summative Assessment

Assessment is an ongoing practice that takes place before, during, and after instruction. **Formative assessment** is an integral part of classroom instruction that takes place throughout the school year to inform teachers and guide them as they make instructional decisions (Swearingen, n.d.). Boston (2002) defines formative assessment as "the diagnostic use of assessment to provide feedback to teachers and students over the course of instruction" (p. 1). Formative assessment includes a variety of things such as teacher-made tests, teacher observations, and student assignments. Teachers use the results from formative assessment to adapt their teaching to meet their students' needs (Boston, 2002). Typically, students receive feedback from formative assessment that helps them understand what they need to learn to succeed. This feedback can come from the teacher or from peers who respond to student work and thereby assist in the process. Black and William (1998) argue that ongoing systematic formative assessment can increase achievement when it is effectively integrated with teaching and learning.

Summative assessment is the way in which teachers find out what students know at the end of a lesson, unit, or school year. In education, summative assessment is most often a test whose purpose is to measure student outcomes and provide accountability to schools and districts. According to the National Research Council (2001), "the teacher makes summative judgments about a student's achievement at a specific point in time for purposes of placement, grading, accountability, and informing parents and future teachers about student performance" (p. 1). Examples of summative assessment include performance assessments (which can be activities undertaken by the students where their performance is used as an outcome measure), portfolios, and end-of-unit tests.

Diagnostic Assessments

Teachers often consider diagnostic assessments within the framework of formative assessment. To better meet the needs of their students, teachers need to find out what students know in order to plan for instruction. The purpose of diagnostic assessment is to measure students' strengths, weaknesses, knowledge, and skills (Swearingen, n.d.). Many teachers give diagnostic assessments the first week of school in a variety of subjects. These assessments are based on the content students were supposed to learn in the prior grade. Teachers can individualize diagnostic assessments, based on one student's unique needs, or administer them to an entire group. For example, a second-grade teacher might have students listen to a story and write a retelling of that story to measure comprehension. The math teacher might give a timed test of simple algorithms to see if the students know their math facts. Diagnostic assessments can be norm referenced or criterion referenced. Teachers can also use alternative assessments to find out what students know.

Diagnostic Language Assessments

Schools throughout the United States use a variety of diagnostic language assessments (see Figure 4.2), both norm referenced and criterion referenced. These assessments are used to ascertain ELLs' English proficiency levels in order to appropriately place them in programs to meet their needs and to exit them from such programs when they are fully proficient in English. Language assessments generally determine ELLs' proficiency in listening, speaking, reading, and writing. To decide which students need to receive

FIGURE 4.2 Diagnostic Language Assessments

Test	What Is Tested?	Tasks	Implications/Problems
Bilingual Syntax Measure (BSM) BSM I (K–2) • 22 items • Five levels of English ability • BSM II (3–12) • 26 items • Six levels of English ability	Oral Language Ability: • Language dominance • Language proficiency	Students look at cartoon pictures (What's he doing?) Responses rated for: • grammatical correctness based on conversational norms • students not expected to produce complete sentences • pronunciation not rated	• Test does **not** measure literacy (reading/writing about academic content). • Young students may be confused. • Older students may be offended by cartoons that have nonhuman characters. • Ungrammatical responses are marked low, e.g. (to a picture of a sailor mopping a deck), a student must say, "He is mopping" or "He's mopping" (progressive verb). "He mopped the deck" is not acceptable. Or (to girl dancing in field of flowers with eyes closed), an acceptable response is "She is sleeping."
Language Assessment Scales (LAS) LAS I (K–5) LAS II (6–12) Five categories: • Fluent • Near Fluent • Limited • Partially Deficient • Non-English	• Pronunciation • Vocabulary • Syntax • Pragmatics • (Claims to) measure conversational and academic proficiency	• Distinguish 6 minimal pairs (pot/dot). • Name objects in pictures. • Listen to short story (very short) and answer questions.	• Test tasks are contrived. • Rough measures of what students can do. • Tests language out of context. • Writing tasks (on one form) are very short. • Measures oral language. • Reading tasks are too short.
Bilingual Index of Natural Language (BINL) • Grades K–12	• Fluency (total number of words used) • Average sentence length (total number of words divided by the total number of sentences) • Total index of language ability (the sum of scores assigned to various features of the 10 language samples) • Average level of complexity (divide the total index of language ability by the total number of sentences)	• Student selects one of 40 pictures and tells a story about it or another picture until 10 separate sentences are obtained. Responses are recorded.	• Doesn't correlate well with other tests.

(continued)

FIGURE 4.2 (continued)

Test	What Is Tested?	Tasks	Implications/Problems
Student Oral Language Observation Matrix (SOLOM) • Five levels	• Comprehension • Fluency • Vocabulary • Pronunciation • Grammar	• Teacher observes the student.	• Informal tool—used if no test available in L1. • Checklist needs to be developed to facilitate administration.

California English Language Development Test (CELDT)
• K–12
• Administered upon school entry and annually thereafter
• Five levels of proficiency:
  ◦ 1= beginning
  ◦ 2=early intermediate
  ◦ 3= intermediate
  ◦ 4=early advanced
  ◦ 5=advanced
	• Listening
	• Speaking
	• Reading
	• Writing
	• Understanding of some basic structures of language—phonemes, morphemes, syntax
		• Teacher gives directions and observes how well the student follows directions.
		• Examiner says words and the student repeats. Examiner notes pronunciation, etc.
		• Student listens to a prerecorded story and retells. Retelling is scored on a rubric to indicate whether the student understands the basic structure of narrative text.
		• Students write in response to pictorial stimuli.
			• Raw scores are converted into scale scores. Students are placed using overall proficiency scores.
			• Teachers may not understand the meaning of the proficiency scores in specific areas such as listening/speaking, reading, and writing.
			• Because students' scale scores reside on a range of scores between students at the beginning of each proficiency level, those in the middle and those at the end, there may be confusion about developing appropriate instruction based on individual scores and performance descriptions (provided by the publisher).

language assessments, schools in many states administer a home language survey to all entering students. This survey asks parents about the languages spoken at home. Figures 4.3 and 4.4 are examples of home surveys used in Vermont and California. In California, if parents enter a language other than English for any of the first three questions (see Figure 4.4), their children are given the CELDT upon entering school and then annually to evaluate their progress in English.

The CELDT

The California English Language Development Test (McGraw-Hill, 2004) is administered to students who have been identified as ELLs, initially by the Home Language Survey, and who have not been previously assessed for English language proficiency in a California public school. Parents or guardians fill out a Home Language Survey (see Figures 4.3 and 4.4 for two examples of home language surveys) when students first register to enroll in a public school. There are four questions on the Home Language Survey in Figure 4.4. Two questions refer to the language the parents speak the most often to the child and the

FIGURE 4.3 Vermont Primary/Home Language Survey

Vermont Department of Education
Primary/Home Language Survey

Directions:

1. Interview the parents/guardians of all new students (including preschool and kindergarten) at the time of enrollment and record all information requested.

2. Provide interpreting services whenever necessary.

3. Please check to see that **all questions** on the form are answered.

4. **If a student's survey indicates a native or home language other than English,** his or her English language proficiency should be evaluated by a **qualified Bilingual or ESL teacher**. Give one copy of this form to the ESL teacher who will then assess oral proficiency, literacy, and academic background.

5. For any survey indicating a language other than English, please send one **legible** copy of the student's survey to: Coordinator of ESL/Bilingual Program
   State Department of Education
   120 State Street, Montpelier, VT 05620-2501

6. Place the original survey form in the student's permanent file.

Student Information			
First Name:	Last Name:	Date of Birth:	Gender: F ☐ M ☐
Country of Birth:	Date of Entry in U.S.:	Date **first** enrolled in **any** U.S. school:	

School Information		
Current School:		
Enrollment Date:	Current Grade:	Person Conducting Survey:

Questions for Parents/Guardians	Response
What is the native language of each parent/guardian?	
What language(s) are spoken in your home?	
Which language did your child learn first?	
Which language does your child use most frequently at home?	
Which language do you most frequently speak to your child?	
What other languages does your child know?	

Primary/Home Language Survey (Revised 9/22/03)

Source: From *Primary/home language survey,* by Vermont Department of Education, 2003. Retrieved August 27, 2005, from http://www.state.vt.us/educ/new/html/pgm_esl.html

FIGURE 4.4 Home Language Survey

FRESNO UNIFIED SCHOOL DISTRICT
HOME LANGUAGE SURVEY
English

Date_____School_____Student Number_____

Birthdate_____   Country of Birth_____

Foreign Born Status: If foreign born, year first entered USA_____ Years attended school in USA _____

The California Education Code requires that schools determine the language(s) spoken at home by each student. This information is essential in order for schools to provide meaningful instruction for all students. If a language other than English is spoken in the home, the District is required to do further assessment of your son/daughter.

Your cooperation in helping us meet this important requirement is requested. Please answer the following questions. Thank you for your help.

NAME OF STUDENT: _____
                    FIRST   MIDDLE   LAST
GRADE: _____ AGE: _____

Which language did your son or daughter learn when he or she first began to speak? _____

What language does your son or daughter most frequently use at home? _____

What language do you use most frequently to speak to your son or daughter? _____

Name the language most often spoken by the adults at home_____

Parent telephone number_____   _____
                                                   SIGNATURE OF PARENT OR GUARDIAN

From: MULTI 008 Home Language Survey
Revised 2/01   Distribution: original to Student CUM; FAX copy to Language Assessment Center

Source: From *Home language survey,* by Fresno Unified School District, 2001. Retrieved August 27, 2005, from http://multilingual.fresno.k12.ca.us/assmctr/HLS/lanindex.htm

language the parents themselves speak the most often in the home. The other two questions refer to the language the child first spoke and the language the child speaks the most often in the home. If responses to any of the first three questions are a language other than English, the child is administered the CELDT. Initial assessments are scored either at the school site or at the district level and then submitted to the test publisher for official scoring.

All students, except kindergarteners and first graders, are tested in listening and speaking, reading, and writing. Students in kindergarten and first grade are tested in listening and speaking only. Test results are issued in raw scores and scale scores that are translated into proficiency levels. Each area of language (listening and speaking, reading, and writing) has five levels of proficiency. Level one identifies the student as a beginning speaker of English, level two as early intermediate, level three as intermediate, level four as early advanced, and level five as advanced. All results from the previous school year are reported to the districts and school in November of the following school year. All results are also posted on the California State Department of Education Web site in February (http://www.cde.ca.gov).

The SOLOM

The Student Oral Language Observation Matrix, or SOLOM (San Jose Unified School District, n.d.), is not a test but a set of structured tasks given to students in a standard way. There is a rating scale that teachers can use to assess their students' command of oral English language based on what they observe students doing on a continual basis in a variety of situations. There are opportunities for teachers to observe students as they engage in class discussions, playground interactions, and encounters between classes. The teacher matches the student's language performance to descriptions on a five-point scale for each of five areas: comprehension, fluency, vocabulary, pronunciation, and grammar. The scores for the individual areas or domains can be considered individually or as a combined total score with a range from 5 through 25. A score of approximately 19 or 20 can be considered proficient. The SOLOM score is derived from situations where a student can participate in oral language tasks expected in the classroom at his or her grade level. Therefore, the score should approximately represent grade level oral language proficiency.

The SOLOM (Figure 4.5) can be used to track annual progress because it describes a range of proficiency from nonproficient to fluent. Once teachers know the criteria for the various ratings and observe their students' language practices with those criteria in mind, the SOLOM has great value. First, it helps teachers focus on language development goals. Second, it keeps them aware on an ongoing basis of how their students' language development goals are progressing. Finally, the SOLOM reminds teachers to set up oral language use situations that allow them to observe students, provide them feedback, and scaffold the language development activities.

As noted above, language can be assessed in a standardized format as in the CELDT or in standard tasks using the SOLOM. The CELDT provides teachers with descriptions of the language expected of students at levels 1, 2, 3, 4, or 5 in listening and speaking, reading, and writing. The CELDT also provides teachers with an overall score. For example, if a student is identified as being a 2 overall, that could mean that his listening and speaking score is a 2, his reading a 1 and his writing a 1. For kindergarteners and first graders, an overall score only represents a listening and speaking score. Thus, teachers need to research the scores in each area of language to get clearer pictures of their students' performance on this principally oral language test.

The SOLOM provides teachers more authentic data, based on standard tasks. There is room for teacher judgment as well as opportunities for teachers to observe students on an ongoing basis in a variety of tasks completed over time. Add to this bank of data more authentic assessments, and teachers can begin to develop curriculum and tasks that are much more focused on developing all of the language arts—listening and speaking, reading, and writing.

FIGURE 4.5 Student Oral Language Observation Matrix (SOLOM)

Skill	Level 1	Level 2	Level 3	Level 4	Level 5
A. Comprehension	Cannot be said to understand even simple conversations.	Has great difficulty following what is said. Can comprehend only social conversation spoken slowly and with frequent repetitions.	Understands most of what is said at slower-than-normal speed with repetitions.	Understands nearly every-thing at normal speed, although occasional repetition may be necessary.	Understands everyday conversation and normal classroom discussions.
B. Fluency	Speech so halting and fragmentary as to make conversation virtually impossible.	Usually hesitant; often forced into silence by language limitations.	Speech in everyday conversation and classroom discussion is frequently interrupted by the student's search for the correct manner of expression.	Speech in everyday conversation and classroom discussions is generally fluent, with occasional lapses while the student searches for the correct manner of expression.	Speech in everyday conversation and classroom discussions is fluent and effortless; approximating that of a native speaker.
C. Vocabulary	Vocabulary limitations so extreme as to make conversation virtually impossible.	Misuse of words and very limited vocabulary make comprehension quite difficult.	Student frequently uses wrong words; conversation somewhat limited because of inadequate vocabulary.	Student occasionally uses inappropriate terms and/or must paraphrase ideas because of lexical inadequacies.	Use of vocabulary and idioms approximate that of a native speaker.
D. Pronunciation	Pronunciation problems so severe as to make speech virtually unintelligible.	Very hard to understand because of pronunciation problems. Must frequently repeat in order to make himself or herself understood.	Pronunciation problems necessitate concentration on the part of the listener and occasionally lead to mis-understanding.	Always intelligible, although the listener is conscious of a definite accent and occasional inappropriate intonation patterns.	Pronunciation and intonation approximate that of a native speaker.
E. Grammar	Errors in grammar and word order so severe as to make speech virtually unintelligible.	Grammar and word order errors make comprehension difficult. Must often rephrase and/or restrict himself or herself to basic patterns.	Makes frequent errors of grammar and word order that occasionally obscure meaning.	Occasionally makes grammatical and/or word order errors that do not obscure meaning.	Grammar and word order approximate that of a native speaker.

Source: San Jose Unified School District (n.d.). *Student Oral Language Observation Matrix.* San Jose, CA: Region VII Comprehensive Center. Retrieved December 1, 2004, from http://www.helpforschools.com/ELLKBase/forms/SOLOM.shtml

Issues of Bias and Validity in Assessing ELLs

When contemplating assessment for ELLs, teachers must look at what is being measured. Because tests generally measure language in addition to content, it stands to reason that ELLs who are not yet proficient in English will encounter difficulty when they are assessed in that language (Mid-Atlantic Equity Center, 1998/9). Researchers have long shown that assessment can be biased in many ways (Laing & Kamhi, 2003, Valdés & Figueroa, 1994). Although standardized tests should not be the only outcome measure used to demonstrate what ELLs know, it is important to look at the validity of any classroom assessment. Two areas of validity related to assessment are cultural and linguistic validity. In addition, when discussing norm-referenced standardized tests it is also important to consider the norming group and whether it is representative of the group that is being assessed.

Solano-Flores (2002) defines cultural validity as "the effectiveness with which an assessment addresses the socio-cultural influences that shape student thinking and the ways in which students make sense of items and respond to them" (p. 1). He describes sociocultural influences as including students' values, beliefs, experiences, communication patterns, teaching and learning styles, and other factors that constitute students' cultural background knowledge as well as their socioeconomic conditions and that of their cultural groups (Solano-Flores, 2002). He argues that test developers need to take into account the sociocultural contexts that impact the way students make sense of the world and therefore the tests they take. Assessments may also demonstrate bias by including stereotypes and/or inadequate representation of minorities (Hambleton & Rodgers, 1997).

Children who are assessed in a language other than their native language experience some sort of linguistic bias related to the difference among the language used by the assessment and the assessor, the language used by the child, and the language of the expected response (Laing & Kamhi (2003). This is often seen in language assessments that purport to delineate among various levels of language proficiency (Oller, 1979). Because we know that every test assesses language in addition to content (Mercado & Romero, 1993), it makes sense that if a student is not proficient in the language of the test, his or her performance will be affected (Basterra, 1999). Although it might seem like a good idea to translate tests into the students' native language, such translations are not equivalent to the original exams because literal translations pose cultural, linguistic, and interpretation problems (Avalos, 2006).

Abedi (2001, 2006) and Bailey (2000) argue that the linguistic complexity of test items may threaten the validity of standardized tests when they are given to ELLs. Factors that influence linguistic complexity include new vocabulary, the use of idioms, the use of complex syntactical structures, and the use of genres that are unknown to the test takers. And assessing some content areas, such as reading (as opposed to math and science), requires more English proficiency (Bailey, 2000).

We must also take into consideration the fact that standardized tests are normed against a sample of test takers who are supposed to be representative of the population of students who take the same exam. Often the samples include limited numbers of ELLs nationwide, and therefore may not be representative of the group taking the exam (Basterra, 1999). Therefore, results compared against those of the normed group are not accurately interpreted (Avalos, 2006).

Authentic Assessment

There are many definitions of authentic assessment, but most educators agree that it consists of tasks that look like real-world activities. Wiggins (1990) states that "assessment is authentic when we directly examine student performance on worthy, intellectual tasks" (p. 1) and argues that it differs from traditional assessment, which is dependent on "substitutes" from which teachers (and researchers) make inferences about such performance. The use of authentic assessment integrates teaching, learning, and assessment as students learn and practice how to apply the knowledge and skills learned in class; it can also improve teaching and learning (Wiggins, 1990).

Authentic assessment, sometimes known as performance assessment, provides teachers with information about students on an ongoing basis. In the assessment process, teachers are encouraged to consider and value not only student strengths, but also areas of need. It is important that we start with the strengths of ELLs to help them understand how much they know, rather than what they don't know (Gibbons, 1993; Perez & Torres-Guzmán, 1996; Villa & Thousand, 2003). In 1994, the International Reading Association and the National Council of Teachers of English offered a list of issues to think about when considering all assessment. For example, in addition to students being the primary consideration in assessment, all data gained from assessment is to be used to improve teaching and learning. Teachers should use assessment to reflect on and allow for critical inquiry into curriculum and instruction. They should also use it to recognize and reflect on the interdependence among school, home, and society. Assessment must be equitable, valid, involve multiple perspectives and sources of data, and include parents as active participants. The teacher, however, is the agent of all assessment. Therefore, teachers must understand why they assess and how to best gather information about their students. Assessments should reflect and be an integral part of the school community; they are tools used to improve learning for all students. All stakeholders in a community must have a voice in assessment—parents, administrators, students, teachers, policy makers, and the public.

Because it is so critical that assessment data inform instruction, experienced teachers interviewed in a study on assessment knowledge and practices responded that they depended on authentic practices to guide instructional decisions on an ongoing basis (Quiocho, Dantas, & Mackintosh, 2001). The study model depicted in Figure 4.6 shows how ongoing assessment is used to guide instruction yet must be tempered with a sensitivity that takes into consideration students' cultures and languages.

The process is a recursive one where teachers use multiple pieces of data to guide instructional planning and assist in monitoring student performance. This process helps teachers make decisions about how and when to supplement classroom instruction with primary language as well as when English Language Development (ELD) or Specially Designed Academic Instruction in English (SDAIE) is appropriate. All this must occur in a learning environment supportive of students, an environment where there are high expectations for all. In this environment, teachers scaffold student learning to ensure that students can and do reach expectations. Assessment that is thorough and thoughtful helps teachers not only to teach the standards but also to go beyond the standards (Ladson-Billings, 1994). Finally, assessment should begin and end with students. Students need to know their strengths as well as the teacher's plans to address their areas of need. After assessment at the end of a unit of study, students need to know how the intervention or

FIGURE 4.6 ELD Instruction: Ongoing Assessment Guiding Instruction

Prior knowledge and understanding of students' culture and language

Ongoing assessment:
Use of multiple tools
to gather information;
Monitor student
understanding during
and after teaching; and
Guide/inform decision
making

Decision-making process:
Instruction based on
knowledge of students'
interests, strengths, and
needs; Instruction grounded
in primary language,
ELD, and/or SDAIE
strategies

Creating a supportive learning environment with high expectations for student growth

Source: From *A work in progress model of assessment for English language learners,* by A. Quiocho, M. L. Dantas, and D. Mackintosh, 2001. Paper presented at the annual meeting of the International Reading Association, New Orleans, LA.

plan affected their achievement. Figure 4.7 presents a classroom model that works to benefit students (Quiocho, Dantas, Mackintosh, & Rodriguez, 2002).

The Use of Portfolios

Teachers can use portfolios to assess student progress over time. In portfolio assessment, teachers, students, and parents use portfolios as a record of student learning (Grace, 1992). The students participate in the assessment process by assessing their own work and

FIGURE 4.7 "Work in Progress" Classroom Assessment Model

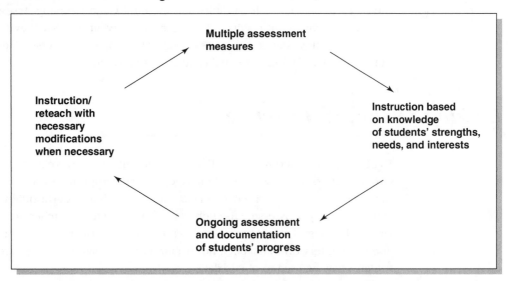

Source: From *Multiple perspectives on assessment and instruction of second language learners,* by A. Quiocho, M. L. Dantas, D. Mackintosh, and L. Rodriguez, 2002. Paper presented at the annual meeting of the International Reading Association, San Francisco, CA.

keeping track of their own growth. Ideally, both students and teachers choose what goes into the portfolio, which may contain any or all of the following: anecdotal records and notes of student behaviors and progress; checklists, which record student progress; teacher-made tests and assessments; assessment reports; student artifacts, such as student writing samples, responses to literature, projects; and pictures of student projects and activity.

Teachers can organize portfolios in many ways, but most teachers arrange student work chronologically and/or by content or curriculum area. Once the portfolio is organized, the teacher can use it to evaluate student progress toward the mastery of specific standards or goals. The teacher then adds her or his evaluative comments to the portfolio, including future needs (Grace, 1992). Portfolio assessment is NOT used to compare students to one another; rather it is used to compare the student's current work with what he or she did in the past as a means of assessing growth and therefore to help the teacher make appropriate decisions about the direction of future instruction.

Ensuring Quality in Assessing ELLs

How do we ensure that the assessments we use with ELLs are accurate and demonstrate high quality? The Northwest Regional Educational Laboratory (NWREL, 2001) suggests that quality student assessments must arise from clear and appropriate learning targets. In other words, teachers must clearly define student expectations, which, in turn, must be aligned to the appropriate content standards. Quality student assessments must also "serve a focused and appropriate purpose" (NWREL, 1998, p. 1) that delineates why the learning targets are being assessed and who will use the results and for what purposes.

It is also important for the assessment method to be appropriate to the learning target. Teachers need to be careful to choose assessments that match the learning. Finally, it is critical to eliminate bias and distortion in assessment (NWREL, 1998). Teachers can do this by evaluating the quality of the assessment and whether it measures what it says it does and by examining reliability, validity, fairness, equity, and sampling. Assessments must demonstrate consistent results over time, measure what they say they measure, and be accessible to all students regardless of cultural or linguistic diversity. Figure 4.8 demonstrates NWREL's four keys to quality student assessment.

Linking Theory to Practice

To obtain a clear picture of how ELLs can manipulate receptive as well as productive language, teachers must assess oral language, reading comprehension, content area understanding and mastery, written language, and overall ability (Carrasquillo & Rodriguez, 1996). A variety of assessments such as teacher-made tests; teacher observations; student work consisting of writing samples, lab reports, and performances as part of a group; questionnaires; interviews; anecdotal notes; and transcribed audio conversations with other students may be used to obtain data.

Teachers should select an assessment based on what is already known about a student along with any additional information needed about classroom performance. An informal oral language sample is an excellent place to start. Teachers should consider

FIGURE 4.8 Good Quality Assessments

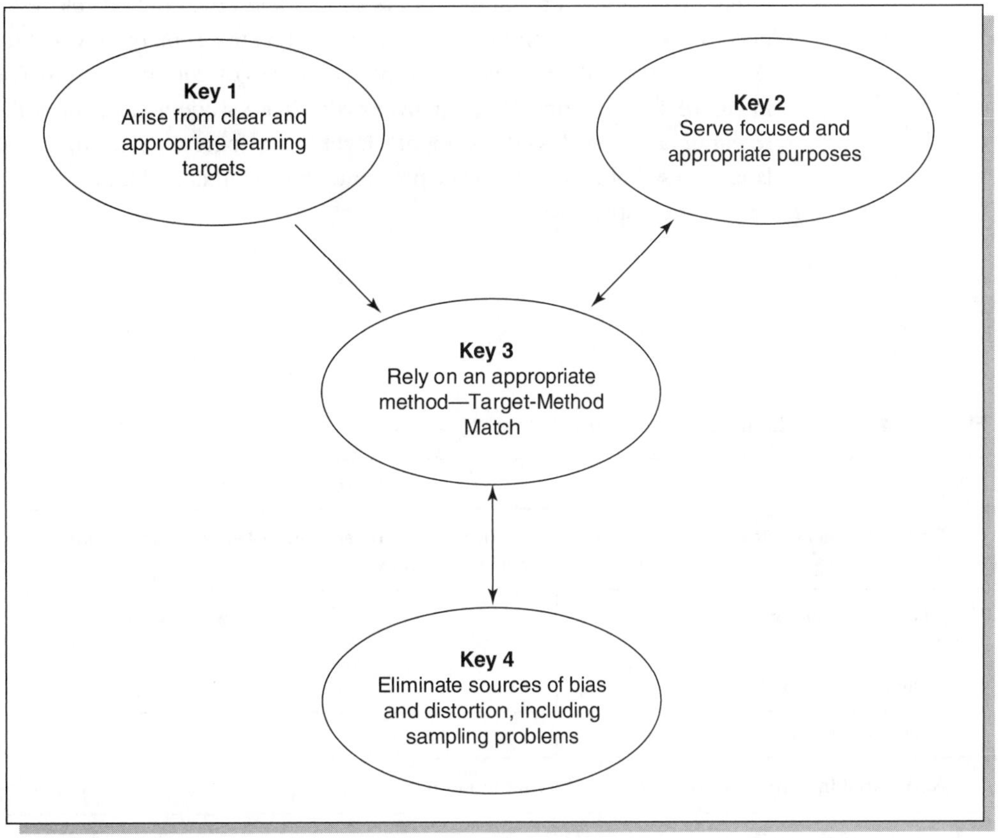

Source: From *Keys to quality student assessment*, by Northwest Regional Educational Laboratory, 2001. Retrieved September 5, 2005, from http://www.nwrel.org/assessment/toolkit98/keys.html

results from a standardized oral language assessment, if available, as an informational reference and review language proficiency levels to ensure that they know what functions of language have been tested.

Teachers can supplement the standardized information by creating an assessment context in which they can obtain an oral language sample from authentic classroom experiences. They can make the classroom tasks or experiences contextual, purposeful, spontaneous, and interactive (Gibbons, 1993). The tasks children are asked to do should also be cognitively demanding yet communicative in nature (Cummins, 1994). The tasks need to be a part of the normal school activities and require more than one-word answers. Children should have a clear purpose for using language; that is, they should understand what they need to accomplish with their language. Tasks such as a retelling and barrier games can serve as authentic assessments (Gibbons, 1993).

Retelling

Teachers can use a tape recorder to record students' language and write anecdotal notes while tape recording a language sample. The anecdotal notes inform teachers about the kinds of things that are happening that cannot otherwise be observed. Evaluating the forms or surface structures of language is important when assessing the concept of language proficiency. Although teachers should keep the context relaxed and informal, they need to assess each component of language (syntax, semantics, vocabulary) separately to determine the effectiveness and appropriateness of communication. The assessment sheet in Figure 4.9 (Gibbons, 1993) analyzes whether a student can accomplish the assigned retelling task as well as the student's level of competency. The sheet also analyzes formal language structures: vocabulary, pronunciation, language fluency, and accuracy of use of the grammatical structures.

FIGURE 4.9 Oral Language Assessment Sheet

Name:		Date:		
1. Ability to carry out the task	**Yes**	**Yes, but with limited competence** (see additional information below)		**No demonstration**
Did the child demonstrate the ability to . . . • understand the task				
• carry out the task				
2. Additional information on aspects of formal language				
Vocabulary/Pronunciation		**Fluency**	**Accuracy**	

Source: From *Learning to learn in a second language* (p. 45), by P. Gibbons, 1993, Portsmouth, NH: Heinemann.

Barrier Games

Gibbons (1993) also suggests that teachers use barrier games as an integral part of class-room instruction as well as assessment. A barrier game refers to an activity where information is shared through language. Students are required to work with decontextualized language, which places a higher linguistic demand on them. Teachers can use barrier games as an assessment to determine if and how students can use language in decontextualized, cognitively demanding situations (Cummins, 1994). Students will eventually be asked to perform in linguistically demanding yet decontextualized situations, such as exams or written essays, throughout their schooling. To determine the types of scaffolds ELLs need to help them accomplish such tasks, teachers should expose them to assessment tasks similar in nature to help guide instruction.

Barrier games direct students to classify objects or describe a picture that another student, separated from them by a barrier, draws without looking at the picture being described. Students may also describe objects and arrange them as well as describe their features and note characteristics that are similar or different. Students can look at two similar pictures that contain minor differences and describe what the differences are. They may give directions to another student who then draws a map based on the directions. Students can also sequence a set of pictures as a group and tell why they placed each picture in a specific place in the sequence. When using barrier games as an assessment, teachers should tape record student language and transcribe it for analysis. As with the retelling task, teachers will be looking for a student's ability to complete the assigned task and the formal language the student used to accomplish the task. The functions of oral language (Gibbons, 1993; Halliday, 1989; Peregoy & Boyle, 2005) can serve as a guide when analyzing oral language samples, such as those collected during retellings and barrier games (see Figure 4.10).

Assessing Reading Comprehension

Running records, where teachers listen to students read and keep track of miscues that contribute to inaccurate understanding of text, are also an excellent way to assess students. However, teachers should supplement running records with information gathered from watching and talking with students. Teachers can observe students and record performance in many ways. Here we suggest checklists, think alouds, reading pictures, and conferences (Hurley & Tinajero, 2000; O'Malley & Pierce, 1996; Peregoy & Boyle, 2005; Trussell-Cullen, 1998).

Checklists

Teachers can develop checklists by examining and describing the purposes of the tasks they ask students to perform in the classroom and listing them on a sheet of paper with room to elaborate about student performance on those tasks. Teachers need to decide on a recording system that will be the most useful for them. For example, do they want to count how many times a student performs a part of the task? Do they want to rate the quality with which the student performs the parts of the task? Teachers should create the checklist simultaneously with the objective for the task in which they want students to engage. They should decide whether they want information about students working

TOURO COLLEGE LIBRARY

FIGURE 4.10 Functions of Language

Functions	Classroom Experiences
Instrumental: I want; language as a means of getting things, of satisfying needs	Child clarifying instructions from morning routines; asking for supplies in play store or kitchen; asking for book in class library
Regulatory: Do as I say; controlling the behavior, feelings, or attitudes of others	Developing pantomimes and role-playing routines with partners or in groups; determining steps for completing projects
Interactional: Me and you; social interaction; getting along with others	Working in cooperative and collaborative groups on projects, art activities, and play
Personal: Here I come; pride and awareness of self, expressions of individuality	Sharing and telling about oneself; dictating language experience stories to others; sharing personal experiences
Heuristic: Tell me why; seeking and testing knowledge	Asking the teachers and students how something works; explaining the ideas in a story or retelling the story
Imaginative: Let's pretend; making up stories and poems; creating new worlds	Using wordless picture books to create new stories; using pictures to create stories; using creative dramatics to act out original ideas
Informative: I've got something to tell you; communicating information, description, ideas	Sharing ideas about what should be studied in a project or theme cycle; explaining what happened during a school event or describing a favorite television show
Divertive: Enjoy this; jokes, puns, riddles, language play	Telling riddles and jokes during special time devoted to this purpose

Source: From *Reading, writing & learning in ESL* (4th ed., p. 124), by S. F. Peregoy and O. F. Boyle, 2005, New York, Longman.

collaboratively or making choices independently and construct the instrument using what they want to know. Figure 4.11 presents one example of a checklist that focuses on the performance of four students. The teacher wants to know whether students can decide what to do independently with syntactical structure after they have read and practiced a story. There is room on this instrument for a check mark and information that elaborates on the observation.

Think Alouds

Teachers can use think alouds to assess reading or writing. In a think aloud, the teacher models for a student what he or she is thinking as he or she reads or writes. It is the first step in helping students become metacognitive and reflective about their own thinking (Costa, 2001; Daniels & Bizar, 1998). For example, let's say the teacher is reading aloud from the book *Grandfather's Dream* (Keller, 1994). The story takes place in the Mekong Delta in Vietnam.

FIGURE 4.11 Example of an Observational Checklist

Purpose for Observation:		To note how often students in a group of four are able to reorder words from their reading books into sentences that are syntactically correct.		
Student	Never independently	Acts by watching others	Sometimes independently	Always independently
Javier				
Gorge				
Chi				
Maribel				

The teacher places a map of Vietnam on the table and locates the Mekong Delta, telling the student that she has never been to Vietnam, so she wants to make sure where the country is located on the map and just where the Mekong Delta is located in the country. The teacher places a removable dot on the map to mark the Mekong Delta.

The teacher begins to read: "'The new dikes are built,' Grandfather announced as he dropped a piece of fish into Nam's bowl" (p. 5). "I wonder," says the teacher, "what a dike is. I have never been in a country where there is a dike. I remember reading about dikes in Holland. I think they are walls that keep the water from flooding the lands. I wonder if that is right. I wonder how important a dike is to this story. I'm just going to use what I think I know a dike is and say it's a wall to keep the land from flooding. I think the dike is important here because the author uses that word right away. I am also going to substitute the word *walls* for *dikes* and see if it makes sense." The teacher reads: "'The new [walls to keep the land from flooding] have been built,' Grandfather announced as he dropped a piece of fish into Nam's bowl." The teacher continues in this fashion reading a small chunk of text each time. The teacher stops after reading the chunk of text and thinks aloud. After the teacher finishes modeling the process, the student then tries. This assessment provides the teacher with information about how students process text, deal with new vocabulary, and know what questions to ask when they don't understand text. Teachers can follow the same process with writing (Trussell-Cullen, 1998).

Reading Pictures

When children begin to read in their primary language, they use pictures as clues to text meaning. As they begin to write, they connect their writing to the pictures they draw. As they learn about the mood of literature, they use pictures to understand this abstract aspect that affects responses to literature. As ELLs learn a second language, they use artifacts and pictures to learn the names of objects to begin to understand the language. Using picture reading can tell teachers if ELLs are learning to name objects in the second language. Having students produce their own pictures can give teachers insights into ELLs' response to the original text.

For example, the teacher sits with a small group of students or one on one with a student and they look at the first page of the story *The Tortilla Factory* (Paulsen & Paulsen, 1995). The text reads: "The black earth sleeps in winter." The teacher prompts, "Let's look at the picture. What do you think the author means when he says the black earth sleeps in winter? What do you see in the picture?"

The students are encouraged to take the time to look at the picture and think about what they see. The picture has the effect of one that has been painted. The colors are dark. The tilled earth is brown with rows of black streaks. A light, perhaps coming from a small house, glows bright in the background against the hills. A bright spot with a red glow is settled at the tip of long, low, flat plains that end in a row of low hills. The red spot and the surrounding glow brighten the slightly darkened sky.

The teacher then prompts the students to make connections between what they have named and the text. "How does the picture help us 'see' the winter? What happens during winter? Where in the picture can we see the earth sleeping? Why do the authors use the word *sleeping*? How do the colors help us 'see' the text in our mind's eye?"

When students read text and are encouraged to visually represent the story or some of its key elements, they demonstrate their ability to transfer understanding from the verbal to the visual realm. Teachers can use students' pictures as assessment when they are prompted to retell the story or a story element in a retelling, using the picture as a reference. The picture retelling represents the level of student response to text as well as thoroughness of understanding.

Conferences

The value of small group and individual conferences cannot be overemphasized. It is essential for all students, but ELLs, in particular, to be able to have private time with their teachers. During conferences teachers can interview students, ask questions, prompt them to talk about their work, provide feedback on work, and make recommendations to students for improvement.

Teachers can initiate conferences, but students need to be taught that it is okay to ask the teacher for a conference. ELLs may have to be taught how to ask for a conference and how to ask questions in the conference to get the input they need. When teachers initiate a conference, they are trying to find out how things are going, what kind of help the student requires, and the best way to begin the assistance process. When students initiate a conference they ask for help; however, they need to be able to articulate the kind of help they require at that specific time. Teachers need to give the following considerations to ELLs during conferences.

There should be wait time, that is, time when the teacher will wait for the students to formulate their thoughts and to find the language necessary to express thoughts. Students should be taught how to ask for wait time so they can articulate what they want to say.

There should also be observation time for teachers to note what is going on with ELLs. What are they actually doing? What part of the tasks are the students dealing with during the observation? What does the teacher perceive as a challenge at that moment? Teachers can record data collected during the observation time as anecdotal notes and use them when they conference with individual students or with a small group.

FIGURE 4.12 An Example of a Conferencing Checklist

	DATES			
Student	**9/20**	**9/21**	**9/22**	**9/23**
Marisol	xx	xx	x	x
Javier	x	xx	x	x
Chau	x	x	xx	x

Open-ended questions work best during conferences. Combining open-ended questions with think time encourages students to use more language to express themselves. The more ELLs practice at communicating their challenges and concerns as well as what they have learned, the more capable they become at manipulating academic language.

Probing student thinking is also helpful. Ask: "Can you tell me more? What else do you remember? What happened next? What do you want me to know the most about what you are writing or reading? How is this connected to . . . [what is being taught]? Tell me more."

Roving conferences where the teacher spends a minute or two with each student provides him or her more time to make individual contact. Questions asked should be directed at the work in which the students are engaged at that moment. A roving conference might become a chat check (Trussell-Cullen, 1998). Teachers can construct a list of student names to help them remember with whom they chatted and when. The list might look like Figure 4.12.

Assessing Student Writing

As with all student work, writing must begin with assessment. It makes sense for teachers to start with benchmark samples of student writing and also to decide what kinds of products will be collected from students to make decisions about the kinds of instruction to implement. Initially, students should view writing as a data-gathering exercise. That is, before a writer can write fluently about any topic, the writer must conduct some research, verify a few facts, and consider the audience for whom the writing is meant. Once the author has gathered data either from outside sources or from within her- or himself, the drafting can begin.

In the classroom, teachers should match writing genres with reading genres to build students' schema about the structure of text. For example, if the materials students are reading contain personal narratives, then teachers would want to begin by having students write personal narratives. They would then analyze the writing products for organization as well as for narrative structure.

All writing should begin with talk about the topic. Students can think on their own, pair their ideas with a partner, and share their personal experiences with the larger group. The teacher will want to "capture" their ideas and language by writing students' thoughts on a "shopping mall" chart of words and ideas. With the guidance of their teacher, students can develop organizational prompts to guide their writing and use them as they shop for words and ideas from the mall to compose their own writing.

The narrative structure *problem solution* is yet another way to organize text and provide a starting point from which to empower ELLs through the writing process. Campbell (2004) notes that problem posing seeks to help students understand the world they live in and critically analyze their real-life situations. When students participate in service learning projects such as working together to clean up a lot in the community or cooperate with the State Fish and Game Division to test the water in a local lagoon on a consistent basis, they feel empowered to write about their experiences. The act of being actively involved in improvement in their community provides students with ideas, language, and opinions about what the problem really is and what can be done to address the problem. Lots of talk naturally follows such activities. Writing should be next.

Teachers should develop and use rubrics that reflect the standards to assess the writing of their ELL students. For example, Violetta, Dionna, and Tessie, three teachers with whom we worked, work from their state's Language Arts Framework and Content Standards to plan their writing instruction and assessment. Standard 2.2 states that students should be able to write responses to literature by demonstrating an understanding of the literary work and support their judgments through references to both the text and prior knowledge (CDE, 1998). Therefore, the rubric they would use addresses the quality or level of understanding of a story that students demonstrate in their writing, whether students support their responses by quoting words or phrases from the story and how they use their prior knowledge in their responses. In addition to looking at the features of the genre of the writing they are working on, Violetta, Dionna, and Tessie use strategies that focus on fluency, organization, structure, and form. For example, Figure 4.13 is an example of one intervention that Violetta and Dionna used with their students to demonstrate the interdependency of listening, speaking, reading, and writing.

FIGURE 4.13 A Writing Intervention

1. Provide a prompt for the student (S) to read.
2. Have the S retell the story.
3. Look for important words in the retelling, and if there are none there, insert words from reading.
4. Write using language experience where students use their retelling and the vocabulary provided by the teacher to dictate a writing piece based on what they read. The teacher mediates student language.
5. Model how to put that in a writing piece to inform others by modeling writing a piece.
6. Develop a rubric with the child to look at what would make a good piece (what it would look like, sound like, where vocabulary would be most appropriate, how the piece could be engaging).
7. Apply rubric to teacher's writing: Student and teacher rate the writing using the rubric.
8. Provide a high interest reading selection to start students writing either in partners or on their own.
9. Have S retell the story. Teacher writes down the retelling.
10. Select five content heavy words to create a word bank.
11. Have S try writing using the model.
12. Use the rubric to score the writing.
13. Use the student's scored writing piece as a starting point for the next lesson.

Examples from the Field

Classroom teachers implement authentic assessments in their classrooms in ways that best serve their students and the work they need to accomplish. In classrooms where authentic assessment is an integral part of instruction, the focus is on student work and student performance in everyday classroom tasks. Let's walk through a few classrooms and see how teachers are using authentic assessment.

There are 20 ELLs in **Dionna's** classroom. All instruction in the district in which Dionna works must be in English. Dionna uses authentic assessment to guide her instruction. When you walk into her classroom, you may see her taking a running record with an individual student or standing behind one student taking a running record while the others are reading aloud at their own pace. When students are writing, Dionna walks around the classroom conducting 1- or 2-minute conferences with her students. Her conference might sound like this: "Read what you are working on to me. I like your topic and I can tell you are very interested in that topic. What is the most important thing you want me to know about your topic? Great! Write that down. I'll be back to check on you." Then she moves on to another student. She will return to check on that student and he knows it.

Violetta has 36 ELLs in her classroom. Violetta's classroom contains a resource center where students can work with thesauruses and dictionaries in Spanish and English, refer to the class graphic organizer, or use the content area and

> **BOX 4.1 DIONNA**
>
> Dionna is a fifth-grade teacher. She has been in the profession for 5 years. Dionna previously taught second and third grades. She earned her master's degree in language and literacy with a reading specialist credential. She has assumed a leadership role at her school.

Dionna assesses a student as a part of the consistent, ongoing assessment process.

BOX 4.2   VIOLETTA

Violetta has taught more than 10 years in elementary schools. She began her career in urban schools and later relocated to another area in southern California and sought employment in a large unified school district that serves a very diverse population. She is bilingual and uses her primary language, Spanish, to support the ELLs in her classroom and at her school.

cognate word walls to support their reading and writing. Violetta's students are willing to tell you how they see themselves as writers. Javier told me that he thought he was a pretty good writer, but he has "troubles" sometimes. "How do you get help?" I asked. "We have the resource corner," he said and pointed it out, "but if I can't get help there or from my writing buddy, I go to the board and write my name for a conference with my teacher."

The students in Violetta's classroom have learned to self-assess. They know how to get help and where to get it. They know how to ask for individual conferences when they need them. Their requests are honored.

Tessie knows she needs to focus on content area reading and writing. One day she might give her students a cloze passage to fill in after they have spent time reading poetry, literature books, the state-adopted reading texts, and the social studies textbook in the unit in which they are studying about explorers. Her students can often be seen looking up at the ceiling as if searching for words. Their gazes shift to the cognate and content area word walls. Some may shake their heads as they realize they inserted a word that doesn't make sense. They erase the insertion and fill in the blank with another word.

BOX 4.3   TESSIE

Tessie has been teaching for 12 years in K–6 education in a large unified school district. She has a master's degree in educational administration and has mentored new teachers. Her parents came to the United States from Mexico. She is a second language learner who is an advocate for all students but understands how to support ELLs. Tessie has an administrative credential and serves as support for the administrator at her school.

Tessie teaches her students to ask themselves if what they are reading looks right, sounds right, or makes sense. Her students know that when they are finished reading something, they will need to retell what they read to her or to their reading buddy who has a retelling assessment checklist. Tessie's instruction is informed by student assessment. You can hear her say, "Yesterday we were talking about the kinds of ships the explorers used when they left their homelands, and I think you may have been confused. Some of you said the explorers left on steamships. When we think about that time in history, let's ask ourselves if that makes sense." The students think. She gives them wait time. They turn to their thinking/writing partners and discuss whether the answer made sense or not. Finally, they are ready. "No teacher," they respond. "The steam engine wasn't made yet." The conversation continues as Tessie uses what she learned from authentic assessment contexts to teach her students the important concepts of the unit.

Kris is a reading coach. He has looked at the schoolwide language scores and reading scores. He has tracked all the assessments of the ELLs in the school. He analyzes the assessment prompts and the assessment results searching for recurring patterns. He finds a very significant one. He sees that students at levels 2 (early intermediate), 3 (intermediate), and 4 (early advanced) on the CELDT are struggling with the syntax of the English language as evidenced in their running records, informal reading inventories, and writing samples that were calibrated at grade level and across grade levels. He decides they need an assessment that would provide data on how students process specific syntactical structures. He realizes that would be helpful in coaching teachers and provide him the material for the model literacy lessons he delivers in classrooms.

Kris does his research and finds an assessment. The selected assessment will provide specific information to each teacher about how the ELLs in her or his class manipulate

BOX 4.4 KRIS

Kris has been in the teaching profession for 7 years in a large unified school district. He has a master's degree in language and literacy as well as a reading specialist credential. He has served as a reading coach, mentored new teachers, and taught first, third, and fourth grades. Presently he is teaching sixth and seventh graders who struggle with reading.

syntax. This information will then be used to support Kris's in-class model lessons, teachers' instructional practices, and writing conferences to help support students.

Not long after Kris located the assessment and obtained copies for teachers to use, he trains them in administration of the test. The assessment is given to those students Kris has identified as struggling with navigating the syntax of English. He charts the assessment results from each classroom and provides them to each teacher. The teachers sit at their grade level meetings and discuss how to develop the best interventions for groups of students who have common needs. Kris volunteers to help.

Soon, the intervention plans for the struggling students contain descriptions of instruction targeted at working with specific syntactical structure in authentic classroom contexts. Teachers meet with students in small groups, making connections between their work and instruction. Kris also works on this task with small groups of students. The teachers at this school have learned that assessment is the foundation of all instruction. Their students are partners in the assessment process, and the teachers and reading coach are partners in using assessment data and collaboratively developing instructional strategies to meet students' needs.

Summing It Up

Results from different kinds of language assessments, including standardized norm-referenced tests and criterion-referenced assessments linked to a common set of standards, can begin to inform teachers about ELLs' language development. Teachers should start with these data and add information gathered from classroom-based authentic tasks, referred to as authentic assessment.

Sometimes when we talk about authentic assessment, the descriptions sound very much like teaching strategies. That is the idea. Anything that can be used to teach a student can be used to assess a student. With ELLs, we always want to consider the student's language proficiency level so we can scaffold their language by providing necessary content words, waiting as they search for words, or asking probing questions to extend their language. We want to consider how students process information culturally; for example, do they view nature as something to be revered and not destroyed, do they see animals as having human characteristics yet could never "become" animals, or do they greatly value concepts such as family and community? This can affect student performance on a language task. For example, when a researcher asked Steven, a Native American second grader, to pretend he was a monkey and write about it, he was stumped. First, he was puzzled, then became angry, telling the researcher that he was not a monkey. The researcher asked him what he would feed a monkey if he had one as a pet and what he would do to take care of it. Steven immediately began to talk about what he would do. "Great," responded the researcher. "Can you write about that?" He began to write.

It is important to know how students respond to input from members of the classroom community. Will they accept help from their peers or will they perceive help that is being offered as a sign that others do not think they are very smart? Do students feel that they are the ones who should ask for help and not someone else in the class? Do students feel they have to send the bravest one in their group to get help for the entire group? These are important cultural perceptions that can have a negative or positive effect on student performance in language-based tasks.

Building a classroom community where all students feel valued and their voices are respected and honored means that a teacher can gather more accurate data in authentic assessment contexts to inform instructional planning and teaching.

Practical Applications and Individual Inquiries: Cases to Think About and Investigate

1. Talk with a parent, teacher, and administrator about their philosophies of assessing ELLs. What do they feel should happen when ELLs do not score as high as other students in the class or school?

2. Interview two classroom teachers. Ask them which type of assessment is most informative to them: standardized tests or authentic assessments in classroom contexts. Whichever form of assessment the teacher selects, be sure to ask why he or she feels that way.

3. Observe a classroom of your choice. What kinds of assessments does the teacher use with ELLs? Describe the assessments. Find out what the teacher does with the assessment results. Are they used to inform instruction? To conference with students and parents? The administrator? Other teachers?

Chapter Five

Teaching and Learning the Necessary Skills for Literacy Success

I kept confusing skills with strategies. I used to think, "Are strategies the same as skills?" Once I began to look at the expected task first, then identified the skills students needed to be able to accomplish the task, I was able to think about the strategy I would use, or how I was going to teach the skills so students could master them and accomplish the assigned task and other similar tasks. So, now I think that skills are the learning/thinking part and the strategy is a way to teach the necessary skills. It makes sense when I think about it that way.

Nancy, first-grade teacher

This chapter focuses on the importance of teaching reading and writing skills to students to give them the tools they need for literacy success. We discuss skills as "information-processing techniques that readers and writers use automatically and unconsciously as they construct meaning" (Tompkins, 2003, p. 267) and distinguish between skills and strategies, which are covered in Chapter 6. We look specifically at reading and writing skills and how teachers can help ELLs understand those skills involved in specific reading and writing tasks to make meaning of text.

Skills instruction is critical for ELLs in that they are often reading texts in English, a language they are still learning. To effectively teach reading and writing skills, teachers need to analyze the literacy task at hand, identify the skills necessary for the students to use in order to accomplish the task, and then strategize the way the skills are taught to help students learn how to learn, thus accomplishing the task. Furthermore, teachers need to make sure that ELLs have adequate vocabulary to understand the task.

To explore the ways in which teachers can effectively use skills instruction to help their ELLs become proficient readers and writers, we listen to one group of teachers as they define skills and strategies and talk about how they teach skills within the classroom context. We then give an example of how two teachers teach reading and writing skills in context and how their students apply those skills to the literacy tasks required of them. In this chapter we:

- Define skills and strategies within the framework of literacy instruction.
- Distinguish between skills and strategies and demonstrate the relationship between the two.
- Describe how teachers work together to determine skills that are important for ELLs.
- Demonstrate what skills instruction looks like.

Building Background Knowledge About Teaching and Learning the Necessary Skills for Literacy Success

What Are Skills?

There are many ways to define the word *skills.* For example, Harris and Hodges (1995) in the International Reading Association's *The Literacy Dictionary: The Vocabulary of Reading and Writing* define skills as "a general term for those techniques . . . that help a person read or listen for specific purposes with the intent to remember" (p. 245). Eggen and Kauchak (2001) describe skills as "cognitive operations" with specific procedures that can be demonstrated with a variety of examples (p. 280). Doyle (1983) adds that skills are not only taught, but also need to develop through practice.

So what does this mean in terms of literacy instruction for ELLs? Tompkins (2003) lists five types of literacy skills that elementary students need to learn: comprehension skills, decoding and spelling skills, language skills, reference skills, and study skills. These types of skills are intricately linked to state standards and curricular frameworks, which spell out what teachers need to teach. California, for example, has both English language arts standards and a framework for teaching English language arts. It also has a set of standards for English language development (http://www.cde.ca.gov). These standards and the framework guide teaching in public schools in California and specify the specific skills in reading, writing, listening, and speaking that students need to master at each grade level. The standards are valuable for teachers in that they address the skills necessary for students to master. However, the standards and frameworks do not specify how to teach the necessary skills or how to differentiate the instruction for ELLs.

When teaching skills it is important to teach skills in context. Learning that "sticks" takes place in collaborative settings that include looking back or reflecting, much like learning in real life (Shulman, 2004). Shulman and others (Resnick, 1987; Dewey, 1938) advocate bringing the learning in school in line with real-life learning. They argue that learning in school is pursued alone, based on pure reflection with abstract symbols, usually in isolation, and aimed at developing generalizations. Real life, on the other hand, is contextual and situation specific, based on accomplishing tasks with real meaning. Such learning is pursued collaboratively, using the tools others have already developed. Resnick (1989) further observes that schools that teach critical thinking well focus on "socially shared intellectual work, and they are organized around joint accomplishments of tasks so that the elements of the skills take on meaning in the context of the whole" (p. 13). Further, teachers and students who actively engage in learning make the hidden processes of "getting it" overt and obvious. Teachers build skills step by step so everyone can participate, and they organize lessons around particular bodies of knowledge and interpretation rather than abilities.

Thus, one can conclude that teaching should take place in context and that teachers should embed specific skills for accessing the curriculum in collaborative learning in a community (Ladson-Bilings, 1994) where all students can participate because skills are scaffolded step by step. Instruction in schools for all children, but especially for ELLs, should mimic real life. Students learn skills in schools explicitly through direct instruction, many times using unfamiliar content with which they have difficulty connecting. On the other hand, real-life learning is open and regularly organized around opportunities to plan, reflect, and review in the company of others (Shulman, 2004), where wait time (Rowe, 1974) is a habit of mind because giving thinkers and learners time has consistently produced higher levels of cognitive processing.

What Are Strategies?

"Strategies are problem-solving tactics selected deliberately to achieve particular goals" (Tompkins, 2003, p. 267). Thus, teachers must think about what they want students to cognitively learn. It is critical for ELLs to think about the language they must use to learn the skills (Chamot & O'Malley, 1994). Once teachers have decided on the objective and the language, then they can select the strategy or strategies necessary to support ELLs in the zone of proximal development (Vygotsky, 1978), where they guide students in achieving their goals. Therefore, teachers must use thinking strategies such as metacognition to help students understand how to navigate the necessary skills and achieve the objective.

The Relationship Between Skills and Strategies

Different researchers and practitioners describe strategies and skills in a variety of ways. For example, Tompkins (2003) notes that strategies help students achieve their goals. Others define skills as "processes that readers use habitually. Strategies are the processes by which they use their skills under conscious control. Teachers need to know what skills and strategies students possess and consciously develop a strong repertoire in all students" (Temple, Ogle, Crawford, & Freppon, 2005, p. 263). Routman (1994) talks about "bringing skills teaching to the strategic level" (p. 134).

Teachers want to teach skills so that they become part of the student's repertoire of learning strategies, so that they are useful later on. In this kind of teaching, what Routman (1994) calls "teaching for strategies," the skill is taught because the learner has a demonstrated need for that skill. The teacher guides the student to use the skill in authentic contexts. The student, therefore, applies the skill to meaningful contexts. When the student knows when and how to apply the skill, the skill is promoted to the strategy level (Routman, 1994).

Rather than being overly concerned with exact definitions for skills and strategies, teaching for transfer should be the goal of instruction. The question is: Can students transfer what they are learning to their lives? For example, can they stop and think out loud about whether they should spend all of their lunch money on a game they really want or they should eat lunch and save the extra money until they have enough to purchase the game? Will students be able to think critically about the causes and effects of an occurrence in history? How automatically can they know that observation and recording of data is the key to analysis or that waiting to look up unknown words when reading their science text is the best strategy to use rather than fleeing to find a dictionary immediately? In other words, what good is learning a strategy if it does not empower students to learn more information when they need to do so?

Skills can be seen as cognitive habits students acquire as part of learning, and those habits will be used regularly in their lives. For example, distinguishing between cause and effect is a skill. Strategies to teach that skill may vary. Grouping and classifying objects, people, and so forth are skills that we always use in our lives so we can compare and contrast what we see in order to make a good decision.

One way to think about the difference between a skill and a strategy when planning lessons is to think reflectively about the process of learning, placing ourselves in the role of the students. Many times when ELLs face a new or challenging situation, they become paralyzed. The language of the task may be confusing. The steps of the task, especially if there are many steps to accomplishing a task, may present an obstacle to beginning or finishing a task. Students may become indecisive about how to begin, what to say, or where to start. They may seem confused and insecure about what they really know about the task. Hildenbrand and Hixon (1991) and others show that when students think they know nothing about what needs to be accomplished, they resort to using limited strategies. Teachers need to remind ELLs that they possess intelligent behavior, or as Costa (1991) describes it, "Intelligent behavior is knowing what to do when you don't know what to do" (p. 20). It is not that ELLs do not behave intelligently. They are navigating a second language in academic contexts, which can produce feelings of insecurity. Thus, they may shut down and convince themselves that they know nothing about what they are being asked to do.

This is when a preassessment of the necessary skills might reveal the skills students have and don't have. This might be a time to help students set goals and develop a plan to proceed and accomplish the task. This might be a good time to monitor and nurture ELLs as they work through a task, providing feedback and posting help with vocabulary words, sequencing, determining importance, selecting appropriate conjunctions, thinking out loud about cause and effect or comparison and contrast, making connections between their background knowledge and the task at hand, or building their background knowledge. In other words, once you know the demands of the task and assess and identify the skills students possess or do not possess to accomplish the task, the skills students need are taught using strategies they can rely on and use over and over again when necessary. Once students have learned the skills through a strategy or strategies, and they review those strategies consistently, they will learn to self-assess and to be metacognitive or think about their thinking.

Now let's see what two teachers have to say about skills and strategies. We met Dionna in Chapter 4. She and Raeanna (see Box 5.1) sat down with us one afternoon to talk about skills and strategies.

BOX 5.1 RAEANNA

Raeanna has been teaching for 6 years in an urban school. She is a fourth/fifth-grade teacher who serves as a teacher leader at her grade levels as well as a change agent at her school. She earned her master's degree in language and literacy with a reading specialist credential.

Dionna's Perspective

When I first started teaching, I felt that a strategy was a skill that students used to accomplish a task. For example, if a student was having a hard time with vocabulary words in a text, a strategy that could help him or her manage that issue was either reading around the word or finding smaller words inside the word to help him or her figure it out. The skill of knowing which strategies to use and to use them flexibly was what I was defining as skill. As I have been teaching longer, I realize that the skill is the task, for example, comprehension in reading. That is a skill. You need multiple strategies to accomplish that task. I learned this from a piece of text we used in a professional development at my school. I thought it was relevant to this example.

Herrell (2000) showed me how teachers can support students as they acquire language and content. As a teacher in California, I realize that the diversity of our students is not just related to the leveled group we put them in during Guided Reading, but more specifically, it is related to their culture, socioeconomic background, and language experiences prior to and outside of school. For our diverse students to construct knowledge and acquire language based on the skills used for literacy, educators must teach strategies tailored specifically for their population. Unfortunately, today's textbook-driven academic fervor has driven teachers toward losing sight of the skills and forced them to bombard students with a plethora of strategies that don't always affirm the way our students construct knowledge.

Raeanna's Perspective

Strategies are basic approaches to aiding students across the curriculum to support their construction of knowledge. Basically strategies should ensure that the curriculum is comprehensible, aid in contextualizing language, allow students to verbally use new knowledge, lower the affective filter, and encourage active participation within the classroom. The key here is finding a handful of strategies that promote growth across curriculum and are adaptable to students' needs. One of the core reading texts in California's adopted curriculum teaches over 170 strategies throughout the whole year. These strategies, which include graphic organizers, games, and charts, are overwhelming. There isn't consistency throughout the year, and teachers use new strategies when they can easily modify ones that the students have already learned. An educator scaffolds in order to promote continuity, growth, and equity in the classroom, but too many scaffolds and strategies can shift students' focus from learning the skill to relying on the support to understand.

If students relate new information to prior knowledge, then using strategies over a longer time and gradually releasing them will allow carryover when students are constructing knowledge related to skills. For example, the same strategies teachers use to scaffold learning about skills pertaining to prefixes, base words, and suffixes can be carried over and modified when scaffolding the learning of skills related to syllabication. When turning focus toward comprehension, teachers could use the same strategy for making judgments but modify it when introducing solving problems and solutions.

Most importantly, teachers want students to be able to read and write using their newly acquired skills. Students shouldn't need to focus heavily on what strategy to use; it should come naturally. If they construct the knowledge correctly, students can actively adapt their strategies to specific skills. This is the basis of constructing knowledge and connecting prior knowledge to new information.

Linking Theory to Practice: Differentiating Skills Instruction for ELLs

We propose guidelines or a framework for teaching skills to ELLs as a way to link theory and practice. The guidelines can be framed in the following way: (1) find out what students know; (2) preteach critical vocabulary; (3) build on background knowledge; (4) provide explicit instruction in a collaborative setting; (5) plan for language, then model and demonstrate; (6) practice, practice, practice; (7) check for understanding. The emphasis is on creating classrooms where the learning is more like real life and not isolated school exercises. Assessment is an important starting point. From there, we build on what students know and extend their knowledge. We place them in groups where they can learn together, have time to reflect, and decide on what works as a learning community. Teaching mini-lessons about skills, linking skills to strategies, and embedding skills instruction in context is also central to these guidelines. A brief explanation for each guideline follows.

Find Out What Students Know

Before instructing ELLs, teachers must find out what they know. Many teachers start with a question that asks students to reflect on what they know about a topic or what they think they might know about a topic. Teachers should give ELLs time to think about the question as they frame their responses in order to connect to what they know about the world and the topic. When necessary, they should repeat the question to ensure that students understand it. Teachers should allow time for thinking, and then have students share their thinking with a partner. Finally they should take students' responses and record them to refer to during the lesson. Teachers need to encourage ELLs at beginning levels to use their primary language to share their thinking with peers and the class so they can actively participate.

Preteach Critical Vocabulary

Selecting appropriate vocabulary for ELLs to learn before starting a lesson is important in helping them gain access to content. Teachers need to select only the vocabulary necessary to understand concepts taught in the lesson. Having students see the vocabulary in context is more helpful than teaching words in isolation. If students are able to see vocabulary in context, they can begin to make connections during reading. However, as the reading progresses, teachers should point out the pretaught vocabulary to check for comprehension and application of understanding.

Build on Background Knowledge

Starting lessons using what students know helps ELLs make connections between what they know and what is being taught. When students are able to use their background knowledge to learn, they are more willing to share relevant personal experiences with others. As teachers validate students' experiences and their background knowledge making explicit efforts to connect what students know with instruction, unfamiliar information begins to make sense. Making meaning is central to all learning, and building on students' background knowledge facilitates learning.

Provide Explicit Instruction in Collaborative Settings

Because ELLs need additional time to process language, teachers should provide them with opportunities to work with others as they think about their own thinking. Such time also provides ELLs with opportunities to receive comprehensible input (Krashen, 1994) and acquire language in the context of the lesson. ELLs need to develop the necessary skills to become independent, skilled readers and writers. Teachers should use results from ongoing assessment (e.g., observation checklists, anecdotal notes, student learning logs) to decide on appropriate group structures in which to place students. When teachers use results of ongoing assessment to group students, they know which groups need explicit instruction in specific skills (see Figure 1.2 for the flow chart that chronicles the process of using assessment to consistently inform instruction). Students should be trained in collaborative processes—how to ask for help, give positive feedback, take explicit roles, or ask questions to clarify meaning. Collaborative structures help ELLs share information, learn how to support each other, and share what they know with confidence.

Plan for Language, Then Model and Demonstrate

As we suggest in Chapters 1 and 3, all instruction for ELLs needs to have a language objective. Since schooling is about language and learning requires understanding and processing language, all lesson plans must contain language objectives. Once again, teachers use ongoing assessment to identify vocabulary as well as language structures that are critical for discussion, comprehension, and writing. Teachers must teach the necessary language structures as a part of the lesson. They should model the language they want students to use and allow time for students to respond to questions using the necessary language structures. In addition, teachers need to take the time to demonstrate the required tasks, stopping at critical points in the modeling to ensure that students understand what must be done as well as the academic language that must be used. As ELLs learn a second language, they search for models to emulate to note patterns and understand what works and what doesn't work in the second language.

Practice, Practice, Practice

It is important to emphasize the element of time. ELLs need time to think about what they are learning, time to observe and process what they are observing, and time to talk about what they think is happening. They need time to practice. It is illogical to rush through state-adopted material or other texts just to complete required tasks while ELLs remain confused and puzzled about what they should be learning and are at a loss to talk about content learning in their own words or ask critical thinking questions. Practice is important. Providing students with feedback on their products and providing additional practice time to students who require it enhances learning. Practice provides time for additional observation and ongoing assessment to support flexible grouping, differentiation, reteaching, and checking for understanding. See Chapter 4 for an analysis of the assessment process and how traditional tests and test results affect ELLs.

Check for Understanding

An integral part of ongoing assessment is checking for understanding. We emphasize that checking for understanding is an indispensable part of instruction. As students work at a task or the teacher progresses through a lesson, it is imperative that he or she stop at critical points in the lesson where concepts are being developed to assess what students understand and the ideas, vocabulary, or concepts with which they are struggling. Ask questions that encourage ELLs to show or retell what they know about each part of the concept. Provide students with opportunities to re-present or use their imagination to create symbols and pictures that demonstrate understanding. No lesson for ELLs is complete without frequent checking for understanding.

Table 5.1 summarizes each step of these guidelines with suggested ways to implement each step as well as activities to support ELLs.

TABLE 5.1 Suggested Guidelines for Teaching Skills to ELLs

Guideline	How to Get to It	Supportive Activities
Find out what students know	• Ask questions. • Bring in realia or tactile objects and have students handle the objects. Have students use observation and tactile sensations to describe realia using primary language.	• Record all student responses. • Have students work in pairs using think-pair-share to collaborate on information, descriptions. • Have students draw an object or situation they think is similar to the one in front of them. Use this approach to support language development. Go back and label part of the picture, using key vocabulary.
Preteach critical vocabulary	• Have pictures that represent key vocabulary. Select only the few terms that are critical to understanding the concepts of the text. Label the pictures. • Create picture glossaries using a picture and labeled parts when knowing individual parts is critical to understanding key concepts. • Create a short list of critical vocabulary words to provide pairs of students with opportunities to observe the word, look for small words within the word, and think about other words that might be like this word.	• Have students search through magazines for pictures that represent a vocabulary word. • Have students create the picture glossaries as they proceed through the lesson. • Have students work in collaborative groups to create a graphic organizer in which they separate out the parts of the word by syllables, noting what they think each part of the word means, and concluding what the meaning of the word is.
Build on background knowledge	• Make connections to students' personal lives, their communities, and experiences they have in common at school. • Use a metaphor with which students can identify to bridge their experiences and content knowledge.	• Begin with cultural understandings and cultural activities. • Use cultural stories and story structures to help students more readily make connections.

TABLE 5.1 (continued)

Guideline	How to Get to It	Supportive Activities
Provide explicit instruction in collaborative settings	• Place students of varying abilities in the groups so all can participate. • Teach about collaboration, providing students with clear standards for listening and speaking. • Provide opportunities for students to practice with peers.	• Model how to work in a collaborative group. • Start with pairs first, and then combine two sets of pairs. • Teach students how to ask questions, especially clarification questions. • Emphasize wait time so ELLs have enough time to process language.
Plan for language, then model and demonstrate	• When you plan the task for each lesson, note the kind of language you want students to use: asking questions, asking for clarification, comparing and contrasting, noting cause and effect, etc. Teach the language in a mini-lesson, modeling with another student and debriefing with ELLs so they can practice the language. • Be explicit on your modeling. Demonstrate the process step by step. (What does it look like? What does it sound like?) Ask students to summarize each step. Put the process together and write the process on butcher paper for future reference.	• Have three students sit in a circle. Ask a question. The first answers one part of the question. The second student repeats or paraphrases what the first student said, then adds information. The third student does the same. All agree and record their group response. • Have several pairs of students model for the rest of the class in a fishbowl, where the pairs sit in the center of the class and groups of students watch them as they model how to do something. Students have a checklist of behaviors to observe.
Practice, practice, practice	• Provide ample time for students to practice. • Provide checklists so students can see how far they have progressed. • Observe and ask probing questions as you monitor student work. • Provide feedback and time for "do overs" and revisions.	• Stop student work and ask them to assess themselves individually as active learners. • Ask the group to assess themselves as one group. • Provide resource areas in the classroom such as cognate word walls, dictionaries in languages other than English as well as English, graphic organizers and planners, rubrics in "kid" language for students to use as they work. • Have tactile reminders (objects selected for touch) whenever possible to stimulate connections to culture, communities, personal lives.
Check for understanding	• Stop the work periodically and ask clarifying questions when you notice that several students are making the same kinds of errors. • Have students talk about and share how they began and continued through the task especially when they felt stuck. • Use student language to compose a reminder list of what students can do when the work appears hard.	• Monitor and ask questions. • Have students read back to you what they have completed. • Regroup students that need more modeling and demonstration and involve them in a mini-lesson that gets them started on the task again. • Make connections between skills and strategies in mini-lessons by linking skills to strategies. • Post skills on the board. • Have available a list of steps for each strategy being used and review the steps before students begin and with small groups when necessary. • After a lesson, have students talk about the "so what" question. How did the strategy help them learn? What was easy about the strategy? What was hard?

Examples from the Field

Discussing Skills and Strategies with Teachers

A group of 18 teachers sat around a table reflecting on the question posed: Is a strategy the same as a skill? How are they alike? How are they different? Think about your own teaching and respond based on your experiences, comparing and contrasting if need be. At first, they looked at each other. Some smiled, others searched the ceiling of the room as if the answer would be there, and others began thinking and talking to their peers. What follows is their dialogue and thinking about the question.

Kris is clear about the differences between a strategy and a skill. "A skill," he says with conviction, "is much more basic than a strategy. A skill can come from a standard, and we usually use the standards to identify skills we want our students to learn. We know that once a student learns a skill, he can practice transferring that skill to other content areas of learning." He continues, "On the other hand, a strategy is a means to teach the skill. For example, if we want our students to infer, summarize, find critical information in text, by the way," he adds, "to infer, summarize, and determine importance are skills. For example, we use GIST (Getting Information by Summarizing Text) as a strategy to teach the skills of inferencing, summarizing, and determining importance. That's the difference between a skill and a strategy."

Reading, writing, and thinking together during small group instruction.

Dionna nods her head and agrees with Kris. She and Kris work at the same school and that staff has worked collaboratively for 3 years talking about and coming to consensus about the differences between a skill and a strategy.

Raeanna is a fourth-grade teacher in a unified school district in a large city. She teaches a class of very diverse children in an urban school. Raeanna spent a large percentage of her first 4 years in teaching continuing her education and dialoging with other teachers about ways to best instruct her students. The topic of the differences between a skill and a strategy is intriguing to her and she chimes in. "I used to think that skills and strategies were the same, but now that we are talking and I think about it, I think they are different. I find myself thinking about what my students should learn according to the standards and district expectations for fourth graders. Then, I look at how my students perform in reading and writing, the skills they exhibit as described in the standards. Next, I decide how I am going to group them, and which strategies I am going to use with which group. So, now I think strategies and skills *are* different. The strategy teaches the skills. The skills then are what students need to know to learn about unfamiliar content. So, I want to see how two things match up, I need to compare and contrast. That's a skill. The strategy might be a Venn diagram or a 'T' table."

Tessie reflects on the question and responds, "A strategy and skill are different, but they are linked. For example, you might teach visualization as a strategy when you are teaching reading comprehension, then you may take this same strategy and teach math. Although the skills are different (you get skills from the standards), the strategy will link your teaching. As a teacher, I may teach metacognitive strategies to help students understand an abstract concept. The only way to assess whether students can use metacognitive strategies is through a skills assessment. Did the student successfully use the strategies to demonstrate that he or she has acquired the skills? Did the student successfully use his or her prior knowledge to connect skills to other learning? I have noticed that once a student has grasped the strategy, he or she can use the strategy to help learn other skills. I believe that a student has acquired the skill when he or she can successfully activate the strategy and actually use it to transfer learning from one content area to another or from learning one concept to learning another."

Watching Kelli Teach

To look at skills in context, let's look at Kelli as she teaches.

Kelli is a third-grade teacher who works at Edge Lake School. We talked with her about skills and strategies and shared some of Raeanna's perspectives. We also observed her teaching. Kelli agrees with Raeanna about skills and strategies. "For me," she notes, "a skill is infused into a strategy. For example, I know that I need to scaffold the writing of my ELLs. I need to teach them to write a 'how to' paper or how to give clear directions. The skills I need to develop are sequencing, questioning, and how to share and clarify ideas. I have decided that I will use the following scaffolds: First, I will have the students do a hands-on activity so they have the opportunity to observe something they have done and talk about it, thus supporting their learning of academic language. Next, I will have them group, list, label, and categorize information because I know

BOX 5.2 KELLI

Kelli is an elementary school teacher in a large unified school district. She has been a teacher for 9 years and has a master's degree in language and literacy with a reading specialist credential. Kelli's expertise is teaching reading and writing to ELLs through academic content.

that they will have to sequence information and name it in ways that will facilitate their understanding.

"The other scaffold I know my students need, based on my assessment data of their language level and their performance in class, is opportunities to review what they have learned as we proceed through the lesson. I will record their language for them to see as we proceed through the lessons. I will need to engage in ongoing assessment, and in this case I will have them show me words and phrases they think designate the language and concepts they have learned. Next we will number and sequence the important points of our learning. To help us develop transitions that must be included in our writing of directions, we will identify and post signal words for them to use in their writing. Once I have facilitated and reviewed the language learning for this lesson, my students will either write on their own or in partners while I monitor their work, conferencing with individual students and with partners, providing them with positive feedback and continuing ongoing conferences."

We watched Kelli teach her third-grade students. Her mornings begin at 8:00 A.M. with a group with both English-only students and ELLs. At 9:00 A.M. when the English-only students go to English language arts instruction in other rooms, the ELLs stay with her and are joined by students learning English as a second language from the other third grades. She now has a group of 21 ELLs. They get right to work.

The purpose of the day's lesson is to begin writing a "how to" paper. Kelli chose to start the process with a hands-on activity. She decided to provide her students with opportunities to "do" something that is observable. She feels this will help them learn language in real, communicative, and motivating contexts. She begins by asking students what they have done the past 2 days. "Plant seeds," they reply. "And what did we need to plant our seeds?" she queries. Students get out a list of the language they generated as they planted their seeds. The list is not in order and Kelli guides students as they think-pair-share with a partner and decide on the appropriate sequence for planting their seeds. As students discuss the sequence, Kelli walks around the room, questioning and probing. "What did we have to do first? Check your list and agree on what happened after that. Of course, you can get up and go look at your seeds. That may help you remember the sequence." The monitoring and positive feedback continues.

When students are ready, Kelli asks each of the partners to share one thing they agreed on in their partner talk and she records students' language on a large chart where they can all see. Kelli then orders the planting process by numbering the steps after students agree on the sequence. She decides to underline the materials they had to use to plant their seeds and she asks a student to do that with the help of his classmates. Kelli then asks students if they are ready to begin the writing process. They can't wait. They have the language to begin and they start.

Some students write by themselves, others ask to work with their writing partners. While students write, Kelli walks around the room conferencing with individual students and pairs of students. Some of her positive feedback includes: "You are writing that just like our science books. I'm so glad you decided to use the book as a model." "What a great job you are doing with your description and all in complete sentences. What did you do with your partner to decide where you would punctuate?" [This pair of students had been struggling with syntax as they wrote.] They reply, "We thought that if we read it to each other, we would agree on where the punctuation would go." Kelli smiles and gives them a "thumbs up."

She stops and asks students if anyone wants to share how they began their writing. Several students stand up and share. Others listen attentively then return to the task of writing. Kelli continues to monitor and asks several students to read their papers to her. She comments, "Wow! That's a great beginning. I think it helped to hear how other students began their writing. Would you agree?" Students smile and Kelli encourages them to keep going.

While Kelli walks around the room conferencing with students, providing feedback, and listening to them share their writing, she takes anecdotal notes. Her notes will be included in the students' learning folders and her observations will not only become a part of her instructional planning, but also be shared with students and their parents at conferences.

Here are some important observations we made about Kelli's classroom:

- Her students are all actively engaged in partner talk and discussion.
- Her students are enthusiastic about their writing.
- Students have many opportunities to share their writing with peers and with us as well.
- Students all have writing notebooks, which they used to write pieces in a variety of genres including plays, short stories, poems, and chapter books. We were privileged to have them share their writing with us.
- Students share their writing in the circle no matter where they are in the process.
- The focus on sharing and positive feedback creates a community where language is a natural part of the classroom activities and students feel confident and are proud to display their work.
- Students not only write for specific purposes, such as the "how to" paper, which addressed a standard, but also write in areas of interest.
- Kelli refers to students as authors, and when they are ready, they sit in the author's chair to share their writing with their peers.
- Published authors receive positive feedback from Kelli and from their peers.
- When students are sharing their works in progress, she asks them probing questions to encourage them to continue with the writing.
- Students in Kelli's room use learning logs to think about their writing and explore their spelling.
- She places students who need additional work with spelling patterns in a small group, and they work to identify words that help them with their writing. She then places these words on the word wall. Students spell the words aloud in a rhythmic fashion, clapping their hands at the same time. Kelli then helps them with making new words based on the words they cheer for. For example, she says, "If you can read *junk* you can read *skunk*. What pattern helps you spell *chunk*?" Children reply, "unk." "Who agrees, she queries?" All the children in the group give her a "thumbs up" sign and they spell the word *chunk* in their learning log.

After the students in Kelli's classroom have the opportunity to read, talk, write, share, focus on needed skills in small groups, and record what they are learning in their learning logs, Kelli plays a vocabulary game with them using words that will be on their upcoming spelling test. "Show me hem. Tiptoe, mend, crouch, plaid." The children stand up and show her, followed by writing the words in their learning logs. "Can we read now?" they ask. "Absolutely," Kelli replies. They all read books they have self-selected. Enthusiasm prevails, silence settles on the room, and we just smile.

What We Learned from the Teachers

The teachers described in this chapter agreed that skills and strategies are different. Their classroom experiences taught them that they could teach a skill in many ways. But all teachers agreed that the most important thing about a skill is that students can use it for a lifetime to learn new content. A skill helps students make connections between content and concepts. A strategy gives students tools to use to demonstrate that they have acquired the critical skills for learning.

As we talked to teachers and watched them teach, we saw that exemplary teachers were always cognizant of what they wanted their students to learn. They had planned backward from the assigned task (concept to be learned), had assessed their students, and knew which students needed specific scaffolds and which students needed more support than others. The groups in their classrooms were flexible. They taught strategies to help students learn skills to facilitate making connections within and between content, books, and other new learning. Students in their classrooms had choices, and they had a voice in their own learning. Students in their classrooms were co-learners with each other and with their teachers. Students in their classrooms could talk about their learning and what they had to do in their heads to learn content. Students received appropriate instructional scaffolds because their teachers relied on a variety of assessments available to them to make decisions. Teachers talked about student work and reflected on their own teaching. In these classrooms, students were proud of who they are. They willingly shared the work they were doing and worked well together. These teachers built and maintained a literacy learning community.

Practical Applications and Individual Inquiries: Cases to Think About and Investigate

1. Interview a teacher. Ask him or her if there is a difference between a skill and a strategy. Write down the teacher's responses. Compare those responses to your own.

2. Identify a strategy that you have learned about in class. Describe that strategy step by step and note the skills that the strategy will develop. Add how the strategy can help students transfer their learning to other skills.

3. Observe a small group of students working in the classroom. Take observational notes. From your observations, identify the strategies students are using to accomplish the assigned task and the skills the strategies are developing.

4. Interview a few students and ask them what they do to comprehend a passage of text. Analyze student responses and make recommendations for instruction.

Chapter Six

Strategies That Count

I made too many assumptions about my ELLs. Because the ELLs I teach have parents who work at Universities or are employed in the field of biotechnology, I just assumed that my fifth graders could process more content language than they actually could. I assumed that although most of them were very shy, they seemed to get along with other students, so they were doing just fine. Not until I sat with them individually and had them talk to me about two pictures that were alike and yet very different did I realize that I had made assumptions based on little information. Not until I began to analyze the skills and the language students needed to know and use to learn an academic concept and the thinking they had to do to understand the concept did I realize that I had just made too many assumptions. Wow! This is good for me. It pushes me to think more deeply about my students and what I need to do.

James, fifth-grade teacher

In this chapter, we present instructional strategies that we believe are important for the academic success of ELLs. These strategies include a focus on the thinking/learning skills as well as scaffolds to support ELLs as they make meaning from text. Learning is complex and must be mediated for ELLs. It is important to teach language, especially academic language (see Chapter 3), including connections (schemata) to ELLs' background knowledge and primary language vocabulary.

If students don't have the background knowledge in their primary language, then the skills necessary to learn unfamiliar concepts need to be frontloaded for students. All language used during the frontloading process and for teaching grade level concepts should be posted in the classroom and reviewed with students on a consistent basis. When teachers engage in these supportive processes over time, they can gradually remove the scaffolds and create independent learners who can compete with others on an equal basis. It takes time, which makes it important to review the work of Chamot and O'Malley (1994) who look at content-embedded instruction for ELLs. That work challenges teachers to identify the critical concepts associated with grade level content and teach those concepts in depth, at the same time teaching language critical to success in school. In the primary grades, it is important that teachers use the enabling skills that support decoding, fluency, comprehension, and reading of literature as well as writing. Therefore in this chapter we:

- Explain the importance of strategies in planning for instruction for ELLs.
- Elaborate on the definition of strategies.
- Describe the importance of choosing appropriate strategies for ELLs.
- Demonstrate several effective strategies for ELLs.

Building Background Knowledge About Strategies

The Context for Using Strategies with ELLs

Planning for instruction for ELLs is a complex process. No one program or set of strategies will meet the needs of all ELLs. Parts of programs contain pieces that enhance instruction; however, to rely completely on one program and/or a list of strategies means that teachers will not address the unique needs of all ELLs. For teachers to effectively meet the needs of ELLs, they must have a focus on high-quality instruction that addresses their linguistic, cultural, and instructional needs, most often within the context of the regular classroom. With today's push to have teachers highly qualified under No Child Left Behind (NCLB; Public Law No.107-110, 115 stat. 1425, before U.S. Department of Education, 2001) in all classrooms, it is important that these teachers have a major focus on high-quality instruction for all students in all contexts.

Instruction that occurs in classrooms where ELLs are integrated with English-only students is of the utmost importance. While the U.S. Census Bureau (2005) reported that 20% of school-aged children speak a language other than English and 41% of teachers in the United States teach or have taught ELLs, less that 13% of teachers in the United States have received any training or professional development for teaching these students (National Center for Education Statistics, 2002). Although teachers may have been designated as highly qualified under NCLB, if they lack training for working with ELLs or rely only on published programs that may not differentiate instruction to meet the varied instructional needs of ELLs, they may not succeed in reaching all students.

Although published programs adopted for schools under the Elementary and Secondary Education Act (2000) can demonstrate that they are scientifically based, one size does not fit all, and instruction must take into account each student's linguistic and cultural needs. As we discussed in Chapter 3 on language development, it is important to think about the diversity of language itself and how that affects thought and understanding. Students with limited English language proficiency will need more support to make meaning of text, whereas students who are more proficient in English may be able to read the text aloud, but can be challenged to answer questions about complex texts that require them to bring background knowledge to the task of reading.

Teachers must also think about how culture (Chapter 2) affects the ways in which students relate to content in schools and make meaning, sometimes meanings at which we marvel. Given the enormous diversity of students, communities, and cultures, it is illogical to think that any one program can do it all. When teachers work in schools or districts that mandate specific programs, they must analyze the cognitive and linguistic support the program provides ELLs in grade level content, given their languages and cultures. Teachers must also analyze the program's support structures for students during instruction and assessment. Thus, the critical need for assessment, analysis, and scaffolding learning to support real differentiation that has a positive influence academically for ELLs is the basic premise of this text.

What Do We Mean by Strategies?

In Chapter 5, we began our discussion of strategies by defining them as "problem-solving tactics selected deliberately to achieve particular goals" (Tompkins, 2003, p. 267). In this chapter, we elaborate on that definition and make connections to their usage in planning effective differentiated literacy instruction for ELLs.

Strategies are planned activities that help ELLs achieve cognitive and language objectives. They result from systematic planning where the instruction pays attention to the necessary skills students need to learn an objective. Students learn the specific steps of each strategy through modeling by the teacher and other students. For example, as teachers ask their students to make predictions based on the cover of a book to be read aloud, they model this simple strategy so that the student will internalize the process as they read other books by themselves. Teachers need to use the strategies they teach students to understand how the process plays out for their students. They further need to "think aloud" as they use these strategies to demonstrate how they, themselves, are using the strategies and to help the students understand the ways in which the strategies are used.

Teachers must also debrief all strategies taught to students after they have had many opportunities to use the strategies to learn. The debriefing process helps teachers learn from students what worked and what didn't work. Teachers can use that information to inform instruction and revise it to meet students' needs.

Strategies are selected after focused planning and are centered around the learning goal. Each strategy is taught step by step and debriefed throughout. The teacher ties all the parts of the strategy together, asking students how specific strategies can be used to learn other content, that is, how the learning is similar and how it is different.

Choosing Appropriate Strategies for ELLs

Given the nature of differentiated instruction for ELLs, teachers must use multiple means of evaluating students' strengths and weaknesses within cultural and linguistic perspectives. Instruction that begins with multiple assessments provides insight into the language proficiency of ELLs and their ability to write, read, think, discuss, and listen to academic concepts in a second language. Once teachers assess students' particular needs, they will be better able to choose effective strategies for instruction. Really, it is not any one strategy that makes the difference. Rather it is selection of a metacognitive strategy or combination of such strategies that use the strengths of students to address their needs. Teachers may need to modify strategies, and they should also select culturally appropriate strategies for ELLs (see Chapter 2 for a discussion of culturally relevant curriculum).

After students have been assessed and instruction is set to begin, the teacher must choose appropriate strategies to effectively teach the curriculum and then analyze each one for appropriateness to both the task and the students. Teachers must reflect on what they want students to learn (the cognitive objective), the skills students need to know and use to learn the cognitive objective, the steps or processes students go through to learn the cognitive objective (what they have to do in their heads), and the language they have to use to learn the cognitive objective. They then modify the strategy based on assessment data and analysis of the concepts that must be learned, transferred, and mastered, all in the context of the students' linguistic proficiency and cultural competence (see Figure 6.1).

Additionally, in choosing strategies teachers need to pay attention to two phases of instruction for ELLs (Graves & Fitzgerald, 2003): planning and implementation. Teachers must think about scaffolding instruction for ELLs in both of these phases to be prepared to meet students' needs. That is, students need to receive temporary support, or scaffolds, while they are learning new content. We call attention to the ongoing assessment phase of planning and implementation to ensure that authentic data such as language samples, individual reading inventories, and oral and written retellings are collected. Teachers then identify patterns that arise in the authentic data and use those patterns to differentiate instruction for

FIGURE 6.1 How to Modify a Strategy

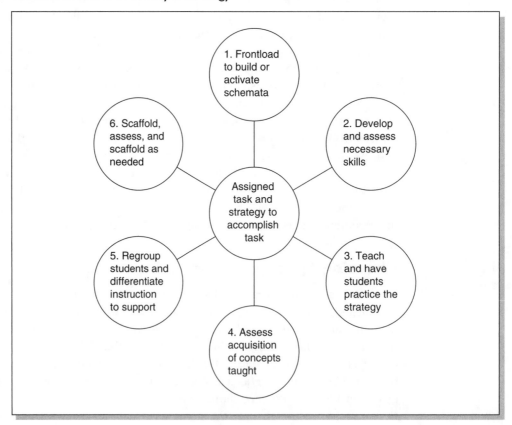

groups of students or for individuals, as needed. For us, differentiating the instruction means to group students to teach them the skills they need to acquire and ensure that they have learned and applied the skills to the completion of an assigned task. Then students should be grouped for opportunities not only to share their thinking with other students in the classroom, but also to get feedback and support from others in the group.

Metacognition

Any discussion of the effective use of strategies to support instruction needs to include a focus on metacognition, which can be an elusive term to define. Blakey and Spence (1990) define metacognition as thinking about thinking in such a way that we know what we know as well as what we don't know. They describe three basic metacognitive strategies: "(1) connecting new information to former knowledge, (2) selecting thinking strategies deliberately, and (3) planning, monitoring, and evaluating thinking processes" (p. 1). Within the framework of instruction, it is often important to directly teach students how to use these metacognitive strategies in order that they may eventually internalize them and use them independently (Scruggs, Mastropieri, Monson, & Jorgenson, 1985).

Metacognition, therefore, is directly related to thinking about learning. It is a critical strategy that supports and gives rise to other strategies. Metacognition, once practiced repeatedly in a variety of different contexts, consistently can serve to increase the self-confidence of ELLs as it helps them to build academic language by making connections to what they already know and focusing on strategies deliberately as they engage in instruction. NCREL (1995) lists several questions that students can learn to ask themselves as they think and act metacognitively during instruction (see Figure 6.2).

Both teachers and students need to be metacognitive—to think about the processes in which they are engaged during the experience, and finally, to reflect on and relate what they have learned to their own thinking. For example, let's look at metacognition in the context of reading. Just as in reading, teachers must become critical readers themselves if they are to teach students to be critical readers, teachers must be metacognitive themselves if they are to teach students to be metacognitive. Graves (1991) emphasizes that teachers must be the chief learners in the classroom, spending a significant amount of their time modeling their own work and talking through their own work with students and showing students how to do something. Once again, critical reading is metacognitive and essential to all comprehension, so metacognition is intricately related to success.

Two key aspects of metacognition are related to the basic metacognitive strategies: knowledge about cognition and self-regulation of cognition (Simpson & Nist, 2002). Readers, for example, have knowledge about cognition when they are aware of their own cognitive resources or what they bring to the task and also knowledge about their ability to regulate those resources. Regulation consists of the capacity to uncover mistakes in what is being read, how to apply different strategies to use with different texts, as well as how to separate important from extraneous information in a given text (Simpson & Nist, 2002).

Critical reading can be considered as the need to question; the skills necessary to select the most appropriate strategies to use to navigate, comprehend, and respond to text; and the ability to summarize (Simpson & Nist, 2002). For the second aspect of metacognition—self-regulation of cognition—readers need to be able to monitor their own comprehension while they are reading and be aware when they don't understand. They develop hypotheses

FIGURE 6.2 Metacognitive Questions to Ask Before, During, and After Instruction

Questions to Ask Before Instruction (Connecting New Information to Prior Knowledge)

1. What in my prior knowledge will help me with this particular task?
2. In what direction do I want my thinking to take me?
3. What should I do first?
4. Why am I reading this selection?
5. How much time do I have to complete this task?
6. What materials will I need?
7. Is this task like any other task I have done?

Questions to Ask During Instruction (Choosing Thinking Strategies Deliberately)

1. How am I doing?
2. Am I on the right track?
3. What information is important to remember?
4. Should I move in a different direction?
5. Should I adjust the pace depending on the difficulty?
6. What do I need to do if I do not understand?
7. Where can I get help?
   a. With vocabulary?
   b. With writing?
   c. With reading?
   d. With anything else?

Questions to Ask After Instruction (Planning, Monitoring, and Evaluating)

1. How well did I do?
2. Did my thinking make sense?
3. Did my thinking produce more or less than I expected?
4. How might I apply this thinking to other tasks?
5. Did I understand everything?
6. Do I need to go back through the task to fill in any "blanks" in my understanding?
7. Could I have done anything differently?

Source: Adapted from Metacognition, in NCREL (1995) *Strategic teaching and reading project guidebook, Revised edition.* Retrieved May 8, 2004, from http://www.ncrel.org/sdrs/areas/issues/students/learning/lrlmetn.htm

about what they have read, test their hypotheses, revise their understanding of text, get the gist of the reading, and evaluate the strategies they are using to make sense of text.

The strategies covered in this chapter are based on the idea of metacognition as one key to success for ELLs. These strategies may not have common titles or names. Many times, they sound like something you may have seen described in other resources as skills. They are processes that focus on what is best instructionally for students given what we know about language, culture, and learning (Banks & Banks, 2003) and the process of making knowledge one's own (Shulman, 2002) to achieve the highest level of literacy.

Metacognition is a critical part of the foundation for strategies that work with ELLs. When teachers use metacognitive strategies, they focus on the cognitive processes that need to occur and/or are occurring while students are learning a concept. Using metacognition means that teachers are aware of the necessary skills students need to learn academic content as well as what the student brings to the task of learning. Within the context of teaching reading, teachers are aware of the differences in the demands of the genres of text they use with students at any specific time as well as the linguistic complexities and cultural context of each text.

Within the framework of metacognition, teachers understand that scaffolding or supporting learning is indispensable to developing skills as well as mastering concepts. Metacognition encompasses the broad ranges, styles, and ways of knowing that are rooted in culture. Its use in instruction helps students understand what it feels like not to know and to label that feeling. Metacognition helps students understand that there is a need to remedy the glitches hampering the comprehension process and that they have tools they can use to take some control over their own learning.

Teachers emphasize metacognition during instruction to teach students that strategies can help them make meaning from text when comprehension breaks down during reading (Harvey & Goudvis, 2000). Understanding how to sort through and select appropriate strategies is especially critical for ELLs, who many times when learning to read in a second language think that being able to crack the code or say the words fast means that one is a good reader.

We want ELLs to go beyond just using strategies in a lesson in the classroom. We want teachers to understand that they should never use strategies because they are "fun." We want teachers to understand that they should select strategies for instruction because they not only help students learn content, but also can be used to learn other content. Teachers choose strategies because they have a clear purpose for learning and transferability from one content area to the other.

Thinking metacognitively is cumulative, and students can "bank" their repertoire of strategies so that it grows and helps them with multiple tasks in school. We want ELLs to understand that the strategies they learn in school always sit in their personal cognitive bank accounts. We want students to know that these accounts have been created with such care and attention that they always know their personal strategy balance and know what and how much to withdraw from their personal account and why the withdrawal is being made. We want ELLs to be able to effectively transfer the use of metacognitive strategies from one content area to another, from one task to the next.

The teacher must spend enough time using strategies to ensure that students have learned the strategies thoroughly. To ensure that the strategies are learned well enough to transfer to other tasks, teachers must record them in such a manner that students can refer to them repeatedly. We recommend that teachers record the processes of the strategies that students use on charts that are prominently displayed in the classroom so that they can be debriefed with students and also so that they can be used for other tasks. Strategies potent enough to support academic content learning must be revisited, reviewed with students, and used again and again to ensure mastery of grade level content. Through teacher modeling, each student must be able to reflect on the strategy learned and say with certainty what was easy and what was hard about each strategy. Each student must learn to say with confidence if he or she would use the strategy as well as how to use the strategy.

Students should not just memorize a fixed number of strategies—are 50 enough or are 100 too many? Strategies help them succeed. It is more important to focus on a few robust strategies that accomplish the cognitive objective and enhance language learning strategies for ELLs. It is more important that teachers analyze the strategies to determine the necessary skills for success. After teachers have analyzed the strategies for skills, they must examine the academic language required to use the skills to learn the concepts and content (see Chapter 3). Skills and language cannot be isolated and/or separated. The focus of instructional practices that utilize appropriate scaffolds to ensure success must be on the integration of learning and thinking while making meaning.

Linking Theory to Practice

Strategies That Count and How They Work

This chapter organizes practice around an analysis of the learning–thinking processes demanded by metacognitive strategies. To best demonstrate this process we present a variety of strategies. As we present the step-by-step processes for each strategy, we offer suggested scaffolds for each one (see Figure 6.3). However, it is important to understand that ELLs will need several scaffolds. As teachers use the suggested scaffold in instruction, they should be observing student learning and consistently checking for comprehension, making anecdotal notes of progress using observational notes or checklists. They can then use these data to regroup students to provide appropriate ongoing instructional support.

Each strategy is presented in the following format (see Figure 6.3 for a list of strategies):

1. The purpose or goals of each strategy.
2. The enabling skills necessary to implement each strategy and understand text as well as the skills to be developed throughout the process of learning the strategy.
3. A description of the instructional process each strategy requires.

FIGURE 6.3 List of Strategies Presented in This Chapter

Strategy 6.1	Connecting Reading and Writing to One's Personal Life
Strategy 6.2	Previewing Text
Strategy 6.3	Summarizing
Strategy 6.4	Inferring
Strategy 6.5	Mediating Vocabulary

STRATEGY 6.1   Connecting Reading and Writing to One's Personal Life

Element	Description
Purpose of the Strategy	Research has shown that ELLs, including those with limited English language proficiency, can benefit from instruction that is context-embedded (Cummins, 1994). Therefore, it makes sense that building schema about a particular text by linking its content to student's lives will help ELLs to better comprehend that text. The purpose of this strategy is to teach ELLs to think through text to support making meaning in reading and obtaining information to make connections to their personal lives.
Thinking Skills	ELLs must have the skills and language to think and talk about what is involved in thinking through text to activate background knowledge. They must be able to: • Observe (look at and listen to) as well as sample (read what they see and process the language as well as be able to talk about) text (written or oral). • Understand and be able to retell information they hear or have read from text. • Sift through text to determine what is important and what is unimportant. That is, they should be able to group, list, categorize, compare, and contrast ideas, concepts, words, and content. • Provide a rationale or reasons for determining importance and unimportance. They should be able to analyze words, ideas, and concepts and to agree, disagree, and/or question what they have read. • Prioritize and sequence the important information, provide a rationale for what they have done, and be able to clarify meaning making. • Synthesize what they have read. They need to get the gist of text, the critical supporting information and then summarize what they have read in their own words. • Make connections between text being read, other texts they have read in other classes, and their own cultural texts, stories, and experiences. • Find relationships between what was read and content/concepts to be learned and hypothesize about what they are reading and predict what is to come next in the text. They must be able to identify causes and effects, that is, what happened in the past to cause the present as well as what is happening in the present that will shape the future. • Make predictions about the future value of what they have read by either creating a new perspective or combining perspectives and provide support and give reasons for new perspectives.
Comments	As you review the thinking/learning skills involved in this one strategy alone, you can see the complexity thinking about text demands. When students have to learn and apply the skills, the process is much more difficult. Therefore, it is imperative that teachers understand the primary languages their students speak and know how to scaffold the language as well as the cognitive concepts they all bring to the classroom. It is also important to note that one strategy that really counts addresses a variety of skills, supporting the notion that teachers should select strategies for their potential to affect learning.

(continued)

STRATEGY 6.1   (continued)

Element	Description
Goals	The following are the goals or the reasons we must teach students to make connections between what they are learning and their own personal lives. This strategy helps ELLs to: 1. Discover and make meaning from what is read or heard and discuss meaning in relation to their academic learning and personal experiences. 2. Recognize and identify perceived biases in text and address the personal cultural understandings of those biases. 3. Understand in practical ways that information gained during reading will eventually be used to support their writing because reading and writing cannot be separated.
Process of the Strategy	1. Select a short piece of grade level text that has cohesion, that is, contains a logical beginning, middle, and end and "hangs together" logically. 2. Preview the section you will be reading, talking aloud about how reading will never make sense if you don't look it over first and ask yourself what you think you know about what you are going to read. 3. Turn headings, charts, and pictures into questions and write those down. 4. Support student learning by creating a modified K-W-L (Ogle, 1986) chart to keep track of predictions and questions as well as summaries made throughout the modeling process. 5. Model aloud how you make sense of text by reading short portions of the selected piece of text to student(s), stopping to question the text and think and talk aloud about which parts of the text are important or unimportant. 6. Summarize each section or piece as you proceed through the text. 7. Write the summaries for future student reference in the "L" section of the K-W-L chart. 8. Add another column and place a "P" for Predictions at the top of the column. 9. Predict what you think will come next in the text and why you think that is reasonable. Write that in the "P" section of the modified K-W-L chart. 10. Use only short pieces if the student is at the beginning stages of acquiring English as a second language. Pause often, use redundancy of terms, and consistently check for student understanding asking "either/or" questions (Terrell, 1977). 11. Show the student the text, pointing out important vocabulary words, phrases, graphs, charts, maps, etc., to highlight connections between the written words and the meaning of the text. 12. Depending on the level of language acquisition of the student(s), read the text to the student or have the student read a short portion of the text, thinking and talking aloud as he or she reads. 13. Record student summaries, analyzing them with students and noting why each summary is a good or "could be improved" summary. 14. Have the students predict what might be coming next in the text and why that is reasonable.

STRATEGY 6.1   (continued)

Element	Description
Scaffolding	How to Observe and Sample Text (use as needed; not necessarily in the order presented).

- Have the students talk aloud about observing as they preview the text.
- Provide a format for this to happen such as think-pair-share where students think quietly about a question and jot down words to trigger their ideas.
- Next, have students pair with another student to talk about their ideas. Finally, they share their ideas by pairs with the large group, expanding on ideas that have already been shared and are similar to theirs. The purpose of the sharing is to have students learn about sharing new ideas and expand on others instead of repeating the same ideas over and over again.
- Note that the process of think-pair-share also has to be scaffolded. In other words, many scaffolds must be scaffolded; students must see the teacher model his or her ideas so they can see that their ideas have legitimacy. Many times ELLs do not think their ideas are acceptable and are reluctant to share them openly.
- Select partners carefully. Teach all students how to listen to others' ideas, to respond positively to ideas, and to ask questions to clarify someone else's ideas.
- Model the sharing process if you expect students to expand on ideas already shared. How to expand on someone else's ideas is important to model.
- At the end of the sharing process, prompt and ask the students questions as you debrief the text with them. Ask questions such as:
  a. "Why do you think that is important? What else did you see in the text that makes you think that is really important? Let's look back together at the text to find words or phrases that seemed important to you as you read and let's talk about why you think they are important."
  b. "Let's write the words and phrases down so we remember them."
  c. "Which words seemed hard or confusing for you? Let's examine them, put the text together again, and see if we can make sense of them."
  d. "How is what you just read about like something you have experienced at home, at school, or in the community?"
  e. "What caused that to happen? How do you know? What do you think will happen next—in the future? Let's talk about why you think that is a reasonable thing to say. Is there anything we can find together in the text that helped us to think that might happen?"
  f. "Let's decide together how we could summarize what you just read. Remember we want it your own words, not the author's. Let's practice together, then you try it on your own."
  g. "What do you think will come next? What is your prediction? Why?"

(continued)

STRATEGY 6.1 (continued)	
Element	**Description**
Scaffolding	h. "Could you use this strategy when you read other things? Why do you think so? What was hard about this process? What could I have done to help you work through the process more easily?" i. "What should I do to help you learn how to use this strategy on your own when you read? What one thing can I do better the next time you try this?"
Comments	Be systematic in your instruction. Explicitly model what students should accomplish in each step. Provide opportunities for students to be interactive, to talk to others, and to write short phrases or poems to ensure engagement in learning. Check for understanding, stopping to engage in a one-minute conference with students about their thinking and their work. Provide positive feedback, noting one thing at a time that students should revise or improve. It can be overwhelming to ask students to change too much at once. Support ELLs and push them to accomplish their very best. Be consistent about modeling and monitoring feedback to promote learning for transfer and mastery.

STRATEGY 6.2	Previewing Text
Element	**Description**
Purpose of the Strategy	ELLs must understand that a reader needs to look over or preview every piece of text before reading. Previewing the text gives the reader a sense of the "playing field," the length of the text, the graphics included in the text, and what graphics mean to the organization of the text. Learning to preview text also helps a reader understand how to use the preview to develop predictions and verify them.
Thinking Skills	Teaching students to preview text encourages them to use learning/thinking skills. They must be able to: • Observe the length of the entire text. • Begin to think about a strategy that might help to navigate the text. • Learn to identify and observe charts, graphs, maps, diagrams, and pictures and to understand how they are related to and fit into the entire text. • Generate questions about text by first skimming and scanning the text and then ask questions using the results of skimming and scanning. ELLs must learn the skills of skimming, scanning, and asking questions, especially if they are learning to read in a second language and have not had the opportunity to learn how to read proficiently in their primary languages. • Understand that the smaller parts (details) of text may be integral to understanding the entire selection. Specific details are used to provide support or elaboration for their own thinking about text. • Understand that previewing text precedes activation of prior knowledge (asking what you think you know about what you are going to read).
Goals	The strategy of previewing text will help ELLs to: 1. Learn that cracking the code is just one part of the reading process. 2. Understand that asking questions about what you are going to read is a critical first step in the process. 3. Understand that comprehending larger pieces of text is the result of comprehending smaller chunks first. 4. Understand that readers process small chunks of text; they must recall what they read to see where it fits into understanding the entire selection. 5. Understand that information from smaller chunks of text must be summarized and recorded to ensure future recall. 6. Understand that efficient readers read to answer questions generated prior to reading. 7. Learn how to ask different types of questions and understand what kind of information one expects to receive if he or she asks a particular type of question.

(*continued*)

STRATEGY 6.2   (continued)

Element	Description
Process of the Strategy	1. Look over the selection to be read with students, noting the titles, graphs, charts, maps, and pictures. 2. Have students count the number of pages to be read and teach them that good readers do not always read text a single page at a time. Rather, they read text in sections, stopping as they go along to ask themselves if what they are reading is making sense. 3. Model how to generate questions from subheadings, charts, graphs, or pictures. 4. Help students generate questions from the previewing process. Have students try to generate a question about a title with a partner. 5. Write the questions down and remind them before they read that they will be reading to answer questions. 6. Post student questions. 7. Have students read to answer one question first, and share their answers with a partner. 8. Have students identify the type of question they answered and evaluate whether it was a good question and why or why not. 9. Have students test whether their question was useful: When I asked that question, did I get the kind of information I wanted? 10. If you want students to answer questions that the publisher has generated at the end of the reading selection, ask students to read the questions. 11. Ask students to identify the types of questions they are being asked. 12. Ask students what they think they have to do in their heads to answer the types of questions asked.
Comments	Questioning is a critical part of previewing text. When you ask students to make predictions about the text, be sure that you ask them to elaborate on their answers. You may prompt them by providing a few words to get them started. Or have them think and talk to a partner. Avoid giving the answers to students because they are struggling with the language. Instead, focus on the language objectives of your lesson and frontload the language for students by previewing and teaching vocabulary as well as the thinking and processing skills. It is by teaching thinking skills that we can best help ELLs to develop academic language.
Scaffolding	Use as needed and not necessarily in the order presented: • Model previewing for students, using the context of the text that they are going to read. • Talk through what you see and how you decide what you use to generate a question. For example, "As I look at this reading, I think, Wow! This is a lot of stuff. So I ask myself, what should I do now? What if I ask a question about what I am going to read? That's what I am going to do. When I get finished, you will look over a small part of the text and generate a question too. When I read I should read to answer my question. So, let me start. Let's see if my question makes sense to you."

STRATEGY 6.2   (continued)

Element	Description
Scaffolding	• Before students generate their own questions, teach them about the types of questions asked in books. Use QAR (Question Answer Relationships; Raphael, 1982). Ask students to generate "right there" questions first. Right there, or text explicit, questions are answered by directly locating the answer in the text. That is, the language of the question is the same as the language in the text. • Next, model "think and search" questions. Then have students generate their own think and search questions. Think and search, or text implicit, questions are questions where students have to draw conclusions and infer the answer because the language of the question and the language of the text are different. • Finally move on to "on my own" questions and "between the author and me." On my own, or script implicit, questions refer to how students bring their own experiences to the text and reflect on them. Between the author and me requires that students think about the work itself. Students express how they are affected by the way the author talks about something in the text. They express their perceptions of what the author has done with the story in the text and may question the author's thinking or biases. • This scaffold provides multiple opportunities for the teacher to model question asking for students and provide enough time for them to practice generating their own questions about experiences and stories that are familiar to them. • After you have scaffolded question asking with in depth lessons on QARs (Question-Answer Relationships), have students work in pairs to generate their own questions. Ask them to identify the type of question they asked and why they think it's that particular type of question. The test is: Did they get the kind of information they thought they would get by asking that particular question? • Have students post their questions for group review and referral over time. Each time students have to generate questions, review the language of each type of question to remind them of the language and skills they should use. • Support and guide students as they generate questions using the text, providing immediate feedback. Continue to post questions for students to review.
Comments	Instruction for this strategy may be conducted in a large group. However, to assess whether students are really able to apply the skills and thinking, instruction in all of the strategies must be followed up in a small group and again later in a large group. In other words, skills must be reviewed, practiced, and reviewed again to help students become automatic in applying the thinking/learning skills.

STRATEGY 6.3   Summarizing

Element	Description
Purpose of the Strategy	Students must learn how to synthesize information and be able to put the information in their own words. The process of summarization means that students learn to determine the important facts or information, are able to sequence the information, and can put it in their own words. Note that summarizing has also been included in Strategy 6.1. For example, when students are taught to activate their background knowledge, they need to summarize what they know and how that is related to what they have read.
Thinking Skills	The following skills need to be applied as students summarize text during and after they read. They must be able to: • Observe and acknowledge all the elements in text. That is, students should not skip anything as they read yet realize that some of the details of the text may be dismissed as not providing enough or appropriate elaboration for the main ideas of the text. • Sort through the details of the text. • Determine which details are not needed and why that is so. • Talk about their own thinking. How did they decide to select the ideas and details they selected? What makes them think those specific details are important? What key words or phrases led to that conclusion? • Determine what is most important in the text. • Prioritize important statements from most important to least important. • Clarify the meaning of important statements. • Paraphrase information from each chunk of the text in their own words. • Provide information to others. • Describe and debrief what they have learned. • Restate the important facts in their own words.
Goals	Summarizing, a strategy that students have to be able to use competently for the rest of their lives, will help ELLs to: 1. Understand that learning content means that you can say what you have learned in your words and it makes sense. Others can understand your summary. 2. Understand that summaries must be clear and include the necessary information so that the other person does not have to go back to the text to get additional information. The summary is sufficient. 3. Understand that to be able to share information with confidence comes from understanding content to the extent that the knowledge is yours.
Process of the Strategy	1. Select a short piece of text that is connected to content students are learning to model for them. 2. Survey the text to determine the type of text structure.

STRATEGY 6.3 (continued)	
Element	**Description**
Process of the Strategy	3. Explain and illustrate the types and structure(s) of the text. For example, if the text is narrative, use a story map. For expository texts, think about the structure(s): for comparison/contrast, use a "T" bar; for cause and effect, use circles and arrows; for sequential text, use a timeline. Remember that a piece of expository text will have more than one text structure. This will be evident in upper grade textbooks or selections.
	4. Use a graphic organizer that makes the most sense to your students and above all helps illustrate and thus facilitate the organization of the text.
	5. Select a chunk of the text to model for students.
	6. Demonstrate how to question text and decide on what the text is really saying.
	7. Write down what you and students decide is the content of the text and questions that can be answered as you proceed through the text.
	8. Proceed through the text using questions, graphic organizers, think-pair-share, and other interactive activities that support student engagement and motivate students to learn content.
	9. Stop and have students decide what information can be deleted from their summaries and what information is needed.
	10. Help students prioritize information in terms of importance.
	11. Have students put information they have read and discussed in their own words.
	12. Have students check that their summaries are in their own words and that the summaries tell enough about what they have read that others do not have to go back to the book for more information.
Comments	Notice that, once again, questioning is a critical enabling skill that should be frontloaded for students before the lesson along with any content concepts you consider critical to transfer and mastery of grade level content.
Scaffolding	Use as needed and not necessarily in the order presented:
	• The principal scaffold involves mediation by an adult. It includes activating background knowledge, modeling thinking, and modeling questioning.
	• Mediation (Santamaria, Fletcher, & Bos, 2002) as a scaffold needs an adult such as a teacher, a trained instructional assistant, or parent. The adult works one on one with one or two students or a small group of three to five students. The adult checks for understanding often throughout the process to ensure that ELLs reflect on their own thinking and are able to talk about their own thinking as they are learning the skill of summarization.
	• Mediation can be done with a large group of students; however, checking for understanding using think-pair-share where students think about the text, pair with another student to talk about their thinking, then share with the entire group is important for engagement. If mediation is done with a large group, feedback is important and

(continued)

STRATEGY 6.3	(continued)
Element	**Description**
Scaffolding	writing student responses for ongoing reference must occur to support thinking, practice, feedback, and learning the skill.

- If students are at beginning levels of language acquisition, adjust the chunk of text selected to ensure that input in the second language is not overwhelming.

- Before mediating the text with students, preview the text or the section of the text. If the topic is not obvious, tell students what it is and then activate background knowledge. Note that some students' background knowledge may need to be built (see below).

- K-W-L charts (what I KNOW, what I WANT to know, what I LEARNED) where students share what they know or think they know about the topic about which they are going to read is effective to illustrate and validate students' background knowledge.

- As you check for understanding, you may learn that some students do not have the background or schema for the text. These students should be regrouped after the lesson to build background knowledge by involving them in hands-on activities that use manipulatives or drama activities such as mime or freeze posing (tableau). Other background building experiences include the use of pictures or video clips where students can see something important about the topic they will be learning—what it might look like and sound like. Many times these experiences will trigger what students already know but are not aware of, and they are able to activate their background knowledge. It is not that ELLs are missing the same kinds of life experiences English-only students have. It is just that they have to negotiate language that supports the process of sharing conceptual understandings. Thus, building background knowledge as a scaffold is critical.

- The adult mediating student learning should always model his or her own thinking and teach students how to talk about their own thinking. This means that ELLs may need to be given the language structures to use to talk about their thinking and be held accountable for using that academic language, or CALP—cognitive academic language proficiency (Cummins, 1994) with partners or in their small group. Thus, the teacher must monitor the use of CALP in discussion by providing feedback and prompting students to delve deeper into text to clarify vocabulary and understanding.

- As students progress through text, the adult who is mediating student learning should ask students questions such as: "How do you know that? What word(s) made you think of that? Show me the words or phrases. What in your experience made you think that? Show me" (see QARs).

- The use of small groups is another scaffold that facilitates language and learning. However, students in the group have to be taught the skills of listening, paraphrasing or repeating, and then extending.

- One more structure teachers can use to support these communication skills is one Kagan (1994) calls "round robin." Round robin works best with three students. The teacher asks a question about the section of text students will be analyzing. The first

STRATEGY 6.3   (continued)

Element	Description
Scaffolding	student gives his or her response, after spending at least 2 minutes thinking and "gathering" the language necessary to share his/her thoughts. The second student repeats what the first said and adds his/her thoughts. The third student does the same. Next, the group agrees on what they should share with the larger group. They write their response down and one of the students in the group shares the group response. • Another scaffold that works well for summarization is GIST (getting information by summarizing text), a modification of Cunningham's (1982) strategy entitled "generating interactions between schemata and text" (Quiocho, 1997). In this scaffold, the teacher first previews the text. Next, students work in pairs. Pairs should be structured in ways that support beginning students. That is, one student should be at a higher level of language acquisition than the beginning student. One student reads while the other listens. The listener then asks the reader a question about what he or she read (questioning has to be taught first). The reader responds. The listener and the reader have to agree on what the text said. They write that down. Together they predict what will come next in the text. The listener then becomes the reader and reader becomes the listener. The process continues until the selected text has been covered and summarized. To support GIST, the teacher must select the size of the chunk of text with which students will be working. • An additional scaffold that must be provided for beginning or early intermediate students is the materials scaffold (Santamaría et al., 2002). In this scaffold, the teacher selects texts that are written at a lower readability level for beginning students and early intermediates. The text is selected to provide initial exposure to content and at a later time, these students will work with grade level text, locating key vocabulary words, phrases, and sentences.

STRATEGY 6.4   Inferring

Element	Description
Purpose of the Strategy	Students need to infer, that is, to visualize and think beyond text. It means that students draw conclusions using what they have read and make applications about what they have read to their own lives, cultures, and the world. Students are taught to see relationships among texts, themselves and text, their cultures, and the world. Students are taught to think beyond the written words. They understand that their experiences are valid and can be used to detect biases in texts. Keene and Zimmerman (1997) note that when making inferences we, as readers, have *to go beyond literal interpretation and to open a world of meaning deeply connected to our lives. We create an original meaning, a meaning born at the intersection of our background knowledge (schema), the words printed on the page, and our mind's capacity to merge that combination into something uniquely ours. We go beyond the literal and weave our own sense into the words we read. As we read further, that meaning is revised, enriched, sometimes abandoned, based on what we continue to read. (p. 149)*
Thinking Skills	The following thinking skills are taught to students when they are taught to infer. They must be able to: • Observe and analyze text to determine importance in text. • Read between and beyond the lines of text. • Draw conclusions from text and make connections among texts, their own experiences, and the world in which they live based on analysis of text. • Make reasonable predictions during the reading. As they read, readers test, analyze, and revise their predictions based on new information encountered in the text. • Combine background knowledge and information from text to answer questions they have about text or questions they have generated before reading. • Make connections between conclusions drawn during the reading and cultural beliefs and knowledge. • Provide support (text, world, self, culture) for all inferences made before and throughout the reading and writing processes. • Make critical judgments about what they have read.
Goals	Instructional strategies for inferring will help ELLs to: 1. Understand that reading means to go beyond the text. 2. Understand that all inferences must be substantiated from text, self, culture, and the world. 3. Learn the language that inference requires. 4. Know that feelings or response to text give rise to inferences. 5. Know that inferences can come from the cover of and illustrations in a text and that they are more open-ended than predictions.

STRATEGY 6.4   (continued)

Element	Description
Goals	6. Infer themes from a story and know that the inferences made can and will be different among students.
	7. Know that facts from text give rise to inferences.
	8. Know that questioning, analysis, comparisons and contrasts, and inferences are inseparable.
	9. Know that visualization supports the process of making inferences.
	10. Understand that rereading is critical to verifying the basis for inferences and clearing up any misconceptions.
Process of the Strategy	1. Select a text (short story, big book, chapter book, textbook).
	2. Model for students how you make inferences by asking questions about a text and making inferences, providing support and elaboration for inferences made.
	3. Have students practice with a partner. Provide multiple opportunities for students to watch you model the process, practice, and then debrief the process. That is, what worked well? What was hard? What else could we do?
	4. Monitor and give clear feedback to student partners.
	5. Have partners share their inferences with the whole group, providing support for inferences.
	6. Probe and provide feedback as partners share.
	7. Record all inferences.
	8. Debrief the thinking process with students.
	9. Write it down and post to review each time students need to make inferences.
Comments	Modeling for students how to support their inferences is a critical part of teaching this skill. What we want is for ELLs to be articulate and to draw upon what they know and have learned to elaborate on inferences. We also want them to have the skills for searching the text to locate words, pictures, phrases, and sentences that support their inferences.
Scaffolding	Begin the process with the use of wordless picture books. Provide student support in the following manner:
	• Ask students to look at the pictures and describe what they see in each picture. Ask probing questions such as, "What else do you see? Where is it? Where is (are) the person(s) in relation to it? What do you think that means? Why? What conclusions can you draw based on what we have seen? What might the character in the story be saying? What makes you think that? Why?"
	• Have students work in partners to generate answers.

(*continued*)

STRATEGY 6.4 (continued)

Element	Description
Scaffolding	• Write down student responses and review them as you go along. Before students make inferences based on the next picture, review what they said about the first picture to ensure that there is an appropriate sequence of events.
	• Debrief with students what they had to do to make inferences and make a list of the skills as they give them to you.
	• Each time before students engage in an activity that requires them to infer information from text, review the list with them and remind them to use the skills.
	• Stop them as they work to ask about the skills required to infer meaning from text.

STRATEGY 6.5	Mediating Vocabulary

Element	Description
Purpose of the Strategy	Because ELLs are learning English as a second language, teachers are concerned about vocabulary development. Learning another language if you are literate in your first language is much easier because you have the knowledge of what language is and what a learner does with it to make sense of school. However, if students are learning to read and write in a second language, the process is much more difficult. Therefore, vocabulary development should focus on three mega skills: making vocabulary connections between a student's primary language and English, learning how to break up words in English and look for patterns in the words, and finally testing predictions made about vocabulary in the context of a sentence to see if the predictions make sense.
Thinking Skills	When understanding the content vocabulary, students need to learn how to arrive at meaning without running to a dictionary to look up the word definitions. They must be able to: • Make connections between unknown vocabulary and known words. • Understand the origins of words to facilitate making connections between parts of words and entire words in context. • Understand that in some languages, such as Spanish, there are cognates or words that mean the same in both languages and cognates can help with comprehension or words and text. An example is important–importante. There are almost 2,500 cognates between English and Spanish. • Apply knowledge about onsets and rimes, morphology, and etymology. • Validate knowledge of the sounds of the English language, the patterns as they appear in words, and the meaning that can be inferred based on sound and pattern knowledge. • Predict what a word might mean based on analysis of similarities between the unknown and known words. • Substitute the predicted meaning of the word, and use the substitution in context to see whether it makes sense and is, therefore, probably the meaning of the word.
Goals	This strategy is used with ELLs because it stresses the importance of contextual meaning. It does students no good to look up words in a dictionary, copy the definitions and write the words in sentences. There are many practices in vocabulary instruction that support making meaning. The purpose for vocabulary mediation is to teach ELLs to: 1. Explore the opaqueness of language, that is, to understand that it is possible to manipulate language. 2. Develop the confidence to take risks and manipulate language without fear of "errors." 3. Learn that authors use the conventions of the English language to place clues for readers in the texts they write. For example, authors will use commas, phrases, or words such as "for instance," "or," "which is," etc. to signal that the definition of a word is in the body of the text or follows the unknown word as signaled by a comma. For example, "The valise, a suitcase, stood next to the door."

(continued)

STRATEGY 6.5   (continued)

Element	Description
Goals	4. Identify a cognate or a word that means the same in two languages to facilitate connections between languages. For example, information and información have the same meaning although they are spelled differently. Be careful to let students know, however, that all words that look and/or sound alike are not the same.
Process of the Strategy	When we teach ELLs about vocabulary it is important to include what we know about word study and the primary languages students speak. There are many vocabulary strategies that do not entail copying a list of words and looking up the definitions (see Allen, 1999). However, remember that most of the vocabulary strategies have been developed for use with native English-speaking students in mainstream classrooms. For ELLs, three things need to be included in instruction to mediate vocabulary: analysis of the word itself, how the word functions in context, and connections to the primary language.

1. Select words that are intricately connected to the selection students will be reading. Selecting too many words or having students work with words on worksheets will not teach students strategies to decode unfamiliar vocabulary or infer and test meaning.
2. Present the word to students in context, in a sentence as it appears in the text.
3. Have students read the sentence with you.
4. Place the word in isolation and look at the parts of the word.
5. First, have students look for units within the word that they recognize or know.
6. Next, create a graphic organizer of the word parts to help students see the individual components.
7. Teach the parts of the words that are unknown to students.
8. Illustrate commonalities between words by showing words that are like the word(s) being analyzed using onsets and rimes, bound morphemes (affixes), and etymology (origins of words) if related to the primary languages of students.
9. Based on what has been analyzed, have students predict the meanings of the word.
10. Place the word back into the context of the sentence from the text.
11. Substitute students' predictions. Ask them if the substitution in the sentence makes sense.
12. Mediate students' thinking if the substitutions do not make sense in the context of the sentence by asking clarifying questions.
13. If the word being analyzed is a cognate, call that to students' attention, using the word *cognate*. Post the word on a cognate word wall for student reference.
14. Have students write the sentence in context and the meaning that worked in a personal dictionary.
15. Review all vocabulary taught and post words in the classroom. Before students go out to recess or home at the end of the day, play a brief word game with them. For example, give them a word meaning and have them work with a partner to match |

STRATEGY 6.5   (continued)

Element	Description
Process of the Strategy	the meaning to the word. You may want to give an inaccurate meaning, one that is not contained in any of the words posted to see if students can recognize what is not there.
Comments	Reviewing vocabulary for ELLs is critical. Each time you come across any of the vocabulary when reading other genres or pieces of literature, stop and ask students if they remember what the word might mean. If the meaning is different, engage in the word analysis process again. ELLs are challenged when they encounter words with multiple meanings, and that has to be mediated and illustrated in context.
Scaffolding	Use as needed and not necessarily in the order listed: • When mediating vocabulary with ELLs, make sure that you plan for additional scaffolds during the planning phase. Have students work with a partner, after you have trained them in partner work, to ensure engagement in the task. • Model every step of the instructional process required to complete the task or accomplish the cognitive objective. • Mediate the students' language by drawing comparisons between the language they speak to each other as well as words derived from their primary languages. • Check for comprehension every step of the way. • Provide opportunities for students to share their thinking after you have shared yours. This means that the classroom should be set up in ways that foster a climate of risk taking. All students must be trained to be supportive of the thinking of others. • Validate what students get "right" and mediate any misunderstandings. • Reteach in small groups or on an individual basis to support transfer and mastery of learning. • Teach students the procedures of the classroom to support classroom management and the ease of working with small groups of students on a regular basis. Regardless of grade level, instruction in flexible, small groups is the best way to ensure that ELLs give and receive feedback on their learning. • Use drama such as *still poses*. For example, after students have had the opportunity to study words, have them work with a small group of students to illustrate the word in context. They set themselves up and freeze. The rest of the class guesses the word being demonstrated and provides reasons why they think the pose demonstrates the word. • Have students illustrate the meaning of words studied and enter the illustrations and definitions in illustrated dictionaries that the entire class can use. • Use graphic organizers whenever possible to encourage students to visualize language.

(continued)

STRATEGY 6.5 (continued)	
Element	**Description**
Scaffolding	• Make comparisons between the students' primary languages and English. For example, the constants in the Spanish language are the vowels that never change in sound. In contrast, the vowels of the English language are short, long, or become a schwa. These changes are like moving targets for ELLs. Therefore, they need to understand the patterns of English, that is, when the sound is predictable and when it is not. ELLs must also learn that the context will affect words to the effect that they are pronounced differently in context. For example, read and read (short e sound), record and record (long e sound), produce and produce (short o sound). Because these unpredictable sounds of the English language will be a challenge to ELLs for a long time, they need to be explicitly mediated and reviewed consistently over time.

A Word About Word Work

The topic of literacy for ELLs conjures up thoughts about how students learn to process or "read" the alphabetic code, especially if their primary languages do not use alphabetic symbols. Teachers know they need to address the issue of how ELLs master the sounds and symbols of English, the language of instruction. How this happens is of concern to many teachers. Teaching ELLs to recognize and decode symbols in English automatically presents obstacles to teachers. Ensuring that students understand and can apply basic concepts about print such as directionality, capital letters, and punctuation must also receive warranted attention. Teachers usually begin with phonemic awareness.

In their work on the National Literacy Panel on Language-Minority Children and Youth, August and Shanahan (2006) note that a critical area of research for them was to investigate how to build the English proficiency skills of second language learners because the ability to develop skills to navigate text is crucial and depends on strong English proficiency. Because typically developing children are hardwired for their primary language by age one, they need to learn oral language and literacy in a second language if they are expected to catch up to their classmates whose primary language is English, especially when instruction is delivered only in English (Riches & Genesee, 2006). Thus, ELLs must not only be phonemically aware, but also be able to match sound to symbol and understand how to manipulate a second language in a variety of ways. ELLs must also be able to process the concepts presented in text, literally comprehend text, infer meaning, and apply their understanding to a variety of situations.

In their research, August and Shanahan (2006) found that the word-level literacy skills of ELLs (e.g., decoding, spelling) are much more likely to be at levels equal to monolingual English speakers. However, this is not the case for text level skills (e.g., reading comprehension, writing). These skills often do not reach levels equal to monolingual English speakers. The research makes it evident that learning the phonology, syntax, and semantics (lexicon) of the English language is of utmost importance to learning English, and ELLs do make progress in this area. For example, the authors observed students "reading," that is, decoding text yet unable to retell the story at the completion of the reading or answer comprehension questions. Inferential questions were difficult to answer. Comprehension is an area of need and prompts referrals to student study teams and special education classes. Lesaux and Geva (2006) note that:

> The large number of studies that examined factors that influence reading comprehension demonstrated that many variables at both the individual (e.g., background knowledge, motivation) and contextual (e.g., story structure, home literacy, demographics) levels influence the second language reading comprehension of language minority students. Although these studies typically did not include a direct comparison between language minority students and native speakers, these same variables have been shown in other work to relate to monolinguals' reading comprehension. (p. 63)

In addition, August and Shanahan (2006) note that there are similar proportions of ELLs and monolingual speakers classified as poor readers. What does instruction look like? What is the difference in instructing ELLs and English-only students? Let's watch Kelli at work.

Examples from the Field

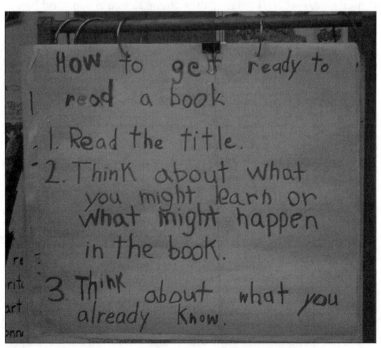

Strategy chart: How to get ready to read a book.

Kelli Teaches Word Work

It is 9:00 A.M. on a Tuesday morning and the tinkle of a small bell can be heard. A group of ELLs quietly enters Room 16, a third-grade classroom, at Edge Lake School. Some of the students she taught during the previous hour remain in their seats while others leave. Today Kelli, the teacher, is reviewing seed planting with her students. She begins by placing pictorial prompts on the flip chart in the front of the group where everyone can see. She asks her students to look at the pictures and talk to their partners about what they see. "What do you notice?" she asks. A moment or two of silence settles in the air followed by the soft hum of whispering voices that rise in volume and enthusiasm. Kelli is developing academic oral language in her students. She then adds the vocabulary words and asks, "What patterns do you see in this list of words?"

Previously, Kelli had provided her students with instruction in phonemic awareness, teaching them how to isolate sounds, match them to words, substitute one sound for another, blend sounds to make words, and rhyme words. She engaged her students in hands-on activities where they made words using onsets and rimes. Kelli was systematic in the rimes she used. She provided a variety of scaffolds that included flexible groups where students could provide each other feedback and she could monitor their learning progress, reteach and model for small groups, as well as provide more in-depth feedback and modeling for struggling individual students.

In the seed planting activity, Kelli encouraged her students to use what they had previously learned about making words. Once the students saw the pattern in the vocabulary list, one student walked to the classroom content area word wall, located the word on the word wall, and led his classmates in a cheer for the word.

Next, Kelli asked her students how they could use the patterns they discovered. "To spell words when we write," they chime in as a group. "And how does that work?" queried Kelli.

Aida: *Teacher, teacher, I found the pattern.*

Kelli: *Tell me.*

Aida: *It's "unk."*

Kelli: *What can you do with that ending or rime?*

Aida: *I can spell "junk."*

Kelli: *Great! Anything else?*

Aida: *"Skunk." Can we come up there and write more words?*

Kelli: *Of course. Bring your writing partner with you.*

Aida goes to get Ramón and they walk up to the chart paper. Kelli encourages them to think and spell out loud for their classmates. She asks the rest of the class to watch and listen very closely because she will be asking them to agree or disagree with Aida and Ramón. They also must be able to explain why. The students get ready and huddle with their partners.

The girls think out loud and say, "If we can spell 'junk,' we can spell other words like that. Can we write them?" They start: "chunk," "hunk," "trunk," "bunk," "dunk," "shrunk." Kelli asks the class what they think about the list the girls have created using the pattern the entire class identified. They show her a thumbs up signal and she asks them to think about ways they can use the words on their classmates' list to write about seed planting. The students know what to do. They take out a sheet of paper, partners face each other, their heads come together and they begin to talk about sentences that will work using the list of words on the board. They begin to compose. Their sentences include the following:

I cover my seed with a hunk of dirt but I threw a chunk of the dirt in the trash.

When I plant my seed I take a chunk of dirt to cover the roots.

I planted my seed and my plant shrunk.

I dunk my seeds in water before I plant them.

Kelli validates their work, noting that their words made sense, reminding them that is a strategy to use if you are uncertain whether a vocabulary word "works." Kelli then reviews other words students have had in previous lessons to ensure that they cannot only find the words on a list, but also tell her what they mean. She asks students to come up to the chart and show her a word. The rest of the class shows agreement or disagreement with a thumbs up (yes) or a thumbs down (no) signal. Kelli starts: "Show me *hem*. Show me *mend*. Show me *plaid*. Show me *crouch*. Show me *tiptoed*."

August and Shanahan (2006) noted that strategies used with English-only students to teach word work can work most of the time with ELLs. However, the instruction must be scaffolded or supported before, during, and after each lesson. We add that previous learning be revisited and connections made for students so they can begin to see that the words they learn are part of a tapestry that supports their reading and writing. The level of scaffolding needed is dependent on how students are processing the second language. To determine the level of support necessary, ongoing assessment must occur. There has to be consistent checking for comprehension accompanied by differentiated modeling for different groups of students and corrective feedback that builds on students' strengths. Kelli does that as she teaches her students phonemic awareness, phonics, spelling, and moves immediately into writing—the application of the knowledge of word work.

Practical Applications and Individual Inquiries: Cases to Think About and Investigate

1. Conduct an Internet search on the concept of metacognition. As you proceed through the research, develop your own practical definition of metacognition and apply your definition as you work with a small group of students. Keep notes about what happened. What worked? Where did you struggle? Share your experiences with a small group in your class.

2. How do you see yourself using metacognition as a future classroom teacher? Discuss this issue with a partner and write a short response to this question.

3. Select an ELL student with whom to work. Assess the student and determine which strategy discussed in this chapter would best serve your student, using his/her strengths to support the areas of need. Follow the process of the strategy step by

step. Keep notes on how the instruction went. What worked well? What was difficult to do? Suggest ways that you might adapt the strategy to best meet the individual needs of your ELL student.

4. Select a grade level text aligned with your state standards. Think about the students at that particular grade level. Plan how you will make the content in the text comprehensible for students. That is, how will you break up the text? What kinds of questions might you ask your students to guide them through the text and remember the content?

5. Develop a lesson plan using one of the strategies suggested in this chapter. Adapt the strategy to best suit your students and deliver the lesson to students. Check for understanding to assess their success. Did they meet the objectives of the lesson? How do you know—what is the evidence?

Chapter Seven _____

Making Content Accessible Through Standards-Based Instruction

It doesn't matter to us where our students come from. We all know that every one of

our students is capable of the best, and it is up to us to give them our best. We believe in

our community, our parents, and our kids. We work together, we believe in each other,

and we give it all we have.

Kris, reading coach and fourth-grade teacher

This chapter focuses on the process of scaffolding instruction to provide access to standards-based content curriculum. We discuss scaffolding from the perspective that (1) scaffolds are temporary and supportive structures that help students accomplish a task they would not have been able to accomplish without the scaffold or support; (2) a scaffold must place a learner in the zone of proximal development (Vygotsky, 1978), which is different for each student and therefore needs to be differentiated, where students can learn content that is unfamiliar; and (3) a scaffold eventually must be dismantled and taken away with responsibility for completing the learning task taken over by students.

We argue that ELLs must be taught grade level content and that content cannot be watered down. Instead, teachers need to differentiate instruction based on student needs, using the scaffolding process to determine the numbers and types of scaffolds ELLs require to learn grade level content. Given the move in California and the nation toward standards-based content instruction, it is important that teachers look for ways to ensure that their students have access to that instruction.

To explore how teachers can teach standards-based content in ways that differentiate instruction to meet student needs, we will look at one school's reform process and how the teachers at that school support their students by scaffolding instruction. We will present what this process looks like and how it provides content access, understanding, and mastery of learning where students are able to and will take over the responsibility for completing an assigned task and can extend the task and apply their learning to other academic areas. In this chapter we attempt to:

- Explain how the alignment of materials and standards creates comprehensible instructional input for students.
- Demonstrate the process of scaffolding student learning that supports standards-based instruction and ensures that grade level content is accessible for students.
- Embed ongoing assessment in standards-based instruction.

Building Background Knowledge About Making Content Accessible Through Standards-Based Instruction

BOX 7.1 OVERVIEW OF THE CELDT

Although California Education Code has long mandated language testing for those students whose home language is not English, Assembly Bill 748 established the CELDT as a response to federal guidelines for No Child Left Behind. The purpose of the CELDT is to identify students as ELLs and to measure their annual progress toward fluent English proficiency. It measures listening, speaking, reading, and writing. Students are assigned a proficiency level for each skill tested, based on the results of the exam (California Department of Education, 2004). These proficiency levels are beginning, early intermediate, intermediate, early advanced, and advanced. Schools (and teachers) use these proficiency levels as a guide for ELD instruction.

This chapter is also informed by the work at Edge Lake School, where the issues of equity and social justice influenced the dialogue at the school about pedagogy and created the nucleus for all instruction, specifically instruction aimed at meeting the needs of ELLs. This chapter is further based on our ongoing work in K–12 classrooms with teachers and their students who were learning English as a second language, all at different English proficiency levels as measured by the California English Language Development Test (CELDT).

We learned a lot about how to make content accessible to ELLs through the use of standards-based instruction by planning with small groups of teachers, individual teachers, the school reading teacher, and the building administrator as they dialogued about the best ways to meet the needs of their ELLs. Because teachers and schools in California are guided by a series of content standards (see http://www.cde.ca.gov for a listing of available content standards; these are revised every 7 or so years under the auspices of the California State Board of Education and include all subject areas as well as ELD), these serve as a frame on which teachers design curriculum. We argue here that within this framework of mandated content standards as it relates to education for ELLs, it is important to discuss the complex issue of scaffolding instruction to ensure access to the curriculum and both ELD and content learning (García, 2003). It is also critical that teachers are aware of the need to plan thoughtfully, to address all the areas of language (reading, writing, listening, speaking, and thinking) as well as content, and to focus on differentiating instruction in ways that best serve ELLs (Chamot & O'Malley, 1994; Dutro & Moran, 2003; Herrera & Murry, 2005).

Some skills that are important to teach throughout the curriculum include inferencing, visualization, questioning, and determining importance to ensure students comprehend text (Harvey & Goudvis, 2002). These skills are considered the basics that teachers need to teach to their students to ensure that they will be successful in the increasing challenges that face them as school gets more complex.

In addition to specific skills, it is also important to explore student identity and teacher expectations according to that identity. Delpit (1995) and Gay (2000) suggest ways for teachers to think about students who see themselves as different because of their unique cultures. When teachers work to plan lessons and units that are culturally relevant to their students' lives (Gay, 2000; Ooka Pang, 2004), they help students to comprehend these lessons more easily.

As we already discussed extensively in Chapter 3, another important factor to consider is the language of instruction and how students make sense of that language, especially if it is not their native language. Research suggests that when ELLs are learning to read in English, the use of their primary language to scaffold the content can help activate background knowledge and serve to increase comprehensible input (Pérez & Torres-Guzmán, 2002). Furthermore, we can use the student's primary language in ways that do not amount to translation and therefore promote ELD (Ulanoff & Pucci, 1999). All this should take place within a balanced program consisting of word work, independent reading, guided reading, writing, and effective assessment (Cunningham & Allington, 2003). Teachers can make grade level content accessible to ELLs when they engage in a complex planning process that takes into account language, content, and scaffolding.

Another important issue is the role of assessment (see Chapter 4). To assess ELLs effectively and accurately, teachers must pay attention to instruction as well as scaffolding and language (Quiocho & Ulanoff, 2005; Quiocho, Dantas, & Mackintosh, 2001). It is critical to look at language and scaffolding, because research shows that when ELLs are assessed, not only is the content measured, but so is their language proficiency, making it difficult to determine whether students miss questions because they don't know the content or because they don't have the language (Mercado & Romero, 1993). Therefore, within instruction as in assessment, language really matters as a scaffold (Rodgers, 2000). When designing differentiated instruction for ELLs, teachers need to reflect on the process of scaffolding and examine when a scaffold is really a scaffold and when a scaffold is supporting student learning. This means that teachers also need to explore whether a scaffold is helping students access the curriculum and then make important decisions about keeping, changing, or abandoning specific scaffolds if they are not supporting student learning throughout a lesson or unit (Rodgers, 2000).

In our work with teachers, we attended grade level meetings. At these meetings, teachers talked about the need to pay attention to the value of what they were teaching students and to use students' backgrounds and interests as a starting point for their teaching. Teachers made the commitment to act from the information research provided them and from data they obtained through ongoing assessment. In this chapter, we suggest a variety of ways to make content accessible through standards-based instruction.

Linking Theory to Practice

Teaching is complex. The lives of teachers are filled with spontaneous decision making, sessions of intense planning, and many hours of reflection on their practice. Teachers are also held accountable for student success. They are expected to make content accessible and teach to standards, doing the best job possible. The multitude of expectations can sometimes seem overwhelming. Yet, teachers know that somehow they must find a way to do it all.

District- or school-adopted materials can be aligned thematically or topically with literature, a balanced language arts program, and standards-based instruction to ensure that all students have access to the core curriculum, and content can be made accessible to students through standards-based instruction.

Moreover, when teachers have to work with a variety of materials such as those adopted by their districts or schools for mainstream classrooms as well as special adoptions for special education and/or ELLs, they immediately know they have a dilemma that must be resolved. There are only so many days in a school year and so many hours in a school day. During this contact time with students, teachers must take into consideration what students know (based on multiple assessments), meet the individual needs of all students in their classes, and yet cover the material. Teachers know that materials are the resources that support their teaching. Yet many times they place a great deal of importance on the value of the adopted materials. Teachers can be more efficient and effective in their teaching if they collaborate with peers on aligning the materials, standards, and instruction.

One School's Guiding Principles

Once more we return to Edge Lake School, a K–5 school in southern California, not far from the Mexican border. It is a small school with approximately 620 students, 74% of whom are ELLs. Edge Lake teachers provide primary language support for students who are at the beginning levels of learning English. However, they provide the bulk of instruction in English, the policy of the medium-sized unified district. Edge Lake staff set out to *change* their practice to more effectively work with all students more than 2 years ago, initially supported by grant funding that focused on raising reading test scores. Although the grant expired at the end of the 2002–03 school year, the school and district supported the change process at Edge Lake by providing local funding for an additional year. Edge Lake serves as an example of how teachers can make content instruction accessible through teaching to and with standards.

The Change Process at Edge Lake

The change process at Edge Lake was guided by some powerful concepts that helped the teachers work together to meet the needs of their students. The following are examples of those concepts.

- Teachers held high expectations for all students with the understanding that students can meet high expectations only when they are afforded access to the core curriculum with support mechanisms (scaffolds) provided appropriately, based on ongoing assessment.
- Teachers worked to provide access to grade level content for all ELLs, regardless of language proficiency level.
- Teachers consistently provided students with opportunities for previewing content, teaching and reteaching content, as well as reviewing and extending content learning throughout the day, specifically in language arts classes, ELD classes, and extended classes where students are mixed by language and language levels.

- Teachers focused on reading and writing across the curriculum with no priorities given to one process over another. They saw reading and writing as interrelated and used as a means to support thinking and comprehension.

- Teachers also decided to focus on a few, robust comprehension strategies that encompass a variety of critical thinking skills to support comprehension development, including inferential thinking and critical thinking using metacognition or thinking about a specific function such as reading or writing while actively engaged in the act.

- Teachers also focused on standards taught through standards-based topic modules developed from grade level content standards considered the basics of learning or starting points rather than ending points.

- They also focused on the California English Language Development Standards as developmental guidelines rather than indications of terminal expectations for performance.

- The reading teacher/literacy coordinator served as a mentor for teachers and modeled in-classroom ELD instruction.

- The reading teacher/literacy coordinator also conducted monthly professional development workshops/classes based on school goals and the school plan as well as teacher needs in the implementation phase of the grant.

- Teachers worked to calibrate student writing in specific genres across grade levels to inform themselves and to shape attitudes about expectations for ELLs.

- The site principal participated as co-learner in the curriculum and all other phases of the change process. The staff at Edge Lake engaged in a teaching and learning community.

- Teachers gave students opportunities to learn grade level content across three time slots in the school day (reading/language arts, ELD, and enrichment).

The teachers at Edge Lake developed a series of *guiding principles* for instruction that helped them develop the models/lessons described in this chapter. All instruction at Edge Lake was conducted in English along with the primary language of students, Spanish, which was used to elaborate on concepts, clarify directions, facilitate vocabulary understanding, and activate students' background knowledge. The teachers all agreed to these principles and used them to guide all planning. They developed guidelines for ELD, SDAIE, and the cognitive academic language learning approach—CALLA (Chamot & O'Malley, 1994).

ELLs in ELD programs received instruction exclusively in English in all content areas, in many cases by teachers who had been specially trained in second language acquisition and development. At the elementary level, this included literacy instruction as well as other content areas, and the goal at all levels was full English proficiency (Peregoy & Boyle, 2004). Note that ELD is often used interchangeably with English as a Second Language (ESL), a term that has been in use much longer than ELD and generally refers to in-class or pull-out programs that teach English to ELLs.

At Edge Lake School, the ELD guidelines gave meaning to the school's structured English immersion (SEI) program, which was developed to meet state mandates. Edge Lake School implemented SEI to help develop ELLs' English proficiency before they are placed in mainstream English classrooms. The guidelines included teaching English language arts (ELA) alongside ELD and focused on teaching for transfer to ensure that students

FIGURE 7.1 ELD Guidelines for Instruction and Transfer

1. The stated purpose of SEI is to help ELLs develop English proficiency.
2. Enrichment classes provide schema development, study skills, and metacognitive strategies to students showing mastery of the English language.
3. There are five major aspects of language: phonology (the sound system), morphology (how words are built), syntax (the structure of sentences), semantics (the meaning of words), and pragmatics (the use of language in social context).
4. ELD focuses on syntax and semantics.
5. ELA focuses on all five aspects with importance on phonology and morphology.
6. Transfer in ELD should follow the progression of listening/speaking to writing and lastly reading.
7. Transfer in ELA should follow the progression of reading to writing and lastly listening and speaking.
8. The ELD framework follows four aspects:
   a. Mastery of the sound system of a language, its syntax and semantics, plus knowledge of vocabulary.
   b. Mastery of the appropriate forms, registers, and styles of language for different social/academic contexts.
   c. Discourse competence and the ability to connect spoken words in a meaningful way and relate them appropriately to a topic.
   d. Strategic competence, the ability to compensate (self-correct) for breakdowns in communication.

Source: Developed by the literacy team at Edge Lake to provide staff with principles to reflect on their instruction.

BOX 7.2 WHY USE STRUCTURED ENGLISH IMMERSION?

In June 1998, California voters approved Proposition 227, which mandated that students be taught "overwhelmingly in English." It further mandated that schools offer ELLs a curriculum called structured English immersion (SEI) for one year, with a possible second year, so that they could become proficient enough in English to participate successfully in mainstream English classrooms. Proposition 227 did not, however, define SEI, leaving that up to local school districts. Districts defined SEI in a variety of ways, some including primary language support.

successfully mastered listening, speaking, reading, and writing in English. Figure 7.1 summarizes the ELD guidelines for instruction and transfer.

Teachers also developed guidelines for SDAIE, which is intended for students already at an intermediate level of English language proficiency. ELLs in SDAIE programs are taught content matter entirely in English, but that content is organized to promote second language acquisition at the same time students are learning challenging grade level content (Peregoy & Boyle, 2004). There is a special focus on scaffolding or *sheltering* the curriculum to provide students with access to the content. In some cases, teachers use the students' primary language to support content understanding, but as previously mentioned, in ways that don't include direct translation. It is important to note that some also refer to SDAIE as sheltered instruction. Figure 7.2 summarizes the key aspects of SDAIE that serve as guidelines for Edge Lake teachers.

Teachers further used CALLA (Chamot & O'Mally, 1994), an instructional approach that focuses on the explicit instruction of learning strategies as well as the development of critical thinking skills. These strategies and critical thinking skills serve to promote second language acquisition to the point where ELLs develop high levels of English proficiency (Herrera & Murry, 2005). The teachers at Edge Lake School included key aspects of CALLA in their guiding principles for effective instruction (see Figure 7.3).

Teachers also explored ways in which ELD, SDAIE, and CALLA impact instruction, generating overarching guiding principles for designing effective instruction for ELLs.

FIGURE 7.2 Key Aspects of SDAIE

1. Cognitive development and language development are tied.
2. School subjects are what children need to discuss in school, so content areas provide opportunity for meaningful communication and transfer.
3. Language assessments, content, and instruction are linked to allow students to develop language used in schools (CALP).

Source: Developed by the literacy team at Edge Lake.

FIGURE 7.3 Key Aspects of CALLA

1. Plan for learning using metacognitive strategies.
2. Engage all material using cognitive strategies.
3. Interact in academic discourse and monitor dialogue.
4. Utilize integrated material to develop deeper understanding.

Source: From *The CALLA handbook: Implementing the cognitive academic language learning approach*, by A. Chamot and J. M. O'Malley, 1994, Reading, MA, Addison-Wesley.

These principles focus on the use of cognitive strategies, language and content objectives, student/teacher dialogue, and the explicit teaching of metacognitive strategies, such as connecting new information to former knowledge (see Chapter 6 for a more complete description of cognitive and metacognitive strategies). The teachers at Edge Lake also used features from *A Developmental English Proficiency Test* (ADEPT; California Reading and Literacy Project, 2001) results to guide their instructional decisions. Figure 7.4 summarizes the guiding principles for designing instruction for ELLs at Edge Lake School.

The teachers at Edge Lake School use these guiding principles to center their curriculum design and instruction. As teachers work together, in both grade level meetings and whole faculty meetings, these guidelines serve as a framework for success at their school.

FIGURE 7.4 Guiding Principles for Designing Instruction Using ELD, SDAIE, and CALLA Strategies

1. ELD must be part of an overarching metacognitive strategy using cognitive strategies to reach mastery.
2. Instruction must focus on specific areas of language transfer that relate back to content areas.
3. Discourse within context should be the main focus of transfer to other literacy events. Semantic structure must be assessed and used for instruction. Classroom settings must allow for dialogue between teacher/student and student/student with monitored scaffolds.
4. Metacognitive strategies must be taught explicitly through all content areas to ensure utilization of strategies for language transfer. Planning must consider content-obligatory objectives (ELA standards/ELD benchmarks) and tie to content-compatible objectives (theme/ADEPT features) for language to be used in context.

Examples from the Field

Small-group strategy instruction.

As the faculty at Edge Lake School used the guiding principles to design curriculum, they began to align curriculum in different ways to meet the needs of their students. A first step was to look at their language arts curriculum and their ELD curriculum to look for connections between units and lessons. The following examples demonstrate the process of aligning mainstream, grade level materials by themes and stories with materials selected by the district to be used with ELLs. They show the ways in which the teachers at Edge Lake began to look at the connections between reading and ELD. At Edge Lake School, teachers use the Houghton Mifflin Reading Series, *A Legacy of Literature*, and the Hampton-Brown ELD series, *Into English!* The following charts (Figures 7.5 through 7.10) show that this alignment can first occur by sitting down with peers to examine materials they use at a specific grade level to see how the units and stories relate to one another. The charts list the specific chapters and units in alignment between the two texts for K–5 grade levels. Teachers use the charts to plan thematic lessons in reading and ELD.

The next step was to dialogue with peers about which skills and content area topics to cover at each grade level and how to align those with the standards, the materials, and the reading,

BOX 7.3 A WORD ABOUT THE CHOICE OF TEXTS

We used specific publishers' materials, Houghton Mifflin and Hampton-Brown, because these materials were adopted by the district and used at the schools in which we did our work. Other districts in the same state and in other states will use the materials adopted by their schools and districts. These examples show how teachers aligned, adapted, and modified adopted materials to ensure that ELLs received instruction in grade level content with the necessary instructional scaffolds.

writing, and oral language development processes. A blank indicated that no story in the ELD materials aligned with the mainstream materials. This provided an opportunity to include authentic storytelling from students' cultures, poetry, or songs that addressed the theme being studied. Figure 7.5 demonstrates the process for kindergarten. It is important to note that this alignment was between the state-adopted reading program and the ELD program used at the school.

Aligning Skills and Topics with Standards and Materials

The next step in the alignment process occurred when teachers examined the alignment charts they had previously created to identify the skills they needed to teach at each grade level, using the *California English Language Arts Framework* (California Department of Education, 2007/1999) and Content Standards (CDE, 1998) as well as the California *English Language Development Standards* (CDE, 2002).

As a group, the teachers at Edge Lake identified what they referred to as *power standards*. Power standards are those standards taught at one or more grade levels. In addition, teachers looked at other standards that are embedded in the power standards, that is, if the power standards were taught, other standards would be included in instruction. As we listened to the teachers talk at their grade level meetings, we learned that they felt it was not logical to teach standards in a linear fashion, beginning with the first until they reached the last. They knew that if they proceeded to teach standards in that manner, they would probably never reach the end of the standards document. They knew that some standards and skills are more important than others and some are probably more challenging for ELLs, so they targeted those standards.

FIGURE 7.5 Houghton Mifflin Alignment Guide for Hampton-Brown *Into English!* Kindergarten

Houghton Mifflin Theme	Hampton-Brown Level A
Theme 1: Look at Us!	Unit 1: A Rainbow
Theme 2: Colors All Around	Unit 1: A Rainbow
Theme 3: We're a Family	Unit 4: Close to Home
Theme 4: Friends Together	Unit 3: My World, Your World
Theme 5: Let's Count!	
Theme 6: Sunshine and Raindrops	Unit 2: Changing Times Unit 8: Caring for Our World
Theme 7: Wheels Go Around	Unit 5: On the Move
Theme 8: Down on the Farm	Unit 7: Country Days and Country Ways
Theme 9: Spring Is Here	Unit 8: Caring for Our World
Theme 10: A World of Animals	Unit 7: Country Days and Country Ways

Note: Themes used by textbook publishers were replicated as alignment themes to avoid confusion by teachers when using published materials.

FIGURE 7.6 Houghton Mifflin Alignment Guide for Hampton-Brown *Into English!* Grade 1

Houghton Mifflin Theme	Hampton-Brown Level A
Theme 1: Look at Us!	Unit 1: A Rainbow
Theme 2: Colors All Around	Unit 1: A Rainbow
Theme 3: We're a Family	Unit 4: Close to Home
Theme 4: Friends Together	Unit 3: My World, Your World
Theme 5: Let's Count!	
Theme 6: Sunshine and Raindrops	Unit 2: Changing Times Unit 8: Caring for Our World
Theme 7: Wheels Go Around	Unit 5: On the Move
Theme 8: Down on the Farm	Unit 7: Country Days and Country Ways
Theme 9: Spring Is Here	Unit 8: Caring for Our World
Theme 10: A World of Animals	Unit 7: Country Days and Country Ways
Houghton Mifflin Theme	**Hampton-Brown Level B**
Theme 1: All Together Now	Unit 2: A Walk in the Woods Unit 6: Farm Fresh
Theme 2: Surprise!	
Theme 3: Let's Look Around!	Unit 1: Best Foot Forward Unit 4: Under Construction
Theme 4: Family and Friends	
Theme 5: Home Sweet Home	Unit 4: Under Construction Unit 5: Just Around the Corner
Theme 6: Animal Adventures	Unit 2: A Walk in the Woods
Theme 7: We Can Work It Out	Unit 4: Under Construction Unit 6: Farm Fresh
Theme 8: Our Earth	Unit 3: One to Grow On
Theme 9: Friends	Unit 2: A Walk in the Woods Unit 6: Farm Fresh
Theme 10: We Can Do It!	Unit 4: Under Construction

FIGURE 7.7 Houghton Mifflin Alignment Guide for Hampton-Brown *Into English!* Grade 2

Houghton Mifflin Theme	Hampton-Brown Level C
Theme 1: Silly Stories	
Theme 2: Nature Walk	Unit 6: Ship to Shore
Theme 3: Around Town	
Theme 4: Amazing Animals	Unit 1: Wild! Wooly! Wonderful!
Theme 5: Family Time	Unit 3: Let's Celebrate Unit 5: Once Upon a Storm
Theme 6: Talent Show	Unit 2: Hands on the World Unit 4: From Field to Table

FIGURE 7.8 Houghton Mifflin Alignment Guide for Hampton-Brown *Into English!* Grade 3

Houghton Mifflin Theme	Hampton-Brown Level D
Theme 1: Off to Adventure!	Unit 3: To the Moon
Theme 2: Celebrating Traditions	Unit 4: Communities in the USA
Theme 3: Incredible Stories	Unit 3: To the Moon
Theme 4: Animal Habitats	Unit 5: Operation Conservation
Theme 5: Voyagers	Unit 3: To the Moon
Theme 6: Smart Solutions	Unit 2: Food for Thought

FIGURE 7.9 Houghton Mifflin Alignment Guide for Hampton-Brown *Into English!* Grade 4

Houghton Mifflin Theme	Hampton-Brown Level E
Theme 1: Journeys	Unit 3: Coast to Coast
Theme 2: American Stories	Unit 2: Water, Water, Everywhere! Unit 5: Around the World in 80 Days
Theme 3: That's Amazing!	Unit 5: Around the World in 80 Days
Theme 4: Desafíos (Problem Solvers)	Unit 2: Water, Water, Everywhere!
Theme 5: Heroes	Unit 5: Around the World in 80 Days
Theme 6: Nature: Friend and Foe	Unit 1: Bloom and Grow Unit 2: Water, Water, Everywhere! Unit 4: Fly Like an Eagle

FIGURE 7.10 Houghton Mifflin Alignment Guide for Hampton-Brown *Into English!* Grade 5

Houghton Mifflin Theme	Hampton-Brown Level F
Theme 1: Nature's Fury	Unit 4: Blast Off
Theme 2: Give It All You've Got	Unit 2: On the Way to the USA
Theme 3: Voices of the Revolution	Unit 3: Liberty and Justice for All Unit 5: Native Land
Theme 4: Person to Person	Unit 2: On the Way to the USA
Theme 5: One Land Many Trails	Unit 1: History Hot Unit 2: On the Way to the USA
Theme 6: Animal Encounters	

Because they knew they assessed writing in the fourth grade, the teams of teachers planned backwards, looking at what fourth graders must know upon entry to that grade level to support their writing. Analysis of student data in reading and writing revealed that reading comprehension and response to literature had to be the goal of instruction. Table 7.1 summarizes the list of skills that the teachers generated by analyzing the results of the fourth-grade state assessment in writing. These skills are those the teachers felt that they should expose students to before they entered the fourth grade. They included skills that are specific to content standards as well as others still deemed important by the teachers.

Next, the teachers identified the power standards for each grade level and connected those standards to a specific topic module or, in the case of primary grades, a skills module. For example, Table 7.2 describes the power standards identified for first and second grade.

The alignment process continued as teachers looked at critical skills students needed to master. They identified the skills as something they needed to emphasize as students engaged in metacognitive strategies. Teachers participated in book clubs where they spent time reading about necessary comprehension skills. They read *Strategies that Work* by Harvey and Goudvis (2000) as well as *Mosaic of Thought* by Zimmerman and Keene (1997) and planned their next module with the learnings from those books in mind. Table 7.3 is an example of a fourth-grade topic module alignment guide, which is an overview of the alignment process, displaying the results of their collaborative reading and work. Note that transfer from this module to other areas of study is a part of the module.

Teachers also developed metacognitive strategy planning guides for 2-week third-grade units that focused on teaching students how to think about different text structures (see Figures 7.11 through 7.14). The unit guides identified features students must know about text structures and helped teachers to plan lessons. They also identified cognitive competencies— what students must be able to understand or do as they read and write. The guides listed different genres and the purposes for writing in those genres. Figures 7.11 through 7.14 include guides for narrative text, persuasion, expository text, and response to literature and summarize the different phases of the unit and the specific components covered.

TABLE 7.1 Writing Skills Students Need Exposure to Before Grade 4

General Category	Specific Skills
Literary Response and Analysis	1. Be able to distinguish common forms of literature. a. Be able to determine the underlying theme of the author's message and support your statement.

Writing Strategies	1. Be able to include a topic sentence with paragraph formatting, including facts and details.
	   b. Be able to revise drafts.
	   c. Engage in the writing process.

Writing Applications	1. Write narratives.
	   a. Setting/character
	   b. Details
	   c. Problem/solution
	2. Use sensory details to support story.

Written Oral Conventions	1. Sentence variations. 2. Syntax. 3. Tense agreement. 4. Run-on and complete sentences.
Punctuation	1. Capitalize titles of books, stories, etc. 2. Use commas appropriately. 3. Capitalize proper nouns. 4. Spelling.
Listening and Speaking	1. Retell a story. 2. Respond to questions in complete sentences. 3. Beginning/middle/end of story. 4. Knowledge of audience.
Reading Comprehension	1. Ask questions about and support answers connecting prior knowledge to the topic to be read.

TABLE 7.2 Power Standards in Language Arts for Grades 1 and 2

Standards	Power Standards and Modules
Reading	**Power Standards for First Grade** 1.9. Segment 4 to 5 letter single syllable words into their components (e.g., splat=/s/p/l/a/t/; rich=/r/i/ch/ 1.15. Read irregular word families (e.g., -ake, -old, -ind, -ild), read common two-vowel word families (-oat, -eat)
Writing	1.1. Select a focus when writing that integrates the content of the module and provides opportunities for students to practice their reading/spelling skills.
Reading Comprehension	**Power Standards for Second Grade** 2.4. Orally use context clues to resolve ambiguities about word and sentence meaning. 2.5. Confirm predictions about what will happen next in a text by identifying key words.

(continued)

TABLE 7.2 (continued)

Standards	Power Standards and Modules
Reading	1.10. Generate the sounds from the long vowel patterns and from two vowels, plus soft "c" and "g," and blend them into recognizable words. 1.12. Use knowledge of vowel diphthongs (e.g., oo, oi, oy) and r-controlled (ar) letter sounds to associate words. 1.13. Read compound words. 1.14. Read inflectional forms (e.g., -s, -ed, -ing) and root words (e.g., look, looked, looking).
Written and Oral English Language Conventions	1.3. Identify and correctly use singular possessive pronouns (e.g., my/mine, his/her, hers, your/s) in speaking. 1.4. Distinguish between declarative, exclamatory, and interrogative sentences. 1.5. Use an exclamation point, period, or question mark at the end of a sentence.
Listening and Speaking	1.2. Model asking questions for clarification and understanding.
Speaking Applications	2.2. Retell stories using basic story grammar relating the sequence of story events by answering who, what, where, when, why, and how questions.
Literary Response and Analysis: Genre Writing	3.1. Identify and describe the elements of plot, setting, and character(s) in a story.

Source: California State Department of Education. (1998). *English-language arts: Academic content standards for kindergarten through grade 12.* Sacramento, CA: Author. Retrieved January 12, 2008, from http://www.cde.ca.gov/be/st/ss/engmain.asp

TABLE 7.3 Houghton Mifflin Topic Module Alignment Guide for Hampton-Brown *Into English!* Grade 4

Dates: 11/11/02–1/24/03. Assessment Week: 10/30/02–11/13/02					
Topic Module 3	**Focus Activities and Skills**				
Metacognitive Strategy	Determining Importance Questioning (see skills link)				
Writing Genre	Expository Writing • Nonfiction Summary and Response • Compare and Contrast • Persuasion				
Literary Genre	Historical Fiction/Realistic Fiction				
Literacy Concept	Focus on: Problem/Solution Cause and Effect				
Topic	Newcomers to California (Immigration)				
Primary Topic	Changes to land and people				
Next Topic Module Focus	Changes to values and cultures (California joins the United States)				
Selected Reading	Read Aloud	Into English	Anthology	Social Studies	Science
	Stowaway to California	Coast to Coast Unit 3	Problem Solvers Unit 4	Unit 2	Unit A, Ch. 5 Protecting and Preserving Ecosystems

TABLE 7.3 (continued)

Dates: 11/11/02–1/24/03. Assessment Week: 10/30/02–11/13/02		
Topic Module 3	**Focus Activities and Skills**	
Text Focus	How immigration changes land and people	
Text Analysis	Summarization, Activate prior knowledge, Critique and Evaluate	
Writing Applications	Inform Evaluate	
ELA Standards	Integrate English Language Arts Standards into the reading, writing, listening, and speaking	
ELD Standards • Refer to standards for groups of students who scored at specified levels of language acquisition • These levels also corresponded to the district benchmarks of ELLs	Level 1: Beginner	
	Level 2: Early Intermediate	
	Level 3: Intermediate	
	Level 4: Early Advanced Speaker	
	Level 5: Advanced Speaker	

End Assessments to be used with school-developed rubrics that were genre specific, organization specific, and conventions specific	Formative Pieces of Assessment
	  1. Nonfiction Summary and Response—Explorers
	  2. Confirm Opinion (compare and contrast)—Priests and Indians
	    a. Infer opinions
	  3. Evaluate and Persuade—Students choose topics
	  4. Summative Assessment Piece
	  5. Persuasion—Persuade Mexican citizens to move to Alta, CA	

Nature of Concepts	**Concept**	
1. Transfer concept to be integrated across the content areas	Immigration changes values and land	
a. Primary concept to be included across the content areas	Changes to the land in California (Spanish Explorers)	
b. Secondary concept to make connections between content, adopted materials, and literature	Changes to the people native to California (Missions)	
c. Tertiary concept to make connections to other student learning	Changes to cultures in California (Ranchos)	
Other Skills	**Specifics**	
Language Skills	Specific for each class and groups of students within the class as determined by district benchmarks.	
Skills—Link to the Topic of the Module	1. Predict, discriminate between important and unimportant details, retell a story or small pieces of information from expository text. 2. Activate prior knowledge, focus on fact and opinion, identify/assess/support answers. 3. Organize, explain/convince, summarize.	
Matching Genres	Teachers decided that learning the features of genres students would encounter in other reading and writing in school would be much more efficient if they matched reading genres with writing genres in their teaching. They give examples of genres as needed.	

Source: Developed by the literacy team at Edge Lake.

FIGURE 7.11 Metacognitive Strategies: Activating Prior Knowledge and Schema

Features (Students must know how to)	Cognitive Competency (Students must understand)
1. Parts of the Story	**1. Activating Prior Knowledge (Schema)**
a. Setting	a. Text-to-self connections
b. Character	b. Text-to-text connections
c. Solution	c. Text-to-world connections
d. Problem	d. Schema activation
e. Agitator	e. Discriminate between important/ unimportant events
f. Protagonist	f. Develop purpose
2. Sequence/Chronology	**2. Interpretation**
a. Main idea	a. Differences between various texts
b. Supporting details	b. Retelling
c. Beginning	c. Text purpose
d. Middle	d. Reading purpose
e. End	**3. Fix-Up Strategies**
f. Central theme	a. Building background knowledge with realia
g. Moral	b. Model metacognition
3. Organize Ideas	c. Pair students to practice metacognition
a. Compare/contrast	**4. Writing Purposes**
b. Cause/effect	a. To inform
c. Clarify	b. To explain
d. Identify	c. To describe
e. Describe	d. To trace
f. Relate ideas	e. To compare
g. Summarize	f. To respond
4. Text Forms of Narrative Writing	
a. Fairy tales	
b. Fables	
c. Myths	
d. Legends	
e. Picture books	
f. Author studies	
g. Letters	
h. Auto/biographies	
i. Folktales	

Source: Summary of 2-week focus in third grade on narrative text, by K. Quiocho and T. Steele, Edge Lake Elementary School.

FIGURE 7.12 Metacognitive Strategies: Synthesizing and Questioning

Features (Students must know how to)	Cognitive Competence (Students must understand)
1. Describe	**1. Questioning**
a. Text genres	a. Construct meaning
b. Characteristics of text	b. Discern fact/opinion
c. Length/format	c. Find answers
d. Headings/subheadings	d. Solve problems
2. Analyze	e. Locate specific information
a. Compare/contrast	f. Utilize new information
b. Critique/evaluate	g. Determine resources
c. Explain	h. Clarify confusion
d. Define	i. Propel research
e. Respond	**2. Synthesize**
f. Question	a. Connect information
g. Organize	b. Relate observations/understanding
h. Order	c. Construct meaning
i. Convince	d. Build on prior perspectives
j. State/defend	e. Evaluate viewpoints
k. Validate/invalidate	f. Summarize through main points
l. Debate	g. Generalize/judge
m. Influence	h. Read with personal understanding
n. Cause/effect	i. Stop, collect, review, and record information
o. Support	j. Infer personal meaning
3. Research	**3. Fix-Up Strategies**
a. Take notes	a. Activate prior knowledge
b. Skim/scan	b. Visualize
c. Cue vocabulary	c. Infer
d. Recognize theme	**4. Writing Purposes**
e. Distinguish fact/opinion	a. To contrast
f. Identify/assess/support	b. To compare
g. Utilize varying text	c. To persuade
h. Frame a question	d. To state
i. Locate information	e. To analyze
j. Provide context	f. To interpret
k. Summarize	g. To critique
4. Text Forms of Persuasive Writing	h. To illustrate
a. Contemporary literature	i. To respond
b. Auto/biography	
c. Non/fiction	
d. Journals	
e. Periodicals	
f. Bibliographies	
g. Letters and supporting text	

Source: Summary of 2-week focus in third grade on persuasive writing, by K. Quiocho and T. Steele, Edge Lake Elementary School.

FIGURE 7.13 Metacognitive Strategies: Activating Prior Knowledge and Schema Visualization

Features (Students must know how to)	Cognitive Competency (Students must understand)
1. Distinguish Elements of Text	**1. Activating Prior Knowledge (Schema)**
a. Problem/solution	a. Text-to-self connections
b. Setting	b. Text-to-text connections
c. Main character	c. Text-to-world connections
2. Identify	d. Schema activation
a. Central ideas	e. Discriminate between important/ unimportant events
b. Themes	f. Develop purpose
c. Symbols	g. Interpret personal reasoning
d. Similarities	h. Predict
e. Differences	i. Retell
f. Continuity	j. Identify text variations
g. Moral	k. Identify different text and purpose
h. Characteristics	**2. Visualization**
i. Character traits	a. Create mental pictures
3. Respond	b. Utilize text language
a. Who	c. Link language to pictures
b. What	d. Place themselves in the story
c. Where	e. Use imaginative thought process
d. When	f. Use reflective thinking
e. How	**3. Fix-Up Strategies**
f. Why	a. Listen to music
g. Sequence	b. Talk about how we feel or what we thought about
4. Clarify	c. Listen to poetry
a. Restate	d. Ask how it makes you feel
b. Support	e. Note transfer to longer pieces
c. State evidence	**4. Writing Purposes**
d. Interpret	a. To respond
5. Summarize	b. To discuss
6. Text Forms of Response to Literature	c. To analyze
a. Grade-appropriate picture books	d. To state
b. Wordless books	e. To describe
c. Short stories	f. To critique
d. Poetry	
e. Folktales	
f. Fairy tales	
g. Pictures/maps/diagrams/charts	
h. Rhyme	

Source: Summary of 2-week focus in third grade on response to literature, by K. Kinsella and S. Harvey. Adapted and compiled by K. Quiocho, Edge Lake Elementary School.

FIGURE 7.14 Metacognitive Strategies: Inferring and Determining Importance

Features (Students must know how to)	Cognitive Competence (Students must understand)
1. Describe	**1. Infer**
a. Order	a. Create meaning
b. List	b. Draw conclusions
c. Categorize	c. Use visual information
d. Compare/contrast	d. Support ideas with facts
e. Problem/solution relationship	e. Move from prediction to clarification
f. Answer/questions	f. Imply
g. State	g. Identify theme/motive
h. Discuss	h. Support impressions
i. Clarify	i. Validate schema
j. Analyze	j. Create purpose
k. Support	**2. Determine Importance**
2. Research	a. Distinguish important from unimportant
a. Process varied information on a similar topic	b. Discern fact/opinion
b. Take notes	c. Move from obvious to obscure
c. Understand visual literacy	d. Show insight
d. Organize information	e. Hypothesize
e. Use informational text	f. Generalize
f. Distinguish fact/opinion	g. Discern main ideas/points
g. Restate	h. Confirm predictions
h. Simplify	i. Relate relevance
i. Frame a question	**3. Fix-Up Strategies**
j. Utilize a wide variety of resources	a. Activate prior knowledge
k. Understand features of resources	b. Visualize
l. Skim/scan	**4. Writing Purposes**
m. GIST	a. To inform
3. Summarize	b. To explain
4. Text Forms of Expository Writing	c. To describe
a. Paragraphs	d. To discuss
b. Historical fiction	e. To analyze
c. Editorials	f. To trace
d. Articles	
e. Manuals	
f. Textbooks (science, history/social science)	
g. Encyclopedias	
h. Informational poetry	
i. Maps	
j. Diagrams	
k. Auto/biography	

Source: Summary of 2-week focus in third grade on expository text, by K. Kinsella and S. Harvey. Adapted and compiled by K. Quiocho, Edge Lake Elementary School.

TABLE 7.4   Challenging Language Areas for ELLs at Edge Lake School

Language Area	What Students Must Know and Understand	Features of a Syntactical Miscue
Phonology	Recognize that letters have associated sounds and be able to pronounce, blend, and segment those sounds to decode unknown words.	• Difficulty in pronouncing words. • Correspond unknown sound to letter. • Problems segmenting or building words. • Beginning, middle, or end difficulty in decoding words.
Syntax	Understand the correct structure of either written or spoken language and understand when language is structured incorrectly.	• Substituting a word that distracts from the meaning. • Incorrect structure of spoken or written language. • Problems using language conventions (periods, commas, etc.) in either reading or written work. • Lack of sentence variations. • Inability to regulate reading rate for the purpose of clarity. • Misuse of prosody in speech or oral reading.
Semantics	Attach words to meaning or concepts, and understand that meaning varies from concrete to abstract.	• Reading words fluently, but experiencing difficulty in defining meaning. • Not using context to infer meaning. • Inability to restate or retell. • Difficulty inserting new words into text.
Morphology	Recognize that words are built on meaningful units that are sometimes alone, but often appear in combination with other units (suffixes, prefixes, roots, onsets, rimes, blends, diagraphs, diphthongs, etc.).	• Not recognizing a word when it is seen in a different text or print. • Difficulty in analyzing a word attached to an affix, root, contraction, etc. • Unable to chunk longer words and make sense of text.
Pragmatics	Understand that language is derived from social context and is determined by a function of interaction, literary context, or situation based on background knowledge of the context.	• Not using background knowledge to comprehend text. Difficulty in clarifying messages related to contextual meaning. Unable to state differing viewpoints or determine a reading purpose.

Understanding the Role of Assessment

Using ongoing assessment, the teachers at Edge Lake identified common miscues across grade levels. In addition to state language and achievement assessments, teachers used observational checklists, anecdotal records, and student writing samples to guide their instruction. Table 7.4 identifies the specific language areas that were challenging for ELLs at Edge Lake School.

Once teachers identified "trouble spots" in language use, they met to *backward plan* their instruction to target student needs and work toward success. They used the following lesson plans as models from which to build their own unit plans. In these lesson plans, the letters that precede a skill refer to the ELLs' language proficiency level according to the CELDT. The levels are as follows: B = Beginner, EI = Early Intermediate, I = Intermediate, EA = Early Advanced, and A = Advanced.

LESSON 7.1 | # First-Grade Model Lesson

Working Backwards for Differentiation

Purpose of This Lesson Model
- To look at backwards planning to ensure differentiation for ELLs
- To base planning on California Reading and Language Arts Content Area Standards
- To base planning on ELD Standards

Standards Addressed in This Model Lesson
2.1: Reading Comprehension
Identify text that uses sequence or other logical order.
2.3: Follow one-step written directions.
ELD:B: Understand and follow one-step directions for classroom or work-related activities.
EI: Understand and follow simple two-step directions for classroom or work-related activities.
I: Understand and follow multi-step directions for classroom-related activities.

Consider the Following
1. Consider who your students are.
2. Consider what you want your students to learn.
3. Consider the content area in which students will be reading.

Give careful consideration to the materials used to ensure that the focus is on teaching content as well as meeting the requirements of the standards.

Sample Lesson

Concept to Be Learned: That all of life has some kind of pattern for order, and we can see that order in books and stories.

Materials—Books at a Variety of Reading Levels
- Williams, S. (1997). *I Went Walking.* Beginning
- Ancona, G. (1993). *Getting Together.* Beginning
- Castro, E., Flores, B., and Hernandez, E. (1997). *La Tostada.* Beginning

Before Instructing
1. Once you have considered who your students are and what you want to teach them, you will need to look at any *assessments* you have given students (required assessments as well as assessments you have chosen to administer because the assigned assessments did not give you clear information about students).
2. Select a variety of *materials* at different reading levels to ensure that students will be able to comprehend the texts.
3. Decide how you will present the concept to the class through shared reading, and how you will break students into smaller groups to ensure support for ELLs.
4. Describe the product or performance you will use to assess understanding at the end of the lesson. Remember that you will be checking for understanding throughout the lesson.

Preparing Students for the Lesson
1. Tell students what they will be learning and refer to this major concept throughout the lesson, especially when you check for comprehension. Write what they will be learning on a piece of paper and ask them to read it with you. Then ask students if they can remember what the lesson is going to be about.

2. Write the standards on a flip chart in simple terms, tell the students what they will be expected to do, and refer to the standards throughout the lesson.
3. Prepare a display of the materials that includes books, poems, pictures, and art taken from various sources that have a clear sequential pattern. Give children time to look through the materials with a partner.
   - *Scaffold.* Pay attention to how you pair students. You should pair a beginner with an early intermediate or intermediate student. You can pair early intermediates with early advanced and advanced students with EO students. If you decide to pair EO students with ELLs, you need to train the EO students not to do the work for the ELLs. The rationale for pairing students is that one is a little more proficient in English than the other. *There may be EO students who are only a little more proficient in English than the early intermediate or early advanced ELLs, and you can pair them with those students. Remember that grouping for the purpose of learning content should not be random until the students in the class have learned how to support other students' learning rather than enable students who need support.*
4. Give students a purpose for browsing. Tell them you want them to look closely at the art, pictures, and texts to get an idea about the importance of the topic of the book.
   - *Scaffold.* Before students browse in pairs, you will need to help them understand what it means to browse with another person. You will need to generate some questions for them to ask each other about what it is each of them sees in the materials as they browse. Examples of questions are: What do you see? What do you think about this? Write down their questions and comments to use as shared reading of ideas throughout the lesson.
5. Now that students have had time to build and/or activate background knowledge, you should leave the information up on the walls for students to see and use. You are now ready to have students read in a shared reading format and then break students into different groups with different books to provide time for you to support beginners.

Teaching Comprehension According to the Standards

The content to which all learning will relate is how there is order in all things, and stories provide us one example. Students will be expected to follow one-, two-, or multi-step directions.

Analyze the tasks that come directly from the standards and resulting skills that are required. There are several tasks (what students have to do):

- Identify text that uses sequence or other logical order.
- Follow one-step written directions.
- ELD:B: Understand and follow one-step directions for classroom or work-related activities.
- EI: Understand and follow simple two-step directions for classroom or work-related activities.
- I: Understand and follow multi-step directions for classroom-related activities.

Skills and Sample Tasks Required to Master the Skills

Skills	Sample Tasks
Identify texts that use sequence or logical order.	Be able to keep track of first, second, etc.
Follow one-step directions and relate that to sequencing.	1. Be able to listen to directions. 2. Be able to act upon directions. 3. Know first, second, third, etc.
Follow two-step and/or multi-step directions.	Be able to keep track of what comes next while you are doing something else.

Once you have identified the tasks and the skills required to perform the tasks, go back to considering who your students are, their levels of language acquisition, what they can do, and what they can't do. Then decide on the scaffolds needed.

Shared Reading

Select a large book and do a shared reading lesson with the students.

- Use the brainstorming that previously occurred.
- Have students predict what they think will happen based on the pictures.
- Stop when you are halfway through the story and ask students to retell the events.
- Write those down.
- Complete the story and ask students to retell the rest of the story.
- Debrief with children and ask them what you have to do to sequence something.
- Have ELD students follow one-, two-, or multi-step directions. Directions could be, "Come and point to . . ." "Point to . . . . and . . ." etc.

Small Group Guided Reading

For students who can follow multiple directions, do a guided reading lesson with one of the texts. Focus on the skills delineated in the standards.

Link an Activity to the Story

For example, read the story *La Tostada*. Then have children build a tostada following the directions given in the book.

Assessment

Read an unfamiliar story to the students and have them retell the story. You can do this in pairs.

Have ELD students follow one-, two-, and multi-step directions by finding items in a story or anything that is connected to their learning and can be completed step by step as well as in multiple steps.

You are actually assessing the standards as you complete these assessment tasks.

| LESSON 7.2 | **Third-Grade Model Lesson** |

Working Backwards for Differentiation

Purpose of this Lesson Model

- To look at backwards planning to ensure differentiation
- To base planning on California Reading and Language Arts Content Area Standards
- To base planning on ELD Standards

Standards Addressed in This Model Lesson

2.4: Comprehension and Analysis of Grade Level Appropriate Text
   Recall major points in the text and make and modify predictions about forthcoming information.
2.5: Distinguish the main idea and supporting details in expository text.
ELD:B: Identify the main idea in a story read aloud using key words and/or phrases.

EI:Read and orally identify the main ideas and use them to draw inferences about written text using simple sentences.

I:Read and use detailed sentences to orally identify main ideas and use them to make predictions and provide supporting details for predictions made.

EA: Describe the main ideas and supporting details of a text.

A: Describe main ideas and supporting details, including supporting evidence.

Consider the Following

1. Consider who your students are.
2. Consider what you want your students to learn.
3. Consider the content area in which students will be reading.
4. Give careful consideration to the materials used.

Sample Lesson

Content: Science (as written in a variety of texts)

Concept: Corn is important in the lives of many people, because it provides food as well as other materials for existence.

Materials—Books at a Variety of Levels

- Aliki. (1976). *Corn Is Maize: The Gift of the Indians.* Early Advanced, Advanced, English Only
- Soto, G., and Martinez, E. (1993). *Too Many Tamales.* Early Intermediate, Intermediate
- Paulsen, G. (1995). *The Tortilla Factory.* Beginning
- Other expository texts and materials available from the school library on corn as a crop, product, or resource. Look for art prints as well as videos about corn.

Before Instructing

1. Once you have considered who your students are and what you want to teach them, you will need to look at any *assessments* you have given students (required assessments as well as assessments you have chosen to administer because the assigned assessments did not give you clear information about students).
2. Select a variety of *materials* at different reading levels to ensure that students will be able to comprehend the texts.
3. Decide how you will present the concept to the class, and how you will break students into smaller groups to ensure support.
4. Describe the product or performance you will use to assess understanding at the end of the lesson. Remember that you will be checking for understanding throughout the lesson.

Preparing Students for the Lesson

1. Tell/write down the major concept of the lesson—what students will be learning—and refer to this major concept throughout the lesson, especially when you check for comprehension.
2. Write the standards on the board, tell the students what they will be expected to do, and refer to the standards throughout the lesson.
3. Prepare a display of resources that includes books, poems, pictures, and art taken from various materials/genres about corn. Tell students they should browse through the materials with a friend.
    - *Scaffold.* Pay attention to how you pair students. You should pair a beginner with an early intermediate or intermediate student. You can pair early intermediates with early advanced and advanced students with EO students. If you decide to pair EO students with ELLs, you need to train the EO students not to do the work for the ELLs. The rationale for pairing students is that one is a little more proficient in English than the other. *There may be EO*

students who are only a little more proficient in English than the early intermediate or early advanced ELLs, and you can pair them with those students. Remember that grouping for the purpose of learning content should not be random until the students in the class have learned how to support other students' learning rather than enable students who need support.

4. Give students a purpose for browsing. Tell them you want them to look closely at the art, pictures, and texts to get an idea about the importance of corn. Students are encouraged to write down any questions they might have about the use of corn in the United States or in the world. Students should have a notepad so they can jot down what they see in the language that is easiest for them. One of the partners needs to take notes.
   - *Scaffold.* Before students browse in pairs, you will need to help them understand what it means to browse with another person. You will need to generate some questions for them to ask each other about what it is each sees in the pictures, etc. Examples of questions are: What do you see? What do you think about this? I wonder if everyone around the world eats corn. What do you think? Shall we write it down as a question?

5. Have students share their observations in small groups where a recorder writes down the group members' ideas (each idea has to be novel or different).
   - *Scaffold.* Before students get into small groups, remind them about how they work with each other. EO students should be taught not to enable the ELLs to remain silent by dominating the conversation. Have a reliable student make sure that each student or pair of students gets to talk. If you have been careful about the pairing, beginning ELLs will be learning more language while they are listening to others share.
   - Be sure to label objects in pictures for beginners and early intermediate students. They will need additional reference points while they learn the language as well as the content of the lesson.

6. Have class members then do a carousel read of each others' ideas where students walk around the room in the same pairs they were in previously and read the posters of other groups. As each pair encounters new ideas, they may add the ideas to their lists on which they originally jotted down ideas.

7. Next, show students short clips of movies about corn as a crop and what happens to corn after it is harvested. Once again, give students a purpose for viewing the clips: to gather new/more information about how corn is important in the lives of people around the world. Show a portion of the clip(s). STOP. Let students discuss what they saw and add to the information they are gathering. Show a short clip. STOP. Etc.

8. Then, have students get back in their original small groups and have them add more information to their original lists.

9. Now that students have had time to build and/or activate background knowledge, you should leave the information up on the walls for students to see and use and have students keep their lists ready and available for reference. You are now ready to have students read in different groups with different books about the importance of corn in the lives of many people around the world.

Teaching Comprehension According to the Standards

The content to which all learning will relate is the importance of corn in the lives of many people because of the resources it provides.

The standards for the lesson that should be emphasized throughout the lesson, in every task students do, are the following:

1. Recall major points in the text and make and modify predictions about forthcoming information.
2. Distinguish the main idea and supporting details in expository text.

Analyze the tasks that come directly from the standards and resulting skills that are required. There are several tasks (what students have to do):

- Recall factual information.
- Record the facts so they won't be forgotten.
- Make predictions and be able to say why the prediction(s) is/are being made.
- Sort through ideas presented in text.
- Prioritize ideas presented in text.
- Identify sorted ideas as being main ideas or supporting details.
- Make inferences about what is read.

Skills and Sample Tasks Required to Master the Skills

Skills	Sample Tasks
Recall factual information.	1. Remember what is happening in text sequentially. 2. Be able to sequence events.
Record facts as they are recalled and clarified.	1. Know how to clarify your thinking as you state that a fact is important. 2. Know which facts to record.
Make predictions.	1. Be able to make predictions. 2. Write predictions down. 3. Read text in chunks. 4. Go back and check predictions. 5. Make new predictions. 6. Provide rationale for predictions. 7. Check predictions, etc.
Sort ideas that are presented in the text and prioritize as well as classify ideas.	1. Analyze and synthesize ideas. 2. Be able to sort through ideas. 3. Be able to prioritize ideas. 4. Classify ideas.
Make inferences about what is read.	1. Draw conclusions about what will come next based on what has come before. 2. Use information from a variety of sources to draw conclusions.

Once you have identified the tasks and the skills required to perform the tasks, go back to considering who your students are, their levels of language acquisition, what they can do, and what they can't do. Then decide on the scaffolds needed.

Some Examples of Scaffolds You Might Consider

1. *Direct teaching of beginning students and early intermediates.* Model how you make sense of the text you have assigned to them. Remind them to use their lists and to refer to the labels you have placed on pictures, objects, etc.
   - *Scaffold.* Map out student understandings pictorially using a pictomap. Label the objects, people, etc., in the pictomap. Use arrows to show relationships as well as sequence of events.
2. Call students' attention to unfamiliar words. If the words are related to words students might already know in their primary language (e.g., cognates in Spanish), refer to those

words to help them make connections between unfamiliar words and words/concepts they already know in their LI but are unable to communicate in L2.

3. Model in a small group, such as a guided reading lesson. Teach students Directed Reading Thinking Activity (DRTA). This is where students make predictions using all the skills they have applied in the scaffold above, read a small section of the text, check predictions made, delete predictions they think are not feasible after the reading, make new predictions, or change any predictions they have already made.
   - **Scaffold.** To help students remember which of their predictions have been validated through reading the text, write them on a chart for future reference. Use chart paper and not the blackboard, which you have to erase. The good thing about using chart paper is that it can be saved and referred to as a collective memory of things the class has studied. Then you can use the chart paper in future lessons to serve as a reminder of previous content.

4. Pair students—one more proficient than the other. Have students read small chunks of the assigned text. One reads while the other follows along. The listener asks the reader questions about what he or she has read.
   - **Scaffold.** You must model for students how to distinguish between main ideas and supporting details. *Too Many Tamales* and *Corn Is Maize* are perfect books for modeling this process. Using the scaffold above, have students record the main ideas and supporting details they have identified.

5. Once students begin to ask questions, the pair clarifies the meaning of the chunk of text and writes the meaning down. Next, students will classify the meanings they have clarified as either a main idea and integral to the story OR a supporting detail and one that provides more elaboration or explanation for the reader.
   - **Scaffold.** If you want students to be able to sequence the events in a story, you must explicitly model the process. The perfect place to do this is in guided reading groups where you can help students make connections between all of the skills they have learned thus far: activating background knowledge, making and checking predictions, sorting through text for main ideas and supporting details.

6. Another task to be assigned to each pair is to make inferences about what they have read.
   - **Scaffold.** Once again you must model this process and allow students enough time to practice under your supervision so they understand how to make inferences. Inferential comprehension is tested annually on standardized tests beginning in the second grade, and results show that it is a very weak area, especially with expository texts. Therefore, it is imperative that you model the process of inferring with real text, the texts you are having students read to understand the importance of the concept of the lesson being taught. Model and reinforce understanding in guided reading groups. Allow students enough time to sort through information in pairs so when they draw conclusions and make inferences, they will be able to say why, using words, phrases, and sentences from the text to support their reasoning.

7. **Paired reading.** In paired reading, students read together. However, they should read small chunks of text and talk about predictions they can make, main ideas and supporting details selected, sequencing of events, and inferences made.
   - **Scaffold.** If you want students to read in pairs and focus on the text (its content and not other things), you need to model, teach, and monitor the process.

8. **Reading.** Decide how you want students to read the books, using the scaffold listed above. *Round robin reading is NEVER appropriate for ELLs.* Round robin reading often raises ELLs' affective filters (Krashen, 2005) and focuses their attention on pronunciation to the

detriment of comprehending text. Students can read aloud to you as they sit with you, one on one, where you can scaffold their reading by modeling a think aloud. This is especially effective with a struggling reader.

- ***Scaffold.*** Sit with an individual student. Tell the student that you are going to think aloud as you read a small section of the text. The purpose of this scaffold is for them to do the same with you. That way you can think about how to make sense from text. Read a short chunk of text and share with the student how you make sense. Next, have the student try it and give corrective feedback. Continue the process until you are sure that the student has been able to make sense of the text.

Even in guided reading groups, students can read in pairs. The important thing to do in guided reading groups is to teach the strategy and show students how the strategy will help them meet the goal of the lesson and the standards.

With beginning students you will have to walk them through *The Tortilla Factory,* using the pictures and referring to what they found out about corn and its importance with their partners during the prereading phase. Also, bring in realia such as corn on the cob, products that use corn such as tortillas, cereal, etc.

Refer to the levels of the books and the classroom model. Be sure to have students read in chunks and check for comprehension throughout the reading. Emphasize the focus of the lesson throughout all tasks students do: identifying main ideas, using content to arrive at word meanings, and making connections between texts, between text and the brainstorming, and text to self (their own experiences).

Assessment

ELLs should be able to do the following if you have taught them the skills and scaffolded the learning, all the while checking for understanding.

ELD:B: Identify the main idea in a story read aloud using key words and/or phrases.
    EI: Read and orally identify the main ideas and use them to draw inferences about the written text using simple sentences.
     I: Read and use detailed sentences to orally identify main ideas and use them to make predictions and provide supporting details for predictions made.
    EA: Describe the main ideas and supporting details of a text.
     A: Describe main ideas and supporting details, including supporting evidence.

EO students should also be able to:

1. Recall major points in the text and make and modify predictions about forthcoming information.
2. Distinguish the main idea and supporting details in expository text.

You can assess these skills by having students take an unfamiliar text and demonstrate how they would identify major points in the text, make predictions before they read, modify predictions during the reading, and distinguish between main idea and supporting details.

Students should demonstrate these skills to you in pairs while you take anecdotal notes or audiotape the authentic assessment. This can be followed up with a piece of writing such as a letter to the editor of the local newspaper telling him or her how important it is for students to have these skills and how the skills work.

Reading should be linked to writing whenever possible. The writing can be the independent assessment piece after students demonstrate in pairs (another assessment) how they have learned to transfer the skills from one text to another.

It is important to teach for transfer and keep revisiting skills and strategies students have learned. You need to remind students about what they have learned and remind them to use the strategies and skills when they read other materials. Otherwise all of the work can be for nothing.

LESSON 7.3 | Sixth-Grade Model Lesson

Working Backwards for Differentiation

Purpose of This Lesson Model
- To look at backwards planning to ensure differentiation
- To base planning on California Reading and Language Arts Content Area Standards
- To base planning on ELD Standards

Standards Addressed in This Model Lesson

1.4: Vocabulary and Concept Development
   Monitor expository text for unknown words or words with novel meanings by using word, sentence, and paragraph clues to determine meaning.

ELD:B: Read aloud simple words presented in literature and content area texts; demonstrate comprehension by using one or two words or simple sentence responses.

EI: Read simple paragraphs and passages independently.

I: Use knowledge of English morphemes, phonics, and syntax to decode written texts.

EA: Use knowledge of English morphemes, phonics, and syntax to decode and interpret the meaning of unfamiliar words.

2.3: Comprehension and Analysis of Grade Level Appropriate Text
   Connect and clarify main ideas by identifying their relationships to other sources and related topics

ELD:B: Read and orally respond to simple text by answering factual comprehension questions using key words or phrases.

EI: Read and orally respond to simple literary texts and content area texts by answering factual comprehension questions using key words or phrases.

I: Read and use detailed sentences to orally respond to literature by answering factual comprehension questions.

Who Are the Students? Students at the beginning level, early intermediate, intermediate, early advanced, and advanced as well as EO students.

What Do I Want Them to Learn? *(Concept)* Rivers are necessary for all humankind and animals to survive.

Sample Lesson

Content Areas: Social Studies, Reading, and Language Arts

Materials—Books at a Variety of Reading Levels
- Halpern, S. (1992). *My River.* Beginning
- Diaz, K. (1997). *Bringing Water to People.* Early Intermediate
- Diaz, K. (1997). *Nos Traen.* Advanced in Spanish

- Sigue, J. (1997). *The River Is My Life.* Intermediate
- Sigue, J., and Dorantes, R. (1997). *The Rio es Mi Vida.* Intermediate in Spanish
- Nikola-Lisa, W. (1997). *America My Land, Your Land, Our Land.* All levels, Art
- Miller, W. (1997). *A House by the River.* Early Advanced
- Avila, A. (1994). *Mexican Ghost Tales of the Southwest.* For storytelling, Intermediate
- Keller, H. (1994). *Grandfather's Dream.* Early Intermediate
- Cherry, L. (1992). *A River Ran Wild.* Intermediate/Early Advanced
- Pictures of rivers, videos of rivers, art of rivers
- Alarcón, F.X. (1998). *From the Bellybutton of the Moon and Other Summer Poems.* Beginning
- Grade level social studies textbooks (information about rivers and their tributaries)

Before Instructing

1. Once you have considered who your students are and what you want to teach them, you will need to look at any *assessments* you have given students (required assessments as well as assessments you have chosen to administer because the assigned assessments did not give you clear information about students).
2. Select a variety of *materials* at different reading levels to ensure that students will be able to comprehend the texts.
3. Decide how you will present the concept to the class, and how you will break students into smaller groups to ensure support.
4. Describe the product or performance you will use to assess understanding at the end of the lesson. Remember that you will be checking understanding throughout the lesson.

Preparing Students for the Lesson

1. Tell/write down the major concept of the lesson—what students will be learning—and refer to this major concept throughout the lesson, especially when you check for comprehension.
2. Write the standards on the board, tell the students what they will be expected to do, and refer to the standards throughout the lesson.
3. Prepare a display of the materials that includes books, poems, pictures, and art taken from various materials about rivers. Tell students they should browse through the materials with a friend or in pairs.
   - *Scaffold.* Pay attention to how you pair students. You should pair a beginner with an early intermediate or intermediate student. You can pair early intermediates with early advanced and advanced students with EO students. If you decide to pair EO students with ELLs, you need to train the EO students not to do the work for the ELLs. The rationale for pairing students is that one is a little more proficient in English than the other. *There may be EO students who are only a little more proficient in English than the early intermediate or early advanced ELLs, and you can pair them with those students. Remember that grouping for the purpose of learning content should not be random until the students in the class have learned how to support other students' learning rather than enable students who need support to remain silent.*
4. Give students a purpose for browsing. Tell them you want them to look closely at the art, pictures, and texts to get an idea about what happens around rivers. Students are encouraged to write down any questions they might have about rivers in the United States or in the world. Students should have paper and pencil so they can jot down what they see in the language that is easiest for them. One of the partners needs to take notes.
   - *Scaffold.* Before students browse in pairs, you will need to help them understand what it means to browse with another person. You will need to generate some questions for them to ask each other about what it is each sees in the pictures, etc. Examples of questions are: What do you see? What do you think about this? I wonder if this happens on rivers around the world. What do you think? Shall we write it down as a question?

5. Have students share their observations in small groups where a recorder writes down the ideas of the group (each idea has to be novel or different).
    - ***Scaffold.*** Before students get into small groups, remind them about how they work with each other. EO students should have been taught not to enable ELLs to remain silent by dominating the conversation. Have a reliable student make sure that each student or pair of students gets to talk. If you have been careful about the pairing, beginning ELLs will be learning more language while they are listening to others share.
    - Be sure to label objects in pictures for beginners and early advanced students. They will need additional reference points while they learn the language as well as the content of the lesson.
6. Have class members then do a carousel read of each other's ideas where students walk around the room in the same pairs they were in previously and read the posters of other groups. As each pair encounters new ideas, they may add the ideas to the lists on which they originally jotted down ideas.
7. Next, show students short movie clips about rivers and how they affect the lives of people and animals. Once again, give students a purpose for viewing the clips: to gather new/more information about rivers and how they affect the lives of people and animals. Show a portion of the clip(s). STOP. Let students discuss what they saw and add to the information they are gathering. Show a short clip. STOP. Etc.
8. Then, have students get back in their original small groups (if you are using them) and have them add more information to their original lists.
9. Now that students have had time to build and/or activate background knowledge, you should leave the information up on the walls for students to see and use and have students keep their lists ready and available for reference. You are now ready to have students read in different groups with different books about how rivers affect the lives of humans and animals.

Teaching Comprehension According to the Standards

The content to which all learning will relate is how rivers affect the lives of humans and animals.

The comprehension skill to be taught is *to connect and clarify main ideas* (in the various readings about rivers) by *identifying their relationships to other sources and related topics.* While students are reading text, they will have to *monitor expository text for unknown words or words with novel meanings by using word, sentence, and paragraph clues* to determine meaning.

Analyze the tasks and skills required. There are several tasks (what students have to do):

- Connect and clarify main ideas in the reading.
- Identify the relationships of the main ideas to other sources and topics.
- Monitor texts for unknown words.
- Use context (word, sentence, paragraph) clues to determine meaning.

Skills and Sample Tasks Required to Master the Skills

Skills	Sample Tasks
Clarify main ideas.	1. Be able to sort through information. 2. Decide what you need in terms of making sense. 3. Decide what you don't need to pay attention to. 4. Discuss the meaning with a partner or understand the importance of each main idea. 5. ELD: Be able to retell facts. 6. ELD: Use key words, phrases, etc., to retell facts.

(continued)

(continued)

Connect main ideas.	1. Be aware of the concept of main idea. 2. Mark down what is important to the concept while reading. 3. Check notes/lists/charts for connections to ideas that were generated during prereading activities. 4. Be able to explain connections that were made using examples (citing words, phrases, sentences) from ideas gathered from video clips, art, etc., as well as personal experiences.
Monitor/identify unknown words.	1. Be able to identify a word as unknown in terms of meaning. 2. Be able to use context to draw conclusions about possible meanings of unknown words.

Once you have identified the tasks and the skills required to perform the tasks, go back to considering who your students are, their levels of language acquisition, what they can do, and what they can't do. Then decide on the scaffolds needed.

Some Examples of Scaffolds You Might Consider

1. *Direct instruction for beginning and early intermediate ELLs.* Model how you make sense of the assigned text. Remind them to use their lists and to refer to the labels you have placed on pictures, objects, etc.
   * *Scaffold.* Map out the students' understandings pictorially using a pictomap. Label the objects, people, etc., in the pictomap. Use arrows to show relationships as well as sequence of events.
2. Call students' attention to unfamiliar words. If the words are related to words students might already know in their first language (e.g., cognates in Spanish), refer to those words to help them make connections between unfamiliar words and words/concepts they already know in their L1 but are unable to communicate in L2.
3. Pair students—one more proficient than the other. Have students read small chunks of the assigned text. One reads while the other follows along. The listener asks the reader questions about what he or she has read.
   * *Scaffold.* If you want students to ask each other questions, you must teach them the types of questions to ask. You will want to teach them about literal questions and inferential questions. Model with students by first showing them how the questioning process works. Then have them try it with a partner. Debrief after you model and students try the process to ensure that they can question independently.
4. Once students begin to ask questions, the pair clarifies the meaning of the chunk of text and writes the meaning down. Next, students note relationships between what they have read and the information gathered during prereading. They can confirm what they have learned previously (or question) and make lists of those relationships as well as other relationships to experiences in their personal lives. Students should use words, phrases, etc., as elaboration and ways to explain connections made.
   * *Scaffold.* If you want students to draw relationships to the prereading activities as well as to other experiences, you will have to teach them how to do this. You may model, have students try with a partner or small group, debrief, give feedback, model again, etc.
5. Another task for each pair would be to make a list of unfamiliar words. Together, the partners can use words, phrases, etc., to arrive at the meaning of unfamiliar words.
   * *Scaffold.* Once again you must model this process and allow students enough time to practice under your supervision so they understand how to use contextual clues.
6. *Paired reading.* In paired reading, students read together. However, they should read small chunks of text and talk about what they think the text means as well as make connections

to other texts, to self, to the world, to what they have done as a group in the prereading phase of the lesson.

- *Scaffold.* If you want students to read in pairs and focus on the text (its content and not other things), you need to model, teach, and monitor the process.

7. *Reading.* Decide how you want students to read the books, using the scaffold listed above. Round robin reading is NEVER appropriate. Students can read aloud to you as they sit with you, one on one, where you can scaffold their reading by modeling a think aloud. You would do this with a struggling student.

- *Scaffold.* In a think aloud, you sit with an individual student to model the process so that she or he will also be able to think aloud. Tell the student that you are going to think aloud as you read a small section of the text. Read a short chunk of text and share with the student how you make sense. Next, have the student try it and give corrective feedback. Continue the process until you are sure that the student has been able to make sense of the text.

  Refer to the levels of the books and the classroom model. Be sure to have students read in chunks and check for comprehension throughout the reading. Emphasize the focus on identifying main ideas, using content to arrive at word meanings, and making connections between texts, between text and the brainstorming, and text to self (their own experiences).

Assessment

Decide how you will assess student learning at the end of the lesson. Here are a few authentic assessments:

Beginning: Refer to the standard for beginning students. They should be able to do a simple retelling of a story and use words, phrases, and sentences as factual information to support their retellings.

Early Intermediate/Intermediate: Students should be able to produce a map or graphic organizer as a group of what they have read. Using the organizer they should be able to write a compilation of the main ideas of what they have read. They should also be able to demonstrate (either in writing or orally) how they were able to find the meanings of unfamiliar words.

Lessons Learned

This chapter presented a process for addressing the curriculum needs of ELLs in reading and language arts. We based the contents on the work of a group of teachers in kindergarten through fifth grade. The process included the alignment of materials used with students, a close look at standards, and a review of how instruction and scaffolding student needs as they learned would support meeting standards. All planning was done with the needs of students and meeting state standards in mind.

The work of the teachers at Edge Lake demonstrates that teachers need to collaborate with others at their grade levels and across all grade levels at a school whenever possible. The work also shows that collaborative planning can lead to efficient teaching and assessment. Their work further demonstrates that dialogue must focus on student strengths and how reflective teaching can result in a focus on best practices and positive achievement for all students.

Practical Applications and Individual Inquiries: Cases to Think About and Investigate

1. Visit a school and interview the schoolwide reading coach or resource teacher. Find out if there is a state assessment process in place and how the results of that process assess standards and inform teacher instruction.

2. Interview a teacher. Find out whether the school has been engaged in the change process to improve literacy achievement of all students. Find out what that plan is and whether it has been successful.

3. Observe a reading lesson in a classroom. Note the grade level. Look at standards that should be taught at that grade level. Note whether the standards are being taught, which standards are being taught, and how they are being taught.

You Mean I Have to Scaffold the Scaffolds? Learning from Myra and Roberto

I have all these thoughts whirling around inside me. My teacher helps me get them out. I talk about them and she helps me write my ideas down. It's hard. Pero [but], I know she always see me and help me.

Roberto, grade 4

One of the critical issues that we have presented thus far is that *scaffolding is important* in differentiating literacy instruction for ELLs to ensure access to the curriculum at all levels. But sometimes scaffolding, such as preteaching vocabulary, providing extralinguistic clues, or even using the primary language for support is not quite enough to make content accessible for all students. In this chapter, we look beyond basic scaffolding to what we call *scaffolding the scaffolds.* Scaffolding the scaffolds involves going beyond traditional support mechanisms to use things that students know, or don't know, about language to promote deep understanding of both language and content. In this chapter, we present the concept of scaffolding the scaffolds through the work and the academic lives of two students at Edge Lake School, Roberto and Myra. Although both students are ELLs, all instruction in their class happens in English. But, as documented in Chapter 7, teachers use their primary language, in this case Spanish, to clarify the meaning of directions, to make connections between English vocabulary and Spanish cognates or words that mean the same in both languages, and to scaffold newcomers to the school culture and community. In this chapter, we will:

- Describe the learning contexts for Roberto and Myra.
- Demonstrate how their teachers scaffold the scaffolds for both of them.

- Analyze the instructional strategies used and the support provided by their classroom teachers through the work that Roberto and Myra do in class.
- Show how the process of scaffolding the scaffolds helps ELLs gain access to the curriculum.

Building Background Knowledge About Scaffolding the Scaffolds

When teachers plan instruction for ELLs, they need to take into account a variety of things, including the students' prior knowledge and their English proficiency levels. Furthermore, teachers themselves need a wide range of competencies, including content, linguistic, and teaching knowledge to best provide instruction for their students (Dutro & Moran, 2003). Fillmore and Snow (2002) argue that teachers need a great deal of knowledge about language acquisition and development, among other things, to effectively instruct ELLs. Teachers also need "a focused approach to teaching language in every classroom, in every subject area" (Dutro & Moran, 2003, p. 227).

We know that when ELLs have opportunities to learn language in rich, integrated settings, they are most likely to be successful (Flores, Cousin, & Díaz, 1998). Within these settings, it is up to the teacher to adapt her or his instruction to include practices that promote success. García (2003) recommends a variety of instructional practices that support ELLs through literacy learning, including flexible grouping, inquiry-based learning, explicit instruction on language differences and rhetorical conventions, thematic instruction, and teaching for transfer.

To ensure that these instructional practices promote success for ELLs, we need to scaffold instruction to make it accessible to students. We often use the concept of scaffolding student instruction to discuss meeting the needs of all students in the classroom. When it comes to examining the process of scaffolding the reading, language development, and writing for ELLs, we tend to propose an instructional model that works in theory but is not used consistently by classroom teachers. For example, in some classrooms, scaffolding student learning for ELLs means that teachers lower their expectations for them and they do not receive instruction in grade level content. Instead, their school day consists of worksheet activities and decodable texts with content that may be of little interest to students, or teachers use ELD strategies based primarily on the need to meet state or district standards without regard to the linguistic and instructional needs of the students. If teachers are to provide effective instruction in a rich, integrated environment, they instead need to provide scaffolded instruction based on student needs.

Scaffolding Student Learning

The process of scaffolding student learning is generally attributed to Wood, Bruner, and Ross (1976). It was used to characterize mothers' verbal interactions with their children when reading a picture book (Graves & Fitzgerald, 2003). The purpose for the scaffolding was to enable a child to solve a problem, address a task, complete a task, or achieve a goal.

What Woods and his colleagues found was that mothers did not simply tell the child the answer or the solution or define the goal but rather created an instructional scaffold designed to teach and assist the child in learning. Mothers gradually released control of the learning process to the child. Thus, mothers were really supporting the process of learning and mastery in that they provided as much support for their children as frequently as needed to ensure that they could complete the task independently.

This notion of scaffolding holds true in language and literacy instruction. Boyle and Peregoy (1998) describe scaffolding in language acquisition as "special ways adults may elaborate and expand upon children's early attempts to use language" (p. 150) and argue that these adults then serve as experts who help children go beyond what they might be able to do alone. It is important to note that in language and literacy instruction, as it is in all instruction, scaffolding is temporary. An adult works with children in the zone of proximal development (Vygotsy, 1978), a space or a place in the learning process where a child requires the guidance of an adult or more experienced peer who can create individual instructional supports. With support, the child can reach his or her goal, solve a problem, or complete a task. Intrinsic to this level of understanding is instruction that results from ongoing assessment and knowledge of reading processes as well as levels of scaffolds needed to shift student learning to a higher level within their instructional zone.

Scaffolds should not be selected at random but rather are specifically designed to support student learning at a given point in time. Teachers must not only attempt to select scaffolds that are appropriate to the task and the student, but also make efforts to keep the content challenging for the student, yet still accessible. Rather than provide low levels of support or "water down" the curriculum (Au, 1998), teachers who work effectively with ELLs provide challenging curriculum with adequate scaffolds that they withdraw gradually, based on ongoing evaluation of student needs and strengths. For language and literacy instruction, scaffolds should be tied to reading and writing activities that are authentic and functional, provide opportunities for students to engage with predictable and patterned text, model proficient language and literacy skills, and support comprehension (Boyle & Peregoy, 1998).

Linking Theory to Practice

This chapter is once again situated in the context of Edge Lake School. In Chapter 7, we discussed how the staff members at Edge Lake engaged in schoolwide reform surrounding effective literacy practices. We gave examples of how they moved through the reform process to plan successful literacy experiences for ELLs and all students. In this chapter, we take a closer look at how teachers presented two ELLs, Myra and Roberto, with opportunities to learn that facilitated their success. We explore the ongoing dance between teacher and student as they become co-learners and find ways to create bridges to connect prior knowledge with new learning. We examine the assessments used at the school as well successful scaffolds that take Myra and Roberto to a different level "helping them problem-solve with increasing independence on tasks that grow in difficulty" (Rodgers, 2000, p. 89).

As we explored the learning opportunities presented to Myra and Roberto at Edge Lake School, we saw an emphasis on teaching grade level content through conversation, strategic guided reading lessons, mini lessons, and extended discourse. We saw that authentic assessments used in reading and writing at the school made connections to students' lives, their primary language, and content. The teachers at Edge Lake focused on comprehension and higher order thinking skills that allowed students to engage in academically challenging activities and receive appropriate academic support through multiple techniques while learning grade level content. Teachers didn't disregard word work, including vocabulary development, but included it as a part of the balanced literacy program that emphasized comprehension. Literature is important at Edge Lake. Teachers have classroom libraries with a minimum of 300 literature books that are an integral part of the literacy program. Students have opportunities to receive instruction in guided reading along with time for independent reading. In the classrooms we observed, it was clear that students were happy and knew how to work collaboratively. Teachers genuinely liked their students. As Shulman (2003) notes in his taxonomy for learning, what is being learned [and taught] must be not only challenging but also fun.

Meet Myra and Roberto

Myra and Roberto are fourth-grade ELLs. Both Myra and Roberto speak Spanish at home. Their parents are native speakers of Spanish. Roberto immigrated to the United States as a beginning third grader and Myra arrived at the end of the third grade. As is current practice in California, they took the CELDT when they first arrived at Edge Lake School to determine their language proficiency levels (see Chapter 4 for a more complete description of English language proficiency assessment). After the initial screening, Roberto and Myra are retested each year to determine the rate of growth in English proficiency, that is, whether their reading, writing, listening, and speaking skills increased, decreased, or leveled off. Initial exam results are used to identify students as ELLs. Subsequent annual tests look at student progress and readiness for reclassification to fluent English proficient (California Department of Education, 2004).

    The CELDT measures listening, speaking, reading, and writing and reports the English proficiency level that each student has attained. Proficiency levels are reported for each skill on the exam and students are categorized into five levels: (1) beginning, (2) early intermediate, (3) intermediate, (4) early advanced, and (5) advanced. Each skill is scored on a scale of 1–5, with 5 being the highest. Individual skill scores are then compiled into the student's English proficiency level. Results of the test administered in the spring or the end of third grade reveal that Roberto received an overall score of 2 and Myra was classified as 1. Roberto's score includes a listening and speaking score of 3, a reading score of 2, and a writing score of 1. That means that Roberto would be categorized as an early intermediate ELL (2), an intermediate learner in listening and speaking (3), and a beginner in writing (1). Myra received an overall score of 1, placing her at the beginning level of English language acquisition. Her listening and speaking score was 1 (beginning level). She received a 2 in reading (early intermediate) and a 1 in writing (beginner).

    After Roberto and Myra were tested, their teachers (the classroom teacher and the literacy coach) at Edge Lake used the CELDT results to plan effective instruction that would help them to access the curriculum and learn content AND become more proficient in English. It is important to remember that, although Roberto and Myra were not completely proficient in English, their instruction was predominantly in English with some primary language support as needed. Therefore, it was up to teachers to scaffold the curriculum in

FIGURE 8.1 Examining Scaffolds in Place: An Observational Checklist

Instructional Components/Scaffolds	Classroom by Number					
	1	**2**	**3**	**4**	**5**	**Comments**
Manipulatives/models						
Charts/graphic organizers						
Teacher modeling						
Use of primary language						
Small-group instruction						
Peer teaching/coaching						
Activation of background knowledge						
Building of background knowledge						
Context use to support meaning						
Use of representative text to provide overview of content						
Metacognition or thinking aloud to model thinking						
Check for comprehension						
Use of reteaching when necessary as indicated by assessment						
Instructional conversations						
Shared/guided writing						
Interactive writing						
Drama/art						
Focus on syntax usage in a writing context						
Variety of genres of writing						

ways that promote content and language learning. The teachers first examined which scaffolds were currently being used effectively during instruction and whether other scaffolds, those that support or scaffold the scaffolds, were also being used that would serve to provide additional support to Myra and Roberto. The teachers turned the lenses on themselves and used an observational checklist to list and explore the scaffolds already in place. Figure 8.1 is an example of a scaffolding checklist that the teachers used with Myra and Roberto. As they examined their own practice, they used those scaffolds and supporting scaffolds to plan and implement instruction to meet both Roberto's and Myra's needs. The following planning charts show how teachers scaffolded instruction for both students (Tables 8.1 and 8.2).

TABLE 8.1 A Planning Chart for Differentiated Instruction for Roberto

Student Name	What I Know About Each Student	Grade Level	Skills Required	Necessary Scaffolds
Roberto	Primary language is Spanish. Assessment of proficiency in English places him as an early intermediate speaker of English. No assessment of proficiency in Spanish was administered.	Fourth grade	Metacognition. Model how to think about thinking and talk about it out loud.	Ask at least one or two metacognitive questions of Roberto throughout all lessons. Be sure to model for him and let him know that you are modeling so he can learn the language and the processes of metacognition.
	High frequency words are hard for him to remember.		Create a list of high frequency words, such as *a*, *an*, *to*, *for*, *in*, *around*, *the*, *that*, *this*, and show him how these words also function in Spanish.	Use language experience and point out to him how often high frequency words appear in oral language.
	Can decode words that are consistent.		Understand that not all words in English are decodable as they are in Spanish. Use contrastive analysis to demonstrate the differences.	Move him from decodable text to predictable text as an accompaniment to grade level text and grade level content.
	Substitutes vowel sounds in Spanish for vowel sounds in English.		Continue with contrastive analysis to demonstrate the difference in vowel sounds in both languages.	Develop pictorial symbols that go over the sounds the vowels make in Spanish and the sounds they make in English. Avoid stereotypical symbols.
	Enjoys drawing and poetry.		Write his own poetry about the content he is learning in class and add a drawing that "sells" his poem.	Have him copy favorite poems from books to understand the structures. Then, leave words out (CLOZE) for him to substitute and create his own poem, for example, in the same structure Robert Frost might use.
	Doesn't always comprehend what he reads as he focuses mainly on decoding.		Give him smaller chunks of text to read.	Use sketching as he reads to help him visualize. Have him use guiding questions as he reads: who, what, where, when, how, why. Have him work with a partner so he can stop after a small chunk, retell, decide on what text says in his own words and write it down.
	Is learning to be a risk taker.		Help him understand that learning comes from what we think are mistakes.	Share stories with him about famous people, preferably from his culture, who have made mistakes and turned them into successes.

TABLE 8.2 A Planning Chart for Differentiated Instruction for Myra

Student Name	What I Know About Each Student	Grade Level	Skills Required	Necessary Scaffolds
Myra	Spanish is her primary language. Assessment of English proficiency identifies her as a beginning speaker of English.	Fourth grade	Model metacognition for her, demonstrating how to talk about thinking and ask questions when one is not sure.	Always ask one metacognitive question of Myra after modeling one so she learns the language and the thinking.
	Very quiet and afraid to speak out. Relies on her friends to help her communicate.		Train a partner to work with Myra. Teach the student to wait and let her process language and ask questions when she is unable to find the words in English. Make sure the student doesn't do the work for Myra.	Provide Myra with visuals such as pictures and real objects of grade level content so she can observe, identify, and label (with her partner).
	Struggles with sight words.		Start with the high frequency words that are common in both languages, such as *a*, *an*, *one*, *to*, *for*, *from*, *at*, *around*, etc. Show her the words in English and in Spanish. Demonstrate that the high frequency words in Spanish are decodable but not in English so she must "see" them in her head.	Have Myra trace high frequency words in the air or on a cookie sheet covered with shaving cream. Then build the words with sponge letters or sand paper (vowels in one color and consonants in another). The tactile experience many times helps stimulate memory.
	Confuses the vowel sounds in Spanish with the vowel sounds in English.		Use contrastive analysis to demonstrate the differences between the sounds vowels make in Spanish and in English. Post these for Myra to easily refer to in her own personal dictionary, personal word wall, or on a board close to her desk.	Create symbols or use colors to designate the sounds the vowels make in Spanish as opposed to the sounds they make in English. Don't do too many at once.
	Focuses on decoding and not on comprehension.		Provide Myra with smaller chunks of text to process.	Have Myra work with a trained partner. They can read together using neurological impress. Stop at the end of a small chunk. Myra retells. The partner helps clarify meaning; Myra revisits the retelling and puts it in her own words. Write it down and proceed through text that way.
	Does not always have the background knowledge or experiences.		Provide experiences, pictures, and real objects to build background knowledge.	Be sure to name objects, events, people and label them. Ask either and/or questions so she can learn the names. Have her write down the names of events, objects, and people and later turn those into poems to scaffold the writing process for her.

Examples from the Field

Myra's Story

Myra's story is an interesting one that clearly demonstrates the benefits of creating an environment that supports ELLs, using scaffolds to support their language and literacy development. Myra's fourth-grade CELDT oral language score of 3 (intermediate) indicates that she is able to use present, past, and future tenses of speech in an appropriate manner. She is also expected to answer and generate who, what, where, when, why, and how questions correctly. In addition, Myra should be able to answer and ask clarifying questions related to a lesson or topic. Her CELDT reading level 2 (early intermediate) score indicates that she has the ability to segment and blend phonemic sounds, read simple sentences within context containing 25 high frequency words, and retell stories using contextual vocabulary for comprehension purposes. Her writing level 3 (intermediate) suggests that she can use basic tenses in writing sentences and paragraphs using conventional forms of spelling and writing. She should be able to write a simple paragraph following a model and contribute to or manufacture brainstorming activities to write a summation. Myra should also demonstrate increased usage of at least 75 high frequency words in writing.

When Myra's teacher analyzed her writing, she found that although Myra scored a 3 in writing, she needed support. She used short sentences and repetitive sentence

Student conferencing during writing workshop.

structures and repeated the same information in more than one sentence. Myra was learning how to make sense of English syntax. For example, in December 2002, Myra wrote a perspective paper on herself as a member of the Hoopa Indian tribe (see Figure 8.2).

FIGURE 8.2 Myra's Writing Sample Describing Herself as a Member of the Hoopa Indian Tribe

My name is Running Tiger. They named me Running Tiger because I run alot. I belong to the Hoopas. I am nine years old. I live with my mom, dad, and my sister and brother. I clean the log house. I watch the sheeps. I like to eat Samlen. I live with the Hoopas. The Hoopas speek inden langerwesh.

I watch the sheeps. I like to watch the sheeps because I think they are nice. I think there nice because they don't bight. I wish I had a pet like this. I wish I had a pet to because I never had a pet before.

I like to eat samlen. I like to eat Samlen because it is good. I think it good because I like to eat fish. Samlen is good because it is fish. I like it because its fish.

I live with the Hoopas. I live with the Hoopas because I am a inden. I am a inden because I born there. I live with the Hoopas all year long. I live with the Hoopas because it is nice to live with them.

Scaffolds to Support Myra's Writing

At the time she completed this writing sample, Myra had a sense of how to write a complete sentence in English. She needed some work in general fluency and sentence combining. For example, she could combine the following three sentences.

> My name is Running Tiger. They named me Running Tiger because I run alot. I belong to the Hoopas. [Original]
> *I am Running Tiger from the Hoopa Indian tribe and I run a lot.* [Combined]

When teaching sentence combining, Myra's teacher understood that her students needed to know that there are several ways to combine sentences. The teacher decided that the following two were the least complicated to teach fourth graders: (1) adding or compounding the sentences with a conjunction such as *and* or *but*, and (2) using an appositive, a noun or pronoun placed after another noun or pronoun to explain or clarify it (e.g., my aunt, Lucy). She taught the students one device at a time either in a small, guided writing group or in a writing conference.

The next kind of support Myra needed was support in revising her sentences to include a focus on sentence fluency. Her teacher facilitated this by modeling the variety of ways she could write her sentences. The chart in Figure 8.3 helped students dissect their sentences and fill in appropriate words using thesauruses, content word walls, and dictionaries.

Myra was then able to use the chart to facilitate combining repetitive sentences, such as:

> I like to eat salmon. I like to eat salmon because it is good. I think it is good because I like to eat fish. Salmon is good because it is fish. I like it because it's fish.

Myra's next writing sample, shortly thereafter, was the result of an inquiry study on salmon. Because the teachers at Edge Lake School use literature to support the curriculum, as Myra began her inquiry and prepared to write about salmon, the first thing she did was find a book on salmon. She looked at pictures of salmon, read about their features, and got some ideas to support the statement, "I like salmon." An Internet search helped Myra collect some ideas for her writing as well. Riverdale School has a Web page on salmon. It is available at http://www.riverdale.k12.or.us/salmon.htm.

As Myra browsed through the books on salmon and the Web site containing student art on salmon, she began a list of descriptive words about salmon. Figure 8.4 is an example of the process chart she compiled to organize her growing information on salmon.

As she browsed through books and recorded words she could use to describe salmon with more details, her teacher would stop by her desk, have her read through the list of words she was collecting, and ask her to note why she decided to select the

FIGURE 8.3 A Chart to Scaffold Myra's Attempts at Sentence Combining

Adj.	Noun	Prep.	Verb	Series
Daily	chores	for me	include	watching the sheep, helping my mom and dad, and cleaning the log house.

FIGURE 8.4 Myra's Process Chart on Salmon

Appearance	Cooking (How)	Taste (Describe)
Pink flesh	Bake	Sweet
Dark skin	Add brown sugar	Smoky
Spotted skin	Barbecue	Alder wood
Black speckled skin	Fry	Soft
Grayish		Melt in your mouth

words she did. Figure 8.5 shows how this scaffolding helped Myra to write the paragraph.

Myra was able to transfer her learning from her work with teachers on sentence combining to the task of writing about salmon. Making lists and using the Internet were scaffolds that Myra needed to develop as a competent writer. These strategies were scaffolds to develop the sometimes-elusive skill of fluency in writing. All students, and certainly ELLs, need structured assistance to understand how to manipulate the syntactical structures of English. The teachers scaffolding Myra through this and other writing tasks eventually gave her less and less support, until Myra was able to use these tools on her own.

Myra's writing in December demonstrates the scaffolds the teachers used during instruction have helped her writing fluency (see Figure 8.6). This piece flows much better than the previous sample. Additional student supports included rubrics with questions that guided students through their writing from paragraph to paragraph (see Figure 8.7 for an example of one of the rubrics that the teachers used to support Myra). These questions supported the drafting process. Students received input on their drafts in whole-group mini

FIGURE 8.5 Myra's Writing Sample About Salmon

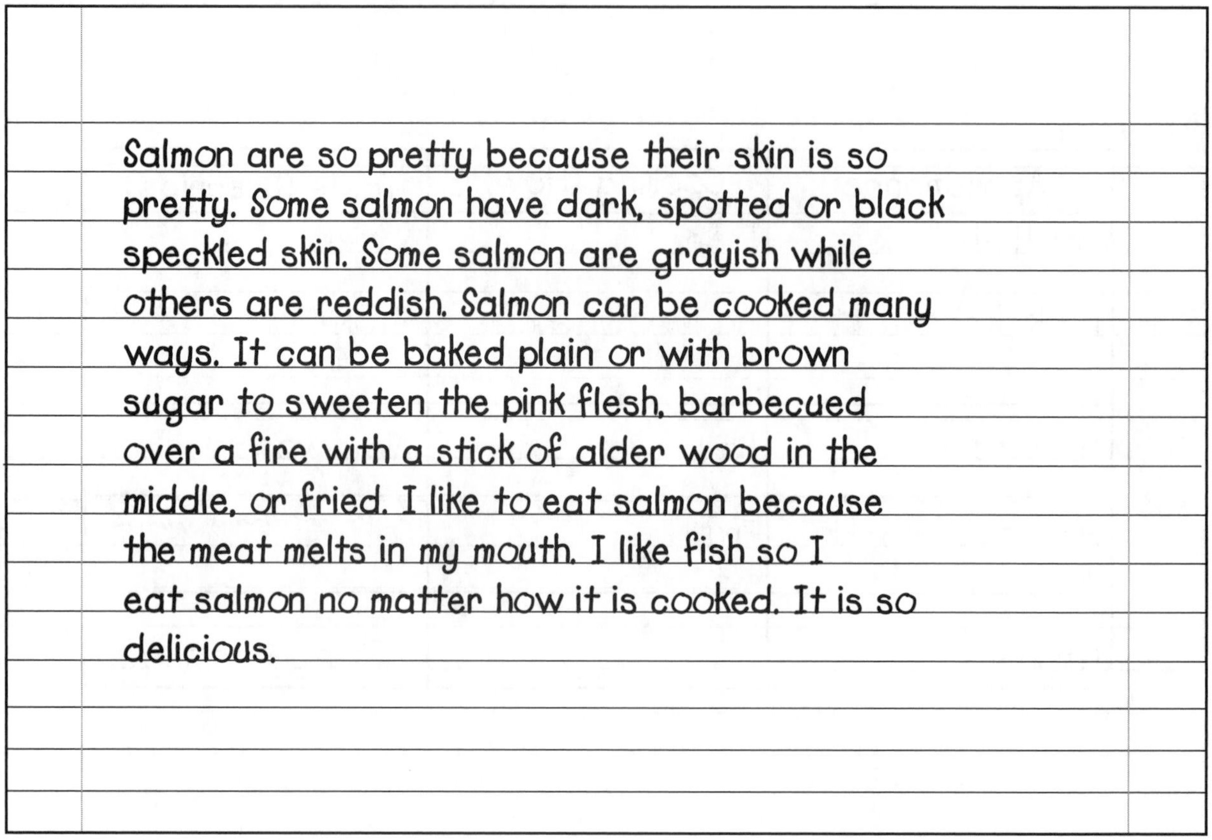

Salmon are so pretty because their skin is so pretty. Some salmon have dark, spotted or black speckled skin. Some salmon are grayish while others are reddish. Salmon can be cooked many ways. It can be baked plain or with brown sugar to sweeten the pink flesh, barbecued over a fire with a stick of alder wood in the middle, or fried. I like to eat salmon because the meat melts in my mouth. I like fish so I eat salmon no matter how it is cooked. It is so delicious.

lessons, where student work without names was used to model revision. Additional input was provided in small, guided writing groups where students and the teacher could talk through the revision process.

Content Area Reading Support for Myra

Based on Myra's informal reading inventory assessment results, Myra's teacher decided that she needed support in comprehension in the content areas. During reading instruction, Myra's teacher spent a good deal of time teaching strategies to support reading, including previewing the text and monitoring comprehension. Her anecdotal notes indicated that when asked to read, Myra started from the beginning of the text and read until the end. She did not practice what she had been taught about previewing the text first, asking herself what she knew about the topic, and making sure she monitored her comprehension as she read. When asked to retell the story and/or to point out the important parts of a passage, Myra was unable to do so. Her inability to answer questions about

FIGURE 8.6 Myra's Writing Sample from December (after scaffolds)

> The Hoopa Indians were similar to the Yuroks. The Hoopas, too, built rectangular wooden houses with slanted roofs. Their villages contained sweat lodges where the fires burned within keeping them very hot. The men gathered in the sweat lodges to think and pray. When they were finished, they would jump into the river next to the village to cool and clean themselves.
>
> Although the Hoopas and the Yuroks spoke different languages, their cultures were very much alike in some ways. They both placed great importance on gaining wealth.
>
> Each year the Hoopas planned two huge celebrations, the White Deerskin Dance and the Jump Dance. During these celebrations the children learned the dances and the traditions of their tribe so they could grow up to be strong leaders.

what she read further indicated that Myra was reading to "get through" the text rather than to comprehend what she had read. Thus, Myra's teacher decided to sit with Myra and several other students who exhibited similar reading behaviors. Her plan to differentiate the instruction for and support these particular students included a modification of the Preview-View-Review strategy (Freeman & Freeman, 1998) with the following steps:

1. Students review what they need to do to preview a text, that is, questions to ask.
2. Students write down the questions they generated.
3. Students read with the purpose of answering the questions generated.
4. Students record answers they located to the questions in their own words and note the page on which they found the answers.
5. Students mark the location of answers within the text with stickies.

FIGURE 8.7 Sample of a Rubric Developed to Guide Writing: Example to Guide the Content Writing About Biomes

---

1. What type of biome was the first mission built on? STOP.
   a. Describe it. Can you see it? How large is it? What material is it made of?
2. If there was a biome built in the rain forest, what would it look like? STOP. THINK. SEE IT IN YOUR MIND'S EYE.
   a. Describe the biome. What was it made of? Why would these particular materials be selected? Why would it be important to select these materials? See the biome in your mind.
3. Compare how the people at both missions would use their natural resources to live.
   a. Use the transition words: alike, at the same time, similarly.
4. Contrast how the people at both missions would use their natural resources to live.
   a. Use the transition words: however, different, on the other hand, in contrast to.
5. Conclusion. Write a conclusion that summarizes both biomes. STOP. Think about the purpose for your writing. It is to inform others who don't know anything about biomes. Have you told them enough? Do you have descriptive details? Should you add more?
6. Sit with your writing partner and read your writing. Check the organization of your writing with the rubric guidelines.

---

6. Students read the text in small chunks as selected by the teacher.

7. Students use context to enhance comprehension. For example, students keep reading and then guess the meaning of a word they didn't know from context.

8. Students check the cognate word wall.

9. Students visualize as they read and read with a partner where one draws as the other reads if they need additional support.

10. Students summarize all they had read in their own words.

Each of the preceding steps, which had initially been taught to the class, was retaught. The teacher modeled for students. Next, the teacher modeled once again with one student. Two students then modeled their thinking, and finally, all the students in the small, guided reading group practiced with their reading partner.

Because Myra's teacher used ongoing assessment to inform her instruction, she was able to determine that several students in her classroom, who had been assessed as level 3 in language development, were focusing on task completion in content area reading rather than on comprehension. The attention to reteaching and thinking about comprehension yielded the following summary of part of Myra and her partner's notes (see Figure 8.8). In this sample, Myra and her partner are not only reading for information, but also looking for causes and effects as well as making predictions.

At an ELD level 2 in reading, Myra was expected to retell stories using accurate vocabulary in context. Myra's summary reveals that she can do that and more as a result of her teacher observing how she was implementing the skills taught and using her observations and assessment data to plan additional scaffolds for Myra and others with similar needs. As soon as she realized that Myra needed reteaching and additional modeling in context, she

FIGURE 8.8 Myra's Summary Notes from February 3, Written with a Partner

February 3, 2003

     We read about three conquistadors from Spain. Their names were Hernando Cortez, Cabrillo, and Vizcaino. The three explorers came on an expedition in galleons to find the Strait of Anian. They came to look for a port, conquer the Indians and their lands, find gold, and be rich. We think there is going to be a war and some of the Natives are going to die. If the Spaniards take over the land, there has to be a war. I would fight if someone was taking my land and conquering me.

brought the small group together and began to scaffold the scaffolds she had previously provided her students.

Summary of the Scaffolds Myra Received

The following supports were provided for Myra:

- Sentence combining to help develop sentence fluency.
- Searching for words in a variety of resources to describe nouns and verbs to develop word choice.
- A writing partner with whom Myra had developed trust and could work well.
- Specific step-by-step teaching of how to read for information.
- Specific teaching of how to ask questions before beginning to read.
- Specific teaching and modeling about how to read to answer questions.
- Direct instruction in note taking.
- Modeling of how to write concise summaries.
- Specific teaching and modeling of how to understand unfamiliar vocabulary words in context.

Myra's case in this classroom is not unusual as her classroom is a busy one and her teacher, with the support of the literacy coach and other colleagues, focuses on making sure students have access to the curriculum and learn how to use strategies to support their learning. She not only scaffolds instruction for her students, but also teaches those students how to use the scaffolding strategies so that they can become independent readers and writers. Constant activity revolves around students talking to each other, asking questions, searching through books, comparing their own writing to the rubric posted on the walls, and a sudden exclamation, "Wow! That's a cognate!" The walls abound with student work. Resources can be seen everywhere to support ELLs and EO students alike. In the middle of all the action is a teacher who stops and talks to each student. She asks questions, smiles, prompts, and says things like, "Just look at me and tell me what you want me to know about this." The student complies. Her language flows easily and fluently. She comments, "I can really see that. Let's work on getting all of that on paper. Do you need help to get started?"

Teacher and student put their heads together and get started. Once the student is comfortable, the teacher's shoulders relax and she smiles. The teacher reminds her, "Remember Marissa can help you if you get stuck. And, I'll be around again." And the buzz continues, a learning buzz of language focused on learning peppered with occasional laughter because someone has read a funny comment or has discovered a cognate in the textbook. It looks like fun and it is.

Roberto's Story

Roberto's story also shows us how a supportive classroom context—along with instruction that not only scaffolds content, but also gives students the strategies and skills necessary to become proficient readers and writers—can make a difference. According to an analysis of his CELDT scores, Roberto, an ELD level 2 in reading, is expected to be able to match vocabulary word to pictures, recognize sound/symbol relationships, use context clues to choose the correct word to complete a sentence, answer some factual comprehension questions, and make inferences after reading a simple text. In writing, as a level 1 student, he is expected to complete a sentence using the appropriate word; respond to a picture prompt by writing words, phrases, or simple sentences that contain at least one English word spelled correctly; and write words or phrases related to the topic, based on sequenced pictures and a sentence starter although the response may contain numerous errors that distort meaning. Roberto's work demonstrates that he can indeed successfully complete all of the above tasks and much more in a supportive environment where his instruction is scaffolded in ways that promote his success.

Roberto's teacher collected samples of his writing from September 2002 to March 2003. The teacher analyzed writing using the length of the writing piece as well as the number of complete ideas expressed. The teacher did not view punctuation as a critical factor because Roberto was at the beginning level in writing proficiency. Roberto did have time to go back and think about conventions, but that was not the focus on writing in his classroom. The teacher's goal was to develop conceptual understanding by scaffolding content area reading and writing. Roberto's teacher considered organization, completeness of thought, and the ability to communicate complete thoughts more important when

FIGURE 8.9 Roberto's Lion Shape Poem

learning to express oneself in a second language. The teacher used several of Roberto's writing samples between September and March to demonstrate how she scaffolded reading and writing to promote growth.

Poetry

One of the areas that Roberto's teacher focused on was poetry, and Roberto actively participated in poetry writing, a task that can be challenging. Roberto's writing begins with graphic organizers and proceeds to *shape writing* that becomes poetry (see Figures 8.9 and 8.10).

The shape poetry resulted from a science unit on animals. Although other students wrote narrative poems about what they learned about lions, Roberto drew a picture and wrote a shape poem. He used words from a content area word wall to compose his poem.

FIGURE 8.10 Roberto's Lion Poem Based on His Shape Poem

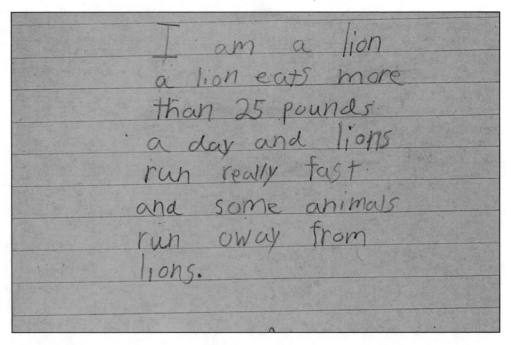

Scaffolds the Teacher Used to Teach Poetry

Roberto's teacher used poetry read alouds as a way to encourage her students to listen to the "music" in language. There was a large collection of poetry books in the classroom, and many students would read them during independent reading.

For this lesson, Roberto's teacher had a variety of books on lions at different readability levels for students to browse through. She selected a book and engaged students in an interactive read aloud. In this read aloud, she read small chunks of informational text, stopped, and asked students to retell to each other what she had read. Next, they shared with the class. As students shared, the teacher added students' new or extended ideas to a chart of information about lions. This shopping mall of ideas was available for all students to refer to and "shop from" as they wrote their poems. As students wrote, the teacher observed and spoke one-on-one with students, encouraging them to "tell me more," "what else can you remember?" and remainding them to use the shopping mall of ideas or the high frequency, cognate, or content word walls to support their writing. At the end of the writing exercise, students read their poems to their reading/writing buddies, receiving positive feedback.

Extending the Writing/Reading Experience

Roberto and his classmates were further encouraged to investigate poetry by collecting poems and creating their own book of personal poems. Roberto's personal poetry book contained 10 poems in October. Some of the poems were pattern poems whereas others were based on the writing of published poets, such as Robert Frost's *Stopping by Woods on a Snowy Evening* (see Figure 8.11).

FIGURE 8.11 Roberto and His Partner's Poem Based on *Stopping by Woods on a Snowy Evening*

Whose forest is these I
think I know. The house
is in the village though;
He will not see me the
Sun set going down
to watch his forest fill
up with snow.

My little forest
must think is queer
To stop without a near house
Between the forest and frozen lake

The forest are louly, dark and deep.
But I have promises to keep,
And miles to go
befor I sleep,
And miles to go
before I sleep.

Beginning Content Area Writing

One subject that Roberto's teacher used as a focus for content area writing instruction was social studies. She taught the students a variety of strategies for writing in the content areas, including the use of graphic organizers and ways to understand expository structures. His teacher also modeled these strategies and often worked with the class to create graphic organizers that would then serve as models for the students' individual work. On September 24, 2002, Roberto created a Venn diagram comparing and contrasting rain forests and deserts. He listed the differences between deserts and rain forests but could find no similarities. His list of characteristics about deserts included words and phrases he could remember:

- dry all year
- lots of animals live there
- (small) animals live
- cat die
- bushies under ground
- eat leaves and fruit seeds
- other animals
- little water to drink
- get wonder

Roberto copied phrases such as "get wonder" and "bushies under ground" from the class graphic organizer. In a conference, Roberto told his teacher that "bushies under ground" meant "bushes on the ground." He demonstrated his developing listening comprehension as well as his progress toward understanding how to take the sounds heard and put them into writing. He used his graphic organizer to write the text in Figure 8.12.

FIGURE 8.12 Roberto's Writing from His Graphic Organizer About Rain Forests and Deserts

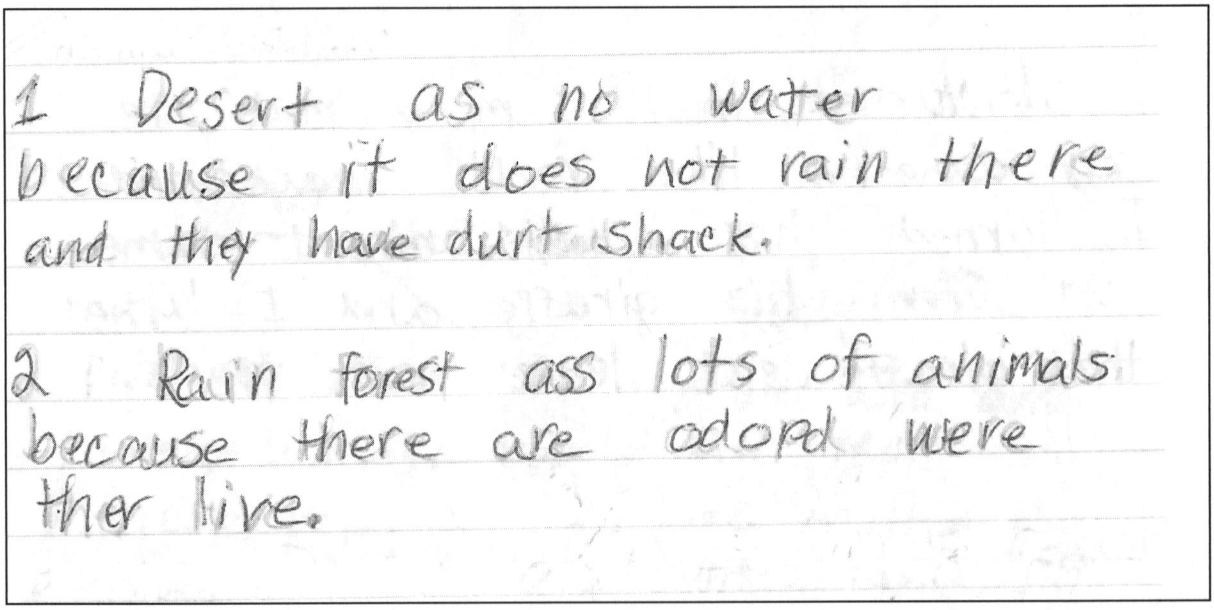

1 Desert as no water because it does not rain there and they have durt shack.

2 Rain forest ass lots of animals because there are odopd were ther live.

FIGURE 8.13 Roberto's Graphic Organizer on Deserts and Rain Forests

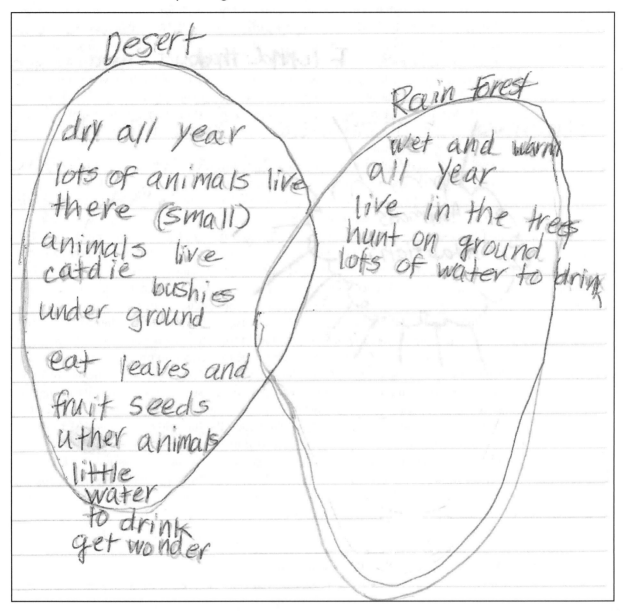

This was Roberto's first exposure to the structure of comparison and contrast, a genre that was taught throughout the year in the fourth grade. Roberto's writing at this stage is typical of an early intermediate student. The phrases are short and there is one short sentence, "lots of animals live there." "Dry all year" is a descriptive phrase that is a complete thought as well, given Roberto's stage of language development. The listing of the rain forest contains one complete communicative thought in "wet and warm all year." Other phrases have no subject or noun, so we are not sure exactly to what or whom Roberto refers when he writes: "live in trees," "hunt on ground," "lots of water to drink" (see Figure 8.13).

Roberto's attempt to use his graphic organizer to write produces two sentences (see Figure 8.12), although it is interesting to note that he uses information in his writing that is not included in his graphic organizer. The first sentence is: "Desert as [has] no water because it does not rain there and they have durt [dirt] shack." His graphic organizer does not contain any information about dirt. He gained that information though small-group discussion. Roberto's listening skills (level 3 or intermediate) serve him well as he works on listening to and learning grade level content. His sentence about the rain forest notes that: "Rain forest ass [has] lots of animals because there [they] are odopd [adapted] were [where] they live." The content is correct—that the animals in the rain forest have adapted to their environment.

Roberto later produces a learning log as a follow-up to the lesson on comparing and contrasting deserts with rain forests (see Figure 8.14).

Roberto is able to produce this long sentence with consistencies such as "lurned" for "learned" where the "ea" is not an easily transferable vowel digraph from another language that has no digraphs. Joining three ideas with the word *and* is also developmental for EO students as well as ELLs. Roberto listens to readings, to class discussions, and to the information shared by the teacher and uses the information gained in his writing. He is in a classroom where he is encouraged to take risks and focus on the communication of content rather than on correctness of spelling and other English conventions.

Roberto wrote his next sample on January 16, 2003, after a 3-week intersession. The text is based on a lesson on the American Indian tribe, the Mojaves. Roberto's teacher provided him with guiding questions that encourage the reflection process during writing. Figure 8.15 provides questions that guide the writing of the introductory paragraph and the second through fifth paragraphs. These guiding questions look like the five-paragraph essay and are simply a scaffold to provide ELLs with some structure in how to proceed when they write in a second language. Remember that the students in this class were writing in personal journals every day and writing responses to literature as well. In other words, this is not the only kind of writing they were doing in this class and would not be the only type. The teacher also provided reflective questions for students to use as they wrote, after she modeled how to use the questions (see Figure 8.16). They became a tool

FIGURE 8.14 Excerpt from Roberto's Learning Log

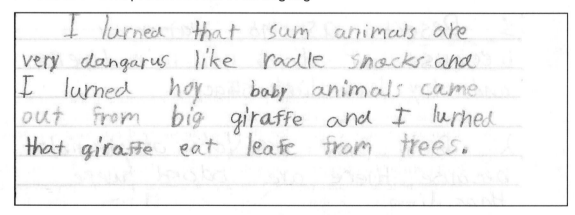

FIGURE 8.15 Questions to Guide Writing

Paragraph 1:	Restate the prompt or the question you are being asked to write about. Follow the restatement with an answer and why you think this is important. Remember, you are looking for the GIST of the big idea. [*Students had been engaged in a process called GIST where they were taught to get information by summarizing the text they were reading.*]
Paragraph 2:	Provide details and explanations to support what you are saying in the first paragraph. Are your details clear? Can the reader "see" what you are saying?
Paragraph 3:	Provide more details for your thoughts. For example, if you are a Mojave child, what else do you do? What is your life like? What does the world around you look like? What does it sound like?
Paragraph 4:	This is where you tell us how it feels to be who you are. Are you proud? Why? Do you have fun as you do now in your real world? How? What does that look like? Sound like? Feel like?
Paragraph 5:	Restate what you told the reader in the beginning of your writing. Restate the prompt in your own words, and make the reader want to live in the time you chose.

FIGURE 8.16 Reflective Questions

Ask yourself:

1. Is my paper easy to read?
2. Do I have enough facts and details to explain what I want to say to the reader?
3. Will my writing take the reader into history?
4. Did I become the person in history?
5. Am I looking through his or her eyes?
6. Did I use the skills of summary—writing only what I need to inform the reader?
7. Did I say what I wanted to say?

for students to think about their writing as they were writing and to know what questions they could ask peers when they needed help.

In the writing sample in Figure 8.17, Roberto has taken the perspective of a Mojave Indian. Although some of the sentences are repetitious, a common characteristic of emerging writers, the sample contains 236 words and 23 complete ideas that are communicated in complete sentences.

This piece of writing was the result of several drafts and conferences with peers as well as the teacher. Roberto used the guiding questions to reflect on the content of his writing. There were three sentences that were not included in the 23 complete ideas because they were, although complete thoughts, repetitive in content. It is important to note that the writing sample did not result from one lesson. Roberto had time to read, talk, and write about the content. The class learned about deserts and the rain forests in

FIGURE 8.17 First Page of Roberto's Sample of Perspective Writing

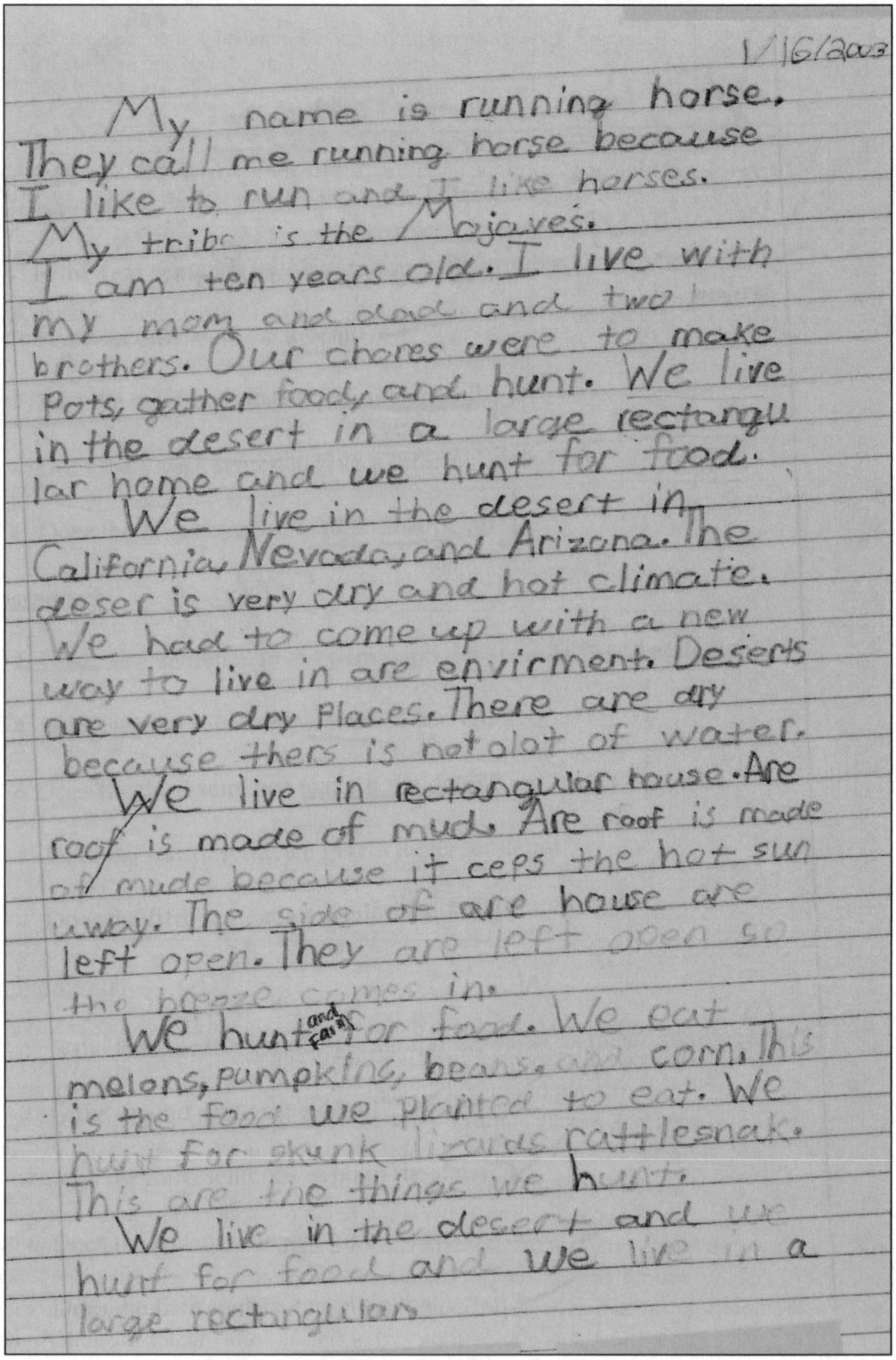

1/16/2003

My name is running horse. They call me running horse because I like to run and I like horses. My tribe is the Mojaves. I am ten years old. I live with my mom and dad and two brothers. Our chores were to make pots, gather food, and hunt. We live in the desert in a large rectangular home and we hunt for food.

We live in the desert in California, Nevada, and Arizona. The deser is very dry and hot climate. We had to come up with a new way to live in are enviroment. Deserts are very dry places. There are dry because thers is not alot of water.

We live in rectangular house. Are roof is made of mud. Are roof is made of mude because it ceps the hot sun away. The side of are house are left open. They are left open so the breeze comes in.

We hunt and farm for food. We eat melons, pumpking, beans, and corn. This is the food we planted to eat. We hunt for skunk lizards rattlesnak. This are the things we hunt.

We live in the desert and we hunt for food and we live in a large rectangular

September. In December, Roberto's learning log is about the Mojave tribe that lives in the desert. Roberto and his class continued to revisit deserts and rain forests and explore how, although they are different from each other, the living things in each of the environments have learned to adapt and survive.

Scaffolds the Teacher Used

Roberto's teacher consistently used scaffolds that supported her students' language and literacy development. For example, she introduced each topic with graphic organizers and developed the topics over time with learning logs, perspective writing, narrative, and other genres. The teacher modeled the guided writing process for students by engaging in shared writing where the teacher and the students compose the piece together. Throughout the composition process, the teacher asked students clarifying questions about the syntax, the use of vocabulary, and the meaning of taking the perspective of another person ("What does it look like? How would you describe it? What does it sound like? What will you hear?").

The teacher introduced each grade level topic with a piece of literature in a read aloud. For example, Roberto's teacher introduced the topic of the conquistadors with Jane Yolan's (1996) book, *Encounter*. Roberto wrote a response to *Encounter*. That was followed by an informational piece about three conquistadors, a learning log, an analytical writing piece supported by guiding questions, and an analytical rubric that supported the structure of comparison and contrast. The teacher taught all rubrics to students before they began their writing. Additionally, she "translated" all rubrics into kid language as she asked students to tell her what they thought each feature of the rubric meant. The teacher rewrote the rubrics based on student feedback and posted them on large charts in the front of the classroom for student viewing and use.

The teachers at Edge Lake School currently use three types of rubrics to assess writing:

- A genre rubric that focuses on the text structure or features of the genre as well as the critical signal words students will be expected to use in their own content area writing.

- A content rubric that focuses on the use of accurate information of grade level content in student writing as well as the organization and sequential progression of the writing.

- A conventions rubric that focuses on capitalization, punctuation, syntactical structure, subject/verb agreement, and spelling.

Rubrics were posted where students could see them and use them as guides while they were writing. Rubrics were explicitly taught, and students used one rubric at a time while writing. They were given time to read and reread their writing, as well as revise and edit writing with peers and in individual conferences with teachers.

Extending the Reading/Writing Process

The teacher and students reviewed all the work the students had completed thus far and how the words they knew, the ideas they had in their heads, the poems they had read, the stories they had read along with the textbook information were sources for them in the reading/writing process. As he continued to write, Roberto started his perspective piece (Figure 8.17) by telling the audience that he is "running horse." He tells us why he has the name—"because I like to run and I like horses." He belongs to the Mojave tribe and is 10 years old. He lives with his "mom and dad and two brothers." His chores are to "make pots, gather food, and hunt." He lives in the desert "in a large rectangular home and we hunt for food." Running Horse lives in the "desert in California, Nevada, and Arizona" where the desert is "very dry and hot climate." He observes that "we had to come up with a new way to live in are [our] environment" noting that deserts are "very dry places" because "thers is [there's] not alot of water." Running Horse describes his house: "roof is of mude [mud] because it ceps [keeps] the hot sun away" and "the side of are [our] house are left open" so "the breeze comes in." Roberto also describes how, in the role of a Mojave, he farms as well as hunts, eats "melons, pumpkins, beans, and corn," and hunts for "skunk lizards rattlesnak."

Roberto is gaining strength as a writer. He has been able to provide his reader with some basic information about the Mojave Indians. He has done well in adopting the perspective of a 10-year-old Mojave child. The ability to adopt the perspective of a character is a valuable skill that supports the process of developing inferential thinking as well as responding to literature (Vacca & Vacca, 2007). Roberto provided the reader with many details about the Mojave Indians. He understood that a writer needs to support statements with details that can be substantiated.

More Content Area Writing

Before students went off track for the intersession, the teacher engaged the students in a unit about biomes. She began with an interactive read aloud and recorded students' important ideas as she read. She made note of vocabulary that was directly related to understanding the content they would be learning and made sure that students understood that vocabulary. She showed students pictures of a variety of biomes. The last sample we collected from Roberto was dated March 28, 2003 (see Figure 8.18), before the students went off track. The concept of rain forests is still a part of this writing sample; however, it is related to the construction of missions, as Roberto continues to make connections in his learning. In addition, the fourth graders at Edge Lake School are still working on comparison and contrast.

The sample from March was preceded by a research organizer on the topic of biomes. The organizer included the different kinds of biomes that the students researched: tropical rain forests, deciduous forests, grasslands, deserts, taiga, tundra, saltwater ecosystems, freshwater ecosystems, and a place for students to write about their favorite biome. Roberto draws his and it looks like a rain forest. In this classroom, students are not only reading social studies and science, but also researching content areas as well as writing about them.

The guiding rubric (see Figure 8.7) for this March writing sample asks students to think about the type of biome on which the first mission was built and to describe the mission and the biome. It also asks students to consider what it would be like if a mission were built in a rain forest. Roberto's teacher continues to connect the content themes that guide her instruction, understanding that guiding themes directly

FIGURE 8.18 Excerpt from Roberto's Content Area Writing About Biomes

March 28, 2003

The first mission called San Diego was built in the grasslan. And is made out of grass and wheat. And we eat little animals. Like burrowing owl and other animals.

If there was a mission in the rain forest it was made out wood. Because went rain alot the wood from the tree can't procte from the rain. Because is to strong the wood for the rain.

The grassland and the tropical rain forest. Are the some of biomes.

support academic language development for ELLs, who need time to become acquainted with the academic language that is used to describe content. They also need many opportunities to write about what has been learned, since using content vocabulary is critical. Teachers should model both reading and writing short pieces as well as longer pieces. Writing must be encouraged and supported by a multitude of resources, including a focus on specific genres as well as guiding questions that develop reflection.

Roberto's March writing sample contains three specific paragraphs comprised of 9 sentences. We can tell by reading this sample that writing comparison and contrast is still difficult for Roberto, as it is for the EO students in the fourth grade. However, because students at this grade level must read text structured in comparison and contrast, it is logical not only to teach this structure, but also to provide students with opportunities to write using comparison and contrast. Roberto's sample contains 11 original communicative ideas and only 3 that are repetitious.

In this piece, Roberto tells us that the first mission was built in the grasslands, made of adobe. He describes the climate of the grasslands as "worm" [warm] where "animals adapted their homes." He goes on to think about building a mission in a rain forest, noting that he would build it out of wood because that's the best material to build a mission if you were in a forest, a logical conclusion. But, as he continues writing this piece, he loses track of whether he is talking about the animals in the biome or in different climates, demonstrating the difficulty he is having.

Roberto demonstrated this in an earlier writing sample where he compared and contrasted the natives and the Spanish conquistadors. Roberto does what developmental writers do. He contains all the similarities in one paragraph and lists the differences in another separate paragraph, demonstrating that integrating comparison and contrast within the same piece takes time and additional opportunities to read the genre, talk about the structure of the genre, and write in the genre. Additional scaffolding activities may be necessary where the teacher models group paragraphs writing in this genre, talking aloud about what should go where and why. Some students will need more time than others, given where they are in the development of academic English as a second language as well as how well they are able to negotiate text written in comparison and contrast format.

The teacher understands that this genre has been a difficult one for her students, but particularly for students like Roberto. It is important to note that this teacher has not given up on Roberto or other students like him. She has not lowered her expectations. Instead, she is using Roberto's writing, as well as that of her other students, to find ways to further support the academic language development of her class. She is finding ways to continue to provide them access to grade level content.

Summary of Scaffolds Roberto Received

The following scaffolds were used to support the development of Roberto's writing:

- Shape writing that eventually led to the writing of narrative poetry based on grade level content.
- Personal poetry based on interest and personal experiences.
- Timed writing where students wrote as many words, phrases, and sentences as they could after listening to a read aloud.
- Teacher modeling of a specific writing genre as a guided writing experience. Understanding the syntactical structure of English was an integral part of the modeling process.
- Debriefing of the guided writing piece by teacher and students where the teacher asked for ways to make the writing more interesting (revision).
- Note organizers that supported comprehension and content learning and were used by students to support the writing process.
- Questions that served as guidelines for student use as they progressed through a writing piece.
- Graphic organizers that illustrated the structure of text and served as references for content area writing.

- Flip notes about content, such as biomes, used as a resource for ideas as well as content vocabulary while writing about structures, such as missions that might be constructed on different biomes.

- Individual conferences that supported student language, thinking, and writing.

Resources in the classroom that supported language and writing development included content word walls and cognate word walls, which highlighted words that have the same meaning in Spanish and in English, such as importante/important, interesante/ interesting, grado/grade. As students encountered cognates in reading narrative or other expository content area texts, the teacher pointed them out, placed them on the cognate word wall for student reference, and integrated them into lessons. Dictionaries in both languages were also available along with thesauruses.

The teacher focused instruction on comprehension. Roberto and his peers received instruction in content area reading and narrative and expository text structures during the reading/language arts time in small, guided reading groups where comprehension strategies were taught explicitly based on assessment data. The teacher also used content vocabulary, text structure, cognate transfer, and instruction in developing and using note organizers to support the writing process as an integral part of Roberto's instruction. She used phonics and phonemic awareness as scaffolds to support fluent reading and writing, and she integrated spelling into the writing process. She used a high frequency word wall during the editing process.

She further supported Roberto in learning grade level content during ELD time by reviewing, reteaching, and extending the content previously taught in reading and language arts. It was during this time that all students wrote about the content they previously learned. In the afternoons, students were mixed in extended classes where students who spoke Spanish as a primary language and English as a second language, at different levels, sat with students who spoke English as a primary language. They learned about text and syntactical structure and engaged in additional comprehension strategies such as inferential thinking and metacognition, where students were taught to think explicitly about the literacy task in which they were engaged. Students also had opportunities to do more writing during this time while receiving feedback from peers and teachers.

Strategies to Scaffold the Scaffold

As we told the stories of Myra and Roberto, we described lessons and scaffolds that their teachers used to support their literacy development. In this section, we highlight three strategies that teachers can use to scaffold instruction for ELLs.

Prediction

What Is It? Students use prediction to project what will come next in text based on the pictures, using what they have heard or know about a topic, and what they have read. Good readers develop the habit of mind where they consistently use prediction in reading and writing to facilitate all other strategies. We selected prediction as an enabling skill that supports scaffolding because it teaches ELLs that they should make predictions throughout the reading process based on what they know (background knowledge) or what they have learned during the reading or writing. As teachers integrate prediction into their instruction and ensure that ELLs can use it consistently, they teach students that predictions are to be shared and discussed to explain and clarify their impressions, rather than to decide whether one student or prediction is more accurate than another. Prediction supports analysis, the basis of thinking and searching through text to discover patterns and use that discovery to enhance comprehension.

Teaching ELLs to predict helps them understand that good readers make connections between what they read or see in their daily lives and their background knowledge. They are able to do this because prediction teaches them to apply background knowledge after it has been activated, make connections between their own experiences and text, make connections among texts they have heard or read, and recognize and describe any disconnects between text they are reading and their own cultural experiences. Students are taught to look ahead in text and make connections with what went before as well as understand that predictions are temporary and have to be validated by textual information, from other media technology such as computers or CDs, and personal experiences that can be shared and elaborated.

Teaching Prediction. Prediction can be taught using the following process:

1. Select a picture book or a story that is a part of the regular classroom instruction to make explicit connections to what is being learned in class.

2. Have students make a prediction about what they think will happen in the story based on previewing the pictures, reading the title of the story, or looking at and reading charts and graphs that are a part of the text. Remember that students may need to learn how to make predictions using the pictures or headings. You should model this first for the group, then let students practice with partners, and then let them try it on their own.

3. Write students' predictions down. It is important that all student language be preserved and referred to throughout the lesson to encourage engagement so students use their language to build academic language.

4. As you proceed through the text either with a read aloud or in a shared or guided reading format, stop students and ask them to think about what they are listening to or reading.

5. Have students retell what they have read or heard first to a partner. Next, have the partners share their retellings with the group.

6. Check the predictions written down with students. Note which predictions were validated and which were not. At this time, guide students through the process of analyzing the predictions that have not been validated. They may delete any predictions they feel don't make sense.

7. Students can add to the predictions list based on what they have read.

8. Continue the process of reading, thinking, validating, deleting, adding, predicting.

ELLs need to be explicitly taught that prediction supports all their learning. Debrief with students and guide them to think about the other content areas. For example, how does prediction help you in math? Is it related to estimating? How is it alike? How is it different? You are actually supporting the thinking and learning processes of which ELLs must be aware. They need to understand that they can apply what they learn about thinking in one content area to learning in another area. That process sets them up for the transfer of skills and eventually independence and mastery of content.

Visualization

What Is It? Visualizing is a strategy that helps readers make the words on the page come alive (Zimmerman & Keene, 1997). ELLs need to learn that authors use words much as an artist uses a paintbrush to help readers create pictures in their heads. Thus, it is critical that teachers mediate vocabulary and phrases, such as those that are meant to help readers "see" through imagery, for ELLs. In addition, authors use other devices to help readers "see" the text. They use graphs, pictures, photographs, maps, and other visual supports such as cutaways, and 3D sketches. However, ELLs must be taught to visualize and be reminded to use visualization as they listen to stories or read text.

We select visualization as an enabling scaffold because it helps students legitimize the pictures they have in their heads. Mediation of critical vocabulary can facilitate the visualization process for ELLs. By teaching ELLs about imagery, we help students understand that their mental imagery is something that is a part of them and always facilitates comprehension of all text. Teaching visualization helps students link their personal experiences from the past and the present to what they are reading. This process helps them understand what it means to activate background knowledge before all classroom lessons, independent reading, and writing. You see pictures in your head of experiences you have had or that are like the experiences you will be reading about. Teaching visualization helps ELLs make connections with text. It supports their imaginative thinking. It also helps them understand that events occur over time and can be "seen" through of the dimensions of time, space, and size.

Teaching Visualization. Visualization can be taught using the following activities:

1. Read aloud a passage with descriptive language to students. Have students take out a piece of paper. Tell students that they will work with a partner who will help them think about and "see" what is being read. You will have to read the passage several times with expression and appropriate pause to provide students time to listen, process the language, think about what was read, and talk with partners about what the picture might look like. One partner draws and the other provides input to help create an accurate depiction using the language of the text. Emphasize that this is not art. Instead, it is a way to "see" text, a strategy readers use to help them make sense of text.

2. Read the passage several times to ensure that students have time to listen, visualize, think, and draw.

3. At the end of the activity, have students post their drawings. Provide feedback about the accuracy of the objects in the pictures in terms of location of people and objects

in relationship to other objects in the picture. Many times students' perceptions of what a vocabulary word looks like differ; for example, a bluff in the desert may resemble a hill or a mountain. If students interpret the word *bluff* as a hill or mountain, show them what a bluff is and have them "fix" their pictures with another color crayon or pen. Then have students help you develop a definition for bluff. Write the definition on a content word wall and have students add it to their personal dictionaries. Thus the visualization process not only makes text come alive, but also supports vocabulary development.

4. Switch partners so that the one who was doing the drawing becomes the supporter. Continue through the short passage in the same manner.

5. Once students have had the opportunity to sketch a passage that you have read repeatedly and have evaluated for accuracy of their drawings, expose them to the following adaptation of sketch to stretch (Whitin, 1996). In this activity, students work with a partner. One reads a small chunk of text while the other sketches. The sketcher can ask to have the passage read again. This is natural and expected because of the complexity of listening and processing the semantics of a second language. After the sketch is complete, have students evaluate the sketch and go back to check text to agree that the sketch accurately represents the text. If students feel that the sketch does not accurately represent the text and vocabulary is the stumbling block, remind them to use the vocabulary strategies you taught them: break the word into meaningful units and analyze the chunks to predict the meaning. Remember, this is not about finishing a story, but rather using a story to scaffold the scaffold you are using in instruction. Once students agree on the accuracy of the sketch, they move on. The reader becomes the sketcher and the sketcher becomes the reader.

At the risk of sounding repetitive, we emphasize that it is important to be systematic and supportive when teaching ELLs. Watch how your students are processing text and representing it. Keep in mind that the purpose for instruction and scaffolding is to create independent learners. All instruction and scaffolds must transfer learning to other content areas and encourage mastery of content information. You will be further informed about student success by authentic assessments such as anecdotal records, checklists, or individual and small-group conferences. Once you have determined that students can talk about and apply the strategies you want them to use, withdraw the scaffolds a little at a time, continuing to observe and document performance.

Cause and Effect

What Is It? Cause and effect is an expository text structure as well as a standard taught across grade levels. It relates directly to comprehension. We selected the cause-and-effect structure as an enabling scaffold because students have to work with events in sequence throughout their school experiences. Learning to order events and sequence them by time is also a lifelong skill and very important to teach ELLs. Thinking and learning about cause and effect helps students understand that what has happened in the past influences the present. Students need to understand that what happens in the present can become a cause and, consequently, affects the future. Understanding cause and effect assumes that students know something about change, time, and space. For ELLs it also means that they learn the key words and phrases that signal cause and effect such as *because, consequently, as a result, influence.* Therefore, it is important to teach conjunctions and other key vocabulary words to ELLs. Understanding cause and effect also helps students think about comparison and contrast. How are two or three incidents the same or different and what is the possibility of one influencing change in the other in the present and over time?

Teaching Cause and Effect. It is best to begin to teach the thinking and language of cause and effect by first starting with concrete objects. Next, use real-life experiences, that is, experiences with which students can identify and interact. Then use pictures and finally, text information. You can illustrate cause and effect with a graphic organizer that uses arrows to indicate cause and effect. Activities like the following are helpful in teaching cause and effect. Drop a book on the floor so it makes a startling, loud noise. Ask students what happened.

> **Teacher:** "What happened?"
>
> **Students:** "There was a loud noise."
>
> **Teacher:** "What caused the loud noise?"
>
> **Students:** "The book dropped."
>
> **Teacher:** "What caused the book to drop?"
>
> **Students:** "You dropped the book on the floor."

The idea is to guide students to think about each part of the act and how one part affects the other. Ask students how the noise affected them. Were they startled? Did they become afraid? Why? The next level of scaffolding involves using real-life experiences to demonstrate cause and effect.

Practical Applications and Individual Inquiries: Cases to Think About and Investigate

1. Observe ELLs in a classroom where instruction is delivered in English. Focus on one student and if possible interview the student. Ask the following questions:
   - Where do you get your ideas for writing?
   - Do you have someone to talk to about your writing?
   - When you are stuck, where do you get help so you can continue to write?

   Write up your observations and make a few recommendations about how you think ELLs can and should be supported in the writing process when writing in their second language.

2. Visit a classroom where there are ELLs. Take anecdotal notes about what the teacher is doing to scaffold the writing of ELLs. Is help visible in the classroom through rubrics, cognates, and content word walls?

3. Interview a teacher who works with ELLs. Find out if there is a writing program used at the school for ELLs.
   - If there is one, find out about it and analyze whether you think the program is one that will produce fluent, organized writers.
   - If the school does not have a formal writing plan, ask the teacher what she does to support student writing. How often do students write? Do they ever receive instruction in the guided writing process? Do they understand and use rubrics to guide their thinking and writing?

Differentiating Instruction for Exceptional ELLs (eELLs)

By Lorri Santamaría

If my teacher only knew that I feel left out. If she knew that she wouldn't have told me not to bother to think about college because I go to special ed classes. I guess I won't go then. School is really confusing. I'm supposed to see what the teachers want me to see, but I see something else. What does that make me?

Eva, grade 6

This chapter addresses differentiating instruction for ELLs who meet the criteria to receive special education services, such as special day classes (SDC), pull-out resource specialist programs (RSP), full inclusion in general education classrooms, and gifted education. In this chapter, these students are referred to as exceptional learners as opposed to students with disabilities, especially because gifted ELLs, who certainly fall into the category, are underrepresented and often overlooked in the literature (Artiles & Ortiz, 2002). Therefore, this chapter emphasizes exceptional education services in lieu of special education services, which carry historically negative connotations, and services that look to deficit models to remedy and assist students referred to as having disabilities.

In most current exceptional education delivery models, students who qualify to receive exceptional education services are excluded from general education classrooms and sent to settings where "experts" can attend to their needs. This perspective is often debilitating to students and counterintuitive to the resources and expertise available at most schools. When general educators (responsible for teaching children without particular educational needs) buy into the "expert" only perspective, they essentially give exceptional learners to "someone else" to take care of, thus giving the responsibility for their success away. This chapter describes how general educators can use differentiated instruction to meet the needs of exceptional learners who are ELLs (eELLs) in the regular classroom. In this chapter, we:

- Provide context for suggested strategies and guidelines using a case study of an exemplary program that uses differentiated instruction for eELLs in the regular classroom.

- Discuss guidelines and a model for appropriate differentiation for ELLs in the general education classroom.

- Explore assessment implications to present perspective and rationale for change.

- Identify practical ways to integrate general and exceptional education services, specifically the value of co-teaching and what it means for exceptional education resources and student learning.

- Explain the scaffolding process for students receiving exceptional education services in order to substantiate scaffolding as a viable strategy for students with or without exceptionalities.

Building Background Knowledge About Differentiated Instruction for eELLs

Welcome to Bienvenidos: A Case Study as Context to Discuss Differentiation for eELLs

Bienvenidos (a pseudonym) Elementary School is a coastal Southern Californian K–6 campus with 422 students, of whom just over 25% are Latino ELLs of Mexican descent. About 30% of the students qualify for free and reduced lunches under federal guidelines. Most of the students who qualify for federal assistance represent culturally and linguistically different groups (e.g., African American, Native American, and Asian Pacific Islander) or are White children living in poverty. There are several exceptional education service delivery models practiced at the school, including three day classes (i.e., K–1, 2–3, 4–6), in-class and out-of-class resource specialist support, speech and language services, and occupational and physical therapy ancillary services. The faculty at Bienvenidos is well seasoned, averaging 12 years of teaching experience, with all but 5% of the teachers having appropriate credentials to teach the grade levels and subjects assigned to them.

Despite the challenges cultural, linguistic, and academic student diversity typically pose for school leadership, Bienvenidos Elementary boasts the following statistics: a good ranking, 8 out of 10 on the California Department of Education's Academic Performance Index, with an overall 42-point improvement over last year's performance, which surpasses the state's target score of 800 for all schools (California Department of Education, 2003).

Although this school fares better than similar schools in most categories, the professional culture at Bienvenidos Elementary follows a typical pattern described in the literature. The school culture fosters separation between general education and exceptional education teachers so that the two programs operate as if they were on two separate campuses. This separation persists because teachers perceive collaboration and change as either too complex or too close to affecting their own individual classroom practices (Peters, 2002).

Several discrepancies for students attending the school exist. First, children who have been identified as having specific learning disabilities, receive support for speech and language difficulties, attend exceptional day classes, or receive in-class and out-of-class resource specialist support do not have complete access to the core academic curriculum. Many of the identified students are Latino/a ELLs. This is in direct violation of the federal legislation No Child Left Behind (NCLB) Act of 2001 (Public Law 107-110) and the 1997 Individuals with Disabilities Education Act (IDEA). Second, teachers do not regularly engage in self-reflection nor do they practice appropriate self-monitoring as suggested by research and literature on the subject, which would be expected in the diverse educational climate at the school. Last, based on biweekly observations, teachers at Bienvenidos (like many nation and worldwide) regularly participate in positive and negative stereotyping based on student ability, ethnicity, class, language, and gender as evidenced by their daily interactions, teaching practices, and staff meetings.

To counter these accepted "ways of being," two forward-thinking teachers, one kindergarten and one first-grade teacher, decided to work collaboratively with local university faculty by combining students in the exceptional education teacher's class with students in the general education classroom. What they learned from this year-long adventure will serve to contextualize and inform the remainder of this chapter (case gleaned from Santamaría & Thousand, 2004).

Differentiation with eELLs: Some Concepts and Definitions

Before discussing management of differentiated instruction for eELLs, we need to first revisit the definition of differentiated instruction. Second, we need to determine who we mean when we refer to eELL students.

Differentiation can best be described as a group of common theories and practices recognizing student differences in background knowledge, readiness, language, learning style, and interests, resulting in individually responsive teaching appropriate to particular student needs (Guild & Garger, 1998). Hypothetically, differentiated instruction is a process approach most suitable to classrooms where students exhibit a wide range of ability levels. The approach addresses content (curricular goals or standards), process (ways in which students negotiate content), and product (what students produce). Differentiation is intended to meet students at personal instructional levels, maximizing growth and resulting in individual success (Hall, 2004). Because recognizing and responding to student differences is subjective, differentiated instruction can be considered a philosophical orientation as much as best teaching practice or theory. In this chapter, I will further explore whether differentiated instruction is appropriate for ELLs with exceptional needs at Bienvenidos Elementary School.

Who are eELLs? It can be argued that all ELLs have exceptional needs by virtue of their learning another language. But according to authors Leonard Baca and Hermes Cervantes it is those ELLs who are in legitimate need of and qualify for exceptional education services independent of English language acquisition that constitute the classification (Baca & Cervantes, 2004). Unfortunately there remains a gross overrepresentation of ELLs receiving exceptional education services due to biased assessment practices related to linguistic and cultural differences based on discrepancies between ELLs and their English-only mainstream peers (Carrasquillo, 1991). Because of this reality, Baca and Cervantes (2004) support bilingual exceptional education services for those who legitimately qualify and ongoing advocacy for students receiving services as a result of inappropriate placement in exceptional education settings. So when we discuss ELLs with exceptional needs, we consider students with particular needs independent of language, according to exceptional, better known as special, education criteria for qualification, as well as students who qualify for exceptional education using biased illegitimate criteria.

Managing Differentiated Instruction for eELLs

At Bienvenidos Elementary School approximately 60% of the students receiving exceptional education services are ELLs and about 50% of those students may not have qualified had they not been acquiring both English and Spanish simultaneously. By their willingness to meet the needs of ELLs in their classrooms, the exceptional education and general education teacher partners at Bienvenidos Elementary School demonstrate their responsiveness to current trends and special education reform. These trends include the movement toward inclusion, the use of a collaborative consultation model, prereferral interventions, and the inclusion of students with disabilities in high-stakes assessment (Baca & Cervantes, 2004). Before their teachers' intervention, students with exceptional needs, both ELLs and EO students, did not have access to general curriculum and did not participate in high-stakes testing. To teach all of the students in the same classroom, differentiation on many levels has to take place every day all of the time. The teachers at Bienvenidos provide an in-depth example of differentiation for practitioners teaching eELLs in primary grades.

The two Bienvenidos teachers profiled in this chapter based their work on that of Carol Ann Tomlinson, who has written extensively on differentiated instruction (Tomlinson, 1995, 2000, 2001, 2003). They both attended inservices on the approach during the previous academic year. To manage differentiated instruction for their diverse learners, they employed five guidelines (Hall, Strangman, & Meyer, 2003) based on the work of Tomlinson, which facilitated differentiation. The teachers' applications of the five guidelines expand its original implications to be more inclusive of culturally and linguistically diverse (CLD) learners.

The first guideline is clarification of key concepts and generalizations. This type of content-based clarification ensures that all learners acquire deep foundational understanding of the academic material being presented. Language arts or mathematics content, based on California content standards (see http://www.cde.ca.gov for a list and description of the most current content standards in place at the state level), was first presented to all students at the same time in general terms using literature, a song, or a skit acted out by the teachers. Then to clarify the concept further, the teachers broke students up into two equally sized, mixed-ability groups to be instructed in two separate classrooms, one classroom per teacher. The groups were then broken up into heterogeneous subgroups and instructed by the teachers, instructional assistants, or parent volunteers primarily using centers where they could teach each learner individually based on her or his particular academic needs. Older student helpers, who served as cross-age tutors, further clarified tough ideas for individual students as needed. If time permitted, teachers reconvened the students into larger groups to still further clarify information learned in order to make pertinent generalizations, adding to students' cumulative knowledge base.

The second guideline is the use of assessment as a teaching tool to extend rather than merely measure instruction occurring before, during, and after learning takes place. In large groups, teachers were able to conduct informal assessment of student knowledge by asking content-based questions of students and by listening to them share known information on a given content area. This allowed the teachers to assess background knowledge and prior learning before beginning more formalized instruction. Later, in smaller groups at centers, teachers continued ongoing assessment during formal instructional time. Teachers used observational checklists, one-on-one content area reviews, and for students with identified exceptional needs, individualized educational program (IEP) objectives. Each child with exceptional needs also brought a communication journal home and back to school so that parents were involved in a more inclusive formative assessment process where their observations and opinions contributed to the teachers' assessment of student learning. By the time report cards or annual IEP meetings were due, teachers had obtained the information they needed to draw summative conclusions and inform future instruction based on whole class as well as individual needs.

Emphasizing critical and creative thinking as global lesson design is the third guideline, which involves process-based student support as needed. The teachers followed through with this component by using California content standards and the material adopted by their district as foundational planning pieces. At first, the teachers complained about having to adhere to standards and the use of the adopted materials, but as they became more proficient in differentiation for particular student needs, they became more fluent in their ability to plan critically and creatively. This involved making standards more accessible to every student on each student's terms. Research-grounded, process-based supports for students included scaffolding by teachers, older students, more proficient peers, or bi/multilingual materials (Santamaría, Fletcher, & Bos, 2002). Instructional assistants also provided process-based supports for students as well as the teachers in their planning and instruction. These individuals were central to the teachers' success in that they became the most fluid supports in the effort, moving between and among teachers, students, parent volunteers, and other adults when and where needed.

The fourth guideline involves the process of engaging all learners within a variety of learning tasks. Engaging all learners sounds almost like a cliché, but when one considers eELLs and other exceptional learners there are many factors to consider. At Bienvenidos, the language of instruction in the classroom was primarily English, but to accommodate ELLs with and without exceptionalities and facilitate access to content area knowledge and content, many modes of demonstrated learning were accepted, including oral responses, body language, visual artistic expression, small-group responses, and translated messages through informal student or instructional assistant interpreters. Centers included visual, auditory, kinesthetic, and tactile activities as well as traditional pen-and-paper tasks. Scaffolds for each activity included assistance by a teacher, aide, or older student; task accommodations and activities; the use of more concrete and explicit language; and materials that were adapted based on student needs (Santamaría et al., 2002).

The final guideline refers to providing a balance between teacher-assigned and student-selected tasks based on assessment data, while incorporating student choice in the classroom. Independent of student competency, the teachers consistently offered choices for their students to make. They embedded these choices in the academic tasks that reflected goals and objectives pursuant to California content standards. Each activity choice satisfied a common or similar goal or objective so no matter which mode of academic expression a student chose to participate in based on their needs, abilities, and interests, it fit the guidelines of learning goals for the entire class.

For this discussion, I describe each guideline separately, but teachers regularly employ one or two, combinations of several, or all guidelines simultaneously, depending on

TABLE 9.1 Guidelines for Differentiation and Teaching eELLs

Guideline	Examples
1. Clarify Key Concepts and Generalizations	Teachers use whole class for direct instruction and small groups for follow-up and reteaching as necessary as a means of ensuring that students understand key concepts and generalizations.
2. Use Assessment as a Teaching Tool to Extend Instruction	Teachers engage the students in large-group discussion where students are provided opportunities to share what they know in a nonthreatening environment. Teachers then plan lessons to meet the needs of the students.
3. Emphasize Critical and Creative Thinking as Global Design	Teachers' lessons are made accessible to all students by differentiating the instruction and scaffolding instruction as needed. Teachers include scaffolds that allow students to engage creatively and critically in the instruction.
4. Engage All Learners Within a Variety of Learning Tasks	Teachers design lessons that utilize a variety of modalities and use resources such as interpreters, when necessary. Students are able to engage in lessons and demonstrate their knowledge in multiple ways, including oral, written, individual, and small group.
5. Provide a Balance Between Teacher-assigned and Student-selected Tasks Based on Assessment Data and Incorporating Student Choice	Teachers use the California content standards to develop lessons. These lessons offer students the choice between a variety of assignments, including oral and written reports, art projects, and individual and group projects.

Source: Based on Hall, T., Strangman, N., & Meyer, A. (2003). Differentiated instruction and implications for UDL implementation. Wakefield, MA: National Center on Accessing the General Curriculum. Retrieved January 19, 2008, from http://www.cast.org/publications/ncac/ncac_diffinstructudl.html

students' needs, content, process, and product. As can be seen from the Bienvenidos example, many different facets of differentiation are often ongoing in effective eELL classrooms. Additionally, differentiation for ELLs with or without exceptionality is specific to the particular language and cultural characteristics presented by each individual learner. Therefore, teachers need to design differentiation to respond to specific and particular students' needs. Table 9.1 describes five guidelines for differentiating instruction for eELLs that were used to meet student needs at Bienvenidos.

Linking Theory to Practice

In What Ways Does Assessment Inform Instruction? Debunking Assumptions and Using Assessment to Address Student Needs

In their work, Baca and Cervantes (2004) discuss what they term unanswered calls for change. This concise list of desired changes for eELLs in classrooms where instruction is differentiated responds to a continued disproportionate representation of CLD learners in exceptional education programs, continued biased assessment practices, continued overreliance on standardized tests, lack of continuity between exceptional and regular education curriculum, and minimal interaction and collaboration between exceptional and general education programs (Artiles & Ortiz, 2002). The participating teachers at Bienvenidos Elementary School responded to these calls for change but realistically had difficulty effecting change in assessment practices driven by national, local, and district initiatives.

Before discussing ways in which assessment informs and drives instruction, we need to identify assumptions about assessments for ELLs, especially those labeled as having special needs. First, many tests rely on students' knowledge of culturally based information, which many ELLs do not know or have cultural access to (Pierangelo & Giulani, 2002). Furthermore, tests in English measure both the content area and language proficiency, so that when a student fails such a test, it is unclear if it is the language or the content that is unknown (Mercado & Romero, 1993). And translating standardized tests poses additional problems.

Traditional assessments used to place ELLs in exceptional education programs are not practical as rarely (if ever) do their results inform academic implications and plans for academic achievement for the students who take them. Furthermore, and especially when you look at the relationship between language and content in tests, one can conclude that their results are arbitrary, leading to labeling that is useless and oftentimes debilitating for students and their families (Collier, 1988; Stainback & Stainback, 1996). Is it any wonder then, that Latino and other ELLs are overrepresented in exceptional education programs (e.g., learning disability resource, special day class) nationally as well as at Bienvenidos? Conversely, ELLs are underrepresented in gifted education programs.

So then what do we make of assessment in the context of differentiated instruction for eELLs? We redefine the construct so that assessment informs instruction, deeming it more appropriate for students while truly allowing and enabling students to demonstrate learning. In this paradigm shift, assessment moves from an oppressive function resulting in inappropriate labeling (thus blaming) and service delivery to a place where it provides clues to teachers as to what students need. In the Bienvenidos case, where content-imbedded assessment that looked at what the students actually did during instruction, these instructional activities began to yield valid information for assessment. Because assessment activities were ongoing, the integration of assessment and intervention ensured involvement of both the exceptional and general educator, and this shift transferred assessment from a place of diagnosis and placement to intervention where it belonged (Baca & Cervantes, 2004).

To further realize this unique way of looking at assessment, the teachers employed several alternative assessments: ecological assessment, descriptive assessment, and advocacy-oriented assessment. Ecological assessment involves direct observations of the students' behavior in their natural environment, in this case school (Anderson & Long, 2002). Ecological assessment also considers group membership as a determinant of student performance. For example, a parent's report of learning may have come because of a student's performance in his or her home environment working at a dinner table with older siblings acting as social scaffolds, where the teacher's assessment is viewed primarily in whole or small groups consisting primarily of the learner's peer group. Another ecological assessment is group membership as a determinant of student performance depending on the ability levels and interaction patterns of the members of the learners' cooperative group.

Descriptive assessment, on the other hand, provides a more holistic view of students by using a variety of data collection methods (e.g., language samples, narrative analysis, rating scales). With this type of assessment, teachers analyze data with full consideration of students' language proficiency, previous academic performance, and an emphasis on the use of multiple measures. Teachers at Bienvenidos, like most in the United States, did not have a lot of time for descriptive assessment, but did use checklists, anecdotal note taking, and the communication journal previously discussed as assessment tools.

The need for advocacy-oriented assessment, usually associated with power and status relations between minority and majority groups (Cummins, 1986), had a clear place in the classrooms at Bienvenidos where some parents and the surrounding learning community considered some of the children more able than others. In this project, which involved the blending of two very different classrooms, both teachers became advocates for all of the students whether ELL, exceptional, or labeled with no apparent exceptionality. This approach, like ecological assessment, perceives the assessment process as inappropriate for ELLs and requires teachers to take precautionary measures when assessing ELLs as well as when interpreting test results for these learners.

Finally, Figueroa and Garcia (1994) offer cautions that teachers should take when assessing ELLs. These cautions, when paired with the testing framework presented in Chapter 4, offer practitioners a more socially just and equitable way of considering assessment for ELLs with and without exceptionality.

One of the first cautions is evaluation of the quality of students' learning experiences. For example, the teachers at Bienvenidos called on their students' preschool teachers for additional background knowledge. Teachers must also be aware that when ELLs are assessed in English, those tests do not necessarily measure the construct they are designed to assess, but instead become a measure of English language proficiency (Figueroa & García, 1994). Furthermore, not all ELLs have identical language backgrounds, which will also influence test results. With these cautions in mind, the teachers at Bienvenidos called on the services of their bilingual instructional assistant, when her language background matched students, to translate during the assessment process. Realizing diminished psychometric qualities of translated tests, another caution, participating teachers took test results with a grain of salt. One more caution teachers responded to was the awareness that the testing context is culturally bound and that student responses could easily be misinterpreted. With these cautions in mind, the teachers at Bienvenidos reinvented the testing process for the learners in their classroom.

Exceptional Education Programs as Resources to the Mainstream: The Value of Co-Teaching

Co-teaching, in this case the general and exceptional education teacher equally sharing fluid teaching responsibilities, is the most readily available way in which exceptional education programs can be considered resources to the mainstream. Another way exceptional education services can add to general education classrooms is the reallocation of resources, including instructional assistants, and the inclusion of ancillary services personnel (e.g., speech/language specialists, occupational therapists) as teaching associates in mainstream classrooms (Santamaría et al., 2002).

Co-teaching is effective for students with a variety of instructional needs, including ELLs (Mahoney, 1997); hearing impairment (Luckner, 1999; Compton, Stratton, Maier, Meyers, Scott, & Tomlinson, 1998); learning disabilities (Rice & Zigmond, 1999; Trent, 1998; Welch, 2000); and high-risk students in a social studies class (Dieker, 1998) as well as in a language remediation class (Miller, Valasky, & Molloy, 1998). To illustrate, Welch (2000) showed that the performance of students with disabilities and their classmates all made academic gains in reading and spelling on curriculum-based assessments in the co-taught classrooms. Mahoney (1997) found that in addition to meeting educational needs "for exceptional education students, being part of the large class meant making new friends" (p. 59). There is, then, an emerging database for preschool through high school levels (Villa, Thousand, Nevin, & Malgeri, 1996) supporting the conclusions that (a) at all grade levels students with disabilities can be educated effectively in general education environments when teachers, support personnel, and families collaborate; and (b) student performance improvements occur in both academic and social relationship arenas.

As predicted by Walther-Thomas (1997), who examined collaborative teaching models in 23 schools across eight districts, co-teaching partners at Bienvenidos also changed the ways in which teachers taught when they moved to a new, larger teaching space to better accommodate their teaching arrangement. When they had only 32 students, the teachers primarily engaged in *team teaching*. They both taught all 32 students together in a whole group by taking turns teaching various aspects of the content, whereas instructional assistants engaged in *supportive co-teaching,* providing support to individual students as needed (Villa, Thousand, & Nevin, 2004). With the unanticipated addition of 10 students during the second week of school, the co-teachers expanded their ways of co-teaching.

For example, they moved from relying solely on their former team-teaching arrangement to using other co-teaching arrangements such as *complementary* or *parallel teaching* at stations (centers). Here they created small heterogeneous groups of students that rotated among stations, each of which was supervised by a teacher, instructional assistant, or student teacher. In this arrangement, all of the adults engaged simultaneously in instruction at centers for part of the day, doing different things in different locations, with students rotating among the centers. Again, they sometimes split the class in half heterogeneously and conducted parallel instruction of groups in the same or different topics in different rooms. These expanded co-teaching configurations allowed for better student management, individualized attention, and the maintenance of high yet differentiated academic standards (Villa et al., 2004).

Most of the co-teaching described in the literature is based on deliberate planning with student characteristics dictating instructional practices (Fletcher, Bos, & Johnson (Santamaría), 1999; Santamaría et al., 2002). Part of the university collaboration involved coaching on multilevel differentiated instruction techniques and authentic assessment. This coaching may have accounted, in part, for these co-teachers' decisions about how to organize and evaluate instruction throughout the day. However, the authors contend that the two experienced professional educators featured in the work also used their already-learned skill to modify lessons on the spot. These observed phenomena of *spontaneous differentiation* have not been addressed in the literature on differentiated instruction thus far (Chapman & King, 2003; Heydon, 2003; Rule & Lord, 2003; Tomlinson, 1999, 2001).

Authentic, multilevel instruction and assessment became the norm in the classroom as teachers moved among a variety of co-teaching configurations to respond to the broad range of student needs (Villa et al., 2004). They planned centers, seat work, and free-play. As a result of the support provided by other adults in the classroom, the teachers were free to meet with small groups and individual students working on specific goals. They put student teachers (who were learning parallel pedagogy in their preservice teaching coursework), university collaborators, ancillary services specialists, and anyone who walked in the door to work to scaffold students at multiple levels of ability to actively engage in the complexities of the day (Santamaría & Thousand, 2004; Santamaría et al., 2002).

Scaffolded Instruction for Exceptional Students

All of the students in the co-teachers' classrooms at Bienvenidos Elementary School experienced a great deal of academic success. Exceptional ELL and other student success was due to the use of a myriad of linguistic, academic, social, and emotional scaffolds. Past scholarly discussions of scaffolding learning for eELLs identified four types of scaffolds: mediated (e.g., expert/novice), task (e.g., steps provided), materials (e.g., story maps or frames), and comprehensible input (e.g., knowledge of concepts in primary language) (Santamaría et al., 2002). These scaffolds take place in what Vygotsky (1978) calls the zone of proximal development or the "place" where students are able to accomplish more than expected with specific appropriate supports and/or assistance. In this chapter, the conversation on academic scaffolds for eELLs includes social and emotional or cultural scaffolds complementing ideas presented in Chapters 2, 5, and 8.

Previously explored scaffolds for eELLs used by participating teachers at Bienvenidos include mediated, task, materials, and comprehensible input. Mediated scaffolds were most frequently used by teachers, instructional assistants, specialists, and older student helpers in their roles as center leaders working in small groups to assist students step-by-step in the learning of new information or the execution of content area tasks. Task scaffolds were used in centers where adults or more capable peers were not assigned and students were expected to work independently. These included cue cards with step-by-step instructions displayed in pictures so students were able to participate in the center regardless of language or ability level. For example, in the listening center the pictures depicted (1) sit down, (2) get a copy of the book from the basket, (3) put headphones on, (4) turn on recorder, (5) follow along by turning pages, and (6) when the bell rings (to change centers) rewind the tape for the next group.

An example of materials scaffolds in the classroom was the use of dotted lines or words written in yellow highlighter pen for young learners negotiating the task of primary penmanship. The most memorable example of comprehensible input as a scaffold was the afternoon when one of the teachers asked ELLs (some with exceptionalities) to share a version of their favorite fairy tale in their native language. Monolingual English speakers were delighted to hear versions of *Cinderella, The Three Pigs*, and *Jack-in-the-Beanstalk* in Spanish, French, and German, and ELLs got a chance to tap into their primary language to better understand the concept of fairy tales in English. Consequentially, as the ELLs read aloud in different languages, their primary language skills were highlighted, which served to scaffold instruction socially and emotionally during the lesson.

What then are social and emotional scaffolds, and why do we need them? Social and emotional scaffolds are really cultural scaffolds communicating to eELLs that they can accomplish whatever is presented to them to complete. These scaffolds are expectations communicated by teachers, adults, and more capable peers (mediated scaffolds) that the learner being supported is valued and that their success matters.

Differentiating instruction for eELLs depends on providing social and emotional support specific to the academic expectations of the learning environment whether classroom instruction, assessment, or socialization are being considered. Multicultural researchers and theorists speculate about what this kind of support looks like and have identified several principles that capture its essence (Ladson-Billings, 1984; Tharp, Estrada, Dalton, & Yamaguchi, 2000). Table 9.2 illustrates ways in which these principles relate to guidelines for differentiated instruction.

The two teachers we observed at Bienvenidos practiced differentiated instruction effectively for the eELLs and ELLs in their classroom, including their evident and noteworthy application of social and emotional principles that accounted for the success of all ELLs. In terms of the first principle, students and teachers producing together, the teachers had an uncanny way of appearing as if they didn't know key concepts only to

TABLE 9.2 Scaffolding Principles and Differentiated Instruction for CLD Learners and eELLs*

Scaffolding Principles for Teaching CLD Learners and eELLs (Standards for Effective Pedagogy and Culturally Responsive Teaching)	Guidelines for Implementing Differentiated Instruction
Teachers and students producing together • Active teaching methods • Teacher as facilitator • Student-controlled *classroom discourse*	**Process** • Emphasizing critical and creative thinking • *Engaging all learners* • Maintaining a balance between teacher-assigned and student-selected tasks
Developing language and literacy across curriculum • Positive perspectives on *parents and families of CLD students* • Small-group instruction and academically related discourse	**Product** • Using assessment as a teaching tool
Making meaning: Connecting school to students • Positive perspectives on parents and families of CLD students • *Cultural sensitivity* • *Reshaping* the curriculum	**Content** • Clarifying key concepts and generalizations **Product** • Using assessment as a teaching tool
Teaching complex thinking • Communication of high expectations • *Culturally mediated* instruction	**Content** • Clarifying key concepts and generalizations **Process** • Emphasizing critical and creative thinking
Teaching through conversation • Positive perspectives on parents and families of CLD students • Student-controlled classroom discourse • Small-group instruction and academically related discourse	**Process** • Emphasizing critical and creative thinking • Engaging all learners • Maintaining a balance between teacher-assigned and student-selected tasks

*Words in italics refer to scaffolding for meeting the needs of CLD learners, including eELLs.

Source: Based on *The dreamkeepers: Successful teachers of African American children,* by G. Ladson-Billings, 1984, San Francisco, CA: Jossey-Bass; *Teaching transformed: Achieving excellence, fairness, inclusion, and harmony,* by R. G. Tharp, P. Estrada, S. S. Dalton, and L. Yamaguchi, 2000, Boulder, CO: Westview Press; *Fulfilling the promise of the differentiated classroom: Strategies and tools for responsive teaching,* by C. A. Tomlinson, 2003, Alexandria, VA: Association for Supervision and Curriculum Development.

"discover" them simultaneously with students. For example, when students first began to make sound–symbol connections, the general education teacher let student discoveries tell her how to react, pretending the discoveries were as new to her as they were to the students. Students were delighted with their joint "discovery."

The two teachers scaffolded the development of language and literacy across the curriculum by their frequent choice of students' native languages during lessons or read alouds. Although neither teacher was bilingual, they had Spanish speakers (e.g., instructional assistants, university collaborators, student helpers) to support ELLs' growth in language arts. ELLs who were not Spanish-speaking received nonverbal support and experienced a celebratory attitude about their and their families' cultural and linguistic differences.

Making connections that explicitly linked students' lives to school was another way in which the teachers scaffolded for social and emotional stability. Students' families were always welcomed and incorporated into lessons, cultural sensitivity was modeled and practiced (there were over six languages, cultures, and ethnicities present in the classroom at all times), and students' language and culture helped teachers to reshape curriculum accordingly, making it more reflective of students' lives.

On the surface, teaching complex thinking does not appear to be scaffolding for social or emotional competence, but in light of the historical absence of its use with ELLs and children with disabilities, it is important to consider its inclusion when differentiating instruction. To teach complex thinking to historically marginalized learners, the teachers at Bienvenidos needed to erase and overcome negative self-talk that precluded these children from benefiting from this kind of teaching and learning. They regularly communicated high expectations to all of the children under their charge, disabled or not. The use of higher order thinking skills beyond rote learning and task orientation, as suggested by differentiation, was used by both teachers to support the possibility of students performing better than they would have without these scaffolds.

Finally, and perhaps most important, teachers consistently used instructional conversation or "talk in which ideas are explored rather than answers to teachers' test questions provided and evaluated" (Cazden, 1998, p. 54) to scaffold social and emotional aspects of student learning. Quiet time did not exist for these young learners. Every learning experience took place within the context of a verbal exchange among students, more capable peers, or adults in the classroom. Students helped to shape instruction by the questions they asked and the answers they generated. Lively conversations were the hallmark of every learning center, every day. English language learners and exceptional learners were surrounded by age-appropriate models and adult support that enabled them to experience classroom success in both language arts and mathematics. Social and emotional scaffolds, therefore, acted as complements to other more standard academic scaffolds.

Lessons Learned

In this chapter, the Bienvenidos case study provided context for suggested strategies and guidelines gleaned from literature and research on ELLs with and without exceptional needs (Santamaría & Thousand, 2004). In addition, I discussed management of differentiation for ELLs with exceptional needs in general education classrooms to present guidelines and a model for appropriate differentiation. I then suggested implications for assessment to provide perspective and rationale for change, followed by a summary of ways to view exceptional education services as resources to student learning via the value of co-teaching, which included practical ways to integrate general and exceptional education services. Finally, I included an understanding of the scaffolding process for students receiving exceptional education services to substantiate scaffolding as a viable strategy for students with and without exceptional needs.

What can we learn from a chapter like this one? Besides equipping teachers who are preservice or currently practicing and those who educate teachers with a more empowering terminology with which to reference children commonly described as being disabled, this chapter offers five lessons for educators working with ELLs. First, we can see by the example provided by the teachers at Bienvenidos ways in which differentiated instruction manifests differently for ELLs with and without special needs. Second, we learned that exceptionality labels for ELLs may be arbitrarily based on the legitimacy of assessment practices and the knowledge base of professionals administering and interpreting test results. Third, we learned that there are a variety of authentic assessments teachers can use to better determine the best ways in which to teach all of their students, especially those who are eELLs. Fourth, we demonstrated ways in which exceptional educators and general educators can work together by reallocating resources whether they be people (e.g., instructional assistants), materials, or space (e.g., classrooms) and by co-teaching. Fifth, we can identify a variety of ways in which to use scaffolding with eELLs and other students who may or may not be labeled as exceptional within the contexts of differentiation using principles for teaching CLD children.

Educators can use the information presented in this chapter to make decisions about teaching and assessment practices for some of the most marginalized learners in U.S. schools: eELLs. Perhaps now, all teachers, regardless of classification, can take back and own the teaching practices that serve these students best and cease from sending eELLs away to "specialists." I hope that after reading this chapter and applying its principles, teachers will attain and maintain academic, social, and emotional success with all of the students in their prospective classrooms.

Examples from the Field

By Sharon H. Ulanoff

Elena is a fourth-grade student. She is 9 years old, was born in Los Angeles, and has attended the same elementary school since kindergarten. She is bilingual. Her native language is Spanish, and she received initial reading instruction in Spanish, transitioning to all-English instruction at the beginning of fourth grade. Before entering kindergarten, she was hit by a car and was in a coma for 8 days. At the time, tests revealed a lateral/frontal hematoma and several broken bones. Shortly after the accident, her IQ was tested to be 110. She had a mild conductive hearing loss and was also diagnosed as having "mildly reduced cognitive status." Upon entering kindergarten, she was placed in a regular

Reading together.

bilingual classroom setting with an IEP. End-of-year comments state that she met her target goals in reading and math. Her entrance documents also contain the comment, "tends to wander away and needs supervision."

At the end of first grade, her teacher recommended testing for exceptional education placement based on her observation that the "child is not progressing in reading class." She also noted that Elena had difficulty remembering material presented both visually and verbally. On the referral sheet she commented, "I am concerned that she does not seem to process directions or information and does not retain much from one day to the next" and checked off that Elena "appears to be achieving below potential." Interestingly, her teacher also commented that she observed Elena looking at her pencil and easily reading the word *Ticonderoga* from its side. The speech therapist reported that Elena is "slow in everything she does according to mom and her classroom teachers." Elena's teachers used this information in planning her instruction (see Table 9.3).

Despite these comments, Elena remained in the regular classroom and received RSP and speech pathology services. Elena is currently engaging in all-English instruction. We observed Elena during several different literacy lessons, both literature discussions and writing lessons/activities. Elena approaches learning and activities in various ways. She is usually slow to start an activity and as she participates becomes more

TABLE 9.3 A Planning Chart for Differentiated Instruction for Elena

Student Name	What I Know About Each Student	Grade Level Concept	Skills Required	Necessary Scaffolds
Elena	Spanish is L1. Was in a car accident before attending K. Although there was no permanent damage, Elena initially had mild auditory and cognitive problems.	Fourth grade	Needs work on attention span and listening skills.	Use varied activities, including short read alouds. Work with speech therapist.
	First-grade teacher said that Elena was not progressing in Spanish reading, but she is able to read environmental print.		Making connections between environmental print and reading texts.	Read the room, use charts and posters as well as big books, shared and guided reading.
	Parents want her to succeed.		Communicating with parents.	Reinforce parental desire for success.
	Starts work slowly and proceeds slowly. Often takes so long to finish work that she gives up (or expects teacher to let her give up); exhibits "learned helplessness."		Needs to work on attention span and following through.	Model and partner reading and writing.
	Understands both English and Spanish.		Making connections between L1 and L2.	Use contrastive analysis.
	Needs support on how to elaborate on ideas in writing.		Drawing on personal interests and background knowledge.	Share and model writing.
	Relies heavily on Spanish syntax and spelling as the basis for her writing in English.		Understanding the structures that do and do not transfer from Spanish to English.	Use contrastive analysis between Spanish and English, free voluntary reading and listening to stories, and journal writing.

interested and efficient. She sometimes uses planning as a strategy, especially in her writing, as she has been taught process writing and writes frequently. Still, her writing samples are often simple and unelaborated (see Figure 9.1, composed on the classroom computer).

One of the scaffolding strategies that her teacher uses is to have Elena engage in shared or modeled writing with a more capable peer (Vygotsky, 1978). Her scaffolded writing samples are generally more elaborate than the ones she writes alone (see Figure 9.2). When she writes alone, she often appears to process things at a slow rate, but this may be due to a sort of "learned helplessness," which Coles (1987) describes as a state where students become defined as not being able to complete academic tasks and therefore become powerless. It may be that this identity as someone who cannot produce work has attached itself to Elena and followed her through school. When she writes with a peer, she still writes more slowly than the rest of the class, but her fellow student helps her to move along at a steadier pace and complete the task in a timely fashion.

Elena's teacher expanded on this strategy when she collaborated with Elena in a modeled writing activity. She chose to do this after she observed Elena complete the writing

FIGURE 9.1 Elena's Writing Sample, Written Alone

A want to be a prynsses to be a
prinses to help people and to mache
them rich and mache them happy and
give them money and thei cood be happy
for eber and they are goen to be rich
for eber and happy

The End

task alone. She gave Elena an individual writing assignment along with the rest of the class. They were to write a letter to a beloved instructional aide who had been transferred to another class. The letters were to be sent to Mrs. Ramirez at the end of the day, so there was already a time frame in place. The students, including Elena, were highly motivated to complete the task.

Elena began to write immediately without planning or stopping to think about what she was going to write. She wrote slowly and methodically in English. Elena paused approximately 15 times during the 15 minutes she worked on her letter (Figure 9.3). Most of her pauses were for 1 or 2 seconds, but she did have two where she paused for 30 seconds or more. When asked about her pauses (after the writing), she said that she was mainly trying to think of what to write, but that one time she did pause to think of how to spell a word (and she did rewrite this word). Her teacher interviewed her after she wrote, and Elena stated that the assignment was a little difficult because it was hard to remember what she wrote. It is interesting to note that Elena struggled with the interview as if she were waiting for the teacher to give up and put the words in her mouth. Her letter, while appearing long, has limited content and is repetitive.

After the interview, the teacher decided to work with Elena so that they could rewrite the letter together, this time with the teacher acting as a more capable other and assisting her performance. She used a few different scaffolds for Elena. First, they planned the letter by brainstorming together and creating a written cluster to serve as an "outline" for the

FIGURE 9.2 Elena's Scaffolded Writing Sample (with a more capable peer)

The Holloween Party

Once upon a time there was a women.

That wanted to have a Holloween party. The women invited her friends. And they like the Holloween Party. And when they opened the door they saw a mummy.

And they srceemed. And they went inside the house. And he nocked on the door. They said who is it. He said your grany. They opened the door. And some body called the police. The mummy came in and ate every body. The police came and put the mummy in jail.

The
n
d

letter (see Figure 9.4). They created the cluster in a collaborative manner also, with each of them alternating adding items to the cluster. This situated the activity in a social context where the teacher was able to scaffold the activity as much or as little as needed. When the cluster was finished, they agreed on an order in which to write the letter (see Figure 9.5). The teacher began the letter and Elena followed. At first, Elena seemed a bit constrained by the task, as if she could not be creative and think of any sentences beyond those that were written in the cluster. By the middle of the second paragraph, however, she began to feel a bit freer and experiment with sentences, structuring her sentences differently than those of the teacher. The teacher then modeled the strategy of rereading to see if the letter *flowed*. The letter does appear to be more cohesive than the solo attempt, despite the two authors. When discussing this task, Elena stated that it was much easier to write with a teacher "because a teacher helps you with your ideas." She also said that making the cluster helped her write the letter.

FIGURE 9.3 Elena's Letter to Mrs. Ramirez, Written Alone

Dear mss. Ramires
thank you For helpen ebre body
en Room.4 were goin to Miss
you so Much did you know you
are my best best Frend. I, am
a bery bery bett Frend of
you I wish I cood know
your aDress and Fone number
Oh did you know my sister
Rosalinda has glases and
she looks Prefle licke claudie
I wish you were my teacher
again ebre Time I,am goin
to thick wer you were here
and ebre time a thinck of
you I,am goin to se the Foto
of you ebre ebre time.

Love

To
mss.
Ramires

FIGURE 9.4 Elena's Brainstorming Cluster, Co-constructed with the Teacher

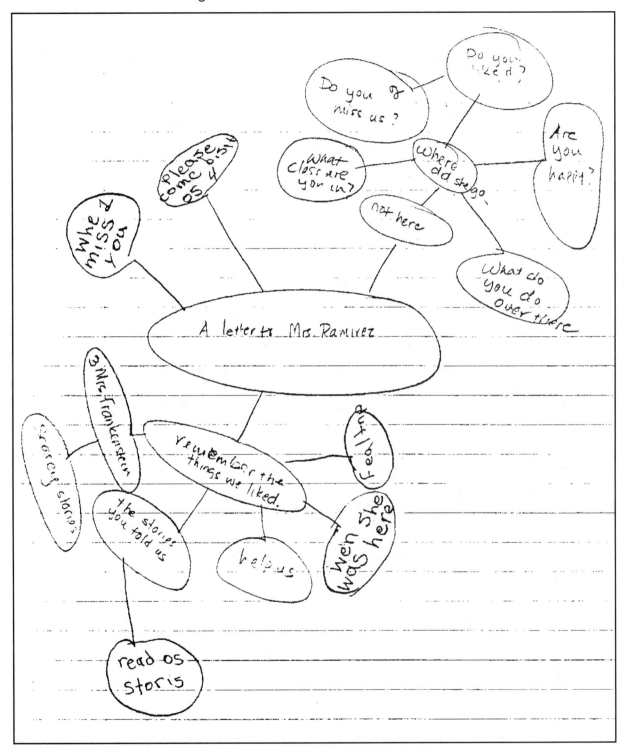

FIGURE 9.5 Elena's Letter to Mrs. Ramirez, Co-constructed with Teacher

Dear Mrs. Ramirez,

We miss you! Do you miss us? Where did you go because you are not here? Whath class are you in? Which teacher do you work with? Do you licke it? What do you do over there? Are you happy? How do you feal? Did you know I Feai bad becose your hot hear?

I remember all the things that you did when you were here. I remember the stories you told us? I remember when you read us books. I well never forget wen you were here. I can still see you dressed as Mrs. Frankenstein, tell us scarey stories. Thanck you for helpen us in the fealtrip. Thank you being our teacher.

Please come, bisit us. We are still learning to read. Were goin to bisit you to? Next week we are on vacation. in vacation I am goin to Mexico were are you goin? Have a good vacation!

It is clear from Elena's story and letter that she was able to perform in more grade-appropriate ways when given support and scaffolding that targeted her strengths as well as her needs. Boyle and Peregoy (2005) argue that literacy scaffolds should be embedded in a social context that supports shared communication and the negotiation of meaning. Despite Elena's tendency to work so slowly that her responses are limited, when faced with targeted scaffolding, she was able to perform in appropriate ways.

Practical Applications and Individual Inquiries: Cases to Think About and Investigate

1. Reflect on Elena's story. How did the teacher's scaffolding help her to be a better writer? What other scaffolds could Elena's teacher use to help her? How will she be able to take the scaffolds away when Elena is ready to work on her own?

2. Visit the Council for Exceptional Children Web site at http://www.cec.sped.org/
    *   Examine the Professional Standards.
    *   Visit some of the discussion forums.
    *   Read the latest issue of *CEC Today Online*.
    *   Write a one- to two-page reflection on your visit to the CEC Web site and how what you learned will help you to differentiate instruction for eELLs.

3. Visit an exceptional education classroom (this can be a special day class or one where eELLs are mainstreamed). Take anecdotal notes about what the teacher is doing to scaffold the work of eELLs. Describe the ways that the teacher scaffolds instruction for individual students. Describe the context of the classroom and how it helps (or doesn't help) eELLs gain access to the curriculum.

4. Interview an exceptional education teacher. Ask about her or his philosophy of teaching and learning and what she or he thinks is important in teaching eELLs. Ask the following questions:
    *   How do students get referred for exceptional education services?
    *   How does an IEP get completed?
    *   How do you work with eELLs (e.g., special day class, pull-out program, inclusion program)?
    *   What resources are available for teaching eELLs?
    *   What scaffolding strategies do you use to ensure that eELLs have access to the curriculum?

Chapter Ten _____

Putting It All Together

As a teacher in California, it is important to realize that the diversity of our students is not just related to the leveled group we put them in during guided reading, but more specifically it is related to their culture, socioeconomic background and language experiences prior to and outside of school. In order for our diverse students to construct knowledge and acquire language based on the skills used for literacy, educators must teach strategies tailored specifically for their population.

Dionna, elementary teacher

Throughout the previous nine chapters, we explored a variety of issues related to the planning and delivery of effective differentiated literacy instruction for ELLs. As teachers, we need to make sure our students have access to the curriculum to be successful in school. Acknowledging the differential needs of the students in today's schools is the first step toward providing quality instruction and ensuring student success. We know that the ELLs in schools today bring a wide range of background knowledge with them to class and that teachers can help them make connections to the classroom context and to the required content.

Figure 10.1 describes what we call our model for a new pedagogy (Quiocho & Ulanoff, 2005). It begins with the students themselves and then outlines how teachers find out what they need to know to plan and implement effective differentiated literacy instruction for ELLs.

In this chapter, we:

- Reflect on what was learned about differentiating literacy instruction for ELLs.
- Align the components of the model for a new pedagogy (Quiocho & Ulanoff, 1995) with the chapters of this text.
- Examine additional samples of ELLs' work from Edge Lake School, where teachers use the model we present.

FIGURE 10.1 A New Pedagogy for Planning and Delivering Differentiated Instruction to ELLs

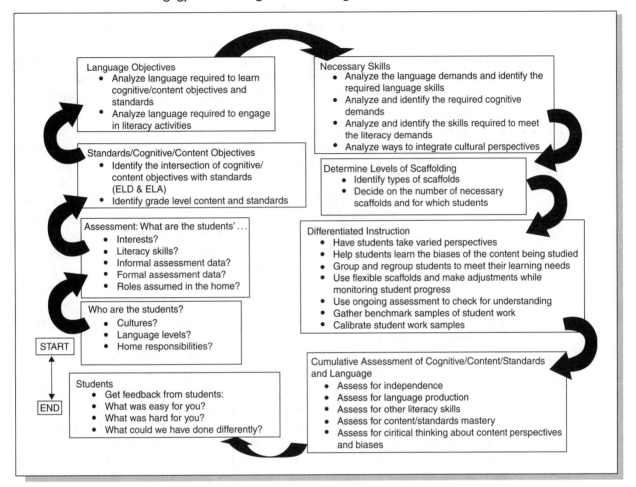

Language Objectives
- Analyze language required to learn cognitive/content objectives and standards
- Analyze language required to engage in literacy activities

Standards/Cognitive/Content Objectives
- Identify the intersection of cognitive/content objectives with standards (ELD & ELA)
- Identify grade level content and standards

Assessment: What are the students'...
- Interests?
- Literacy skills?
- Informal assessment data?
- Formal assessment data?
- Roles assumed in the home?

Who are the students?
- Cultures?
- Language levels?
- Home responsibilities?

START

END

Students
- Get feedback from students:
- What was easy for you?
- What was hard for you?
- What could we have done differently?

Necessary Skills
- Analyze the language demands and identify the required language skills
- Analyze and identify the required cognitive demands
- Analyze and identify the skills required to meet the literacy demands
- Analyze ways to integrate cultural perspectives

Determine Levels of Scaffolding
- Identify types of scaffolds
- Decide on the number of necessary scaffolds and for which students

Differentiated Instruction
- Have students take varied perspectives
- Help students learn the biases of the content being studied
- Group and regroup students to meet their learning needs
- Use flexible scaffolds and make adjustments while monitoring student progress
- Use ongoing assessment to check for understanding
- Gather benchmark samples of student work
- Calibrate student work samples

Cumulative Assessment of Cognitive/Content/Standards and Language
- Assess for independence
- Assess for language production
- Assess for other literacy skills
- Assess for content/standards mastery
- Assess for ciritical thinking about content perspectives and biases

What Have We Learned About Differentiated Literacy Instruction for ELLs?

We have learned many things about differentiating instruction for ELLs. First, we learned that we need to guide such instruction not only by what we learn about our students' language and literacy skills through assessment, but also by the cultural ways they construct knowledge. To motivate and engage students, we must activate or build their background knowledge about topics and concepts taught and also consider how we give students control over their own learning (Banks & Banks, 2003) through instruction. We learned that while teachers engage in the planning process, they have to think critically about pedagogy that is equitable and socially just for all students, and they have to accept and build on students' experiences to facilitate learning and understanding (Banks & McGee Banks, 2003; Shulman, 2003).

We learned that alignment of content and language development standards (for ELLs and EO students) serves to ensure that ELLs have access to all of the elements of the core curriculum. Language development and language objectives for lessons and unit plans are critical and must be clearly identified in the planning process. In this way, teachers are able to anticipate and plan for scaffolds that appropriately support student performance and help students to make connections as they transfer knowledge from the learning process to real life (Shulman, 2003). We learned that some students need more scaffolds or supports than others do, making the differentiation process one that is dependent on student needs. Teachers need to determine and revise plans for differentiation by constantly checking for understanding and facilitating academic language. Teachers can determine students' needs in the classroom by using authentic assessments such as checklists, running records, anecdotal records, and by reviewing student work using rubrics to which students have had access.

Furthermore, student groups should be flexible and responsive to students' academic needs. The purpose of grouping is to focus on students as they learn critical concepts in a collaborative setting. Although all groups have choices and may follow a variety of different processes to learn content, there should be opportunities for groups to share the processes they used to learn the same concept.

In our model for a new pedagogy (see Figure 10.1), we base differentiated instruction on the "I'll get you what you need to learn this" model and not on an inflexible model where criteria for forming groups are predetermined and membership is static. A static model assumes that no growth has occurred in student achievement. Moreover, we suggest that teachers respect students' background experiences and share knowledge construction processes. In this model, scaffolds naturally bring into play content integration (Banks & McGee Banks, 2003). Teachers also use content from other fields or disciplines to scaffold student learning and support knowledge construction. Through a natural course of reading and thinking critically about content, teachers can address prejudice reduction (Banks & McGee Banks, 2003) throughout planning, assessment, scaffolded instruction, and finally, mastery of academic concepts and content. In addition, we suggest the following elements as context for our model for a new pedagogy.

Teaching from a Multicultural Perspective

The perspectives of multicultural education (Banks & McGee Banks, 2003) provided a foundation for the research in which we engaged. Banks and McGee Banks base their work on the premise that children bring cognitive, linguistic, personal, and cultural strengths to school. Banks (in Diaz, 2001) describes multicultural education as a "metadiscipline." He challenges those who teach and study multicultural education to deeply examine social issues and develop a commitment to multiculturalism and multicultural education organized around transformative knowledge. In Banks's pedagogy, students examine issues, concepts, and ideas from multiple perspectives. This process of critical thinking resides in the heart of the curriculum. His goal is that teachers and students who study multiculturalism together emerge committed to social action that will eventually transform society and make it an inclusive one. Other multicultural educators (Grant, 1995; Diaz, 2001; Sleeter & Grant, 2002; Sleeter, 1992; Nieto, 1999a, 1999b; Gollnick & Chinn, 1998) emphasize the value of and respect for students' knowledge, culture, language, and ways of communicating. It is "educators and students [who must] accept the responsibility to be active participants in society's efforts to accept and advocate the positive values of social equality and equity" (Grant, 1995, p. 9). Thus, we suggest that teachers organize literacy instruction around the principles of multicultural education.

Promoting Multilingualism

We further suggest there is a need to examine literacy acquisition from a multilingual stance rather than from a traditional, English-only perspective (Bernhardt, 2003; Bernhardt & Kamil, 1995; Bossers, 1991; Brisbois, 1995; Carrell, 1991; Halcón, 2001; Moll, 2001; Diaz & Flores, 2001; de la Luz Reyes, 2001; Bartolomé & Balderrama, 2001; Berzins & López, 2001). Second language literacy has traditionally been viewed as comparable to first language literacy acquisition; however, as Bernhardt (2003) notes, "the mere existence of a first language (regardless of whether it is only oral, or oral and literate) renders the second language reading process considerably different from the first language reading process because of the nature of information stored in memory" (p. 112).

Bernhardt further refers to cultural memory; for example, a Japanese reader brings a different understanding to the word *breakfast* than students from other cultures. For some, breakfast means eggs, bacon, cereal, fruit, or rolls. To the Japanese reader, it means soba or hot soup. Page space as well as space between words or other factors such as right to left directionality does not readily explain the differences in reading in the first language and the second language (Bernhardt, 1986, 2003; Brown & Haynes, 1985; Hayes, 1988; Kern, 1994). Such differences have a direct effect on literacy acquisition and point to a need to look at cognitive and social literacy processes in light of a "literacy/language network that already exists" (Bernhardt, 2003, p. 113) in children when they come to school. In addition, Trueba, Cheng, Ima, and Trueba (1993) and Valdés (1996) caution that minority children who leave their countries of origin to come to the United States experience not only a language change but also a change of the basic social unit in which they live. The current focus is on language as the principal factor. Language is dynamic and changes over time.

Understanding Culture

Children's cultural experiences with text and their families also affect how they "see" the world as revealed to them in typical school tasks. Cheng (in Trueba et al., 1993) cites examples of preschool children who were puzzled by questions asked by teachers who expected traditional answers. For example, a Cambodian child who was asked which bedroom she slept in responded with a puzzled look and asked, "What do you mean?" When the teacher repeated the question, the child responded, "Everywhere." This example clearly indicates that when educators have perceived ideas about what children should know, there will be a misinterpretation of the student's knowledge base. Another example is the story of the Chinese-speaking preschooler who pointed to two pencils when asked with what she would eat. Many times real-life experiences clash with school experiences for ELLs.

Using Assessment Appropriately

Assessment conducted in a traditional manner does not always reveal the strengths of ELLs (Mercado & Romero, 1993). Traditional assessment instruments focus on the forms of language and thus "exacerbate difficulties in the assessment of non-English-proficient children, because communication is culturally bound and must be assessed with respect to the social and cultural contexts in which it occurs" (Cheng, in Trueba et al., 1993, p. 49). Mercado and Romero (1993) remind us that "When students' weaker language is used to measure knowledge of content, their linguistic competence contaminates the results" (p. 145). It then appears illogical to make judgments about the achievement of ELLs based on results from traditional assessments, because the results are flawed and do not provide robust data to make instructional, grouping, and placement decisions. There is a need to use authentic, context-embedded assessments that are more culturally aligned and classroom-based to obtain information about the achievement of ELLs, a challenge teachers face on a regular basis.

The model for a new pedagogy provides students with opportunities to openly voice what worked and what didn't work for them in instruction and practice (Ladson-Billings, 1994). We learned that we will continue to learn more as we observe and continue to work with students and teachers. We are cognizant that there are no easy answers; instead thoughtful practice that is systematic and planned to meet the needs of students must prevail in a context where students and teachers are co-learners. We learned that the minute we thought we had found what might appear to be the answers, something new and unexpected happened or we met students who still struggled or needed more support than we had anticipated. As you read what we have to say about differentiating literacy instruction for ELLs, know that as you are learning so are we. We know that we will continue to observe students and learn from them. Only as reflective lifelong learners can we continue to revise our practice to create literacy instruction that is equitable and socially just.

Linking Theory to Practice

Figure 10.1 represents a model of the essential elements necessary for planning and delivering effective instruction to ELLs. The model is informed by the work of Villa and Thousand (2005), among others, who focus on the universal design format of planning to ensure that classrooms and schools are inclusive. This format is in concert with our own research as well as that of Banks and McGee Banks (2003), where all planning starts with students, their cultures, and their identities. Let's take the elements individually to make the connections between our model and the various topics presented in this book transparent.

The Students, the Teachers, and the Classroom

The teachers with whom we worked began their planning by examining the cultural and linguistic contexts in which they teach, essentially looking at the students they teach and where they teach to better understand how to make their curriculum congruent with that context. They also used that information to plan ways in which to make the curriculum accessible to their students. The kind of things the teachers took into account included:

- The language background and language proficiency level of each student. In Chapter 8, we showed how Roberto's and Myra's teacher used their language proficiency levels as one data point to guide instructional differences.

- The cultural background of the student. In Chapter 2, we discussed why teachers need to take issues of culture into consideration when planning for effective instruction.

- The background knowledge each student brings to the classroom context. Although building on background knowledge is important for all students, it is especially critical for ELLs who may have content knowledge but lack linguistic labels or need to learn the content itself. Making connections to prior knowledge and situating instruction in context facilitates learning.

Culturally and Linguistically Appropriate Diagnostic and Ongoing Assessment

The schools we worked with started the data analysis and planning process by first acknowledging their students' backgrounds, strengths, and needs. They looked at the variety of assessments used in their schools. For example, one of the schools in which we did our research focused on data obtained from results of the following assessments administered to all ELLs:

- The CELDT (California Department of Education, 2001) Form A, which provided an English language proficiency level score (an overall proficiency score as well as proficiency levels in listening/speaking, reading, and writing). Whereas listening and speaking scores were available for kindergarten and first grades, listening/speaking, reading, and writing scores were available for grades 2 through 12.

- The ADEPT Test (Alisal School District, 2001), which provided specific scores for expressive and receptive language usage. The ADEPT focused on survival language and provided teachers with data about the ways their students used English syntatical structures supported by semantics. The teachers then used that data to mediate content-related vocabulary words as well as the words that hold the syntax together, such transition words or coordination words.

- Informal reading inventories such as Johns (2005) Basic Reading Inventory, which provided data on miscues, retelling, and comprehension questions based on word lists and graded paragraphs.

- RESULTS (California Reading and Literature Project, 1997), which is an assessment program with a variety of informal tests of phonemic awareness and phonics and includes word lists and graded paragraphs.

- Writing samples about grade level content, which were used by grade level teams as benchmarks for student writing portfolios and also to help determine the necessary scaffolds and supports required for individual students.

An examination of multiple pieces of data related to school change—such as student achievement, consistency of instruction across grade levels supported by professional development, a culture of change, and articulation (horizontally and vertically) between grade levels—showed that school personnel had actively engaged in the change process. The teachers at Edge Lake School focused on the cultures of their students (Banks &

McGee Banks, 2003; Hernandez, 2000), on multiple assessments as ways to collect data and make curriculum decisions that were data driven, and on using standardized as well as authentic classroom assessments to discover strengths, noting breakthroughs and struggles (Stefankis, 1998). The teachers at the school studied the data as a group, clearly moving from engagement to commitment (Shulman, 2003). They identified necessary skills and scaffolds for their students.

When we look at Edge Lake School in comparison to schools with similar socio-economic, linguistic, and cultural diversity, we see that students at this school demonstrated remarkable growth in test scores. Teachers did not teach to test; rather, they emphasized the skills students need to develop as individual learners.

Language and Content Standards and Objectives

It is critical that teachers examine and understand the relationship between ELD standards and ELA standards. According to Carr and Lagunoff (2006), ELD standards serve as a sort of "onramp" that leads to the mastering of ELA standards, which is naturally the main objective of differentiated literacy instruction for ELLs. As mentioned in Chapter 3, we know that learning to read in a second language differs in many ways from learning to read in one's native language. Lessons for ELLs, therefore, must address language and content objectives in order to promote success. Chapter 7 demonstrates how the teachers we examined used both sets of standards to plan and deliver literacy instruction. Although those teachers used the California ELD and ELA standards, their work serves as an example for teachers from other states.

Skills, Strategies, and Scaffolds

The critical elements that propelled the change at the schools in which we worked have been demonstrated in this book through the analysis of the work of students such as Roberto and Myra. We learned about Roberto and Myra by observing them in a variety of learning contexts and analyzing their work. We concluded that the instruction Roberto and Myra received, the support they were provided, and their improvement characterized the growth made by the ELLs at their school. When differentiating literacy instruction for ELLs, teachers must look at the tasks they are assigning their students in order to ascertain the specific skills and strategies necessary to make sense of the task. Figure 10.2 highlights the relationship among skills, strategies, and each task itself.

Differentiated Instruction Revisited

In this text, we advocate for differentiated instruction as a critical part of planning for curriculum that supports literacy success for ELLs. To use differentiated instruction effectively, teachers must recognize, respect, and use students' varying background knowledge as well as their experiences or lack of experiences with schooling. Teachers must recognize that all students come to school with different interests and learning styles, and the goal of differentiated instruction is academic success that stems from meeting each student where he or she is and assisting and monitoring each student in the learning process (Schumm & Arguelles, 2006).

FIGURE 10.2 Skills, Strategies, and Scaffolds

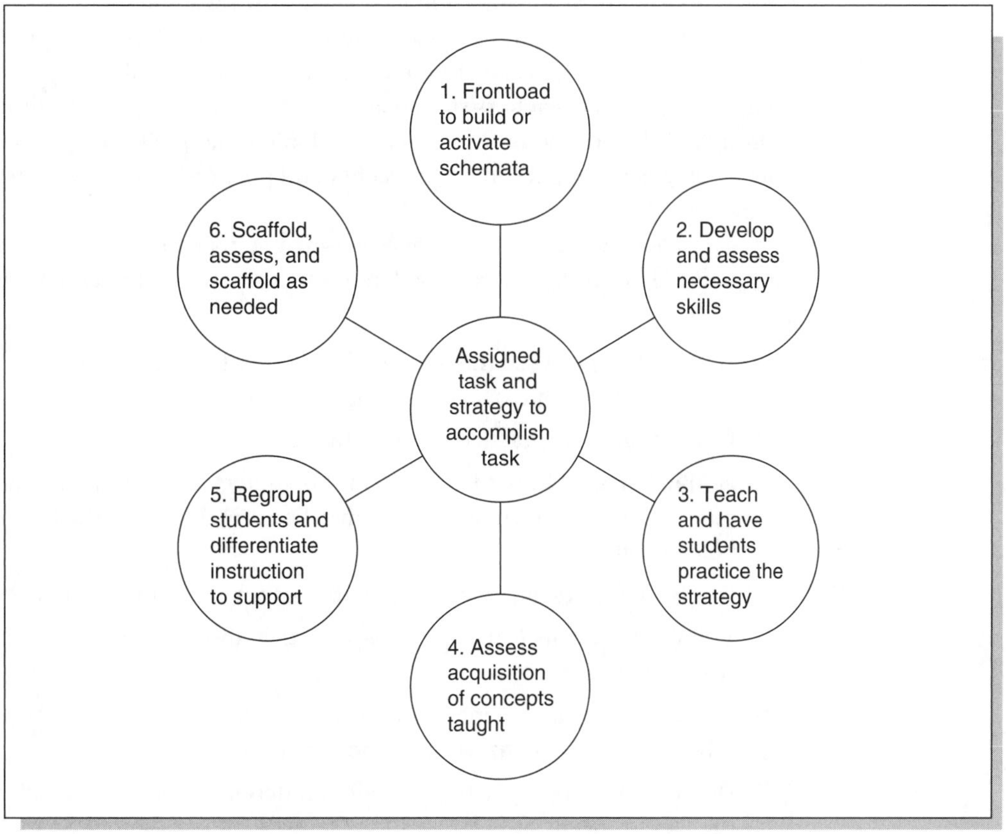

Differentiated instruction varies according to students' needs; however, the goal is always to ensure that we are teaching ELLs the core curriculum. Teachers can vary and differentiate instruction by paying attention to several practices. The first is grouping. The teacher must decide how to group students to achieve maximum learning results. Will ELLs learn best in pairs, as individuals, in a small group, or in large groups? Consider the cognitive and language objectives of the lesson. Should the groups be of mixed abilities or same abilities to support maximum student language development and learning? How will the teacher ensure that when students are placed in same ability (homogeneous) groups that the grouping structure is temporary and flexible, not permanent? The objectives of instruction, the structure of the required task, and the focus on mastery of content are central to the makeup of group structures.

Next, teachers must select the strategies to use based on their knowledge of students' experiences, backgrounds, linguistic strengths, and cultural ways of knowing. They should select materials appropriately. Content and materials should not be watered down, but be at students' instructional reading levels to provide multiple opportunities to scaffold comprehension and writing as students read and write. Students should work with more challenging materials after they have had time to work with books, articles, diagrams, models, or research materials that first provided them comprehensible ways to learn content.

It is important that teachers are trained in and understand the dynamic processes of differentiated literacy instruction for ELLs. Knowing students and their experiences is an important factor, assessing for academic knowledge is a basic component, selecting appropriate strategies is key to effective instruction, and taking the time to bring it all together is critical. Teachers should allow enough time for ELLs to process information through discussion, demonstrations, questioning, and multiple opportunities to build academic language, practice, receive teacher and peer feedback, and debrief all learning activities.

The following practical list of questions that teachers should consider when selecting instructional practices was expanded from a list of questions by Schumm and Arguelles (2006):

1. Why do I want to use this strategy or activity? Is it because students will like it? Will they learn academic concepts using the strategy?

2. Is the strategy or practice research based?

3. Do I understand how to implement this strategy or activity step by step so I don't miss any indications that students may be struggling with the language or concepts being taught?

4. Is this strategy or activity aligned with district and state standards?

5. Will what students learn from this strategy translate into positive results on summative assessments?

6. Is this strategy or activity best implemented in whole class or small groups? What other structures might work for individual students?

7. Do I have the appropriate materials at different instructional reading levels to support the literacy needs of ELLs?

8. Have I planned enough time for students to think, discuss, and construct learning?

9. Have I assessed and determined the skills students possess so I know what kind of support to provide and to whom?

10. Will I need additional help from peers, community members, or instructional assistants to be efficient and effective in implementing this strategy or activity?

11. Have I trained students to know how to help each other when misunderstandings occur?

12. Do I know which students require modifications and adaptations based on their identified learning disabilities (e.g., ELLs with IEPs)?

13. Do I have the assessment devices necessary to monitor student progress on an ongoing basis?

14. Will students require support at home to learn?

15. Have I planned for ways to support parents' abilities and resources to help their children?

16. Will this strategy or activity promote student learning of skills required by standards?

17. Can the strategy or activity be easily implemented given the realities of my classroom?

Teachers who work with ELLs are encouraged to consistently reflect about why they decide to use the groupings they use, the instructional strategies and materials they select, as well as how they can best monitor student achievement.

Summative Assessment Linked to the Content and Language Standards

Summative assessments are administered at the end of lessons, units, or at the end of the school year. Teachers can use the results to communicate to students, parents, administrators, schools, and districts about student progress. They can also use the information obtained from summative evaluation to support revision of grade level or schoolwide curriculum. They must consider the multiple factors that constitute summative evaluation, such as the language and cognitive needs of the student population and whether instruction explicitly addresses student needs. If the summative test is traditional, teachers must consider the validity and reliability of the instrument, the standards that are being tested, the types of questions, and the language used in test directions.

In Chapter 4, which discusses assessment for ELLs, we suggest that authentic assessments of student learning provide the clearest view of student achievement and improvement. Standardized assessments are traditionally used as part of the summative process of reporting student progress in most school districts. However, the teachers at Edge Lake School understood the limitations of traditional testing and added authentic instruments such as rubrics, checklists, anecdotal notes, assessments that provided feedback on nontransferable skills such as syntax and grammar, and informal reading inventories to provide a broader view of student strengths and areas of need. They used the results of the additional assessments to further inform instruction and support the differentiation process. The belief was that students must learn in supportive contexts where instruction was differentiated and improvements in traditional summative assessments would occur because ELLs would have developed skills to help them become independent learners and not because they had become good test takers.

Because the curriculum at the school was designed to improve literacy achievement and meet state standards, it made sense that teachers used this data to inform their teaching, support student learning, and show improved literacy achievement in summative evaluation. On the state standards test, the ELLs at Edge Lake met state standards as a subgroup of the entire school population. Summative evaluation, when supported by other assessments, is part of a larger curriculum design to help ELLs meet state content standards at every grade level.

Examples from the Field

In previous chapters, we examined the contexts and instructional planning that allowed the students at Edge Lake and Blue Eagle Schools to succeed (see Table 10.1). Roberto, Myra, Elena, and the others have moved on to middle school and high school. They left their elementary schools after completing the fifth grade, reading at grade level and scoring as early advanced students in English proficiency. We were curious to see whether other students achieved the same results. In this section, we will look at some writing samples (the teachers' choice for use as examples of schoolwide assessment) from Cindi, Daniel, and Ignacio, ELLs who were also students at Edge Lake School.

Reading workshop: Opportunities to question and think aloud.

TABLE 10.1 A Planning Chart for Differentiated Instruction for ELLs

Student Name	What I Know About Each Student	Grade Level Concept	Skills Required	Necessary Scaffolds
Ramón	Spanish is L1.*	Fourth grade	Understanding the similarities and differences between English and Spanish. Using cognates is helpful. Understanding the meaning units in English is helpful.	Use cognates to make connections between L1 and L2.
	Involved in soccer in the community.		Understanding how soccer strategies are related to learning strategies.	Uses soccer stories and strategies.
	Parents want him to succeed.		Communicating with parents.	Reinforce parental desire for success.
	Syntax is difficult in writing; L1 vowel sounds substituted for L2 vowel sounds.		Understanding what transfers and what doesn't.	Conference. Use analogies between L1 and L2. Post reminders and expect student to use them.
	Getting the "gist" of a reading and comprehension of main idea is difficult.		Understanding that the meaning of larger pieces of text is facilitated by processing smaller chunks of text first.	Use think alouds.

* L1 refers to the student's primary language or the language he or she speaks the most often.

TABLE 10.1 (continued)

Student Name	What I Know About Each Student	Grade Level Concept	Skills Required	Necessary Scaffolds
	Needs support on how to elaborate on ideas in writing.		Drawing on personal interests and background knowledge.	Begin writing in poetry about grade level content. Conference often with teacher and peers. Use post writing graphic organizers and rubrics.
Chau	Vietnamese is L1. Parents expect her to do well in school. Is a relentless worker. Asks questions often when she doesn't understand. Willing to take risks with language.	Fourth grade	Understanding that structures (syntax, semantics) do not transfer from Vietnamese to English.	Work on morphological units and demonstrate how words are made in English to address her curiosity and desire to learn the second language.
	She is angry sometimes because she is frustrated with making sense of L2 (English).		Understanding the meaning units in English is helpful. Acquiring an "ear" for the language is critical. Voluntary free reading is necessary.	Share stories of how others struggle to learn a second language and have succeeded. Use stories of ethnic authors.
	Syntax is difficult in writing. Needs additional help to elaborate and support main ideas in writing.		Noting how authors "use" English in their writing. Keeping a journal of phrases that are either misunderstood or sound "good."	Begin with poetry. Conference and ask her to read her writing. Focus on positives of writing, having her work on one area of difficulty at a time. Allow time for her to read and talk about one piece of work. Observe when she becomes frustrated and let her put the piece away to revisit later.
Luz	Tagalog is L1. Parents try to speak only English at home. Attended school in the Philippines and studied Tagalog, Spanish, and English.	Fourth grade	Understanding that knowing three languages is an asset and that all languages have form, function, and use that may differ, but are essential.	Use cognates when necessary. Work on morphemes, both bound and unbound as they appear in grade level text, and assist in decoding unfamiliar words. Encourage parents to read in the L1 at home.
	Has adapted well to the English curriculum. Is inquisitive about language. Needs support in elaboration of ideas writing.		Noting how authors "use" English in their writing. Keeping a journal of phrases that are either misunderstood or sound "good."	Provide positive feedback. Use graphic organizers or other organizational charts to illustrate the structure of grade level text and what authors do to help readers "see" the message they are trying to convey.
Aída	Spanish is L1. Parents only speak Spanish and do not write or read Spanish. They want Aída to do well but are unable to help her at home.		Understanding that knowing two languages is an asset and that all languages have form, function, and use that may differ, but are essential.	Use primary language support when appropriate and cognates to make connections between oral language and written language. Encourage parents to tell stories in the L1 at home.

(continued)

TABLE 10.1 (continued)

Student Name	What I Know About Each Student	Grade Level Concept	Skills Required	Necessary Scaffolds
Aída	Is shy and afraid to speak out—fears making errors.	Fourth grade	Understanding that it is okay to wait and think about what you are going to say before you say it. Practicing taking risks with language.	Provide time for her to process information in her primary language. Talk no more than 10 minutes and allow her to process in Spanish for at least 2 or 3 minutes. Review information again in English prompting Aída to fill in vocabulary that is important to concept understanding—a kind of oral "cloze" procedure. Post word walls and let her use a personal word wall of cognates and other vocabulary essential to content understanding and to writing.
	Comprehension of main ideas is difficult.		Understanding that the meaning of larger pieces of text is facilitated by processing smaller chunks of text first.	Use a think aloud, illustrating how you think about making sense as you read. Model and let Aída try this process with coaching, not telling.
	Elaboration of main ideas in writing needs support.		Noting how authors "use" English in their writing. Keeping a journal of phrases that are either misunderstood or sound "good."	Begin with poetry writing, encouraging her to use both languages as she writes her poems about content. Conference, asking her what she wants to say and then helping her fill in the blanks with appropriate vocabulary. Have her work with a supportive partner who has been taught how to wait and support but not tell her the answers or do the work for her.
Dire	Native California Indian Tribe member. English is his primary language.	Kindergarten	Understanding that parents expect their children to be independent, find their way to school and back home without escorts.	Encourage and support his tribal culture through Native songs, poems, stories, use of drums, attention to powwow rituals.
	Sees writing as drawing.		Understanding that drawing is a part of writing. Let him observe the role of drawing in books and talk about how the drawing helps the reader understand the story.	Show him how writing is different from drawing. Encourage him to mix writing and drawing.

254

TABLE 10.1 (continued)

Student Name	What I Know About Each Student	Grade Level Concept	Skills Required	Necessary Scaffolds
	Is a keen observer and curious about many things in the classroom such as the ant farm, books, music.		Understanding that areas of interest such as the ant farm can be found in books and on the Internet. Understanding that music is a form of communication.	Use oral language as a way to scaffold him into reading. Have him dictate stories.
	Parents believe his educational growth is the school's responsibility.		Communicate regularly and consistently with parents in the home to establish cordial relationships.	Involve Dire in home visits.
	Is also an auditory learner who likes to listen to stories.		Understanding that storytelling helps us understand how stories are constructed and that Native stories have a different structure than Western stories.	Use story maps to visually show how stories in different cultures are structured. Add pictures and drawings.
	Will engage in activities when he feels confident and ready.		Understanding that interest and observation are cultural ways of knowing for the children of this tribe. Encourage Dire's curiosity.	Help him understand that it is okay to observe. Ask questions about his observations to increase interest.
Teddy	Is withdrawn and shy. Needs nurturing and time to heal after his mother's death.	Kindergarten	Understanding that tragedies make us sad and that is a natural response.	Provide a safe place to be alone in the classroom or with others.
	Responds to firm requests with anger and perceived stubbornness.		Understanding that drawing about how one feels is a way to put our feelings into visual symbols so we can feel better.	Help Teddy to express how he is feeling and that he needs some space for a short time.
	Calms down when listening to music.		Understanding that music is communication that tells stories just like books do.	Help Teddy create poems and songs that can be communicated with drums and chants.
	Likes to copy words from the room environment.		Understanding that lists of words can be turned into poems, songs, and stories.	Use language experience creating his own stories through dictation. This becomes his reading.

(continued)

TABLE 10.1 (continued)

Student Name	What I Know About Each Student	Grade Level Concept	Skills Required	Necessary Scaffolds
Ricardo	Spanish is L1. Was instructed in English in K, changed schools and began instruction in Spanish in first grade, moved again and was placed in English instruction in second grade.	Fifth grade	Needs to build CALP in his L2.	Develop vocabulary through use of visuals.
	Very good with math, especially problems that call for understanding spatial relationships.		Understanding how to use what he knows about spatial relationships in math to make meaning of text.	Use math word problems.
	Parents want him to succeed.		Communicating with parents.	Reinforce parental desire for success.
	Relies heavily on L2 and has trouble with both reading and writing.		Understanding what transfers and what doesn't.	Conference. Use analogies between L1 and L2. Post reminders and expect student to use them.
	Getting the "gist" of a reading and comprehension of main idea is difficult.		Understanding that the meaning of larger pieces of text is facilitated by processing smaller chunks of text first.	Use think alouds.
	Needs support on how to elaborate on ideas in writing.		Drawing on personal interests and background knowledge.	Begin writing in poetry about grade level content. Conference often with teacher and peers. Use post writing graphic organizers and rubrics.
Esteban	Spanish is L1. Was enrolled in L1 reading K–2 and then in a transitional reading class for third grade. Very verbal in both English and Spanish, but more comfortable in Spanish.	Fifth grade	Listening and speaking English in meaningful conversations with peers in order to receive comprehensible input.	Use cooperative group work.
	Relies heavily on Spanish syntax and spelling as the basis for his writing in English.		Understanding the structures that do and do not transfer from Spanish to English.	Use contrastive analysis between Spanish and English. Allow free voluntary reading and listening to stories. Use journal writing.
Roberto	Primary language is Spanish. Assessment of proficiency in English places him as an early intermediate speaker of English. No assessment of proficiency in Spanish was administered.	Fourth grade	Metacognition. Model how to think about thinking and talk about it out loud.	Ask at least one or two metacognitive questions of Roberto throughout all lessons. Be sure to model for him and let him know that you are modeling so he can learn the language and the processes of metacognition.

TABLE 10.1 (continued)

Student Name	What I Know About Each Student	Grade Level Concept	Skills Required	Necessary Scaffolds
	High frequency words are hard for him to remember.		Create a list of high frequency words such as *a, an, to, for, in, around, the, that, this,* and show him how these words also function in Spanish.	Use language experience and point out to him how often high frequency words appear in oral language.
	Can decode words that are consistent.		Understand that not all words in English are decodable as they are in Spanish. Use contrastive analysis to demonstrate the differences.	Move him from decodable text to predictable text as an accompaniment to grade level text and grade level content.
	Substitutes vowel sounds in Spanish for vowel sounds in English.		Continue with contrastive analysis to demonstrate the difference in vowel sounds in both languages.	Develop pictorial symbols that go over the sounds the vowels make in Spanish and the sounds they make in English. Avoid stereotypical symbols.
	Enjoys drawing and poetry.		Write his own poetry about the content he is learning in class and add a drawing that "sells" his poem.	Have him copy favorite poems from books to understand the structures. Then, leave words out (CLOZE) for him to substitute and create his own poem, for example, in the same structure Robert Frost might use.
	Doesn't always comprehend what he reads as he focuses mainly on decoding.		Give him smaller chunks of text to read.	Use sketching as he reads to help him visualize. Have him use guiding questions as he reads: who, what, where, when, how, why. Have him work with a partner so he can stop after a small chunk, retell, decide on what text says in his own words and write it down.
	Is learning to be a risk taker.		Help him understand that learning comes from what we think are mistakes.	Share stories with him about famous people, preferably from his culture, who have made mistakes and turned them into successes.
Myra	Spanish is her primary language. Assessment of English proficiency identifies her as a beginning speaker of English.		Model metacognition for her, demonstrating how to talk about thinking and ask questions when one is not sure.	Always ask one metacognitive question of Myra after modeling one so she learns the language and the thinking.

(continued)

TABLE 10.1 (continued)

Student Name	What I Know About Each Student	Grade Level Concept	Skills Required	Necessary Scaffolds
Myra	Very quiet and afraid to speak out. Relies on her friends to help her communicate.	Fourth grade	Train a partner to work with Myra. Teach the student to wait and let her process language and ask questions when she is unable to find the words in English. Make sure the student doesn't do the work for Myra.	Provide Myra with visuals such as pictures and real objects of grade level content so she can observe, identify, and label (with her partner).
	Struggles with sight words.		Start with the high frequency words that are common in both languages such as *a, an, one, to, for, from at, around,* etc. Show her the words in English and in Spanish. Demonstrate that the high frequency words in Spanish are decodable but not in English so she must "see" them in her head.	Have Myra trace high frequency words in the air or on a cookie sheet covered with shaving cream. Then build the words with sponge letters or sand paper (vowels in one color and consonants in another). The tactile experience many times helps stimulate memory.
	Confuses the vowel sounds in Spanish with the vowel sounds in English.		Use contrastive analysis to demonstrate the differences between the sounds vowels make in Spanish and in English. Post these for Myra to easily refer to in her own personal dictionary, personal word wall, or on a board close to her desk.	Create symbols or use colors to designate the sounds the vowels make in Spanish as opposed to the sounds they make in English. Don't do too many at once.
	Focuses on decoding and not on comprehension.		Provide Myra with smaller chunks of text to process.	Have Myra work with a trained partner. They can read together using neurological impress. Stop at the end of a small chunk. Myra retells. The partner helps clarify meaning, Myra revisits the retelling and puts it in her own words. Write it down and proceed through text that way.
	Does not always have the background knowledge or experiences.		Provide experiences, pictures, and real objects to build background knowledge.	Be sure to name objects, events, people and label them. Ask either/or questions so she can learn the names. Have her write down the names of events, objects, and people and later turn those into poems to scaffold the writing process for her.

TABLE 10.1 (continued)

Student Name	What I Know About Each Student	Grade Level Concept	Skills Required	Necessary Scaffolds
Elena	Spanish is L1. Was in a car accident before attending K. Although there was no permanent damage, Elena initially had mild auditory and cognitive problems.	Fourth grade	Needs work on attention span and listening skills.	Varied activities, including short read alouds. Work with speech therapist.
	First-grade teacher said that Elena was not progressing in Spanish reading, but she is able to read environmental print.		Making connections between environmental print and reading texts.	Read the room, use charts and posters as well as big books, shared and guided reading.
	Parents want her to succeed.		Communicating with parents.	Reinforce parental desire for success.
	Starts work slowly and proceeds slowly. Often takes so long to finish work that she gives up (or expects teacher to let her give up); exhibits "learned helplessness."		Needs to work on attention span and following through.	Modeled and partner reading and writing.
	Understands both English and Spanish.		Making connections between L1 and L2.	Use contrastive analysis.
	Needs support on how to elaborate on ideas in writing.		Drawing on personal interests and background knowledge.	Share and model writing.
	Relies heavily on Spanish syntax and spelling as the basis for her writing in English.		Understanding the structures that do and do not transfer from Spanish to English.	Use contrastive analysis between Spanish and English, free voluntary reading and listening to stories, and journal writing.

Cindi's Writing Development

Cindi came to school in second grade as an ELD level 2 in writing. That means she was able to use phonemic spelling and illustrate and write about a personal experience using some writing and spelling conventions. She could complete graphic organizers requiring simple writing forms and could incorporate high frequency words (25) correctly in her writing. At the end of fifth grade, Cindi showed improvement in how she organized her thinking and her writing.

In the fifth grade, Cindi was an overall ELD level 4 on the CELDT, but a 3 in writing. This means that according to the district benchmarks, Cindi could use basic varied tenses in writing sentences and paragraphs using conventional forms of spelling. A level 3 should be able to write a simple paragraph following a model. Note that scaffolded guiding writing is critical for students at level 3 in writing. At level 3 or intermediate level in writing, Cindi could contribute to or manufacture brainstorming activities to write a summary. She could use high frequency words (75) accurately. Let's look at Cindi's work in writing.

During the time of our observations, Cindi's class was writing about explorers, a common unit in social studies for fifth graders. She had been exposed to guided writing, where the teacher worked with her in a small group consistently thinking aloud about the topic (explorers), generating ideas about the topic, and thinking about how to best describe the person about whom they were writing. The guided writing activity served as a beginning scaffold for ELLs. Cindi used a rubric to guide her writing. Her writing sample is reproduced in (Figure 10.3). No language convention changes were made.

Because Cindi was an ELL working with the writing process, she had a rubric that guided her paragraph by paragraph. The rubric served as a checklist to help her check the following:

- The first paragraph should contain the information that tells the reader who the explorer is, what he did, and how he did it.
- Paragraph 2 develops the exploits of the explorer, explaining where he went, when he went, and the events he experienced in chronological order.
- The third paragraph answers the question why the explorer left his homeland, what caused him to want to leave and how the writer thinks the explorer felt about the voyage he took.
- The last paragraph reflects on the definition of what it means to be an explorer, the different kinds of explorers, and the main reasons for exploration.

We would like to see ELLs write independently without support structures. However, as we consider the complexity of language learning and the abstractness of the writing process as well as the difficulty of English syntax, it becomes increasingly apparent that ELLs need a structure such as a scaffold to begin writing. The syntax with which they struggle is a nontransferable skill. Once ELLs become confident writers and feel free to take risks and share their ideas, the teacher can gradually withdraw the scaffold.

When we analyzed Cindi's writing, we could easily see that she used the rubric as a guide to her writing, which helped give it some organization. She did repeat phrases such as "riches, spices, gold and conquer new land and people." She did, however, take risks with vocabulary using words like *passionate*. There are a few spelling glitches, which can easily be worked out in a spelling/writing conference where the teacher first talks to Cindi about the positives of using more picturesque words like *passionate*. The teacher can ask Cindi to read her writing to her and teach her how to combine sentences or use a thesaurus to find other ways to talk about riches, spices, gold, and conquering new lands.

Cindi's writing sample is certainly not perfect, but it is important to note that she started at the phonemic writing stage and that she used illustrations, some graphic organizers, and only 25 high frequency words at that time. Cindi developed as a writer in English. She will continue to develop as a reader and writer in a supportive sixth-grade classroom where the teacher will continue to use scaffolds but also remove them when appropriate to encourage Cindi to "own" her writing.

FIGURE 10.3 Cindi's Writing Sample About Explorers

> My explorer is Cristopher Columbus. Christopher Explored the unknown world. He did it by sailing in ships called galleons. Cristopher Columbus sailed for almost all his life.
>
> He sailed all over the unknown world to England, and the Canary Island across the Mediterranean sea and along the coast of Africa. He sailed to the unknown world in 1492. Christopher Columbus was passinate about being a sailor. He really wanted to go sailing with is uncle when he was a kid.
>
> He went to get riches, spices, gold and conquere new land and people. He read Travels of Marco Polo again and again he was fascinated by the stories. Christopher Columbus was happy on his voyages. He wants to get riches, spices, and gold for spains monaches.
>
> An explorer is someone who sails and trades things for other things and conquere new land and people. The different kinds of explorers are Leif Erickson, Marco polo, Portugal, Vespucci, Balboa, Magellan, and De soto. The main reasons for explorations are trading for riches, spices and gold and to conquere land and people. Columbus told Spain's monarchs that he would get them riches, spices, gold, and conquere new land so that he could go sailing.

Daniel's Writing Development

In the fourth grade, Daniel tested as level 2 or early intermediate in writing. In the fifth grade, he was evaluated as being level 3 or intermediate in writing. He was in Cindi's class and benefited from guided writing instruction as well. Daniel used the same rubric that Cindi used. In his piece on explorers, he chose to write about Magellan. He approached his writing in a different way. Let's look at his writing sample (Figure 10.4). Again, the sample has not been corrected.

Daniel started his sample with an interesting beginning, transferring what he knew about narratives to his writing piece. The quality of this piece is similar to that of Cindi's writing. His piece is different because he uses one repetition—that Magellan sailed west around the Americas. He reflects on Magellan's work, adding that Magellan probably felt good about his exploration efforts. As small an observation as that is, it is a beginning reader response.

Daniel's writing needs were scaffolded in a manner similar to Cindi's. He leaves out details that explain events as well as cause and effect factors. The absence of these

FIGURE 10.4 Daniel's Writing Sample About Explorers

> Long ago there was an explorer. The explorer was named Magellan. He was one of the best explorer in the whole world. He explorer new land by sailing west around the Americas.
>
> Magellan sailed the tip of Brizil. He went around the Pacific Ocean. He started sailing in 1519. Magellan stop at the Phillippines Island. He stayed there for a few months.
>
> The reason for expiation was to find a way to reach Asia by sailing west around the Americas. Magellan stayed in the Phillippiines island. In the Phillippines island there was a war. Magellan went to the war and died there.
>
> An explorer is a person that travel to find new things. Columbus sailed to a different land just like Cortes. The Vikings went to the Americas to find gold. Magellan also traveled around the world. I think Magellan felt good of his journey around the world.

elements is typical in beginning writers. Daniel profited from individual and small-group conferences that occurred in his classroom at the time of our research. He also bene-fited from explicit lessons modeling how to revise a piece of writing to elaborate on ideas and utilize the visualization strategies in which his class engaged to support comprehension.

Daniel will continue to need support such as personal word walls, guided writing in a small group, guided writing with a partner, small-group and individual conferences to sup-port revision and editing to scaffold his writing until he becomes more fluent as a writer and takes over organization and word choice on his own. Daniel developed as a second language writer at Edge Lake and needs to be placed in a supportive sixth-grade class where student writing is honored and supported, where scaffolds are put in place as stu-dents need them and withdrawn to create independent writers.

Ignacio's Writing Development

Ignacio is a level 4 in English language proficiency and early advanced in writing. District level benchmarks describe a level 4 as a student who uses basic varied tenses in writing sentences and paragraphs using conventional forms of spelling and writing. He can write a simple paragraph using a model, brainstorm ideas, and use high frequency words accu-rately. Let's look at Ignacio's writing as a fifth grader (Figure 10.5). He chose to write about Christopher Columbus and began his writing with a graphic organizer. His writing sample is also presented without corrections.

Ignacio's writing is more organized than either Cindi's or Daniel's writing, yet he too lacks details that help create a clear picture of the causes and effects between the main events. He seems to be more fluent in expressing his ideas using more syntactically accu-rate sentences. He uses one repetition and has a few subject–verb agreement miscues. He does have a response to the topic of explorations. He adds "I think" to his writing, noting that explorations must be exciting.

Ignacio will continue to grow in a supportive atmosphere where conferencing occurs on a regular basis; pictures, drama, and graphic organizers are used to support brainstorm-ing and the connections of ideas; and writing is looked at as personal thinking and not a task in completing a specified number of writing assignments.

Important Factors to Consider as We Reflect on Writing Development

Cindi, Daniel, and Ignacio developed as writers in classrooms where their teachers under-stood the need to scaffold ELLs as they learned to read and write in a second language. The teachers focused instruction in reading on determining importance, questioning, sum-marizing, visualizing, and in content area writing supported with graphic organizers, cog-nate word walls, guided writing, and individual as well as small-group conferences. They developed rubrics with student input using "kid" language, and posted them for everyone to see and use. The previous chapters of this book illustrated the differentiated literacy instruction these students received that supported them through the second language literacy learning process.

FIGURE 10.5 Ignacio's Writing Sample About Exploration

My explorer is named Christopher Columbus. He was an explorer by telling Queen Elizabeth to let him have ships and 50 men. The Queen told a man to research it. The guy did not like Christopher Columbus so he did not research it. One day the king came and told the Queen that the war was over and that's how he got his 3 ships and his 150 men.

Christopher sailed to Cuba then to America. Christopher sailed in 1492 to Cuba. He arrived in 1504 so I think it took him 12 years to get there. Christopher is my favorite explorer that lived because he sailed to Cuba and America.

I think Christopher sailed west because he thought by sailing west he will get to China. He wanted to find a better route to China by sailing west, but instead he got to Cuba. The thing that caused the explorer was to find new routes, gold and spices. I think voyages are very exciting.

An explorer is a person that sails to find new stuff in new places. There is a lot of different kinds of explorers in teh world. I will name three of them. First is Magellan, second, Marco Polo, and the third one is Hernando Cortes. I think the main reason for exploring is to show other people that you can find new things and to prove that. That's the main reason for exploration.

Practical Applications and Individual Inquiries: Cases to Think About and Investigate

1. Just as we learned from Myra, Roberto, Cindi, Daniel, Ignacio, and the rest of the students in this book, we urge you to learn from your students. Spend some time researching their academic histories if they are newcomers to the school or your classroom. If they are students who have been in this country for several years but are still not proficient in English, examine their test data, look at authentic work samples they have produced, and talk to them to get to know them and their experiences. Try to find out what they are interested in. Try to glean from them what is easy for them and what is hard as they work on school tasks. Make connections between their cultures and the content being taught in school. Bring their language into the classroom and use it to compare and contrast words and concepts. Always reflect on the differences in learning/processing styles they may possess and how that affects your teaching.

2. Revisit the model for a new pedagogy (see Figure 10.1), making a conscious effort to begin all planning with the knowledge about your students, their strengths, and their needs in mind. Make specific plans for ways to support them as they process meaning. Use the list of questions on page 250 to reflect on the strategies you want to use, the manner in which you group students, and the variety of materials you will need to implement differentiated instruction effectively.

3. As educators, we must become lifelong learners. As the world becomes smaller and our classrooms much more diverse, the more there is to learn about the children we

FIGURE 10.6 Linking Assessment and Instruction

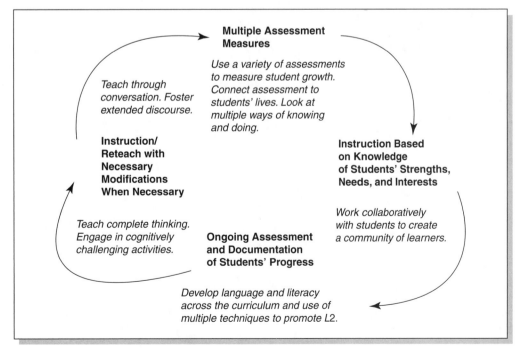

Multiple Assessment Measures

Use a variety of assessments to measure student growth. Connect assessment to students' lives. Look at multiple ways of knowing and doing.

Instruction Based on Knowledge of Students' Strengths, Needs, and Interests

Work collaboratively with students to create a community of learners.

Instruction/ Reteach with Necessary Modifications When Necessary

Teach through conversation. Foster extended discourse.

Teach complete thinking. Engage in cognitively challenging activities.

Ongoing Assessment and Documentation of Students' Progress

Develop language and literacy across the curriculum and use of multiple techniques to promote L2.

teach. If you are in a school where inclusive practices are a part of the regular school day, work collaboratively with the exceptional education teacher to ensure that you are both doing what you were hired to do—teach. Teach and support all of the children in the classroom. Use the process of scaffolding instruction for exceptional students. Note the progress made by the eELLs we feature in Chapter 9 when their teachers engaged in reflective practice and appropriate scaffolding.

4. Keep in mind that organizing for differentiated literacy instruction for ELLs needs to be linked to state, district, and school standards within the context of student needs. Keep expectations high. As teachers, we need to take into account both the language proficiency level and instructional needs for each of our ELLs. Moreover, we need to use multiple assessments to find out what our students know and to build on that knowledge to ensure that they meet grade level standards. Figure 10.6 reminds us of one way to look at the assessment/instruction process.

5. Finally, be thoughtful about materials, activities, or strategies you use to support student learning. Consider the scaffolding process (Figure 10.2) as you plan and implement differentiated literacy instruction for your ELLs. Never set limits for your students or yourself. Together, you, your colleagues, and your students can do wonderful things.

References _____

Abedi, J. (2001). *Validity considerations in the assessment of LEP students using standardized achievement tests.* Paper presented at the annual meeting of the American Educational Research Association, Seattle, WA.

Abedi, J. (2006). Psychometric issues in the ELL assessment and special education eligibility. *Teachers College Record, 108*(11), 2282-2303.

Adams, M. J. (1990). *Beginning to read: Thinking and learning about print.* Cambridge, MA: MIT Press.

Adger, C. T., Snow, C. E., & Christian, D. (2002). *What teachers need to know about language.* McHenry, IL: Delta Systems and CAL.

Alisal School District. (2001). *Alisal District English Proficiency Test (ADEPT).* Alisal, CA: Author.

Allen, J. (1999). *Words, words, words: Teaching vocabulary in grades 4-12.* York, ME: Stenhouse Publishers.

Allington, R. L. (2002). *Big brother and the national reading curriculum: How ideology trumped evidence.* Portsmouth, NH: Heinemann.

Allington, R. L., & Woodside-Jiron, H. (1999). The politics of literacy teaching: How "research" shaped educational policy. *Educational Researcher, 28*(8), 4-13.

Anderson, C. M., & Long, E. S. (2002). Use of a structured descriptive assessment methodology to identify variables affecting problem behavior. *Journal of Applied Behavior Analysis, 35*(2), 137-154.

Artiles, A. J., & Ortiz, A. O. (2002). *English language learners with special education needs.* Washington, DC: Delta Systems.

Astin, A. W., Banta, T. W., Cross, K. P., El-Khawas, E., Ewell, P.T., Hutchings, P., Marchese, T. J., McClenney, K. M., Mentkowski, M., Miller, M. A., Moran, E. T., & Wright, B. D. (1996). 9 principles of good practice for assessing student learning. *AAHE Assessment Forum, July 25.* Retrieved September 7, 2005, from http://www.colum.edu/info/assessments/pdfs/learning-outcomes

Athanases, S. Z. (1998). Diverse learners, diverse texts: Exploring identity and difference through literary encounters. *Journal of Literacy Research, 30*(2), 273-296.

Au, K. (2002). Multicultural factors and the effective instruction of students of diverse backgrounds. In A. E. Farstrup and S. J. Samuels (Eds.), *What research has to say about reading instruction* (pp. 392-413). Newark, DE: International Reading Association.

Au, K. H. (1993). Multiethnic literature and the valuing of diversity. In K. H. Au (Ed.), *Literacy instruction in multicultural settings* (pp. 175-190). New York: Harcourt Brace.

Au, K. H. (1998). Social constructivism and the school literacy learning of students of diverse backgrounds. *Journal of Literacy Research, 30*(2), 297-319.

August, D., & Shanahan, T. (2006). *Developing literacy in second language learners: Report of the national literacy panel on language-minority children and youth.* Mahwah, NJ: Erlbaum.

Ávalos, M. A. (2006). No two learners are alike: Learners with linguistic and cultural differences. In J. S. Schumm (Ed.), *Reading assessment and instruction for all learners* (pp. 59-86). New York: Guilford Press.

Baca, L. M., & Cervantes, H. T. (2004). *The bilingual special education interface* (4th ed.). Upper Saddle River, NJ: Pearson Merrill Prentice Hall.

Bailey, A. (2000). Factors influencing the English reading test performance of Spanish-speaking Hispanic children. *Reading Research Quarterly, 26*(4), 371-391.

Baker, A., & Greene, E. (1977). *Storytelling: Art and technique.* New York: R. R. Bowker.

Baker, K. (1992). Ramírez et al.: Led by bad theory. *Bilingual Research Journal, 16*(1&2), 63-90.

Banks, J. A. (1999). *An introduction to multicultural education.* Boston: Allyn & Bacon.

Banks, J. A. (2001). Approaches to multicultural curriculum reform. In J. A. Banks and C. A. McGee Banks (Eds.), *Multicultural education: Issues and perspectives* (4th ed., pp. 225-246). New York: Wiley.

Banks, J. A. (2002). *Teaching strategies for ethnic studies* (7th ed.). Boston: Allyn & Bacon.

Banks, J. A. (2007). *An introduction to multicultural education* (4th ed.). Boston: Allyn & Bacon.

Banks, J. A., & Banks, C. A. M. (2003). *Multicultural education: Issues and perspectives* (4th ed.). New York: Wiley.

Bartolomé, L. I., & Balderrama, M. V. (2001). The need for educators with political and ideological clarity: Providing our children with "The Best." In M. de la Luz Reyes and J. Halcón (Eds.), *The best for our children: Critical perspectives on literacy for Latino students* (pp. 48-64). New York: Teachers College Press.

Barton, B. (1986). *Tell me another: Storytelling and reading aloud at home, school and community.* Portsmouth, NH: Heinemann.

Barton, B. (2000). *Telling stories your way: Storytelling and reading aloud in the classroom.* Portsmouth, NH: Heinemann.

Basterra, M. del R. (1998-1999). Using standardized tests to make high-stakes decisions on English language learners: Dilemmas and critical issues. *Equity Review.* Retrieved January 1, 2008, from http://www.maec.org/ereview1.html

Bernhardt, E. B. (1986). Cognitive processes in L2: An examination of reading behaviors. In J. Lantolf and A. Labarca (Eds.), *Research in second language acquisition in the classroom setting* (pp. 35-51). Norwood, NJ: Ablex.

Bernhardt, E. B. (2003). Challenges to reading research from a multilingual world. *Reading Research Quarterly, 38*(1), 112-117.

Bernhardt, E. B., & Kamil, M. L. (1995). Interpreting relationships between L1 and L2 reading: Consolidating the linguistic threshold and the linguistic interdependence hypotheses. *Applied Linguistics, 16,* 15-34.

Berzins, M. E., & López, A. E. (2001). Starting off right: Planting seeds for biliteracy. In M. de la Luz Reyes and J. Halcón (Eds.), *The best for our children: Critical perspectives on literacy for Latino students* (pp. 81-95). New York: Teachers College Press.

Bialystok, E. (2002). Acquisition of literacy in bilingual children: A framework for research. *Language Learning, 52*(1), 159-199.

Bissex, G. L. (1980). *Gyns at wrk: A child learns to read and write.* Cambridge, MA: Harvard University Press.

Black, P., & William, D. (1998). Inside the black box: Raising standards through classroom assessment. *Phi Delta Kappan, 80*(2), 139-148. Retrieved February 19, 2006, from http://www.pdkintl.org/kappan/kbla9810.htm

Blakey, E., & Spence, S. (1990). Developing metacognition. ERIC Digest No. ED327218. Syracuse, NY: ERIC Clearinghouse on Information Resources. Retrieved January 6, 2008, from http://www.eric.ed.gov/ERICDocs/data/ericdocs2sql/content_storage_01/0000019b/80/22/b5/bb.pdf

Bliatout, B. T., Downing, B. T., Lewis, J., & Yang, D. (1988). *Handbook for teaching Hmong-speaking students.* Folsom, CA: Southeast Asia Community Resource Center.

Bond, L. A. (1996). Norm- and criterion-referenced testing. *Practical Assessment, Research & Evaluation*, 5(2). Retrieved January 2, 2008, from http://PAREonline.net/getvn.asp?v=5&n=2

Bossers, B. (1991). On thresholds, ceiling, and short circuits: The relation between L1 reading, L2 reading, and L1 knowledge. *AILA Review, 8*, 45-60.

Boston, C. (2002). The concept of formative assessment. *Practical Assessment, Research and Evaluation, 8*(9). Retrieved February 19, 2006, from http://pareonline.net/getvn.asp?v=8&n=9

Boyle, O. F., & Peregoy, S. F. (1998). Literacy scaffolds: Strategies for first- and second-language readers and writers. In M. F. Opitz (Ed.), *Literacy instruction for culturally and linguistically diverse students* (pp. 150-157). Newark, DE: International Reading Association.

Brisbois, J. (1995). Connections between first- and second-language reading. *Journal of Reading Behavior, 24*, 565-584.

Brown, T. L., & Haynes, M. (1985). Literacy background and reading development in a second language. In T. H. Carr (Ed.), *The development of reading skills* (pp. 19-34). San Francisco, CA: Jossey-Bass.

Burke, C. (1987). The reading interview. In Y. M. Goodman, D. J. Watson, & C. L. Burke (Eds.), *Reading miscue inventory: From evaluation to instruction* (pp. 179-185). New York: Owen.

Burke, C. (2005). The reading interview. In Y. M. Goodman, D. J. Watson, & C. L. Burke (Eds.), *Reading miscue inventory: From evaluation to instruction* (pp. 134-137). New York: Owen.

California Department of Education. (1997). *English-language arts content standards for California Public Schools kindergarten through grade twelve.* Sacramento, CA: Author. Also available online: http://www.cde.ca.gov/board/pdf/reading.pdf

California Department of Education. (1998). *English-language arts: Academic content standards for kindergarten through grade 12.* Sacramento, CA: Author. Retrieved January 12, 2008, from http://www.cde.ca.gov/be/st/ss/engmain.asp

California Department of Education. (1999). *English language development standards.* Sacramento, CA: Author. Also available online: http://www.cde.ca.gov/standards/eld.pdf

California Department of Education. (1999/2007). *Reading/language arts framework for California public schools.* Sacramento, CA: Author. Also available online: http://www.cde.ca.gov/cdepress/lang_arts.pdf

California Department of Education. (2001). *California English Language Development Test (CELDT).* New York: McGraw-Hill.

California Department of Education. (2002). *English language development standards for California public schools.* Sacramento, CA: Author.

California Department of Education. (2003a). *California English Language Development Test, Form C.* New York: McGraw-Hill.

California Department of Education. (2003b). *Academic performance index.* Retrieved June 5, 2004, from http://www.cde.ca.gov/ta/ac/ap/index.asp

California Department of Education. (2004). *California English Language Development Test (CELDT): Communications Assistance Packet for School Districts/School.* Sacramento, CA: Author. Retrieved October 10, 2004, from http://www.cde.ca.gov/ta/tg/el/assistancepkt.asp

California Reading and Literature Project. (1997). *RESULTS.* Berkeley, CA: University of California.

Calkins, L. M. (1986). *The art of teaching writing* (New ed.). Portsmouth, NH: Heinemann.

Campbell, D. E. (2004). *Choosing democracy: A practical guide to multicultural education* (3rd ed.). Upper Saddle River, NJ: Merrill Prentice Hall.

Carnoy, M. (1974). *Education as cultural imperialism.* New York: David McKay.

Carr, J., & Lagunoff, R. (2006). *The map of standards for English learners, grades K–5: Integrating instruction and assessment of ELD and ELA standards in California* (5th ed.). San Francisco: WestEd.

Carrasquillo, A., Kucer, B., & Abrams. R. (2004). *Beyond the beginnings: Literacy interventions for upper elementary English language learners.* Clevedon, UK: Multilingual Matters.

Carrasquillo, A. L. (1991). *Hispanic children and youth in the United States: A resource guide.* New York: Garland Publishing.

Carrasquillo, A. L., & Rodriguez, V. (1996). *Language minority students in the mainstream classroom.* Bristol, PA: Multilingual Matters.

Carreiro, P. (1998). *Tales of thinking: Multiple intelligences in the classroom.* Portland, ME: Stenhouse Publishers.

Carrell, P. (1991). Second language reading: Reading ability or language proficiency? *Applied Linguistics, 12,* 159–179.

Cazden, C. B. (1988). *Classroom discourse: The language of teaching and learning.* Portsmouth, NH: Heinemann.

Celce-Murcia, M. (1991). Grammar pedagogy in second and foreign language teaching. *TESOL Quarterly, 25*(3), 459–480.

Chall, J. S. (1983). *Stages of reading development.* New York: McGraw-Hill.

Chamot, A. U., & O'Malley, J. M. (1994). *The CALLA handbook: Implementing the cognitive academic language learning approach.* Reading, MA: Addison-Wesley.

Chamot, A. U., O'Malley, J. M., & Cunningham, J. W. (1982). Generating interaction between schemata and text. In J. A. Niles and L. A. Harris (Eds.), *New inquiries in reading research and instruction. Thirty-first yearbook of the national reading conference* (pp. 42–47). Rochester, NY: National Reading Conference.

Chapman, C., & King, R. (2003). *Differentiated instructional strategies for writing in the content areas.* Thousand Oaks, CA: Sage.

Cheng, L. (1987). English communicative competence of language minority children: Assessment and treatment of language "impaired" preschoolers. In H. Trueba (Ed.), *Success or failure? Learning and the language minority student* (pp. 49–68). New York: Newbury/Harper & Row.

Chomsky, C. (2001). Stages in language development and reading exposure. In S. W. Beck and L. N. Oláh (Eds.), *Perspectives on language and literacy: Beyond the here and now* (pp. 51–75). Cambridge, MA: Harvard Educational Review.

Chomsky, N. (1957). *Syntactic structure.* The Hague: Mouton.

Chomsky, N. (1968). *Language and mind.* New York: Harcourt, Brace and World.

Clay, M. M. (1975). *What did I write? Beginning writing behaviour.* Portsmouth, NH: Heinemann.

Clay, M. M. (1993). *An observation survey of early literacy achievement.* Portsmouth, NH: Heinemann.

Cline, A., & Necochea, J. (2003). My mother never read to me. *Journal of Adolescent and Adult Literacy, 47*(2), 122–126.

Coles, G. (1987). *The learning mystique: A critical look at "learning disabilities."* New York: Fawcette Columbine.

Coles, G. (2000). *Misreading reading: The bad science that hurts children.* Portsmouth, NH: Heinemann.

Collier, C. (1988). *Assessing minority students with learning and behavior problems.* Lindale, TX: Hamilton Publications.

Collier, V. P. (1992). A synthesis of studies examining long-term language-minority student data on academic achievement. *Bilingual Research Journal, 16*(1&2), 187–212.

Collier, V. P., & Thomas, W. P. (1988). *Acquisition of cognitive-academic second language proficiency: A six-year study.* Paper presented at the annual meeting of the American Educational Research Association, New Orleans, LA.

Collier, V. P., & Thomas, W. P. (2004). The astounding effectiveness of dual language instruction for all. *NABE Journal of Research and Practice, 4*(1), 1–20.

Compton, M., Stratton, A., Maier, A., Meyers, C., Scott, H., & Tomlinson, T. (1998). It takes two: Co-teaching for deaf and hard of hearing students in rural schools. In *Coming together: Preparing for rural special education in the 21st century.* Conference Proceedings of the American Council on rural Special Education, Charleston, SC. (ED 417901).

Cooperative Children's Book Center. (2003). *Children's books by and about people of color published in the United States.* Madison: University of Wisconsin. Retrieved May 9, 2004, from http://soemadison.wisc.edu/ccbc/pcstats.htm

Costa, A. (1985). *Developing minds.* Alexandria, VA: Association for Supervision and Curriculum.

Costa, A. (1991). *The school as home for the mind.* Palatine, IL: Skylight.

Costa, A. (2001). *Developing minds: A resource book for teacher thinking* (3rd ed.). Alexandria, VA: Association for Supervision and Curriculum Development.

Council on Interracial Books for Children. (n.d.). *10 quick ways to analyze children's books for racism and sexism.* Retrieved May 9, 2004, from http://www.birchlane.davis.ca.us/library/10quick.htm

Crawford, A. (2003). Communicative approaches to second-language acquisition: The bridge to second-language literacy. In G. García, (Ed.), *English learners: Reaching the highest level of English literacy* (pp. 152-181). Newark, DE: International Reading Association.

Crumpler, T. P., Bertelsen, C. D., Bond, E. L., & Tierney, R. J. (2003). *Interactive assessment: Teachers, parents, and students as partners.* Norwood, MA: Christopher-Gordon.

Cummins, J. (1981). Primary language instruction and the education of language minority students. In California Department of Education Office of Bilingual/Bicultural Education, *Schooling and language minority students: A theoretical framework* (2nd ed., pp. 3-49). Los Angeles: Evaluation, Dissemination and Assessment Center, California State University, Los Angeles.

Cummins, J. (1986). Empowering minority students: A framework for intervention. *Harvard Educational Review, 56*(1), 18-36.

Cummins, J. (1989). *Empowering minority students.* Sacramento, CA: California Association for Bilingual Education.

Cummins, J. (1991). Interdependence of first- and second-language proficiency in bilingual children. In E. Bialystok (Ed.), *Language processing in bilingual children* (pp. 70-88). Cambridge, MA: Cambridge University Press.

Cummins, J. (1994). Primary language instruction and the education of language minority students. In C. F. Leyba (Ed.), *Schooling and language minority students: A theoretical framework* (2nd ed., pp. 3-46). Los Angeles: EDAC, CSULA.

Cummins, J. (2003). Reading and the bilingual students: Fact and fiction. In G. García, (Ed.), *English learners: Reaching the highest level of English literacy* (pp. 2-33). Newark, DE: International Reading Association.

Cummins, J. (2005). Teaching the language of academic success: A framework for school-based language policies. In C. F. Leyba (Ed.), *Schooling and language minority students: A theoretico-practico framework* (3rd ed., pp. 3-32). Los Angeles: LBD Publishers.

Cummins, J. (n.d.). *Putting language proficiency in its place: Responding to critiques of the conversational/ academic language distinction.* Retrieved August 16, 2004, from http://www.iteachilearn.com/cummins/converacademlangdisti.html

Cunningham, P. M., & Allington, R. L. (2003). *Classrooms that work: They all can read and write* (3rd ed.). New York: Allyn & Bacon.

Daniels, H., & Bizar, M. (1998). *Methods that matter.* York, ME: Stenhouse Publishers.

Darling-Hammond, L. (2000). *Transforming urban public schools: The role of standards and accountability.* (ERIC Document Reproduction Service No. ED459290).

De la Luz Reyes, M. (2001). Unleashing possibilities: Biliteracy in the primary grades. In M. de la Luz Reyes and J. Halcón. (Eds.), *The best for our children: Critical perspectives on literacy for Latino students* (pp. 96-120). New York: Teachers College Press.

Delgado-Gaitán, C., & Trueba, H. (1991). *Crossing cultural borders: Education for immigrant families in America.* London, England: The Falmer Press.

Delpit, L. (1995). *Other people's children: Cultural conflicts in the classroom.* New York: New Press.

Dewey, J. (1938). *Experience and education.* New York: Macmillan.

Diaz, C. F. (2001). *Multicultural education for the 21st century.* New York: Longman.

Diaz, E., & Flores, B. (2001). Teacher as sociocultural, socio-historical mediator: Teaching to the potential. In M. de la Luz Reyes and J. Halcón. (Eds.), *The best for our children: Critical perspectives on literacy for Latino students* (pp. 29-47). New York: Teachers College Press.

Dieker, L. (1998). Rationale for co-teaching. *Social Studies Review, 37*(2), 62-65.

Doyle, W. (1983). Academic work. *Review of Educational Research, 53,* 159-199.

Droop, M., & Verhoeven, L. (2003). Language proficiency and reading ability in first- and second-language learners. *Reading Research Quarterly, 38*(1), 78-103.

Dulay, H. C., & Burt, M. K. (1974). Errors and strategies in child second language. *TESOL Quarterly 8*(2), 129-136.

Dulay, H. C., Burt, M. K., & Krashen, S. (1982). *Language two.* Oxford: Oxford University Press.

Duthie, C. (1996). *True stories: Nonfiction literacy in the primary classroom.* Portland, ME: Stenhouse Publishers.

Dutro, S., & Moran, C. (2003). Rethinking English language instruction. An architectural approach. In G. G. García (Ed.), *English learners: Reaching the highest level of literacy* (pp. 227-258). Newark, DE: International Reading Association.

Dyson, A. H., & Genishi, C. (1994). *The need for story: Cultural diversity in classroom and community.* Urbana, IL: NCTE.

Edelsky, C. (1986). *Writing in a bilingual program: Había una vez.* Norwood, NJ: Ablex.

Edinger, M., & Fins, S. (1998). *Far away and long ago: Young historians in the classroom.* Portland, ME: Stenhouse Publishers.

Egan, K. (1986). *Teaching as storytelling: An alternative approach to teaching and curriculum in the elementary school.* Chicago: University of Chicago Press.

Egan, K. (1988). *Teaching as storytelling.* London: Routledge.

Eggen, P. D., & Kauchak, D. P. (2001). *Strategies for teachers: Teaching content and thinking skills* (4th ed.). Boston: Allyn & Bacon.

FairTest. (2005a). *Criterion-and standards-referenced testing.* Cambridge, MA: Author. Retrieved September 3, 2005, from http://www.fairtest.org/facts/csrtests.html

FairTest. (2005b). *Norm-referenced achievement tests.* Cambridge, MA: Author. Retrieved September 3, 2005, from http://fairtest.org/facts/nratests.html

Figueroa, R. A., & García, E. (1994). Issues in testing students from culturally and linguistically diverse backgrounds. *Multicultural Education, 2*(1), 10–19.

Fillmore, L. W., & Snow, C. E. (2002). What teachers need to know about language. In C. T. Adger, C. E. Snow, and D. Christian (Eds.), *What teachers need to know about language* (pp. 7–54). McHenry, IL: Delta Systems.

Fletcher, T., Bos, C., & Johnson (Santamaría), L. (1999). Accommodating English language learners with language/ learning disabilities in bilingual classrooms. *Learning Disabilities Research and Practice, 14*(2), 80–91.

Flores, B., Cousin, P. T., & Díaz, E. (1998). Transforming deficit myths about learning, language and culture. In M. F. Opitz (Ed.), *Literacy instruction for culturally and linguistically diverse students* (pp. 27–38). Newark, DE: International Reading Association.

Foorman, B. R., Fletcher, J. M., Francis, D. J., & Schatschneider, C. S. (2000). Response misrepresentation of research by other researchers. *Educational Researcher, 29*(6), 27–37.

Freeman, D. E., & Freeman, Y. S. (1992). *Whole language for second language learners.* Portsmouth, NH: Heinemann.

Freeman, Y. S., & Freeman, D. E. (1998). *ESL/EFL teaching: Principles for success.* Portsmouth, NH: Heinemann.

Fresno Unified School District. (2001). *Home language survey.* Fresno, CA: Author. Retrieved August 27, 2005, from http://multilingual.fresno.k12.ca.us/assmctr/HLS/lanindex.htm

Garan, E. M. (2002). *Resisting reading mandates: How to triumph with the truth.* Portsmouth, NH: Heinemann.

García, E. E., & Curry-Rodriguez, J. E. (2000). The education of limited English proficient students in California schools: An assessment of the influence of Proposition 227 on selected districts and schools. *Bilingual Research Journal, 24*(1&2), 1–21.

García, G. (2003). *English learners: Reaching the highest level of English literacy.* Newark, DE: International Reading Association.

García, G. E. (2003). The reading comprehension development and instruction of English-language learners. In A. P. Sweet and C. E. Snow (Eds.), *Rethinking reading comprehension* (pp. 30–50). New York: Guilford Press.

Gardner, H. (1999). *The disciplined mind: What all students should understand.* New York: Simon & Schuster.

Gay, G. (2000). *Culturally responsive teaching: Theory, research and practice.* New York: Teachers College Press.

Gay, G. (2002). Preparing for culturally responsive teaching. *Journal of Teacher Education, 53*(2), 106–116.

Genesee, F., Lindholm-Leary, K., Saunders, W. M., & Christian, D. (2006). *Educating English language learners: A synthesis of research evidence.* New York: Cambridge University Press.

George, M., Rafael, T. E., & Florio-Ruane, S. (2003). Connecting children, culture and text. In G. G. García (Ed.), *English learners: Reaching the highest level of English literacy* (pp. 308–332). Newark DE: International Reading Association.

Gibbons, P. (1993). *Learning to learn in a second language.* Portsmouth, NH: Heinemann.

Givens, A. (Ed.). (1998). *String souls singing: African American books for our daughters and our sisters.* New York: W. W. Norton.

Gollnick, D. M., & Chinn, P. C. (1998). *Multicultural education in a pluralistic society* (5th ed.). Upper Saddle River, NJ: Merrill/Prentice Hall.

Goodman, K. (1986). *What's whole about whole language?* Portsmouth, NH: Heinemann.

Grace, C. (1992). *The portfolio and its use: Developmentally appropriate assessment of young children.* ERIC Document Reproduction Service No. ED351150. Retrieved August 19, 2006, from http://ericae.net/edo/ed351150.htm

Grant, C. (1995). *Educating for diversity: An anthology of multicultural voices.* Boston: Allyn & Bacon.

Graves, D. (1982). *Writing: Teachers and children at work.* Portsmouth, NH: Heinemann.

Graves, D. (1991). *Build a literate classroom.* Portsmouth, NH: Heinemann.

Guild, P. B., & Garger, S. (1998). *What is differentiated instruction? Marching to different drummers* (2nd ed.). Alexandria, VA: Association for Supervision and Curriculum Development.

Gutiérrez, K., Baquédaño-López, P., & Tejeda, C. (1999). Rethinking diversity: Hybridity and hybrid language practices in the third space. *Mind, Culture and Activity, 6*, 296–303.

Halcón, J. (2001). Mainstream ideology and literacy instruction of Spanish-speaking children. In M. de la Luz Reyes and J. Halcón. (Eds.), *The best for our children: Critical perspectives on literacy for Latino students* (pp. 65–80). New York: Teachers College Press.

Hall, R. (1964). *Introductory linguistics.* Philadelphia, PA: Chilton.

Hall, T. (2004). *Differentiated instruction.* Retrieved May 1, 2004, from http://www.cast.org/ncac/index

Hall, T., Strangman, N., & Meyer, A. (2003). Differentiated instruction and implications for UDL implementation.

Wakefield, MA: National Center on Accessing the General Curriculum. Retrieved January 19, 2008, from http://www.cast.org/publications/ncac/ncac_diffinstructudl.html

Halliday, M.A. K. (1989). *Spoken and written language.* New York: Oxford University Press.

Halliday, M.A. K. (1973). *Exploration in the functions of language.* London, UK: Arnold.

Halliday, M.A. K. (1975). *Spoken and written language.* Oxford, UK: Oxford University Press.

Hambleton, R., & Rodgers, J. (1997). *Item bias review.* ERIC Digest. Retrieved February 20, 2006, from http://www.ericdigests.org/1997-1/bias.html

Harris, T. L., & Hodges, R. E. (1995). *The literacy dictionary: The vocabulary of reading and writing.* Newark, DE: International Reading Association.

Harvey, S., & Goudvis, A. (2000). *Strategies that work: Teaching comprehension to enhance understanding.* York, ME: Stenhouse Publishers.

Hayes, E. B. (1988). Encoding strategies used by native and non-native readers of Chinese Mandarin. *Modern Language Journal, 71,* 188-195.

Heath, S. B. (1983). *Ways with words: Language, life and work in communities and classrooms.* Cambridge, MA: Cambridge University Press.

Hefflin, B. R. (2002). Learning to develop culturally relevant pedagogy: A lesson about cornrowed lives. *The Urban Review, 34*(3), 231-250.

Hernandez, H. (2000). *Multicultural education: A teacher's guide to multicultural context, process and content* (2nd ed.). New York: Prentice Hall.

Herrell, A. L. (2000). *Fifty strategies for teaching English language learners.* Upper Saddle River, NJ: Merrill.

Herrera, S. G., & Murry, K. G. (2005). *Mastering ESL and bilingual method: Differentiated instruction for culturally and linguistically (CLD) students.* Boston, MA: Pearson.

Heydon, R. (2003). Literature circles as a differentiated instructional strategy for including ESL students in mainstream classrooms. *Canadian Modern Language Review, 59*(3), 463-475.

Hildenbrand, L., & Hixon, J. (1991). Video assisted learning of study skills. *Elementary School Guidance and Counseling, 26*(2), 121-129.

Houk, F.A. (2005). *Supporting English language learners: A guide for teachers and administrators.* Portsmouth, NH: Heinemann.

Hudelson, S. (1986). ESL children's writing: What we've learned, what we're learning. In P. Rigg and D. Enright (Eds.), *Children and ESL: Integrating perspectives* (pp. 23-54). Alexandria, VA: Teachers of English to Speakers of Other Languages.

Huitt, W. (1996). Measurement and evaluation: Criterion-versus norm-referenced testing. *Educational Psychology Interactive.* Valdosta, GA: Valdosta State University. Retrieved September 3, 2005, from http://chiron.valdosta.edu/whuitt/col/measeval/crnmref.html

Hurley, S. R., & Tinajero, J.V. (2000). *Literacy assessment of second language learners.* Boston: Allyn & Bacon.

Individuals with Disabilities Education Act (IDEA). 20 United States Congress 1412[a] [5]).

Irvine, J. J., Armento, B., Causey, V. E., Jones, J. C., Frasher, R. S., & Weinburgh, M. H. (2001). *Culturally responsive teaching: Lesson planning for elementary and middle grades.* New York: McGraw-Hill.

Johns, J. (2005). *Basic reading inventory: Pre-primer through grade twelve and early literacy assessments* (9th ed.). New York: Kendall Hunt.

Johnson, D.W., Johnson, R.T., & Holubec, E. J. (1994). *The new circles of learning: Cooperation in the classroom and school.* Arlington, VA: ASCD.

Kagan, S. (1994). *Cooperative learning* (2nd ed.). San Juan Capistrano, CA: Kagan Cooperative Learning.

Kamil, M. L., Mosenthal, P. B., Pearson, P. D., & Barr, R. (2000). *Handbook of reading research* (Vol. III). New York: Erlbaum.

Keene, E. O., & Zimmerman, S. (2007). *Mosaic of thought: The power of comprehension strategy instruction* (2nd ed.). Portsmouth, NH: Heinemann.

Keller, H. (1994). *Grandfather's dream.* New York: Greenwillow Books.

Kellough, R. D., & Kellough, N. G. (1999). *Secondary school teaching: A guide to methods and resources, planning for competence.* Upper Saddle River, NJ: Prentice Hall.

Kern, R. G. (1994). The role of mental translation in second language reading. *Studies in Second Language Acquisition, 16,* 441-461.

Konold, T. R., Juel, C., & McKinnon, M. (1999). *Building an integrated model of early literacy acquisition.* Ann Arbor, MI: Center for the Improvement of Reading. Retrieved July 29, 2003, from http://www.ciera.org

Krashen, S. D. (1987). Encouraging free reading. In M. Douglass (Ed.), *Claremont reading conference 51st yearbook.* Claremont, CA: Claremont Graduate School.

Krashen, S. D. (1991). *Writing: Research, theory and applications.* Torrance, CA: Laredo Publishing.

Krashen, S. D. (1994). Bilingual education and second language acquisition theory. In C. F. Leyba (Ed.), *Schooling and language minority students: A theoretical framework* (2nd ed., pp. 47-75). Los Angeles, CA: EDAC.

Krashen, S. D. (2003). Three roles for reading for minority-language children. In G. García (Ed.), *English learners: Reaching the highest level of English literacy* (pp. 55-70). Newark, DE: International Reading Association.

Krashen, S. D. (2005). Bilingual education and second language acquisition theory. In C. F. Leyba (Ed.), *Schooling and language minority students: A theoretico-practical framework* (3rd ed., pp. 3-32). Los Angeles: LBD Publishers.

Krashen, S. D., & Biber, D. (1988). *On course: Bilingual education's success in California*. Sacramento, CA: CABE.

Krashen, S. D., & Terrell, T. D. (1988). *The natural approach: Language acquisition in the classroom.* Hemel Hempstead: Prentice Hall.

Kucer, S. B. (1989). *A writing interview.* Unpublished paper. Los Angeles, CA: USC.

Kucer, S. (2001). *Dimensions of literacy: A conceptual base for teaching, reading, and writing in school settings.* Mahwah, NJ: Erlbaum.

Ladson-Billings, G. (1994). *The dreamkeepers: Successful teachers of African American children.* San Francisco, CA: Jossey-Bass.

Ladson-Billings, G. (1995). But that's just good teaching! The case for culturally relevant pedagogy. *Theory Into Practice, 34,* 159–165.

Laing, S. P., & Kamhi, A. (2003). Alternative assessment of language and literacy in culturally and linguistically diverse populations. *Language, Speech, and Hearing Services in Schools, 34,* 44–55.

Lesaux, N. K., & Geva, E. (2006). Synthesis: Development of literacy in language-minority students. In D. August and T. Shanahan (Eds.), *Developing literacy in second language learners: Report of the national literacy panel on language-minority children and youth* (pp. 53–74). Mahwah, NJ: Erlbaum.

Liebling, C. R. (1998). *In the beginning: Helping all children achieve early literacy.* Portsmouth, NH: EMC Research Corp. Retrieved December 27, 2008, from http://www.eric.ed.gov/ERICDocs/data/ericdocs2sql/content_storage_01/0000019b/80/15/72/d2.pdf

Lindholm-Leary, K., & Hargett, G. (2006). Student Oral Language Observation Matrix (SOLOM). In K. Lindholm-Leary and G. Hargett (Eds.), *Evaluators toolkit for dual language program.* Washington DC: Center for Applied Linguistics. Retrieved December 30, 2007, from http://www.cal.org/twi/EvalToolkit/appendix/solom.pdf

Lu, M. (1987). *Multicultural children's literature in the elementary classroom. ERIC Digest.* Bloomington, IN: ERIC Clearinghouse on Reading English and Communication. Retrieved December 26, 2007, from http://www.ericdigests.org/1999-2/literature.htm

Luckner, J. (1999). An examination of two co-teaching classrooms. *American Annals of the Deaf, 144*(1), 24–34.

Lyman, F. T. (1981). The responsive classroom discussion: The inclusion of all students. In A. Anderson (Ed.), *Mainstreaming digest* (pp. 109–113). College Park: University of Maryland Press.

MacSwan, J., Rolstad, K., & Glass, G. V. (2002). Do some school-age children have no language? Some problems of construct validity in the Pre-Las Español. *Bilingual Research Journal, 26*(2), 216–238.

Mahoney, M. (1997). Small victories in an inclusive classroom. *Educational Leadership, 54*(7), 59–62.

Mathis, J. B. (2001). Respond to stories with stories: Teachers discuss multicultural children's literature. *The Social Studies, 92*(4), 155–160.

McArdle, P., & Chhabra, V. (2004). *The voice of evidence in reading research.* New York: Brookes Publishing.

McGinley, W., Kamberelis, G., Mahoney, T., Madigan, D., Rybicki, V., & Oliver, J. (1997). Re-visiting reading and teaching literature through the lens of narrative theory. In T. Rogers and A. O. Soter (Eds.), *Reading across cultures: Teaching literature in a diverse society* (pp. 42–68). New York: Teachers College Press.

McTighe, J., & Ferrara, S. (1998). *Assessing learning in the classroom.* Washington, DC: National Education Association.

Mercado, C., & Romero, M. (1993). Assessment of students in bilingual education. In M. B. Arias and U. Casanova (Eds.), *Bilingual education: Politics, practice, research* (pp. 144–170). Chicago: University of Chicago Press.

Mid-Atlantic Equity Center. (1998/9). *Using standardized tests to make high-stake decisions on English-language learners: Dilemmas and critical issues.* Chevy Chase, MD: Author.

Miller, A., Valasky, W., & Molloy, P. (1998). Learning together: The evolution of an inclusive class. *Active Learner: A Foxfire Journal for Teachers, 3*(2), 14–16.

Miller, P. J., & Mehler, R. A. (1994). The power of personal storytelling in families and kindergartens. In A. H. Dyson and C. Genishi (Eds.), *The need for story: Cultural diversity in classroom and community* (pp. 38–54). Urbana, IL: NCTE.

Moline, S. (1995). *I see what you mean.* York, ME: Stenhouse Publishers.

Moll, L. (1998, February). *Funds of knowledge for teaching: A new approach to culture in education.* Keynote address at the Illinois State Board of Education, Twenty-First Annual Statewide Conference for Teachers of Linguistically and Culturally Diverse Students.

Moll, L. C. (2001). The diversity of schooling: A cultural-historical approach. In M. de la Luz Reyes and J. J. Halcón, (Eds.), *The best for our children: Critical perspectives on literacy for Latino students* (pp. 13–28). New York: Teachers College Press.

Moll, L. C., Amanti, C., Neff, D., & González, N. (1992). Funds of knowledge for teaching: Using a qualitative approach to connect home and classrooms. *Theory Into Practice, 31,* 132–141.

Nassaji, H., & Cumming, A. (2000). What's in a ZPD? A case study of a young ESL student and teacher interacting through dialogue journals. *Language Teaching Research, 4*(2), 95–121.

National Center for Education Statistics. (2002). *1999-2000 Schools and staffing survey: Overview of the data for public, private, public charter and Bureau of Indian Affairs elementary and secondary schools.* Washington, DC: U.S. Department of Education, Office of Educational Research and Improvement.

National Center for Research on Evaluation, Standards and Student Testing. (n.d.). Norm-referenced assessment. *Glossary: F–Z.* Retrieved January 1, 2008, from http://www.cse.ucla.edu/products/glossary_2.html

National Reading Panel. (2000). *Teaching children to read: An evidence-based assessment of the scientific research literature on reading and its implications for reading instruction: Reports of the subgroups.* Washington, DC: National Institute of Child Health and Human Development.

National Research Council. (2001). *Classroom assessment and the National Science Education Standards.* Committee on classroom assessment and the National Science Education Standards. J. M. Atkin, P. Black and J. Coffey (Eds.). Center for Education, Division of Behavioral and Social Sciences Education. Washington, DC: National Academy Press. Retrieved February 19, 2006, from http://newton.nap.edu/html/classroom_assessment/index.html

NCREL. (1995). *Strategic teaching and Reading Project Guidebook* (Rev. ed.). Excerpt retrieved May 8, 2004, from http://www.ncrel.org/sdrs/areas/issues/students/learning/lr1metn.htm

NICHD. (2000). *Report of the National Reading Panel. Teaching children to read: An evidence-based assessment of the scientific research literature on reading and its implications for reading instruction* (NIH publication 004 769). Washington, DC: US Government Printing Office. Retrieved February 25, 2007, from http://www.nationalreadingpanel.org

Nieto, S. (1999a). *The light in their eyes: Creating multicultural learning communities.* New York: Teachers College Press.

Nieto, S. (1999b). *Affirming diversity: The sociopolitical context of multicultural education* (3rd ed.). New York: Addison-Wesley.

Nieto, S. (2001). School reform and student learning: A multicultural perspective. In J. A. Banks and C. A. McGee Banks (Eds.), *Multicultural education: Issues and perspectives* (4th ed., pp. 381–401). New York: Wiley.

Northwest Regional Educational Laboratory. (2001). Keys to quality student assessment. *Toolkit98: Standards-based assessment—Nurturing Learning Readings.* Retrieved September 5, 2005, from http://www.nwrel.org/assessment/toolkit98/keys.html

Ogle, J. M. (1986). K-W-L: A teaching model that develops active reading of expository text. *The Reading Teacher, 39,* 564–570.

Oller, J. W. (1979). *Language tests at school: A pragmatic approach.* London: Longman.

O'Malley, J. M. (1993). *Authentic assessment for English language learners.* Boston: Pearson Higher Education.

O'Malley, M., & Pierce, L. V. (1996). *Authentic assessment for English language learners: Practical approaches for teachers.* Boston: Addison-Wesley.

Ooka Pang, V. (2001). *Multicultural education: A caring-centered, reflective approach.* Boston: McGraw Hill.

Ooka Pang, V. (2004). *Multicultural education: A caring-centered, reflective approach* (2nd ed.). Boston: McGraw-Hill.

Orellana, M. F., Reynolds, J., Dorner, J., & Meza, M. (2003). In other words: Translating or "para-phrasing" as a family literacy practice in immigrant households. *Reading Research Quarterly, 38*(1), 12–35.

Paulson, G., & Paulsen, R. W. (1995). *The tortilla factory.* New York: Harcourt Brace.

Peregoy, S. F., & Boyle, O. F. (1997). *Reading, writing and learning in ESL: A resource book for K-12 teachers* (2nd ed.). New York: Longman.

Peregoy, S. F., & Boyle, O. F. (2005). *Reading, writing and learning in ESL: A resource book for K-12 teachers* (4th ed.). New York: Longman.

Pérez, B., & Torres-Guzmán, M. E. (1996). *Learning in two worlds: An integrated Spanish/English biliteracy approach* (2nd ed.). New York: Longman.

Pérez, B., & Torres-Guzmán, M. E. (2002). *Learning in two worlds: An integrated Spanish/English biliteracy approach* (3rd ed.). Boston: Allyn & Bacon.

Peters, J. (2002). University-school collaboration: Identifying faulty assumptions. *Pacific Journal of Teacher Education, 30*(3), 229–243.

Peyton, J. K. (1990). Dialogue journal writing and the acquisition of English grammatical morphology. In J. K. Peyton (Ed.), *Students and teachers writing together* (pp. 67–97). Alexandria, VA: Teachers of English to Speakers of Other Languages.

Peyton, J. K. (1997). Dialogue journals: Interactive writing to develop language and literacy. *Emergency Librarian, 24*(5), 46–48.

Peyton, J. K., & Reed, L. (1990). *Dialogue journal writing with nonnative English speakers: A handbook for teachers.* Alexandria, VA: TESOL.

Peyton, J. K., & Staton, J. (1992). *Dialogue journal writing with nonnative English speakers: An instructional packet for teachers and workshop leaders.* Alexandria, VA: TESOL.

Pierangelo, R., & Giulani, G. (2002). *Assessment in special education: A practical approach.* Boston: Allyn & Bacon.

Proctor, C. P., Carlo, M., August, D., & Snow, C. E. (2005). Native Spanish-speaking children reading in English: Toward a model of comprehension. *Journal of Educational Psychology, 97*(2), 246–256.

Quiocho, A. (1997). The quest to comprehend expository text: Applied classroom research. *Journal of Adolescent & Adult Literacy, 40*(6), 450–455.

Quiocho, A., Dantas M. L., & Mackintosh, D. (2001a). *Assessment of English language learners.* Paper presented at the annual meeting of the International Reading Association, New Orleans, LA.

Quiocho, A., Dantas, M. L., & Mackintosh, D. (2001b). *A work in progress model of assessment for English language learners.* Paper presented at the annual meeting of the International Reading Association, New Orleans, LA.

Quiocho, A., Dantas, M. L., Mackintosh, D., & Rodriguez, L. (2002). *Multiple perspectives on assessment and instruction of second language learners.* Paper presented at the annual meeting of the International Reading Association, San Francisco, CA.

Quiocho, A., & Santamaría, L. (2003, November). *Developing academic language in English for heritage language learners.* Paper presented at the annual meeting of the California Reading Association, San Diego, CA.

Quiocho, A., & Ulanoff, S. (2005). What differentiation should be for English language learners: A new pedagogy. In B. Bartlett, F. Bryer, and D. Roebuck (Eds.), *Stimulating the "action" as participants in participatory research* (Vol. III, pp. 62–72). Brisbane, Australia: Griffith University.

Ramírez, J. D. (1992). Executive summary. *Bilingual Research Journal, 16*(1&2), 1–62.

Raphael, T. E. (1982). Question-answering strategies for children. *The Reading Teacher, 36,* 186–190.

Ray, K. W. (1999). *Wondrous words: Writers and writing in the elementary classroom.* Urbana, IL: NCTE.

Resnick, L. (1987). *Comments during a symposium on implications of the Carnegie task force.* Paper presented at the annual meeting of American Educational Research Association, Washington DC.

Resnick, L. B. (1989). Introduction. In L. B. Resnick (Ed.), *Knowing, learning and instruction: Essays in honor of Robert Glaser.* Mahwah, NJ: Erlbaum.

Rice, D., & Zigmond, N. (2000). Co-teaching in secondary schools: Teacher reports of developments in Australia and American classrooms. *Learning Disabilities Research and Practice, 15*(4), 190–197.

Riches, C., & Genesee, F. (2006). Crosslinguistic and crossmodal issues. In F. Genesee, K. Lindholm-Leary, W. Saunders, and D. Christian (Eds.), *Educating English language learners: A synthesis of research evidence* (pp. 64–108). New York: Cambridge University Press.

Rodgers, E. M. (2000). Language matters: When is a scaffold really a scaffold? *National Reading Conference Yearbook, 49,* 78–90.

Roe, B. D., Alfred, S., & Smith, S. (1998). *Teaching through stories: Yours, mine, and theirs.* New York: Christopher-Gordon Publishers.

Rossell, C. (2004–2005). Teaching English through English. *Educational Leadership, 62*(4) 32–36.

Rossell, C. H. (1992). Nothing matters? A critique of the Ramírez, et al. longitudinal study of instructional programs for language-minority children. *Bilingual Research Journal, 16*(1&2), 159–186.

Rossell, C. H., & Baker, K. (1996). The effectiveness of bilingual education. *Research in the Teaching of English, 30,* 7–74.

Routman, R. (1994). *Invitations: Changing as teachers and learners K–12.* Portsmouth, NH: Heinemann.

Rowe, M. B. (1974). Relation of wait time and rewards to the development of language, logic, and fate control: Part II–Rewards. *Journal of Research in Science Teaching, 11*(4), 291–308.

Rule, A. C., & Lord, L. H. (2003). *Activities for differentiated instruction addressing all levels of Bloom's taxonomy and eight multiple intelligences.* East Lansing, MI: National Center for Research on Teacher Learning. (ERIC Document Reproduction Service No. EC309660).

Salas, R. G., Lucido, F., & Canales, J. (2002). Multicultural literature: Broadening young children's experiences. In J. Cassidy and S. Garrett (Eds.), *Early childhood literacy: Programs and strategies to develop cultural, linguistic scientific and healthcare literacy for very young children and their families, 2001 CEDER Yearbook.* Corpus Christi, TX: Texas A & M University. Retrieved May 9, 2004, from http://80-www.edrs.com.mimas .calstatela.edu/Webstore/Download2.cfm?ID=714707

Samway, K. D. (2006). *When English language learners write: Connecting research to practice K–8.* Portsmouth, NH: Heinemann.

San Jose Unified School District. (n.d.). *Students Oral Language Observation Matrix.* San Jose, CA: Region VII Comprehensive Center. Retrieved December 1, 2004, from http://www.helpforschools.com/ELLKBase/ forms/SOLOM.shtml

Santamaría, L. J., Fletcher, T. V., & Bos, C. S. (2002). Effective pedagogy for English language learners in inclusive classrooms. In A. Ortiz & A. Artiles (Eds.), *English language learners with special education needs* (pp. 133–157). Washington, DC: Center for Applied Linguistics (CAL).

Santamaría, L. J., & Thousand, J. A. (2004). Collaboration, co-teaching, and differentiated instruction: A process-oriented approach to whole schooling. *International Journal of Whole Schooling, 1*(1), 13–27. Retrieved January 19, 2007, from http://www.coe.wayne.edu/ wholeschooling/Journal_of_Whole_Schooling/articles. html

Sapir, E. (1921). *Language.* New York: Harcourt Brace.

Schleppegrell, M. J. (2004). *The language of schooling: A functional perspective.* Mahwah, NJ: Erlbaum.

Schumm, J. S., & Arguelles, M. E. (2006). *No two learners learn alike: The importance of assessment and differentiated instruction.* In J. S. Schumm (Ed.), *Reading assessment and instruction for all learners* (pp. 27–86). New York: Guilford Press.

Scruggs, T. E., Mastropieri, M. A., Monson, J., & Jorgenson, C. (1985). Maximizing what gifted students can learn: Recent findings of learning strategy research. *Gifted Child Quarterly, 29*(4), 181–185.

Shioshita, J. (1997, September–October). Beyond good intentions: Selecting multicultural literature. *Children's Advocate.* Retrieved May 9, 2004, from http://www.4children.org/news/9-97mlit.htm

Short, D. J., & Fitzsimmons, S. (2007). *Double the work: Challenges and solutions to acquiring language and academic literacy for adolescent English language learners: A report to Carnegie Corporation of New York.* Washington, DC: Alliance for Excellent Education.

Shulman, L. (2002). Making differences: A table of learning. *Change, 34*(6), 36–44. Retrieved February 14, 2003, from http://www.carnegiefoundation.org/elibrary/docs/making_differences.htm

Shulman, L. (2003). Making differences: A table of learning. *Carnegie Foundation eLibrary.* Retrieved February 24, 2003, from http://www.carnegiefoundation.org/elibrary/docs/printable/making_differences.htm

Shulman, L. S. (2004). *The wisdom of practice: Essays on teaching, learning, and learning to teach.* San Francisco, CA: Jossey-Bass.

Simpson, M. L., & Nist, S. L. (2002). Encouraging active reading at the college level. In C. C. Block and M. Pressley (Eds.), *Comprehension instruction: Research based best practices* (pp. 365–382). New York: Guilford Press.

Sims Bishop, R. (1997). Selecting literature for a multicultural curriculum. In V. J. Harris (Ed.), *Using multiethnic literature in the K-8 classroom* (pp. 1–19). Norwood, MA: Christopher-Gordon.

Sims Bishop, R. (2003). Reframing the debate about cultural authenticity. In D. Fox & K. Short (Eds.), *Stories matter: The complexity of cultural authenticity in children's literature* (pp. 25–40). Urbana, IL: National Council for Teachers of English.

Skinner, B. F. (1957). *Verbal behavior.* New York: Appleton-Century Crofts.

Sleeter, C. (1992, March/April) Restructuring schools for multicultural education. *Journal of Teacher Education, 43*(2), 141–148.

Sleeter, C. E., & Grant, C. A. (2002). *Making choices for multicultural education: Five approaches to race, class and gender* (4th ed.). New York: Wiley.

Smith, F. (1983). Reading like a writer. *Language Arts, 60*(5), 558–567.

Smith, F. (1986). *Insult to intelligence: The bureaucratic invasion of our schools.* Portsmouth, NH: Heinemann.

Smith, F. (1994). *Writing and the writer* (2nd ed.). Hillsdale, NJ: Erlbaum.

Snow, C. E., Burns, M. S., & Griffin, P. (1998). *Preventing reading difficulties in young children.* Washington, DC: National Academy Press.

Solano-Flores, G. (2002). *Cultural validity: The need for a sociocultural perspective in educational measurement.* Paper presented at the annual meeting of the American Educational Research Association. New Orleans, LA. Retrieved June 6, 2006, from http://www.edgateway.net/cs/cvap/print/docs/cvap/pub_6.htm

Spindler, G., & Spindler, L. (1994). *Pathways to cultural awareness: Cultural therapy with teachers and students.* Thousand Oaks, CA: Corwin Press.

Stainback, W., & Stainback, S. (1996). *Inclusion: A guide for educators.* Baltimore: Paul H. Brooks.

Staton, J. (1983). Dialogue journals: A new tool for teaching communication. *ERIC Clearinghouse on Languages and Linguistics, 6*(2), 1–2, 6.

Stefankis, J. (1998). *Whose assessment counts?* Portland, ME: Stenhouse Publishers.

Sternberg, R. J. (1982). Culture and intelligence. In R. J. Sternberg (Ed.), *Handbook of human intelligence* (pp. 642–719). New York: Oxford University Press.

Swearingen, R. (n.d.). *A primer: Diagnostic, formative and summative assessment.* Retrieved September 5, 2005, from http://www.mmrwsjr.com/assessment.htm

Taylor, O. L. (1990). *Cross-cultural communication: An essential dimension of effective education* (Rev. ed.). Chevy Chase, MD: The Mid-Atlantic Center. Retrieved August 19, 2006, from http://www.maec.org/cross/

Temple, C., Martinez, M., Yokota, J., & Naylor, A. (2002). *Children's books in children's hands: An introduction to their literature* (2nd ed.). Boston: Allyn & Bacon.

Temple, C., Ogle, D., Crawford, A., & Freppon, P. (2005). *All children read: Teaching for literacy in today's diverse classrooms, California edition.* Boston: Allyn & Bacon.

Terrell, T. D. (1977). A natural approach to second language acquisition and learning. *Modern Language Journal, 6,* 325–337.

Tharp, R. G., Estrada, P., Dalton, S. S., & Yamaguchi, L. (2000). *Teaching transformed: Achieving excellence, fairness, inclusion, and harmony.* Boulder, CO: Westview Press.

Thomas, W. P., & Collier, V. P. (1997). *School effectiveness for language minority students.* Washington, DC: National Clearinghouse for Bilingual Education.

Thonis, E. W. (1994). Reading instruction for language minority students. In C. F. Leyba (Ed.), *Schooling and language minority students: A theoretical framework* (2nd ed., pp. 165–202). Los Angeles, CA: EDAC.

Tomlinson, C. A. (1995). *Differentiating instruction for advanced learners in the mixed-ability middle school classroom.* ERIC Digest E536. Retrieved May 1, 2004, from http://www.ed.gov/databases/ERIC_Digests/ed389141.html

Tomlinson, C. A. (1999). *The differentiated classroom: Responding to the needs of all learners.* Alexandria, VA: ASCD.

Tomlinson, C. A., (2000). *Differentiation of instruction in the elementary grades.* ERIC Digest. Champaign, IL: ERIC Clearinghouse on Elementary and Early Childhood Education. ERIC Document No. ED443572. Retrieved May 1, 2004, from http://ceep.crc.uiuc.edu/eecearchive/digests/2000/tomlin00.pdf

Tomlinson, C. A. (2001). *How to differentiate instruction in mixed-ability classrooms* (2nd ed.). Alexandria, VA: Association for Supervision and Curriculum Development.

Tomlinson, C. A. (2003). *Fulfilling the promise of the differentiated classroom: Strategies and tools for responsive teaching.* Alexandria, VA: Association for Supervision and Curriculum Development.

Tomlinson, C. A. (2004). *How to differentiate instruction in mixed-ability classrooms* (2nd ed.). Alexandria, VA: Association for Supervision and Curriculum Development.

Tompkins, G. E. (2003). *Literacy for the 21st century* (3rd ed.). Upper Saddle River, NJ: Merrill Prentice Hall.

Trager, G. (1949). *The field of linguistics.* Norman, OK: Battenberg Press.

Trent, S. C. (1998). False starts and other dilemmas of a secondary general education collaborative teacher: A case study. *Journal of Learning Disabilities, 31,* 503–513.

Trueba, H. T., Cheng, L. R. L., Ima, K., & Trueba, E. T. (1993). *Myth or reality: Adaptive strategies of Asian Americans in California.* New York: Routledge Falmer.

Trussell-Cullen, A. (1998). *Assessment in the learner-centered classroom.* San Diego: Dominie Press.

Ulanoff, S. H. (1995). Dialogue journal writing and the mediated development of writing. In R. F. Macías and R. G. García Ramos (Eds.), *Changing schools for changing students: An anthology of research on language minorities* (pp. 1–33). Santa Barbara, CA: UC Linguistic Minority Research Institute.

Ulanoff, S. H., Gopalakrishnan, A., Brantley, D., Courtney, S., with Rogers, R. (2007). Examining second language literacy development in an urban multi-age classroom. *International Journal of Early Childhood Education, 14,* 53–62.

Ulanoff, S. H., & Pucci, S. L. (1999). Learning words from books: The effects of read aloud on second language vocabulary acquisition. *Bilingual Research Journal, 23*(4), 365–378.

Ulanoff, S. H., & Pucci, S. L. (2005). Where have all the books gone? The evolution of the Spanish print environment in one Los Angeles community. *International Journal of Learning, 11,* 549–556.

Ulanoff, S. H., & Vega-Castaneda, L. (2003, April). *Four years after 227: What about reading instruction for English language learners?* Paper presented at the annual meeting of AERA, Chicago, IL.

Unrau, N. J., & Ruddell, R. B. (2004). *Theoretical models and processes of reading* (5th ed.). Arlington, VA: International Reading Association.

U.S. Bureau of the Census. (2005). *2005 American community survey.* Retrieved June 26, 2007, from http://www.census.gov/acs/www/index.html

U.S. Department of Education. (2001). *No child left behind.* Washington, DC: Author.

Vacca, R. T., & Vacca, J. L. (2007). *Content area reading: Literacy and learning across the curriculum* (9th ed.). Boston: Allyn & Bacon.

Valdés, G. (1996). *Con respeto: Bridging the distance between diverse families and schools (an ethnographic portrait).* New York: Teachers College Press.

Valdés, G. (2005). Bilingualism, heritage language learners, and SLA research: Opportunities lost or seized. *Modern Language Journal, 89*(3), 410–426.

Valdés, G., & Figueroa, R. A. (1994). *Bilingualism and testing: A special case of bias.* Westport, CT: Ablex.

Valle, R. (1997). *Ethnic diversity and multiculturalism: Crisis or challenge.* New York: American Heritage Custom Publishing.

Vermont Department of Education. (2003). *Primary/home language survey.* Retrieved August 27, 2005, from http://www.state.vt.us/educ/new/html/pgm_esl.html

Villa, R., & Thousand, J. (2003). Making inclusive education work: Successful implementation requires commitment, creative thinking, and effective classroom strategies. *Educational Leadership, 61*(2), 19–23.

Villa, R., & Thousand J. (2005). *Creating an inclusive school.* Arlington, VA: Association for Supervision and Curriculum Development.

Villa, R. A., Thousand, J. S., & Nevin, A. (2004). *A guide to co-teaching: Practical tips for facilitating student learning.* Thousand Oaks, CA: Corwin Press.

Villa, R., Thousand, J., Nevin, A., & Malgeri, C. (1996). Instilling collaboration for inclusive schooling as a way of doing business in public education. *Remedial and Special Education, 17*(3), 169–181.

Vygotsky, L. S. (1978). *Mind in society: The development of higher psychological processes* (M. Cole, V. John-Steiner, S. Scribner, & E. Souberman, Eds. & Trans.). Cambridge, MA: Harvard University Press.

Walther-Thomas, C. (1997). Co-teaching experiences: The benefits and problems that teachers and principals report over time. *Journal of Learning Disabilities, 30,* 395–407.

Welch, M. (2000). Descriptive analysis of team teaching in two elementary classrooms: A formative experimental approach. *Remedial and Special Education, 21*(6), 366–376.

Wells, G. (1986). *The meaning makers: Children learning language and using language to learn.* Portsmouth, NH: Heinemann.

Wertsch, J.V. (1990). *Voices of the mind: A sociocultural approach to mediated action.* Cambridge, MA: Harvard University Press.

West, J. O. (1989). *Mexican-American folklore.* Little Rock, AK: August House Publishers.

WestEd. (2001). *A map for teaching and assessing California's English language development (ELD) and English-language arts (ELA) standards for ELLs* (2nd ed.). San Francisco, CA: Author. Also available online: http://web.WestEd.org/online_pubs/ELD/CARR_complete.pdf

Whitin, P. (1996). *Sketching stories, stretching minds: Responding visually to literature.* Portsmouth, NH: Heinemann.

Wiggins, G. (1990). The case for authentic assessment. *Practical Assessment, Research & Evaluation, 2*(2). Retrieved September 5, 2005, from http://pareonline.net/getvn.asp?v=2&n=2

Wiley, T. G. (1996). *Literacy and language diversity in the United States.* Washington, DC: Center for Applied Linguistics and Delta Systems.

Wilkerson, P. A., & Kido, E. (1997). Literature and cultural awareness: Voices from the journey. *Language Arts, 74*(4), 255–265.

Willig, A. (1985). A meta-analysis of selected studies on the effectiveness of bilingual education. *Review of Educational Research, 55*(3), 269–317.

Wood, D. J., Bruner, J. S., & Ross, G. (1976). The role of tutoring in problem-solving. *Journal of Child Psychology and Psychiatry, 17*(2), 89–100.

Yolan, J. (1996). *Encounter.* New York: Voyager HBJ Books.

Zimmerman, S., & Keene, E .O. (1997). *Mosaic of thought.* Portsmouth, NH: Heinemann.

Index

Academic achievement, 10, 32
Academic language, 3, 54, 58, 127, 213
A Development English Proficiency Test (ADEPT), 159, 247
Advocacy-oriented assessment, 228
Alignment, 160-172, 244
Alphabetic principle, 57-58
American Association of Higher Education, 83
Assessment
    AAHE's nine principles, 83-84
    alternative, 227-228
    common miscues, 172
    culturally and linguistically appropriate, 247-248
    cumulative, 19
    current trends, 84
    for eELLs, 224-228, 247
    ensuring quality, 96
    four keys to quality student assessment, 96, 97
    framework of methods and approaches, 85
    guidelines for effective, 83-84
    issues, list of, 94
    kinds of, 86-91
    language learning and content related, 82
    linking instruction to, 265
    multiple, 125
    ongoing, 94, 95, 126-127
    planning literacy instruction, 18
    portfolio assessment, 95-96
    purpose of, 83-84
    scaffolding and language, 155
    summative, 86, 251
    using appropriately, 245-246
    values and beliefs, 31
    "work in progress" classroom model, 95
    writing, 103-104, 211
Authentic assessments, 94-95
    assessment approaches, 97
    defined, 94
    eELLs, 233
    examples from the field, 105-107

as measures of success, 82
standardized tests supplemented, 7
teaching strategies, 107
traditional testing *versus,* 251
types of instruments, 251

Background knowledge
    background building experiences as check, 140
    building on, 114-115, 116
    determining, 14
    metacognitive strategies, 170
    prediction, 215
    sample strategy, 131-134
    standards-based content, 154-155
    strategies, 123
Barrier games, 99
Basic interpersonal communication skills (BICS), 55-56
Behaviorist theory of first language acquisition, 54-55
Between the author and me questions, 137
Biases, 10, 29, 40, 93, 96
Bilingual education, 66-67
Bilingual exceptional education, 223
Bilingual Index of Natural Language (BINL), 87
Bilingual Syntax Measure (BSM), 87

California
    curriculum standards, 18-19
    curriculum design, 154
    language arts skills, 110
    language of instruction, 20
California English Language Arts Framework, 161
California English Language Development Standards, 151, 157
California English Language Development Test (CELDT), 7, 88-91, 154, 190, 247
California Standards Tests (CSTs), 85
CALLA example, 158-159
Caretaker speech, 60
Cause and effects, 139, 216, 218-219
CELDT. *See* California English Language Development Test

Change process, 156-159, 247-248
Chat checks, 103
Checklists, 99-100, 101, 103
Children's literature, 29, 38-43
Classroom community, 29
Cognates, 3, 145, 215
Cognitive academic language proficiency (CALP), 5, 55, 140
Cognitive objectives, 126
Collaborative teaching models. *See* Co-teaching
Color-coded poetry, 63-64
Communicative competence, 54
Communicative language, 54
Community, 29
Comparison/contrast, 139, 206, 207, 213-214
Complementary teaching, 229
Complex planning, 13
Complex thinking, teaching eELLs, 232
Comprehensible input as a scaffold, 230
Comprehensible input (i+1), 60-61
Conferences, teacher-student, 102-103, 105, 106, 120-121
Content, 6, 153
Content-area writing, 206-212
Content-embedded instruction, 124, 131-134, 227
Content specific standards, 14
Content word walls, 215
Contextual meaning, 60, 145
Contrastive linguistics, 60
Controversial issues, 10
Corn, words for, 59
Co-teaching, 228-230
Creation of stories, 34
Critical reading, 127
Critical thinking focus, 10-11, 111
Cultural diversity, 27, 30-31, 44-46, 232, 242
Culturally and linguistically diverse (CED) learners, 224
Culturally responsive teaching, 9-10, 28-33, 38-43, 46-50
Cultural memory, 62
Cultural mismatches, 10
Cultural story structures, 35
Cultural validity, 93

Culture
concept of, 26–27
cultural ways of making meaning,
3–4, 125
culture of children, 26
differentiated instruction
and, 3–5
importance for teaching and
learning, 27–28
language and, 59
learning about, 27
multiple intelligences and cultural
ways of knowing, 11
role of planning, 49
school *versus* real-life
experiences, 245
storytelling, 34
student identity, 155
Cumulative assessment, 19
Curricula, types of, 27
Curriculum standards for California,
18–19
Curriculum, 27

Debriefing process for strategies, 125
Deficit perspective, 45–46, 54, 221
Demonstrated learning,
modes of, 225
Descriptive assessment, 228
Diagnostic assessments, 86
Diagnostic language assessments,
86–88
Dialogue journals, 62–63, 65, 67,
69–80
Differentiated instruction, 2, 3–6
components necessary, 8–14,
29–33
features summarized, 243–244
guidelines for eELLs, 224–226
teacher role summarized,
248–250
Differentiation, 2, 5–6, 223–224, 229
Directed Reading Thinking Activity
(DRTA), 179
Diversity, 25

Ecological assessment, 227–228
Edge Lake School, 22–24
eELLs. *See* Exceptional
ELLs (eELLs)
ELA standards, 248
ELD standards, 248
Elementary and Secondary Education
Act (2000), 124
ELLs (English language learners), 1–3,
61–63, 154, 250
English Language Development
(ELD), 94, 157–158, 160–166
English-only programs, 5

English-only students, 45
Exceptional ELLs (eELLs), 221–224,
227–241

Feedback, 32
First language acquisition, 54–55,
60–62
Flexible grouping, 17
Formative assessment, 85–86
Framework for teaching skills. *See*
Skills instruction guidelines
Frontloading process, 123
Funds of knowledge, 46

Gaps in understanding, 17
Gifted eELLs, 221
Gifted students, instructional models
for, 2, 221, 227
GIST (Getting Information by
Summarizing Text), 118, 141
Grammar worksheets, 66
Graphic organizers, 206–208
Grouping strategies, 45, 102, 115,
140, 244, 249
Group work, 17
Guiding principles for instruction,
147, 156

Hampton-Brown ELD series,
160–166
Heroes, in children's books, 42
Home Language Survey, 88–91
Houghton-Mifflin Reading Series,
160–166

Individualized education program
(IEP), 225
Individuals with Disabilities
Education Act (IDEA), 223
Inferring, 142–144, 171, 179
Initial literacy instruction, 60, 62
Innatist theory of first language
acquisition, 55
Input hypothesis, 60–61
Instruction. *See also* Lesson plans;
Skills instruction guidelines
guiding principles (example),
156, 157
linking assessment to, 265
ongoing assessment, 94, 95,
126–127
planning for, 44–46
questions to ask before, during,
and after instruction, 128
questions to consider, 250
recommended scaffolding
practices, 188
role of assessment, 83, 84
teaching cause and effect, 219

teaching prediction, 216–217
teaching visualization, 217–218
two phases, 126
what exemplary teachers do, 122
Instructional assistants, 228–229
Instructional issues, 13, 28
Instructional needs of ELLs, 4, 7–8,
14–17
Instructional plans, formal, 27. *See
also* Lesson plans
Instruction strategies, 5. *See also*
Strategies
Interactionist theory of first language
acquisition, 55

Japanese culture, 245
Jazz chants, 64
Johns Basic Reading Inventory, 247

Key concepts, 43–44, 224, 226
Kindergarten, 59
Knowledge, 9
K-W-L chart, 132, 140

Language, 28, 53, 59, 100, 155, 172
Language acquisition, 60, 189
Language Assessment Scales (LAS), 87
Language brokers, 18
Language in literacy development,
53–63
Language monitor, 66
Language objectives, 19, 115
Language proficiency
A Development English
Proficiency Test (ADEPT), 159
assessment bias, 93
backward planning for trouble
spots, 172
CELDT, 190, 247
defined, 54
demonstrating knowledge, 61
diagnostic language assessments,
86–88, 247
for eELLs, 228, 232
elements of, 54
example, 157
exceptional education
services, 223
grammatical errors, patterns of, 60
heterogeneous groups, 45
kindergarten instruction, 59
lessons on key concepts, 44
oral language, as predictor, 61
plan for language, then model and
demonstrate, 115
practice, importance of, 115–116
rule-governed acquisition, 55
second language background
knowledge, 124

standardized instruments, 7
teachers' role, 53-54
Language structure, 57-58
Learned helplessness, 45, 235
Learning, real-life contexts, 110-111
Learning and acquiring a second
    language compared, 60
Learning apart from traditional
    school interactions, 46
Learning disabilities case study,
    222-223
Learning process, reflections on, 112
Lesson plans
    components for, 8
    culturally responsive, guidelines,
        43-44
    eELLs, 225, 226
    first-grade model lesson, 173-175
    key concepts in, 43-44
    sixth-grade model lesson, 181-185
    third-grade model lesson, 175-181
Limited strategies, 112
Linguistic bias, 93
Linguistic diversity, 53
Literacy experiences, prior, 60
Literacy instruction, 17-19
Literacy skills, five types, 110
Loaded words, in children's
    books, 42

Mainstream classrooms, 7
Mainstream English speakers, 2-3,
    124
Materials scaffolds, 141, 230
Meaningful context for language
    learning, 60
Mediated scaffolds, 230
Mediating vocabulary strategy,
    145-148, 217-218
Mediation, 139-140
Metacognition, 127-128
Metacognitive strategies, 127-130
    activating prior knowledge and
        schema, 168
    activating prior knowledge and
        schema visualization, 170
    connecting reading and writing to
        one's personal life, 131-134
    inferring, 142-144
    inferring and determining
        importance, 171
    mediating vocabulary, 145-148
    need for multiple strategies,
        125-126
    preassessment, 119
    previewing text, 135-137
    summarizing, 138-141
    synthesizing and questioning, 169
Minority heroes, 42

Mixed-ability students, instructional
    models for, 2
Modeling by teacher, 125, 200
Mothereze, 53
Multicultural children's literature,
    38-43
Multicultural conceptual
    curriculum, 43
Multicultural education, 244-245
Multilingualism, promotion of, 245
Multiple grouping experiences, 3
Music, 64-65

Narrative, structure of, 164, 167
National Reading Panel Report
    (2000), 27
Native American learners, 4, 34, 46-50
Native language. *See* First language
    acquisition
Natural Approach, 65
Natural Order hypothesis, 60
New pedagogy, 13, 17, 242-244, 246
No Child Left Behind (NCLB), 27,
    124, 223
Norm-referenced tests (NRTs),
    84-85, 93
Note organizers, 215
Nouns and adjectives (adjective
    position), 58

Observational checklists, 101, 191
Observation time for teachers, 102
On my own questions, 137
Open-ended questions, 103
Oral language proficiency, 61, 87,
    91-92, 97-98, 194

Pacific Islanders, talk story, 4
Paired reading, 179, 184-185
Parallel teaching, 229
Parents, 29
Participation, 32
Part-to-whole reading, 66
Performance assessment, 94. *See also*
    Authentic assessments
Personal contact, 31
Personalized word banks, 63
Perspective writing, 209-211, 212
Phonemes (sounds), 58
Phonemic awareness, 150
Pictures, reading, 101-102
Planning
    background knowledge about
        strategies, 124
    complex, 13
    for differentiation, 6
    for effective instruction, 44-46
    equitable pedagogy, factors
        involved, 12-13

examples from the field, 19-24
    instructional components
        and, 11-13
    new pedagogy approach, 246
    role of culture, 49
Planning charts, 252-259
    culturally responsive emphasis, 50
    differentiated instruction, 15-16
    eELLs, 235
    language and literacy
        development, 68
    scaffolding, 192-193
Poetry, scaffolding for, 204
Portfolios, use of, 95-96
Power standards, 161, 164-166
Practice, importance of, 115-116
Prediction, 215-217
Prejudice-reduction activities, 10, 244
Previewing text, strategy for, 135-137
Preview-View-Review strategy,
    199-200
Primary language support
    example, 156
Probing student thinking, 103
Problem solution, 104
Proposition 227, 20, 158

QAR (Question Answer
    Relationships), 137
Questioning, 136-137, 169

Racism, 41-42
Readiness levels of students, 6
Reading
    comprehension, assessing, 99
    comprehension, factors
        affecting, 149
    connecting reading and writing to
        one's personal life, 131-134
    content area support example,
        198-201
    critical reading, 127
    language structure, 57-58
    meaning from text when
        comprehension breaks down,
        129
    metacognition and, 127
    part-to-whole reading, 66
    prediction, 215-217
    previewing text, 135-137
    Preview-View-Review strategy,
        199-200
    second language acquisition, 56-57
    skimming and scanning text, 135
    slang words, 58-59
    task completion without
        comprehension, 198-200
    teaching ELLs to read in English,
        61-62

Reading pictures, 101–102
Research organizers, 212
RESULTS (California Reading and Literature Project), 247
Retelling exercise, 97–98, 106
Rice, words for, 59
Risk taking environment, 32, 147
Round robin reading, 140–141, 179–180
Roving conferences, 103, 105
Rubrics for assessing writing, 104
Rubrics for scoring, 32, 33
Rules overemphasis, 66

Scaffolding
    access to language and text, 60–61
    basic assumptions, 153
    content-area writing, 211–212
    defined, 11
    for eELLs, 230–232
    elements summarized, 244
    example, 158
    first-grade examples, 174
    inferring strategies, 143–144
    instructional examples, 150
    learning of skills, 113
    in lesson plans, 44
    materials scaffolds, 230
    mediated scaffolds, 230
    mediating vocabulary, 147
    mediation, 139–140
    metacognition as framework, 129
    multiple grouping experiences, 3
    new pedagogy, 17
    observational checklist, 191
    planning instruction, 126
    previewing text strategy, 137
    principles for CLD learners and eELLs, 231
    scaffolds, 187–189
    sixth-grade examples, 182–183, 184–185
    skills and strategies related, 248, 249
    skills related, 19, 111
    social and emotional scaffolds, 231, 232
    strategy for connecting learning to personal life, 133–134
    student learning process, 188–189
    for summarizing strategy, 139–141
    syntax, 260
    task scaffolds, 230
    teacher examples, 119–122
    techniques listed, 2
    as temporary support, 11
    third-grade examples, 176–177, 178–180

writing fluency, 197
    zone of proximal development, 4, 11
Schoolhouse Rock series, 64–65
Schools, culture of, 27
SDAIE. *See* Specially Designed Academic Instruction in English
Second language acquisition, 54
    demonstrating knowledge, 61
    examples of instructional resources for, 63–66
    facilitated by first language proficiency, 61–62
    factors affecting reading, 57
    first language proficiency related, 59
    how to build English proficiency skills, 148–149
    issues for reading in English, 56
    literacy issues summarized, 245
    reading instruction, 61–62
    reading pictures, 101–102
    use of primary language in, 155
    writing instruction, 62–63
Self-esteem issues, 32–33
Self-image, in children's books, 42
Self-regulation of cognition, 127–128
Semantics, differences in, 59
Sentence combining/fluency, 196
Service learning projects, 10
Sexism, analyzing children's books for, 41–42
Shape poetry, 203
Shape writing, 203
Shopping mall of ideas, 204
Sketch to stretch activity, 218
Skills
    basic for student success, 154
    as cognitive habits, 112
    defined, 109, 110, 111
    discussing with teachers, 118–119, 122
    preassessment, 112
    strategies and scaffolds related, 248, 249
    strategies confused, 109, 113
    strategies related, 111–112
Skills instruction, 19, 109, 114–118
Skimming and scanning text, 135
Slang words, 58–59
Small-group conferences, 102
Social action approach, 28, 244
Social and emotional scaffolds, 231, 232
Social conventions, 58
Social studies, 206
Societal curriculum, 27
Sociocultural influences, 93

SOLOM. *See* Student Oral Language Observation Matrix
Southeast Asian cultures, 59
Spanish, 58, 145, 148
Special education services, 221
Specially Designed Academic Instruction in English (SDAIE), 94, 158–159
Spiraling curriculum, 43
Spontaneous differentiation, 229
Standardized assessment
    accountability, 18–19
    achievement of ELLs, 248
    authentic assessment complementing, 251
    current trends, 84
    eELL language and content proficiency, 227
    formal assessments, 27
    instructional needs of ELLs and, 7–8
    validity for ELLs, 93
Standards-based content, 153–156, 160–172, 174, 177–178, 183
Stations (centers), 229
Stereotypes, 40–41
Still poses, 147
Storyboards, 36–38
Story maps, 139
Storytelling, 34–36, 47. *See also* Talk story
Strategies
    building background knowledge, 124–130
    choosing for ELLs, 125–127
    debriefing, 125
    defining, 111, 125
    discussing with teachers, 118–119, 122
    how to modify, 126
    issues to consider, 249
    metacognition, 127–148
    prediction, 215–217
    recording processes, 129
    selection of, 125
    skills and scaffolds related, 248, 249
    skills confused with, 109, 113
    skills necessary for success, 130
    teaching key concepts, 43–44
Structured English immersion (SEI), 158
Student choice in the classroom, 225, 226
Student expectations, 96
Student identity, 155
Student Oral Language Observation Matrix (SOLOM), 87, 91–92
Students, 9, 14, 24

Substituting words, 64
Substitution drills, 66
Summarizing, 32, 118, 138–141
Summative assessment, 86, 251
Supportive co-teaching, 229
Symbolic curriculum, 27
Syntax, 64, 106–107, 247, 260

Talking circles, 37
Talk story, 4
Task scaffolds, 230
Teacher expectations, 19, 155–156, 232
Teachers, 25, 28, 118–119, 124
Teaching
    co-teaching strategies, 228–230
    culturally responsive for ELLs, 33
    from multicultural perspective, 244–245
    strategies, 19, 107, 111
Team teaching, 229
Text level skills, 148–149
Think alouds, 100–101
Thinking/learning skills, 32–33
Think-pair-share discussion strategy, 36, 45, 133, 139
Timelines, 139

Tokenism, 41
Traditional models of differentiated instruction, 3, 5–7, 227, 245–246
Transfer, teaching for, 111–112
Transitional readers, 58
Translation skills of ELLs, 46, 52
Triad grouping, 45

Validity, in assessment, 93
Values and beliefs, 31
Venn diagrams, 206
Verb conjugation drills, 66
Visualization, 119, 217–218
Vocabulary learning, 3, 114, 145–148

Wait time, in conferences, 102
Word banks, personalized, 63
Word-level literacy skills, 148
Word lists, 63–64
Word study, 146–147
Word substitutions, 64
Word walls, 63, 215
Word work, 150–151
Work samples, 19
Worldviews, 27

Writing
    assessment, 103–104
    checklist (fifth grade), 260
    connecting reading and writing to one's personal life, 131–134
    content-area writing, 206–211
    drafting process, 197–198
    eELLs, 233–241
    examples from the field, 22, 194–196, 202–205, 259–264
    factors to consider, 263
    fluency, 196, 197
    "how-to" papers, 120
    instruction for ELLs, 62–63
    perspective writing, 209–211, 212
    poetry examples, 203–205
    reflection process, 208–209
    rubrics, 197, 200, 211
    scaffolding, 196–198, 202–205
    sentence combining, 196
    shape writing, 203
    skills students need exposure to before grade 4, 165
    strategies, 33

Zone of proximal development, 4, 12, 111, 153, 189, 230